The
Making of
Modern Marriage

The Making of Modern Marriage

MATRIMONIAL CONTROL AND
THE RISE OF SENTIMENT IN
NEUCHÂTEL, 1550–1800

Jeffrey R. Watt

CORNELL UNIVERSITY PRESS

ITHACA AND LONDON

First published 1992 by Cornell University Press.

International Standard Book Number 0-8014-2493-3
Library of Congress Catalog Card Number 92-52775

Printed in the United States of America

Librarians: Library of Congress cataloging information appears on the last page of the book.

♾ The paper in this book meets the minimum requirements of the American National Standard for Information Sciences— Permanence of Paper for Printed Library Materials, ANSI Z39.48-1984.

To Isabella

Contents

Maps and Tables

Acknowledgments

While working on this book, I have received valuable assistance, advice, and criticism from many different sources. I first thank the Swiss government for the generous grant that enabled me to undertake two years of archival research in the city of Neuchâtel. In the summer of 1989, I was able to pursue additional research there thanks to support from the University of Mississippi Graduate School's Office of Research.

I enjoyed many stimulating conversations with scholars in Neuchâtel who generously shared their time and ideas. Several of them read the manuscript in its entirety and offered excellent recommendations on how to improve it. Carlo Augusto Cannata, a law professor at Neuchâtel, was kind in agreeing to oversee my work, and his legal expertise helped illuminate the institution of early modern marriage. I had the good fortune of knowing Gabrielle Berthoud, a local historian who passed away not long ago; I will always remember her generosity in sharing with me her unpublished work on the consistory of Valangin. Philippe Henry, a professor of early modern history, graciously took the time to help clarify the intricate relationships of the legal and judicial institutions of Old Regime Neuchâtel. I am also grateful to Rémy Scheurer, a medievalist at the University of Neuchâtel, for providing vitally important insight to the economic history of Neuchâtel. Two other local historians, Michèle Robert and Raoul Cop, kindly brought to my attention pertinent sources in Neuchâtel's municipal archives and in the public library of La Chaux-de-Fonds. I also thank Michel Schlup, associate director of Neuchâtel's public library, and Robert Darnton for directing me to important sources in the vast documentation of the Société typographique de Neuchâtel in the Bibliothèque de la ville de Neuchâtel. I am also very grateful to Christian and Nicole Quellet for providing me with a quiet setting in which to compose the first draft.

The successful completion of this project depended heavily on the work of past and present archivists. In this regard, I could not have asked for a better reception in Neuchâtel. In the state archives, Jean Courvoisier, the former Archiviste d'Etat, and his excellent staff directed me to the pertinent documents and provided a most pleasant ambience to work in. I especially thank Maurice de Tribolet, formerly the associate archivist and currently Archiviste d'Etat, whose wise advice and patient help in paleography were indispensable for an archival neophyte. In the years that have passed since my stay in Neuchâtel, he has never failed to keep me abreast of new developments in Swiss historiography and has been most diligent in answering my countless letters. For their cheerful assistance, I also thank Jean-Pierre Jelmini, the director of Neuchâtel's municipal archives, as well as the staffs at the public libraries of Neuchâtel and La Chaux-de-Fonds.

On this side of the Atlantic, I am most indebted to Robert Kingdon, my adviser at the University of Wisconsin, who more than anyone else inspired me to enter the field of social history. His meticulous editing, constructive criticism, and constant encouragement have been fundamental contributions to this book. Suzanne Desan and Michael MacDonald read the manuscript, improving its content through their astute scholarly criticism. At the University of Mississippi, Kees Gispen and Robert Haws offered important advice on revision.

Special thanks go to John Ackerman, director of Cornell University Press, for his unwavering support of this project.

More personally, I thank my parents for their genuine interest in my scholarly pursuits. Ironically, it was while doing research on divorce and romantic misadventures that I met my wife to be, Isabella Maurilli. Her moral support and patience have been invaluable since the outset of this work.

Parts of this book have appeared in different form in the *Journal of Family History* 14 (1989): 137–155; the *Journal of Social History* 22 (1988): 129–147; and the *Sixteenth Century Journal* 20 (1989): 89–104. I have also drawn from articles forthcoming in *Calviniana II*, published by the Sixteenth Century Journal Publishers, and in *Calvinus Sacrae Scripturae Professor*, published by Eerdman's. I thank the various editors for their permission to reuse material here.

University of Mississippi   JEFFREY R. WATT

Abbreviations

The
Making of
Modern Marriage

Introduction

This book offers an examination of the institution of marriage in early modern Neuchâtel, a French-speaking principality that converted to the Reformed faith in the sixteenth century and became a Swiss canton in the early 1800s. The most important sources for my research have been the court records of marital disputes in Neuchâtel. A study of long *durée,* my analysis covers the entire early modern period, beginning in 1547, the date of the first extant records of the Protestant matrimonial courts, and ending in 1806, when Neuchâtel passed into the hands of Napoleon. This latter date is a useful cutoff point since local legal practices changed considerably thereafter. It is my aim in examining these records over a two-hundred-fifty-year period to determine whether this early modern county witnessed significant changes in the control of marriage and in the institution of marriage itself.

Marriage and the family are arguably the most fundamental and influential of our institutions. Yet only in recent years have scholars earnestly pursued research on the history of marriage and the family. Now historians have undertaken studies to determine whether there was an evolution from the extended to the nuclear family and have conducted demographic research to establish the average age at marriage for men and women, the percentage of the population that was widowed, and the mean size of families. This research has sparked much debate on the origins of the modern family as we know it.

The early modern period has received special attention from historians of the family. Vivian Fox and Martin Quitt have convincingly

explained why the early modern period has been of so much interest to
historians of the family: it is in the early modern period that we begin
to see systematic records on family events such as marriages, births, and
deaths; much of the pioneering work in family history—by Philippe
Ariès, Lawrence Stone, Edward Shorter, and Peter Laslett, for example—concerns the early modern period; and many historians contend
that the basic features of the contemporary family—close relationships
between parents and children, romantic or affectionate marriage, and
weak kinship ties—originated in early modern Europe.[1]

To be sure, it is not a unanimous view that the early modern period
was a decisive turning point in the history of marriage and the family.
Most historians now agree that in terms of household structure there
was more continuity than change from medieval to early modern Europe. Peter Laslett, for one, has rejected the notions that the family has
evolved from the patriarchal/extended family to the nuclear family,
claiming that the nuclear family was the norm in preindustrial England.
Jack Goody also dismisses the notion that the nuclear family emerged
from the extended family, holding that "small domestic groups are virtually universal"; the important changes that have taken place in the
family "concern the disappearance of many functions of the wider ties of
kinship."[2] On the basis of the Florentine *catasto* of 1427, David Herlihy
and Christiane Klapisch-Zuber found that the nuclear family was the
most common household structure in Tuscany, where extended families
represented only about one-fifth of all households.[3] In short, scholars

1. Fox and Quitt, eds., *Loving, Parenting, and Dying: The Family Cycle in England and
America, Past and Present* (New York, 1980), pp. 6–7.
2. Laslett, Introduction to *Household and Family in Past Time*, ed. Peter Laslett and Richard
Wall (Cambridge, 1972), pp. 1–89, and *The World We Have Lost: England before the Industrial
Age*, 2nd ed. (New York, 1971), pp. 93–95; Goody, "The Evolution of the Family," in *Household and Family in Past Time*, p. 119. Like Laslett, I use "household" to refer to "all persons
inhabiting the same set of premises." I define the "family" as the coresident domestic group.
Live-in servants are therefore members of their masters' families. The "extended family" is a
household that includes the nuclear (or conjugal) family and one or more relatives; see Laslett,
Introduction to *Household and Family in Past Time*, pp. 23, 29, 36. In defining "household,"
some scholars argue that Laslett puts too much emphasis on coresidence and pays too little
attention to other perspectives, especially the factor of production; see, e.g., David Warren
Sabean, *Property, Production, and Family in Neckarhausen, 1700–1870* (Cambridge, 1990), pp.
96–101. Though such criticisms are valid when applied to peasant societies, I find Laslett's
definition useful—since much production took place outside the home in late eighteenth-
century Neuchâtel.
3. Herlihy and Klapisch-Zuber, *The Tuscans and Their Families: A Study of the Florentine
Catasto of 1427* (New Haven, Conn., 1985); Klapisch-Zuber, "State and Family in a Renaissance Society: The Florentine *Catasto* of 1427–30," in *Women, Family, and Ritual in Renaissance Italy*, trans. Lydia G. Cochrane (Chicago, 1985), p. 18. But Richard Goldthwaite holds
that the families of elites did experience nuclearization in fifteenth-century Florence. Studying

now generally reject the traditional view that the European family experienced progressive nuclearization from medieval to modern times.

Several scholars see still further continuity in the family stretching back to the Middle Ages. Herlihy finds that the most fundamental changes in the history of the family occurred not in the modern period but rather in the early Middle Ages. Referring to family structure, he maintains that medieval households were different from those of classical and barbarian antiquity, arguing that "domestic units of antiquity were not commensurable and comparable across society, and that the ancients lacked even the concept of family as a moral unit, common to all levels of the social hierarchy." In other words, Romans did not use the same terminology to refer both to the households of aristocrats, which often included hundreds of slaves, and to the small family units of humble artisans, which may have consisted of only husband, wife, and children. In Roman and barbarian times, households "lacked symmetry, in the sense that different sectors of society possessed fundamentally different domestic units. Medieval families from the seventh and eighth century show much greater commensurability. Apparently for the first time, households could be used as standard units in censuses and surveys. Of course, they continued to vary in size and structure, but the range of variation had become much more restricted."[4]

For very different reasons, Goody also maintains that the most decisive changes in the institutions of the family and marriage took place in the early Middle Ages. Roman law and Germanic customs had permitted Europeans to divorce, practice concubinage, adopt children, and

---

domestic architecture, he maintains that, though kinsmen had lived under one roof or in blocks of houses during the Middle Ages, Florentines began constructing palaces in which only the nuclear family resided, thus facilitating the isolation of the conjugal family from the outside world; *Private Wealth in Renaissance Florence: A Study of Four Families* (Princeton, N.J., 1968). In his work on families in Renaissance Florence, Francis William Kent criticizes Goldthwaite for failing to distinguish between domestic groups and larger family institutions. For patricians of Renaissance Florence, the household and lineage were two complementary family institutions. Moreover, Kent found that, for the families he studied, about one-third were complex or extended, and that those who built palaces had no intention of cutting themselves off from relatives. His findings, like Goldthwaite's, apply only to a very small elite; *Household and Lineage in Renaissance Florence: The Family Life of the Capponi, Ginori, and Rucellai* (Princeton, N.J., 1977), pp. 10–14, 26–27, 227–228. Herlihy and Klapisch-Zuber found that composite households were more common among the wealthy than among the population at large; *Tuscans and Their Families*, pp. 290–298.

4. Herlihy, *Medieval Households* (Cambridge, Mass., 1985), pp. v, 62. Herlihy also maintains that during the early medieval period European families ceased to be dominated by the Roman paterfamilias with his virtually unlimited power over other family members, a change that allowed the advancement of women's legal rights vis-à-vis their husbands; "Land, Family, and Women in Continental Europe, 701–1200," *Traditio* 18 (1962): 89.

marry first cousins and affines. During the early medieval period, the
Roman Catholic church rejected all these practices, even forbidding
marriages as far as the seventh degree of consanguinity and affinity.
Why did these changes occur? Most did not have scriptural backing.
Noting that all these practices were concerned with the inheritance of
family property, the "provision of an heir," and the "maintenance of status" in society, Goody asserts that the church introduced such policies
in order to increase the likelihood that it would inherit property; if believers failed to produce heirs, the church enjoyed greater opportunities
of material aggrandizement. Goody's thesis is provocative, and few have
embraced it entirely.[5]

In another stimulating work, Georges Duby holds that a new and different family model appeared in France in the central Middle Ages. Duby
argues that in the period 1000–1250 there were two conflicting models
of marriage in France—the priestly and the knightly. The priestly
model espoused exogamy, the indissolubility of marriage, and the free
choice of spouses. With their overriding interest in continuing the lineage without dispersing the family property, aristocrats favored endog-
amy, parental control of marriage, and the possibility of divorce and
remarriage. But, by the beginning of the thirteenth century, Duby argues, priests and knights understood marriage in much the same way. A
valid marriage had to be based on the freely given consent of two parties who had reached the age of reason. Men were to have authority over
their wives just as the clergy had dominion over the laity in spiritual
matters, including marriage. Duby takes this union of conflicting mod-

5. The decisive change in the ideology of marriage, Goody argues, occurred in the fourth
century A.D. He also holds that property concerns were behind the call for clerical celibacy, a
view that most historians can accept; Christian leaders opposed clerical marriages at least in
part out of fear that priests might bequeath church property to their children; *The Development
of the Family and Marriage in Europe* (Cambridge, 1983), pp. 36–46, 81, 102, 220–221. In
response to this thesis, Herlihy observes that it is unclear whether the Church would have
profited materially by preventing the wealthy from having heirs. The church depended on
wealthy families for priests and nuns; indeed, its "need for property was no greater than its
need for priests"; *Medieval Households*, p. 13. James Brundage questions whether the church
was actually thinking about inheritance patterns when it set standards on marriage and legitimacy; he doubts that "the Church and its leaders were either cunning enough or farsighted
enough to have implemented a long-range scheme to shape Christian marriage law so as to
maximize the Church's material benefits. It would have required a better-organized and more
efficient system of centralized planning than the medieval Church ever enjoyed to have pro-
jected and implemented such a strategy.... We are more likely dealing with an unintended
result of the Church's urge to protect the sanctity of sex, rather than with policy consciously
created to enrich the ecclesiastical establishment"; *Law, Sex, and Christian Society in Medieval
Europe* (Chicago, 1987), p. 587.

els of matrimony in the High Middle Ages to have established the traditional Christian marriage system that would prevail into modern times.[6]

From other perspectives, however, historians have argued that the early modern period was decisive for the history of the family. One point of great controversy is the role sentiment played among family members in early modern Europe. The modern family is often said to be based on the "love marriage" and on the idea that the closest affection is reserved for members of the nuclear family. Philippe Ariès maintains that the modern family was born in the early modern period, a product of the growing appreciation of children. According to such historians as Lawrence Stone and Edward Shorter, the family underwent significant changes during the Protestant Reformation but the modern family, distinguished by the growth of affective ties within the family and the increased isolation of the nuclear family, appeared only in the late seventeenth or eighteenth centuries. All three of these historians maintain that, at least until the seventeenth century, families did not nurture feelings of affection among their members, the nuclear family enjoyed little privacy from neighbors and kin, and the pervasive influence of the community left individuals little room for self-realization.[7] All this would change, however, during the course of the early modern period.

In tracing the evolution of the family in early modern England, Stone offers an admittedly schematic representation of the gradual separation of the nuclear family from kin and community. He first describes the "open lineage family," which predominated into the seventeenth century. Permeable to outside influences, especially to those of kin, this family was "an open-ended, low-keyed, unemotional, authoritarian institution which served certain essential political, economic, sexual, procreative and nurturant purposes." Stone argues that in the seventeenth century the nuclear family became more separated from kin and that the state and church reinforced patriarchy, thus relegating women to an ever more subordinate position. After 1640, however, various changes "in the state, the society and the Church undermined this patriarchal emphasis, while continuing the decline of external pressures on the increasingly nuclear family." The result was the "closed domesticated nuclear

6. Duby, *The Knight, the Lady, and the Priest: The Making of Modern Marriage in Medieval France*, trans. Barbara Bray (New York, 1983). Duby's thesis, like Goody's, has received criticism; most important the church's views on marriage often had little impact on aristocratic marriage practices.
7. Ariès, *Centuries of Childhood: A Social History of Family Life*, trans. Robert Baldick (London, 1962); Stone, *The Family, Sex, and Marriage in England, 1500–1800* (London, 1977); Shorter, *The Making of the Modern Family* (New York, 1975).

family," which first appeared among the upper bourgeoisie and squirearchy and came to predominate in the eighteenth century, as it filtered down to lower classes. In choosing spouses, individuals now for the first time put more emphasis on affection than on wealth or status. These changes mark for Stone the decisive shift in the evolution of the modern family:

> the four key features of the modern family—intensified affective bonding of the nuclear core at the expense of neighbours and kin; a strong sense of individual autonomy and the right to personal freedom in the pursuit of happiness; a weakening of the association of sexual pleasure with sin and guilt; and a growing desire for physical privacy—were all well established by 1750 in the key middle and upper sectors of English society. The nineteenth and twentieth centuries merely saw their much wider diffusion.[8]

In a more recent work, Stone has modified his views somewhat, especially the negative views on family life before 1700. He acknowledges, for example, that lower down the social scale paternal control over marriages was not so great; many young people married without their parents' consent. Nevertheless, he still contends that, among the upper levels of English society throughout the sixteenth and seventeenth centuries, the influence of parents, kin, and friends on young people's choice of marriage partners was nearly irresistible, mostly because of financial pressures. Stone maintains that between 1660 and 1800 there was a palpable shift in attitudes toward marriage, which promoted more freedom from parents and more emphasis on affection in choosing marriage partners.[9]

In many ways, Shorter's analysis of sentiment in early modern families resembles Stone's. He too envisions marriages of "traditional society"— that society that prevailed until the end of the early modern period—as essentially pragmatic relationships contracted for economic reasons. In these "bad old days," sentiment was not important in one's choice of spouses, and the feelings spouses had for each other did not become strong after marriage. Shorter asserts that only toward the end of the eighteenth century were inner feelings more important in choosing a mate than property, parental wishes, or other factors. Hitherto, property had played a far greater role in the choice of spouses than did

8. Stone, *Family, Sex, and Marriage*, pp. 4–5, 7–9.
9. Stone, *Road to Divorce: England, 1530–1987* (Oxford, 1990), pp. 10, 57–61.

"romantic love," defined as "the capacity for spontaneity and empathy in an erotic relationship." Shorter, however, speaks of a veritable revolution in sentiment in the late eighteenth century which was to change dramatically the nature of the family.[10] Although their chronologies do not coincide exactly, Stone and Shorter agree that only toward the end of the early modern period were affective ties between spouses strong.

Many scholars have arrived at substantially different conclusions about early modern marriage. Historians such as Pierre Bourdieu, Elisabeth Claverie, Pierre Lamaison, and Alan Macfarlane maintain that early modern matrimony was stable and underwent no important changes— that, in the selection of marriage partners, the role played by sentiment vis-à-vis wealth did not change significantly from the sixteenth to the eighteenth century. Macfarlane claims that the modern family predates industrialization; indeed, he holds that the English family system today is roughly the same as it was in 1250, and observes that husbands and wives then, as now, "lived in conjugal units, participated in local and regional markets, devised strategies for passing on land outside customary inheritance patterns, and otherwise behaved like individuals in a capitalist society."[11] Ralph Houlbrooke, Ferdinand Mount, and Linda A. Pollock all support the theory that there was no important change in the family—either in its structure or in the sentiment among family members—from the sixteenth to the eighteenth century.[12]

On the question of sentiment, a host of specialists on early modern Britain find that Stone and Shorter underrate the extent to which personal preference and affection influenced the choosing of spouses in the sixteenth and seventeenth centuries. Though agreeing that marriage was to a large degree property-oriented, G. R. Quaife, for example, argues that court records from seventeenth-century Somerset reveal that love

---

10. Shorter, *Making of the Modern Family*.

11. Macfarlane, *Marriage and Love in England: Modes of Reproduction, 1300–1840* (Oxford, 1986), and *The Origins of English Individualism: The Family, Property, and Social Transition* (Cambridge, 1978), p. 198; Bourdieu, "Les stratégies matrimoniales dans le système de réproduction," *Annales: E.S.C.* 27 (1972): 1105–1125; Claverie and Lamaison, *L'impossible mariage: Violence et parenté en Gévaudan au 17e, 18e et 19e siècles* (Paris, 1982).

12. Houlbrooke, *The English Family, 1450–1700* (New York, 1984); Mount, *The Subversive Family: An Alternative History of Love and Marriage* (London, 1982); Pollock, *Forgotten Children: Parent–Child Relations from 1500 to 1900* (Cambridge, 1983). In dealing with family life in a late medieval urban setting, David Nicholas also sees "continuity in the practical aspects of family life between the Middle Ages and the Industrial Revolution. . . . The modern age seems less revolutionary as its medieval antecedents are explored"; *The Domestic Life of a Medieval City: Women, Children, and the Family in Fourteenth-Century Ghent* (Lincoln, Neb., 1985), pp. 4, 12.

and affection were more significant than Stone and Shorter allow.[13]
Similarly, in his work on English church courts from 1570 to 1640,
Martin Ingram argues for more continuity of family life between the
fifteenth and seventeenth centuries than Stone allows and suggests that
Stone's sources are skewed toward the upper classes. Acknowledging
that wealth was of utmost importance in choosing spouses, Ingram asserts that Stone "exaggerates the strength of parental influence, under-
estimates the role of romantic love and gives inadequate attention to the
middling groups who played such an important part in parish society."
Like Quaife, Ingram avows that personal attraction and inclination were
much more important in matchmaking than Shorter and Stone would
have us believe, a view shared by Houlbrooke, Michael MacDonald, and
Keith Wrightson.[14]

Did the demographic realities of early modern Europe preclude sentimental attachment? In an age of high mortality, some would argue, it
was so common for parents to lose children, children to lose parents,
and husbands and wives to lose each other that one dared not become
too emotionally attached to anyone. Some believe that because of the
ubiquity of death early modern Europeans were hardened to death and
did not suffer over the loss of a spouse or child. Various scholars have
argued against such an assumption. Fox and Quitt point out that we of
the twentieth century have not become inured to the suffering caused
by divorce even though divorce is omnipresent.[15] The fact that death
was so common did not remove its sting, nor did it prevent emotional
commitment. Steven Ozment disagrees strongly with the view that
marriages in Reformation Europe were basically contracted for economic reasons and remained relatively loveless. Citing various anecdotal
sources, such as the writings of Protestant moralists, medical texts, and
sermons, Ozment asserts that twentieth-century standards must not be
applied in evaluating the status of women or the role of affective ties in
sixteenth-century marriages. In his opinion, couples of this period often
did have loving marriages. The fact that parents had authority over their
children's choice of spouses does not, in his mind, preclude marriage

13. Quaife, *Wanton Wenches and Wayward Wives: Peasants and Illicit Sex in Early
Seventeenth-Century England* (New Brunswick, N.J., 1979), p. 243. Cf. Shorter, *Making of the
Modern Family,* pp. 62–68, 146.

14. Ingram, *Church Courts, Sex, and Marriage in England, 1570–1640* (Cambridge, 1987),
pp. 137–141; Houlbrooke, *English Family,* pp. 76–78; MacDonald, *Mystical Bedlam: Madness,
Anxiety, and Healing in Seventeenth-Century England* (Cambridge, 1981), pp. 88–98; Wrightson, *English Society, 1580–1680* (New Brunswick, N.J., 1982), pp. 82–84.

15. Fox and Quitt, *Loving, Parenting, and Dying,* p. 407.

for love. Children were often content to take the advice of their parents on such matters. In short, the fact that young people could not marry without parental consent did not, according to Ozment, inhibit the development of sentiment between spouses.[16]

Still others agree that the family evolved in early modern Europe but deny that marriage practices changed so drastically. The French historian Jean-Louis Flandrin finds that, between the sixteenth and eighteenth centuries, neighborhood solidarity weakened while family solidarity was enhanced. The triad of father, mother, and children increasingly detached itself from other kinsfolk and servants. Though he recognizes an increase in sentiment among family members, Flandrin does not believe that love marriages were common before the twentieth century. The enlightened elite of the eighteenth century dreamed of instituting the love match but were unable to follow these inclinations "as long as their social power remained based on a material patrimony." Though love may have incited men to indulge in concubinage, it was not as yet the basis for marriage. Flandrin concludes that "the revolution of the conjugal system did not take place until after that of the economic system, for only then could the marriage founded on love be instituted without challenging the hierarchical structures of society."[17]

Though he sees the birth of new attitudes toward marriage in early modern England, John Gillis also rejects the linear development Stone and Shorter describe. Gillis believes that people in the sixteenth and seventeenth centuries were capable of romantic love, though affections were very structured and expressed in ways we might not recognize. Getting married was a very public affair, involving the betrothal, the publicizing of the banns, and a big wedding in which entire villages participated. "Because the household was the central unit of both pro-

16. Ozment, *When Fathers Ruled: Family Life in Reformation Europe* (Cambridge, Mass., 1983). Ozment reinforced these views in *Magdalena and Balthasar: An Intimate Portrait of Life in 16th-Century Europe Revealed in the Letters of a Nuremberg Husband and Wife* (New York, 1986).

17. Flandrin, *Families in Former Times: Kinship, Household, and Sexuality*, trans. Richard Southern (Cambridge, 1979), pp. 173, 180, 216. James F. Traer believes that the notion of the "modern family" developed out of the literature of the French Enlightenment. Dramatists, novelists, and philosophes idealized the marriage of inclination and criticized the marriage of convenience that was based on material concerns; *Marriage and the Family in Eighteenth-Century France* (Ithaca, N.Y., 1980), p. 70. Flandrin would no doubt agree but would argue that this new ideal of marriage had not yet been put into practice. In another work, however, Flandrin provides a different picture. Though conceding that the marriage of convenience was the norm, Flandrin claims that within these limits peasants enjoyed considerable freedom in choosing spouses and that love matches were probably more common than we have traditionally thought; *Les amours paysannes: Amours et sexualité dans les campagnes de l'ancienne France (XVIe–XIXe siècle)* (Paris, 1975), pp. 74–75, 95–100.

duction and reproduction, its formation was a major public event, subject to the politics of both family and community." Nonetheless, Gillis does see the new ideal of companionate marriage, first appearing in the mid-seventeenth century, as an idea so revolutionary as to be considered subversive. Such ideals, however, would have little effect on practice until the nineteenth century.[18]

As may be expected, some medievalists have taken umbrage with the austere picture of medieval family life that some early modernists have painted. Barbara Hanawalt provides evidence that premarital sexual flirtation was not uncommon among peasants in late medieval England and that as many as one-third of all women may have been free from parental control in choosing their husbands. Acknowledging that medieval peasants generally did not marry in order to attain connubial bliss, Hanawalt, like Ozment, warns against using twentieth-century standards in evaluating families of earlier generations. Though different from modern marriages, medieval English peasant marriages can best be described as economic and emotional partnerships to which both husbands and wives made vital contributions.[19] Medievalists also caution against basing conclusions about family affection on arguments from silence; as Herlihy suggests, "the medieval family was never dead to sentiment; it is only poor in sources."[20]

Several scholars argue that the medieval church was already calling for modern marriage practices. James Brundage, a specialist on medieval canon law, points out that many of the characteristics of the so-called modern marriage—"including free choice of marriage partner, the rejection of parental permission as a necessary precondition for the marriage of adults, the ideal of conjugal bonding through mutual affection—were also promoted and championed by medieval lawyers and theologians a half-millennium before 1680."[21] Rejecting the view that marital affection was a modern invention, Goody avows that in stressing the importance of consent in marriage the Roman Catholic church favored the love marriage and affection within the family, which both "owe little to the later transformations of feudalism, mercantile capitalism, industrial society, Hollywood or the Germanic tradition."[22]

18. Gillis, *For Better, for Worse: British Marriages, 1600 to the Present* (Oxford, 1985), pp. 4–5, 12–13.
19. Hanawalt, *The Ties That Bound: Peasant Families in Medieval England* (Oxford, 1986), pp. 8–10, 188, 192–193, 200, 219.
20. Herlihy, *Medieval Households*, p. 158.
21. Brundage, *Law, Sex, and Christian Society*, p. 586.
22. Goody, *Development of the Family*, pp. 153, 155.

Intimately tied to this question of conjugal affection is that of the status of women. Historians of marriage have discussed whether the Protestant Reformation had a positive or negative impact on women. That opinions differ on this issue is hardly surprising. On the one hand, Protestant reformers exalted the married state, denied the moral superiority of celibacy, and introduced the possibility of divorce and remarriage, all of which appear on the surface as progressive for women. On the other hand, Protestants eliminated the confessional with parish priests, which might have provided emotional support for women, and abolished the career option of the convent. The British historian Keith Thomas concedes nothing more than a marginal improvement in women's status in seventeenth-century Puritanism vis-à-vis medieval Catholicism: "The Puritans, by their exalted conception of sexual morality, and their protests against wife-beating and the double standard of sexual morality, and their denunciation of the churching of women, with its origin in the primitive view of women as shameful and unclean, had done something to raise women's status, but not really much."[23]

Discussing the social impact of Calvinism in France and Switzerland, Natalie Zemon Davis is even more reluctant to say that the Reformation enhanced the status of women. She denies, for example, that the right to divorce necessarily increased women's legal rights. Under medieval canon law, women had long had the right to petition for separation on the grounds of adultery or for an annulment under certain circumstances. But a traditional double standard that tolerated a man's adultery more readily than his wife's might have vitiated a woman's chances of success either before or after the Reformation.[24] Furthermore, a woman, who may have had custody of children, most likely would have faced greater financial difficulties than a man in the interval between the divorce and possible remarriage. Divorce or legal separation was possible only for very wealthy men and women. At any rate, divorce remained rare in sixteenth- and seventeenth-century Geneva, for example. Nevertheless, Davis notes that the Reformed faith "did promote a certain desexualization of society, a certain neutralizing of forms of communication and of certain religious places so that they became acceptable for women." These gains, though "bringing new tools to women and new experience to both sexes," were acquired at a price. The austere Reformed moral code prohibited much of the recreational

23. Thomas, "Women and the Civil War Sects," *Past and Present* 13 (1958): 43.
24. See also Keith Thomas, "The Double Standard," *Journal of the History of Ideas* 20 (1959): 195–216.

and festive life that laymen and laywomen had enjoyed together under Roman Catholicism. Moreover, the reformers eliminated the role models provided by female saints and the opportunity of living in a convent. According to Davis, by eliminating a separate religious organization for women, the Reformation may have made them a little more vulnerable to subjection from every direction. Consequently, she concludes, it is difficult to establish that the Reformed religion was quicker or more creative in changing sex roles than was contemporary Catholicism.[25]

Stone goes a step farther, asserting unequivocally that the Reformation brought a decline in the status of women. With the increasing separation of the nuclear family from kin and community in the sixteenth century, women were no longer protected by their relatives and were even more at the mercy of their husbands. Stone adds:

> The end of Catholicism involved the elimination of the female religious cult of the Virgin Mary, the disappearance of celibate priests, who through the confession box had hitherto been so very supportive of women in their domestic difficulties, and the closing off of the career option of life in a nunnery. Puritanism was unable to fill the same role for more than a tiny minority of educated female zealots who attached themselves to charismatic preachers; while post-Reformation English society had nothing but contempt for spinsters.[26]

Stone also asserts that the state and the law emphatically prescribed the subordination of wives to ensure law and order and that the Protestant sanctification of marriage made conjugal love a duty, perhaps facilitating the subordination of wives.[27] In short, whereas Thomas acknowledges a minimal degree of improvement in women's status, Stone declares that the English Reformation relegated women to an increasingly subordinate position. Only in the late seventeenth and eighteenth centuries were women freed from the yoke of extreme patriarchy.

Studying seventeenth-century Dutch Calvinists, Simon Schama suggests that Stone has created a false dichotomy in contrasting "patriarchal" and "companionate" relationships. Schama maintains that in marriage Dutch Calvinists did not "subordinate love to obedience but rather exalted it as the indispensable quality for a godly union." Like

25. Davis, "City Women and Religious Change," in *Society and Culture in Early Modern France* (Stanford, Calif., 1973), pp. 90–94.
26. Stone, *Family, Sex, and Marriage*, p. 202.
27. Ibid.

sixteenth-century humanists and moralists, writers in the Dutch Golden Age insisted that "deference to the husband as lord of the household was conditional on his reciprocal obligation to confide the governance of the home into his wife's charge and to abstain from all conduct that would bring house and family into disgrace or ruin."[28] In theory then, Dutch Calvinists promoted loving marriages that were partnerships based on the mutual obligations of husbands and wives.

Ozment also disagrees with the negative assessments of the status of women at the time of the Reformation. While admitting that Protestantism brought an increase in the authority of the male household head, he suggests that the Reformation enhanced the status of women as well as that of men, asserting that most women of Reformation Europe probably found their domestic chores as wives and mothers personally satisfying and were not prevented from working at their own or their husbands' crafts. Ozment maintains that "a wife's subjection to the rule of her husband was not the subservience of a serf to a lord, or a maid to a master, or a child to a parent; despite male rule, an ordered equality existed between husbands and wives." Though Protestants did not have a monopoly on loving marriages, the new Protestant marriage laws, "especially those that recognized for the first time a mutual right to divorce and remarriage, became the most emphatic statement of the ideal of sharing, companionable marriage in the sixteenth century."[29] Unlike Davis, Ozment thus considers the newly established right to divorce and remarry to be the most important manifestation of the mutual respect spouses owed one another. Citing findings from court records, he observes:

Over 40 percent of Zurich's divorce cases in the late 1520s involved the suits of wives against adulterous husbands. In recatholicized Constance, two-thirds of the court cases heard between 1551 and 1620 concerned petitions by single women to have promises of marriage (half with alleged sexual consummation) declared valid. Although the Protestant courts were reluctant to grant divorces and the Catholic courts equally hesitant to enforce promises of marriage acknowledged by only one party, the persistence of such suits suggests widespread impatience with male infidelity and deceit.[30]

28. Schama, *The Embarrassment of Riches: An Interpretation of Dutch Culture in the Golden Age* (Berkeley, Calif., 1988), pp. 421–425. Schama acknowledges, however, that the Puritans insisted more than the Dutch Reformed on a woman's submission to her husband.

29. Ozment, *When Fathers Ruled*, p. 99.

30. Ibid., pp. 56–57; see also Walther Köhler, *Zürcher Ehegericht und Genfer Konsistorium* (Leipzig, 1932–1942), pp. 109, 120; Thomas Max Safley, "Marital Litigation in the Diocese

In Protestant Zurich and Basel, magistrates imposed the same sentences on adulterers and adulteresses, indicating that fidelity was not subject to a double standard. Taken as a whole, the evidence from the courts suggests, according to Ozment, that women did make gains with the advent of the Reformation: having the legal right to divorce and remarry, women were now less likely to endure insufferable marriages.[31]

The different interpretations of the effects of the Reformation on women could in part be the result of geographic variation. The conversion to Protestantism could have elevated the status of women in Germany while denigrating their position in England. As we see in later chapters, there were indeed significant differences between the marriage laws of England and those of German Protestant states. Not infrequently, however, even scholars concentrating on the same geographic area differ about the Reformation's impact on women. Lyndal Roper and Merry Wiesner, for example, disagree with Ozment, claiming that the position of women declined in Reformation Germany.[32] Simply put, family historians have not reached a consensus on the status of women, the affective ties within the family, or the degree to which the family changed between the Renaissance and the French Revolution.

Even among those who agree that the family underwent important changes in early modern Europe, scholars still differ on the causes of change. For Stone and Ariès, the modern family first emerged among the middle and upper classes as a result of ideological changes. Though

---

of Constance, 1551–1590," *Sixteenth Century Journal* 12 (1981):61–78. Ozment is being very selective in choosing statistics. He could have mentioned that in Zurich, from 1525 to 1531, husbands initiated nearly 60 percent of all divorces on grounds of adultery and abandonment; in Basel from 1529 to 1550, husbands sued for divorce in about 60 percent of all cases; from 1550 to 1590, wives initiated the bare majority of divorces, just over 50 percent; statistics from Safley, "Protestantism, Divorce, and the Breaking of the Modern Family," in " *Pietas et Societas*": *New Trends in Reformation Social History,* ed. Kyle C. Sessions and Phillip N. Bebb (Kirksville, Mo., 1985), p. 55. See also Safley, *Let No Man Put Asunder. The Control of Marriage in the German Southwest: A Comparative Study, 1550–1600* (Kirksville, Mo., 1984), p. 175; Adrian Staehelin, *Die Einführung der Ehescheidung in Basel zur Zeit der Reformation* (Basel, 1957), pp. 181–198.

31. In dealing with late medieval England, Barbara Hanawalt arrived at conclusions that resemble Ozment's for Reformation Germany: "Court cases show an absence of malice and a strong tendency to provide and support a wife's interests. Wills indicate a high degree of trust and even affection. . . . The separate space for men's work and women's work did not denigrate the input of the wife relative to that of the husband, nor is there evidence that medieval peasant men thought so"; *Ties That Bound,* pp. 218–219.

32. Roper, *The Holy Household: Woman and Morals in Reformation Augsburg* (Oxford, 1989); Wiesner, "Nuns, Wives, and Mothers: Women and the Reformation in Germany," in *Women in Reformation and Counter-Reformation Europe: Private and Public Worlds,* ed. Sherrin Marshall (Bloomington, Ind., 1989), pp. 8–28.

acknowledging that economics was relevant, Stone maintains that attitudinal changes were most important in determining decreases in illegitimacy, increases in prenuptial conceptions, and changes in the control of morality.[33] He rejects outright Friedrich Engels's contention that love matches were made possible by industrialization and first appeared among the working classes. Stone holds that the love match became common first among the landed, professional, and upper bourgeois classes and trickled down to the working classes only in the late eighteenth and early nineteenth centuries; that the new family appeared before industrialization; and that industrialization did not break up the family as an economic unit, since the first phase of industrial activity involved people, especially women, working at home in cottage industries.[34] Among those who have supported Stone's thesis are scholars who concentrate on the family lives of elites; Randolph Trumbach, for example, found that aristocrats gave increased importance to romantic love in eighteenth-century England.[35]

Still other scholars hold that economic developments, not ideological changes, were behind the making of the modern family. Shorter sees market capitalism as the primary motivating factor behind the "revolution in sentiment." For him, the discovery of affection and the growth in individualism were above all the ramifications of the contemporary shift from the traditional "moral" economy to a modern marketplace economy with its economic egoism. Moreover, the love match first took hold not among the elite but rather among the nascent proletariat, which was untrammeled by property concerns.[36] Rudolf Braun, Hans Medick, David Levine, and many others hold that with the growth in wage labor people enjoyed more freedom from parental control and were able to

33. Stone, *Family, Sex, and Marriage*, pp. 622–643. Stone holds that the imposition of Puritan mores was chiefly responsible for the decline in illegitimacy in seventeenth-century England. In a more recent work, Stone continues to argue that "changing moral attitudes, themselves the outcome of a variety of societal, economic, and cultural influences, and differing from group to group within the society," were mainly responsible for changes in marriage patterns and in premarital sexual activity. When legal changes on divorce finally took place in the nineteenth century, they were the "result of changes in the minds of men in positions of power"; *Road to Divorce*, pp. 13–22.

34. Stone, *Family, Sex, and Marriage*, pp. 658–666. Here Stone is describing what we now generally term protoindustry rather than industrialization; see Chapter 4 of this volume. In his more recent work, Stone continues to hold that the growth of affective individualism in the eighteenth century was most pronounced among the "middling sort," including everyone from wealthy merchants and bankers "down to farmers and small tradesmen and clerks"; *Road to Divorce*, pp. 45, 61.

35. Trumbach, *The Rise of the Egalitarian Family: Aristocratic Kinship and Domestic Relations in Eighteenth-Century England* (New York, 1978), pp. 113–117, 157–160.

36. Shorter, *Making of the Modern Family*, pp. 15, 255–258.

marry younger; since wealth was in wages rather than land, young people no longer had to wait to inherit property before marrying and starting a family. Moreover, Braun argues that, since property was no longer decisive in forming marriages, people could give freer rein to affection in choosing spouses.[37] In their work on the family in central Europe, Michael Mitterauer and Reinhard Sieder maintain that the growing intimacy of nuclear family members stemmed primarily from economic developments whereby the family lost its productive function. The separation of workplace from home was vital in stimulating new ideas about marriage and the family; the formation of marriage was determined less by economic considerations, allowing a greater role for emotion. Mitterauer and Sieder do, however, concede that the Reformation and especially the Enlightenment promoted stronger relationships between husbands and wives and parents and children.[38]

In describing the development of the companionate marriage, Gillis also gives considerable importance to economic changes, though he is just as critical of Shorter as of Stone. He denies that the history of marriage consists of the progress of "the conjugal" by which individuals were freed from the yoke of kin and community. Agreeing with Stone and others that the conjugal ideal was born in England in the mid-seventeenth century, he maintains that this would remain a utopian vision for the rest of the early modern period. Though he asserts that the companionate marriage first appeared among the upper-middle classes, including Puritans, Gillis argues that the changes brought by industrialization were a condition sine qua non for the implementation of the marriage of sentiment. But, contrary to Shorter's thesis, he contends that during the Industrial Revolution the companionate marriage became widely accepted among the "middling sort" but not among "ordinary people," who often rejected "monogamous marriage and the nuclear family in favor of nonconjugal arrangements that for them were more conducive to equitable, fulfilling heterosexual relationships."[39]

Those who believe that the modern family developed in early modern Europe have thus offered a variety of explanations for this change, dif-

37. Braun, *Industrialisation and Everyday Life*, trans. Sarah Hanbury Tenison (Cambridge, 1990), pp. 37–60; Levine, *Family Formation in an Age of Nascent Capitalism* (New York, 1977); Medick, "The Proto-Industrial Family," in Peter Kriedte, Hans Medick, and Jürgen Schlumbohm, *Industrialization before Industrialization: Rural Industry in the Genesis of Capitalism*, trans. Beate Schempp (Cambridge, 1981), pp. 38–73.

38. Mitterauer and Sieder, *The European Family: Patriarchy to Partnership from the Middle Ages to the Present*, trans. Karla Oosterveen and Manfred Hörzinger (Chicago, 1982), pp. 6–7, 60.

39. Gillis, *For Better, for Worse*, pp. 3–14.

fering on whether economic developments or changes in mentality were more important in transforming the family.[40] In dealing with such questions, however, Goody, Medick, Sabean, and others have cautioned against portraying emotion and wealth as mutually exclusive concerns that competed for the attention of family members. These analysts see personal and property relations as closely interwoven in early modern Europe; property often brought family members closer together by forcing them to cooperate, but it also was the source of many conflicts as relatives disputed over land and inheritance.[41] Furthermore, in studying the interplay between family, property, and production, Sabean has questioned the prevailing view that kinship relations were predominant in early modern Europe, declining in importance only with moderni-

---

40. Differences of interpretation are not limited to the topic of family sentiment. Scholars have offered a variety of explanations for differences in family structure. Some have suggested that the existence of joint families—households in which property rights are shared, consisting of parents and two or more married children or of two married siblings—are determined more by cultural than by socioeconomic factors. Frédéric Le Play (d. 1882), a French social reformer who had a profound impact on the study of the history of the family, believed that changes in customs were responsible for transformations in the family. A very conservative thinker, Le Play favored the patriarchal or stem family over the nuclear family, which he considered unstable. Believing that families had traditionally been extended, Le Play blamed the Napoleonic Code for introducing forced equality among heirs, which enabled children to rebel against parents, causing the fragmentation of families into nuclear units; see *L'organisation de la famille* (Tours, 1871). Though they recognize the importance of economic developments, Laslett and Robert Wheaton both agree that cultural factors contribute to the existence of joint families; Laslett, Introduction to *Household and Family in Past Time*, pp. 16–17, 65; and Wheaton, "Family and Kinship in Western Europe: The Problem of the Joint Family Household," *Journal of Interdisciplinary History* 5 (1975): 623. In his influential *World Revolution and Family Patterns* (New York, 1963), William J. Goode also puts a great deal of emphasis on cultural factors in the development of the family. He holds, for example, that the Protestant Reformation altered the family by stressing individualism. Goode goes so far as to say that family structure affects economic development rather than vice versa; industrialization occurred earlier in the West because families were not patriarchal and polygynous, marriages were not arranged, and so on. Concomitantly, the extended structure and strong kinship ties found in the third world hindered the growth of industry. John Shaffer, however, holds that economic factors suffice to determine family structure. The family's goal has always been the survival of the family; with this aim in mind, families have simply modified themselves to adapt to changes in their environment, such as those brought by industrialization; *Family and Farm: Agrarian Change and Household Organization in the Loire Valley, 1500–1900* (Albany, N.Y., 1982), pp. 9–17.

41. Goody, Introduction to *Family and Inheritance: Rural Society in Western Europe, 1200–1800*, ed. Jack Goody, Joan Thirsk, E. P. Thompson (Cambridge, 1976), p. 3; Medick and Sabean, Introduction to *Interest and Emotion: Essays on the Study of Family and Kinship*, ed. Hans Medick and David Warren Sabean (Cambridge, 1984), p. 5. This theme is repeated in several articles included in *Interest and Emotion:* Martine Segalen, "'Avoir sa part': Sibling Relations in Partible Inheritance Brittany," pp. 129–144; Alain Collomp, "Tensions, Dissensions, and Ruptures inside the Family in Seventeenth- and Eighteenth-century Haute Provence," pp. 145–170; Sabean, "Young Bees in an Empty Hive: Relations between Brothers-in-Law in a South German Village around 1800," pp. 171–186.

zation. On the basis of evidence from rural Württemberg, he asserts that kinship ties actually became more important in the late eighteenth and nineteenth centuries—even as mobility increased, the market economy grew, and wage labor expanded.[42]

I should mention the sources on which the aforementioned historians have based their conclusions. Claiming to have examined every possible type of evidence that can provide insight to "changes in value and behaviour at the personal level," Stone lists the following sources: moral and medical tracts, written primarily by theologians or physicians; diaries, autobiographies, and correspondence; biographies and family histories; newspapers and magazines; comments and reports by travelers; and novels, plays, and poetry.[43] Like Stone, Ozment has used personal evidence such as autobiographies and normative sources, particularly moral and medical treatises.

Evidence from diaries and autobiographies can be valuable in approaching the mentality of past ages. Such sources can provide firsthand accounts, sometimes of an intimate nature, of individuals' mores and attitudes. Caution must be used in examining them, however. Those who write autobiographies or keep diaries have always been exceptional; they are generally more introspective than most and may be motivated by feelings of alienation or of mission that others do not share. Evidence from such sources thus does not necessarily reflect the values and behavior of most contemporaries, particularly when a large percentage of the population is illiterate, as was the case throughout the early modern period.

In a similar fashion, moral treatises can provide some useful information on marriage and the family. No doubt such literature can reveal how family members were expected to behave toward each other. They too, however, must be analyzed prudently. Theologians' writings on marriage were often intended to be exemplary; they may therefore show how matrimony ought to have been, not how it really was. In the same manner, creative literature is important in showing what contemporar-

42. Sabean, *Property, Production, and Family in Neckarhausen*, pp. 36–37. Questioning whether kinship relations were always the primary focus of one's life in early modern Europe, as Laslett and others have suggested, Sabean finds that among peasants with little or no property the ties within the nuclear family tended to be weak: most children left home at an early age and were free to marry whomever they chose, and three-generation households were rare. In short, family structure was directly linked to the way property was transmitted; "Aspects of Kinship Behaviour and Property in Rural Western Europe before 1800," in *Family and Inheritance*, pp. 96–111, citing Laslett, *World We Have Lost* (New York, 1965), pp. 78–79; and Gérard Bouchard, *Le village immobile; Sennely-en-Sologne au XVIIIe siècle* (Paris, 1972).

43. Stone, *Family, Sex, and Marriage*, pp. 10, 759.

ies read for pleasure, the substance of which probably reflected their own ideals. But the value of these sources is limited to exposing attitudes of those who were literate.

Only recently have historians begun to see the utility of researching court records for the study of family history. Shorter and Ozment did not consult court records in their research on the history of the family, nor did Stone for *Family, Sex and Marriage*. His *Road to Divorce*, however, was based on court records, as were the works of Ingram, Quaife, and Houlbrooke. All these scholars deal with early modern England, where courts handled cases of marital breakdown quite differently than did contemporary continental tribunals.[44] The records of matrimonial or ecclesiastical courts are most important in evaluating the history of marriage. The decisions rendered for matrimonial litigation illustrate how marriages were contracted, sustained, and dissolved. Court records can be much more informative than statutes. Even though a law may forbid marriages between persons more closely related than third cousins, for example, tribunals may regularly grant dispensations to first cousins. Ordinances may theoretically allow both men and women to file for divorce on the grounds of adultery; yet the court records may show that male plaintiffs far outnumber females, since the latter dare not seek divorces because of their financial dependence. In short, court records may show that marriage practices are not identical to the theories behind the marriage laws.

When using court records as a window to past societies, we must be aware of the social strata from which the litigants came. Were they from a broad range of social backgrounds? If legal procedures were very expensive, one would expect the cost to prevent all but the wealthy from filing suit. Or, the contrary, it might have been the wealthy who most sought to avoid the ignominy often associated with court battles. Specialists in English history have debated this point to get a better understanding of the importance of court records as historical documents. In his work on late medieval court records, R. H. Helmholz concludes that litigants rarely came from either the highest classes or the servile classes. On the basis of fourteenth-century consistory records, Michael M.

---

44. In addition to works already mentioned, see Houlbrooke, *Church Courts and the People during the English Reformation, 1520–1570* (Oxford, 1979), and "The Making of Marriage in Mid-Tudor England: Evidence from the Records of Matrimonial Contract Litigation," *Journal of Family History* 10 (1985): 339–352. Barbara Hanawalt also consulted published editions of court records to supplement coroners' inquests, the principal sources for her study of the late medieval English family. Ozment does occasionally refer to evidence from courts; but this, as we have seen, he has gleaned from secondary works.

Sheehan finds that, though the upper classes were perhaps underrepresented, the registers offer a pretty accurate cross section of late medieval English society, including those who were not free. According to Houlbrooke, the parties who appeared before the courts of sixteenth-century Norwich and Winchester were of social backgrounds ranging from the servile poor to the lesser gentry. Examining English courts in the late sixteenth and early seventeenth centuries, Ingram, like Helmholz, found that most classes except the very rich and the totally destitute were represented; most who appeared before the English courts were from the "middling ranks of yeomen, husbandmen, tradesmen and craftsmen," though female litigants tended to be less well off. Stone, however, found that in the eighteenth century it was becoming less common for poor people to file suit before consistory courts, and rapidly rising legal costs increasingly precluded all but the rich from making appeals to the Court of Arches.[45]

Though the court records for early modern Neuchâtel provide little explicit information on the class or occupations of litigants, my general impression is that a fairly broad range of social backgrounds is represented. Throughout the two and a half centuries of this study, nobles made only rare court appearances (understandable since there were so few of them). Though litigants—or at least guilty parties—generally had to pay court costs, the financial burden must not have been too great, since many servants and day laborers filed suits. Because of these costs, the totally indigent probably were reluctant to initiate judicial proceedings in the sixteenth and seventeenth centuries. In the eighteenth century, however, people who could demonstrate financial hardship could litigate free of charge. Thus, whereas Stone found that fewer people could afford the costs of matrimonial courts in eighteenth-century England, contemporary tribunals in Neuchâtel became more receptive to the poor during the same period. Access to the courts was not restricted to a small elite, and the records accordingly provide valuable insight into popular marital disputes.

Critics may hold that court records cannot show what "normal" marriages were like since they deal with deviant behavior and reflect the

45. Helmholz, *Marriage Litigation in Medieval England* (Cambridge, 1974), pp. 160–161; Sheehan, "The Formation and Stability of Marriage in Fourteenth-Century England: Evidence of an Ely Register," *Mediaeval Studies* 33 (1971): 234; Houlbrooke, *Church Courts and the People*, p. 75; Ingram, *Church Courts, Sex, and Marriage*, pp. 194–195, and "Spousals Litigation in the English Ecclesiastical Courts c. 1350–c. 1640," in *Marriage and Society: Studies in the Social History of Marriage*, ed. R. B. Outhwaite (New York, 1981), pp. 44–45; Stone, *Road to Divorce*, p. 38.

values of judicial authorities, not of the population at large. It is true that these documents are skewed toward conflict. If one studies nothing but divorce cases, one may indeed be tempted to conclude that all marriages are unhappy, loveless affairs. In dealing with so-called deviant behavior, however, tribunals revealed the connubial norms contemporary society sought to uphold. Ingram found that in late Elizabethan and early Stuart England, contrary to common opinion, church courts did not enforce "outmoded or unwanted values": "many of the courts' activities were either in line with the existing attitudes and expectations of honest householders in the parishes . . . or represented a realistic attempt, normally supported by at least a section of local opinion, to nudge the mass of the people towards improved standards of morality and religious observance."[46] Likewise, Rosalind Mitchison and Leah Leneman found that in pursuing illicit sexuality Presbyterian church courts in seventeenth- and eighteenth-century Scotland defended a brand of Calvinist morality which the "mass of the population" embraced.[47] This basically holds true for Neuchâtel's courts, even though they may have lagged a step behind popular mores on marital breakdown and premarital sexual activity.[48] Furthermore, testimony concerning the way promises to marry were made can reveal the role sentiment played in leading up to marriage; and all litigation can show to what extent the courts upheld the interests of women.[49]

In addition to the works on English history, several studies pertaining to the history of marriage in late medieval and early modern Europe have been based on the registers of various courts. Through court records, scholars have studied illicit sexuality, illegitimacy, and marriage patterns in Calvinist Scotland and Renaissance Venice. For the German-

46. Ingram, *Church Courts, Sex, and Marriage*, p. 323.
47. Mitchison and Leneman, *Sexuality and Social Control: Scotland, 1660–1780* (Oxford, 1989), pp. 229–230.
48. At the time of the conversion to the Reformed faith, popular resistance to the control of morals was strongest against mandatory church attendance and the celebration of the eucharist; see Jeffrey R. Watt, "The Reception of the Reformation in Valangin, Switzerland, 1547–1588," *Sixteenth Century Journal* 20 (1989): 89–104.
49. Stone makes the following defense of the use of court records: "It might seem that the evidence is biased towards the pathology of social deviance and moral failure. But it is not only disastrous marriages which appear in court records, since many had started exceptionally well, or were entirely uneventful until a crisis had been triggered by a wholly unexpected act of adultery. In any case, the bias has its positive compensations, for it is only at times of crisis, such as revolutions in society and marital breakdowns in families, that the innermost workings of a social system and the values which support it are exposed to the historian's gaze. Moments of crisis and rupture reveal secrets which in normal times remain hidden since they are taken for granted"; *Road to Divorce*, p. 28

speaking world during the Reformation, Lyndal Roper has consulted court records to evaluate the position of women in Augsburg; Thomas Max Safley has made a comparative study on the control of marriage in Protestant Basel and in Catholic Freiburg and Constance. As for early modern France, Alain Lottin and other historians published a work based on eighteenth-century matrimonial court records from the diocese of Cambrai, and Roderick Phillips has provided an analysis of the matrimonial litigation at Rouen during the French Revolution, a period when extremely liberal divorce laws were in effect.[50]

All these works have been valuable, but no one has yet produced a work that encompasses a period broad enough to perceive long-term changes in the institution of marriage.[51] By covering all matrimonial litigation in early modern Neuchâtel, I am attempting here to fill that void. Although some documents have disappeared, the large majority of pertinent court records have been preserved. Litigation pertaining to marriage was heard primarily before three different tribunals: the matrimonial court of Neuchâtel and the consistory and matrimonial court of Valangin, a small seigneury that was incorporated into Neuchâtel in the late sixteenth century but maintained separate judicial institutions throughout the Old Regime. Valangin's consistorial records have been remarkably well preserved; with only a few short lacunae, the *procès verbaux* are extant from this tribunal's inception in 1547 until its dissolution in 1848. Records of Neuchâtel's *Justice matrimoniale* are intact for the periods 1570–1621 and 1704–1806, though relatively few of its registers have survived for cases prior to 1570 or for the period 1622–1703. Also relevant are records from Neuchâtel's Conseil d'Etat, the principality's supreme legislative body, and from the Quatre-Ministraux, authorities who had jurisdiction over lesser offenses in the city of Neuchâtel. Whereas the records for the former are complete for the entire early modern period, those for the Quatre-Ministraux are extant only from 1715. Taken together, the records of these various institutions provide an excellent basis on which to analyze changes in the control of marriage and in the institution of marriage itself. Moreover,

50. Roper, *Holy Household*; Guido Ruggiero, *The Boundaries of Eros: Sex Crime and Sexuality in Renaissance Venice* (Oxford, 1985); Mitchison and Leneman, *Sexuality and Social Control*; Safley, *Let No Man Put Asunder*; Lottin et al., *La désunion du couple sous l'ancien régime: L'exemple du Nord* (Paris, 1975); Phillips, *Family Breakdown in Late Eighteenth-Century France: Divorces in Rouen, 1792–1803* (Oxford, 1980). David Sabean also made use of court records, in addition to many other archival sources, in his *Property, Production, and Family in Neckarhausen*.

51. The one exception is Stone's *Road to Divorce*. As a work on English history, however, it deals with a country where divorce was all but impossible before the nineteenth century; that was not the case in early modern Neuchâtel.

the quantity of these archival sources is ideal for a case study of this nature. Numbering over 4,100 cases, the documentation related to marriage left by these various institutions is rich enough to allow valuable analysis without being so voluminous as to preclude its perusal.

By covering the entire early modern period, this analysis of matrimonial disputes tests some of the more hotly disputed questions among historians of the family. In an effort to see more clearly whether an evolution occurred in Neuchâtel's matrimonial regime, I divide this work into two periods. The first begins in 1547 with the first extant court record and ends in 1706, just before Neuchâtelois recognized the House of Hohenzollern as their rightful princes. The second begins with the accession of the Prussians in 1707 and ends when Neuchâtel passed into the hands of Napoleon in 1806. Such a division can help us determine whether the eighteenth century was indeed a turning point in the history of marriage, as several historians would have us believe.

Neuchâtel was a small political entity—its population reached 48,000 at the end of the eighteenth century and its boundaries surround no more than 797 square kilometers (roughly 300 square miles). Be that as it may, the work offered here is in no way provincial. Though it would be dangerous to assume that what took place in Neuchâtel occurred all over Europe, this principality's political, religious, and economic developments were not unusual for early modern Europe, especially when compared with those of other Protestant areas. More bluntly, as a principality that witnessed no major political upheavals and was home to practically no famous persons in the early modern period, Neuchâtel is an ideal setting for long-term examination, in the tradition of the *Annales* school, of "motionless history" and the history of the non-famous.

PART I

THE REFORMATION
AND THE
SEVENTEENTH CENTURY

1

The Principality of Neuchâtel

THE POLITICAL AND ECONOMIC STRUCTURE

The state known today as the Republic and Swiss Canton of Neu-châtel has a long and colorful history that predates the Reformation by centuries. Nestled between the Franche-Comté and the Canton of Bern, this former principality includes that part of the Swiss Jura mountains that run parallel to Lake Neuchâtel as far south as the Pays de Vaud (see Maps 1 and 2). In 1033, Holy Roman Emperor Conrad the Salien attacked Neuchâtel and absorbed it into the empire, though it still enjoyed considerable local autonomy because of the unwieldy, inefficient imperial feudal structure. In 1406, Conrad de Fribourg-en-Brisgau, count of Neuchâtel, formed an important alliance with the city of Bern, the powerful neighbor to the northeast. This agreement stipulated that henceforth the city of Bern would provide Neuchâtel with military protection, would receive an annual tax from the county, would serve as arbiter between the counts and their subjects, and could call on Neuchâtelois to provide military support in case of emergency. This powerful ally was to exert considerable influence on Neuchâtel throughout the late medieval and early modern periods.[1] For administrative and judicial purposes, the territory of Neuchâtel was subdivided into political

1. Jean Courvoisier, *Panorama de l'histoire neuchâteloise*, new ed. (Neuchâtel, 1972), pp. 26, 49–50; Léon Montandon et al., *Neuchâtel et la Suisse* (Neuchâtel, 1969), p. 19.

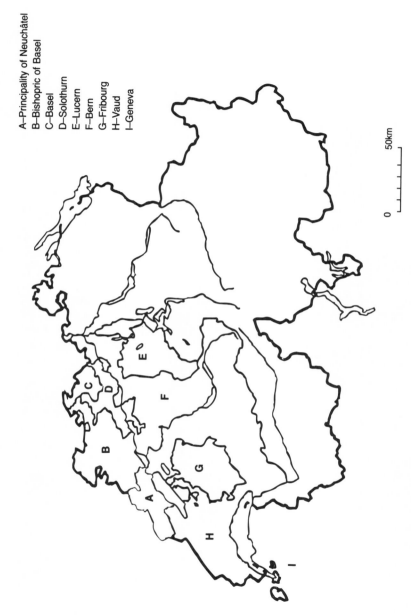

A—Principality of Neuchâtel
B—Bishopric of Basel
C—Basel
D—Solothurn
E—Lucern
F—Bern
G—Fribourg
H—Vaud
I—Geneva

0   50km

Map 1. Neuchâtel and Switzerland in the early modern period

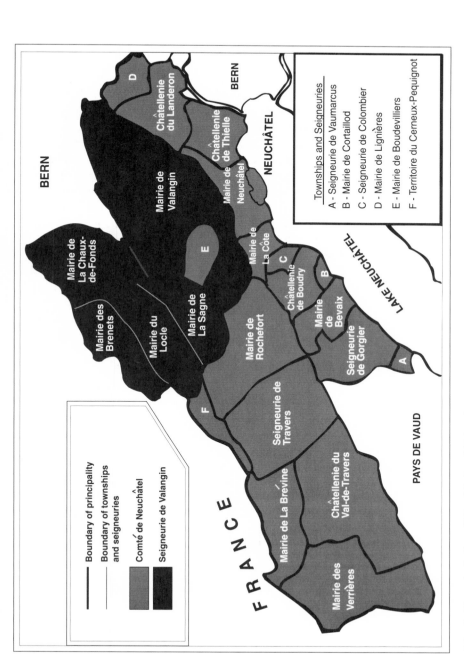

Map 2. The principality of Neuchâtel and Valangin

BERN

BERN

Mairie de
La Chaux-
de-Fonds

Mairie des
Brenets

Châtellenie
du Landeron

D

Mairie de
Valangin

Châtellenie
de Thielle

Mairie du
Locle

Mairie de
La Sagne

E

Mairie de
Neuchâtel

NEUCHÂTEL

Mairie de
La Côte

Mairie de
Rochefort

Châtellenie
de Boudry

C

B

Mairie
de
Bevaix

A

LAKE NEUCHÂTEL

Seigneurie
de Gorgier

F

Seigneurie de
Travers

PAYS DE VAUD

Mairie de La Brévine

Châtellenie du
Val-de-Travers

Mairie des
Verrières

F R A N C E

Townships and Seigneuries

A - Seigneurie de Vaumarcus
B - Mairie de Cortaillod
C - Seigneurie de Colombier
D - Mairie de Lignières
E - Mairie de Boudevilliers
F - Territoire du Cerneux-Pequignot

Boundary of principality
Boundary of townships
and seigneuries
Comté de Neuchâtel
Seigneurie de Valangin

units known as *châtellenies* or *mairies*. Appointed by the count, the *châtelains* and mayors had essentially the same responsibility of overseeing the administration of their districts.[2]

A political division within the principality of Neuchâtel that enjoyed a special status was the small seigneury of Valangin. This tiny county, home to no more than three thousand souls during the early sixteenth century, was from the thirteenth century on a fief under the suzerainty of the count of Neuchâtel. Throughout the centuries, however, the various *comtes* of Valangin had continually asserted their independence of the authority of their lords. Valangin rejoined Neuchâtel at the end of the sixteenth century, at which time the principality of Neuchâtel reached its definitive size.[3] Even after this reunion, however, Valangin continued to enjoy a certain independence, having its own legal institutions and obtaining the title, mainly honorary, of *Comté*. Consequently, the principauté de Neuchâtel et Valangin, as it was called officially throughout the Old Regime, was theoretically made up of two counties.[4]

Though Neuchâtel was under the suzerainty of a count, the authority of this figure declined in the early sixteenth century. In 1504, Jeanne, the last member of the ruling Bade-Hochberg family, married Louis d'Orléans-Longueville, the first Frenchman to serve as Neuchâtel's count. The Orléans-Longueville dynasty ruled in Neuchâtel for two hundred years and remained throughout this period very faithful servants of the French crown. Louis himself was too absorbed in fulfilling his duties toward Louis XII, king of France, to pay much attention to the small principality he had married into. From the time of his marriage until his death in 1515, he paid only a few brief visits to Neuchâtel, a trend that became more accentuated under later counts. During his very long reign, for example, Henri II de Longueville (1595–1663) resided in France and visited Neuchâtel only twice. Consequently, the count's authority passed more and more to his representative, the "governor and lieutenant general," an official who exercised the count's authority in his absence.[5] In exchange for a rather modest tax, Louis and his successors were content to leave the administration of the principality in the hands of municipal authorities, the Quatre-

2. Rémy Scheurer, *Pierre Chambrier 1542(?)–1609: Aspects de la vie d'un homme d'Etat neuchâtelois* (Neuchâtel, 1988), p. 11.

3. Ibid., p. 8.

4. Comité Farel, *Guillaume Farel, 1489–1565* (Neuchâtel, 1930), p. 236; Philippe Henry, *Crime, justice et société dans la principauté de Neuchâtel au XVIIIe siècle (1707–1806)* (Neuchâtel, 1984), pp. 55–56.

5. Scheurer, *Pierre Chambrier*, p. 10.

Ministraux, who became the real masters of the county. The Quatre-Ministraux represented the interests and handled the day-to-day work of the city council of Neuchâtel. To have a voice on the city council, one needed to have the status of "bourgeois" of Neuchâtel. Consequently, as the power of the count declined, that of the bourgeoisie was enhanced.[6]

Thereafter, a potpourri of other groups shared power in the county. The bourgeoisie of Valangin, like that of Neuchâtel, was a ruling elite that enjoyed great influence in that community. The supreme legislative body of the principality of Neuchâtel and Valangin was theoretically the Conseil d'Etat. This institution, which grew out of the feudal tradition of the aid or advice that vassals owed their lords, traditionally was composed of vassals, churchmen, and officials of the count. A dozen men served on this council, usually appointed for life. Until the Reformation, the clergy and nobility each occupied four seats on the Conseil d'Etat, and the third estate was represented by four members of the bourgeoisie of the city of Neuchâtel, members of the Petit Conseil or city council. Another important institution was the Tribunal des Trois Etats, a sovereign court of appeals that dated from the fifteenth or sixteenth century.[7] Originally the twelve judges of this tribunal were the same men who sat on the Conseil d'Etat, though later their memberships were not identical. Despite its name, this tribunal, like the Conseil d'Etat, did not draw its members from a broad cross section of society. It has been estimated that in the mid-seventeenth century, when it began to enjoy legislative as well as judicial powers, the Tribunal des Trois Etats represented no more than 10 percent of the county's population.[8] Beginning in 1592, Valangin had its own Tribunal des Trois Etats, which also consisted of twelve members: four nobles, four mayors, and four bourgeois of Valangin.[9]

6. Courvoisier, *Panorama de l'histoire*, p. 61; Montandon et al., *Neuchâtel et la Suisse*, p. 27. The city council, as described in the eighteenth century, had two different components: the Conseil des Vingt-quatre, or Petit Conseil, and the Conseil des Quarante, or Grand Conseil. Together they formed the Conseil Général, which met twice a month. The Petit Conseil, presided over by the mayor or his lieutenant, also served as Neuchâtel's court of justice. The Quatre-Ministraux, consisting of selected members of the Petit and Grand Conseils, met twice a week and were responsible for preparing and proposing matters to be brought before the councils. They also had the authority to rule on affairs that were not so important as to require action from the Conseil Général; *Almanach officiel* (Neuchâtel, 1773).

7. Rémy Scheurer, Louis-Edouard Roulet, and Jean Courvoisier, *Histoire du Conseil d'Etat: Des origines à 1945* (Neuchâtel, 1987), pp. 7–9, 30.

8. Dominique Favarger, "L'élaboration des lois à Neuchâtel aux XVIIe et XVIIIe siècle," *Musée neuchâtelois*, 1972, 186–212; Louis-Edouard Roulet et al., *Neuchâtel et la Suisse*, p. 186.

9. Henry, *Crime, justice et société*, pp. 77–79; Scheurer, *Pierre Chambrier*, pp. 10–11. Records have survived for the Audiences générales du Tribunal des Trois Etats of Neuchâtel.

A strong, if unofficial, influence within Neuchâtel came from the city of Bern. During the sixteenth century, Bern was often called on to serve as mediator to conflicts between Neuchâtel's bourgeoisie and the count. Bern's influence is aptly illustrated by the occupation of the county of Neuchâtel by various Swiss cantons for a period of seventeen years (1512–1529). At war with France, the Swiss feared that the French might cross through Neuchâtel to attack them. They also considered Neuchâtel a strategic location from which to launch an attack on Burgundy, should they decide to undertake such an offensive. Largely at Bern's initiative, the Swiss decided to occupy the county. Representatives of Bern, Solothurn, Lucern, and Fribourg, the four Swiss cities with which Neuchâtel had formed alliances (*combourgeoisie*), asked the Neuchâtelois to swear fealty to them as their new masters. The Neuchâtelois readily complied, since their sympathies were unabashedly with the Swiss. When the tension between France and the cantons lessened, it was Bern, along with Solothurn, that encouraged the other cantons to agree to the restitution of Neuchâtel to Jeanne, now Louis's widow.[10] This is but one example of Bern's intervention in the political affairs of its weaker neighbor.

Not only was it unimposing politically, Neuchâtel was also backward economically. At the end of the medieval period, Neuchâtel in effect had a subsistence economy. Its land was poor in natural resources, obliging its residents to import iron from the Franche-Comté. Neuchâtel's most important activity was agriculture. Animal husbandry, though it existed in Neuchâtel, did not play nearly as important a role as elsewhere in late medieval Europe. The plague devastated the county in 1349, causing a precipitate fall in population, which in turn effected a significant decline in the amount of land cultivated. As the population began to rebound about 1430, peasants cleared much land in previously unpopulated mountainous areas to be used for animal husbandry as well as agriculture. In spite of their travails, Neuchâtel's peasants produced rather meager yields. In late medieval Neuchâtel, the average ratio of seed to yield for oats has been estimated at 1 to 3.7; today, the same land can

---

These volumes are useful though they are weak concerning details about particular cases, often saying nothing more than whether the decision made in the lower court had been *bien jugé* or *mal jugé*. Regrettably, no records survive for the Tribunal des Trois Etats of Valangin; Gabrielle Berthoud, "Le consistoire seigneurial de Valangin à la fin du XVIe siècle," paper presented at the Société pour l'histoire du droit et des institutions des anciens pays bourguignons, comtois et romands, Geneva, 1977, p. 17.

10. Montandon et al., *Neuchâtel et la Suisse*, pp. 27–31; Scheurer, *Pierre Chambrier*, p. 11.

yield about twenty bushels of oats for every bushel of seed sown. Because of such low yields, Neuchâtel's agricultural production was generally limited to local consumption. To make matters worse, peasants had to pay rents in kind to the count. These rents provided the prince with a fixed income but weighed heavily on the peasants; since payments were in kind, peasants received no relief from the inflation of the fifteenth and sixteenth centuries which would have reduced the burden of payments in specie.[11]

Well into the seventeenth century, Neuchâtel's only important export was wine. The county of Neuchâtel has a long history of wine production, a tradition that probably began in the Gallo-Roman period. Viticulture expanded steadily throughout the medieval and early modern periods, the biggest producer being the count himself. Exporting wine, primarily to Solothurn, was his principal means of obtaining specie apart from borrowing. Neuchâtelois involved in viticulture entered a type of sharecropping agreement whereby the landowner and the worker divided the harvest with one getting one third, the other two-thirds, depending on who bore the costs of cultivation. This working relationship, which existed as early as the thirteenth century, continued to be used in Neuchâtel until the middle of the twentieth century.[12]

Like peasant societies in general, Neuchâtel of the late medieval and early modern periods had artisans who served the needs of the local population. Neuchâtelois would have used the services of carpenters and masons, bakers, drapers, tailors, cobblers, and smiths. Commerce, however, was quite limited. A few shopkeepers could be found, but late medieval commerce was tied to the county's three annual fairs. Until the end of the fifteenth century, only one guild existed in Neuchâtel for all merchants. Only slowly did more specialized guilds appear: the coopers' guild was founded in 1472, followed by that of the merchants of lake products (fishermen, boatmen, and so on) in 1482; smiths, masons, and carpenters formed a guild in 1520. Significantly, these artisanal activities were intended predominantly for local needs.[13]

From the late Middle Ages through the seventeenth century, the county of Neuchâtel was closely linked to the traditions of manorialism. In the fourteenth century, the count of Neuchâtel depended directly on the products from his land to support the needs of his various abodes

11. Rémy Scheurer, "L'économie neuchâteloise au Moyen Age," in *Histoire du Pays de Neuchâtel: De la préhistoire au Moyen Age* (Hauterive, Switzerland, 1989), pp. 263–268, 276.
12. Ibid., pp. 267, 269–271.
13. Ibid., pp. 277–283.

within the principality. The bread, wine, and meat his dependents and he consumed while staying in a particular castle were the products of the land surrounding that domicile. As Rémy Scheurer observes, the count of the fourteenth century very much resembled an early medieval sovereign. By the sixteenth century, he was less bound to the land, so to speak, as he ruled the county in absentia. Be that as it may, the administration of his revenues changed little from the mid-fourteenth to the seventeenth century. The vast majority of his wealth came from revenue from his land, with small supplements from various seigneurial fees. For example, traditionally anyone wanting to buy or sell property in the principality had to receive the count's permission. This custom evolved into the right of the prince to receive 8 percent of the value of property sold. Through *banalités,* the count had a monopoly on services such as ovens, mills, and sawmills, and he taxed those who used these facilities. Moreover, much of the ruling family's income was still paid in kind rather than money in the sixteenth century. At the end of the sixteenth century, for example, the payments the count received in wheat, oats, and wine represented 70–75 percent of his revenue, with payments in money only about one-fourth of the total. Now, however, the count did not actually consume these products; rather, cereals and wine were converted into money at a price fixed by the Conseil d'Etat, which in turn sold the produce. With the strong inflation that affected all of Europe in the late sixteenth century, the counts had a strong incentive to maintain these payments in kind. Simply put, in an era when some European rulers had developed sophisticated bureaucratic and fiscal machinery, Neuchâtel was still very much a seigneury tied to the medieval institutions of manorialism and feudalism.[14]

Not only was the count of Neuchâtel dependent on land for his wealth and power, the city of Neuchâtel itself was no more forward-looking. In fact, residents of the city who became wealthy were those who invested in land for the production of cereals and wine. A good example is Pierre II de Chambrier (1542?–1609), a vassal of the count and one of the wealthiest inhabitants of Neuchâtel. The descendant of merchants who later were ennobled, Pierre based his wealth primarily on income from his land, especially from wine production, not on commercial or industrial activities. After the death of Pierre II, the Chambriers' most important source of wealth was the sale of wine, most of which was sold within the principality of Neuchâtel and Valangin. In-

14. Ibid., pp. 268–269; Rémy Scheurer, and Dominique Quadroni, *Les finances du comté à la fin du XVIe siècle* (Neuchâtel, 1985), pp. 11–14, 16–22, 41–42, 73.

terest from loans was a distant second among the family's sources of revenue, generating a little less than half that of wine sales, while sales of livestock brought in about a fourth the income from wine production. Moreover, the inventories of the Chambriers' possessions have shown that in the early seventeenth century even the wealthiest Neuchâtelois rarely purchased anything produced outside their native county. As Scheurer has aptly observed, in this society which had by no means conquered poverty, wealth was understood in terms of well-stocked granaries, wine cellars, and smokehouses that ensured a family's security from one harvest to another. Even the most affluent members of this society remained firmly tied to grain production, viticulture, and animal husbandry.[15] Throughout the sixteenth and seventeenth centuries, Neuchâtel continued to have a rather backward economy, exporting little beyond some wine and a few head of livestock.

THE CONVERSION TO PROTESTANTISM

The most important cultural development in sixteenth-century Neuchâtel was the conversion to Protestantism, a religious change for which Bern was largely responsible. Having converted to the Reformed faith in 1528, Bern sought to promote this new faith wherever its political influence was felt. Neuchâtel was too closely tied to Bern to avoid its newly found converting zeal. Guillaume Farel, the French reformer vigorously supported by Bern, arrived in Neuchâtel in December 1529. A consummate zealot and propagandist for the Reformed faith, he and other colleagues aggressively preached in favor of renouncing the Roman church. The city of Neuchâtel was the first locality in the principality—in fact, one of the first French-speaking cities anywhere—to embrace the Reformed faith: on 4 November 1530 the bourgeoisie voted by a small majority in favor of Protestantism. Bern and the Reformed bourgeois hoped that the Reformation would follow a course similar to that it had taken in Bern; that is, they envisioned the imposition of Protestantism on all inhabitants of the county, with threats of fines for those who continued to practice Roman Catholicism. Several years were needed, however, for Protestantism to be generally—though never totally—accepted throughout the county. And even then,

15. Scheurer, "L'économie neuchâteloise," p. 283, and *Pierre Chambrier,* pp. 34–36, 43, 72, 78.

the success of the reformers was in large part due to the support of Bern: the Protestants were able to consolidate their strength in the county of Neuchâtel only after Bern's conquest of the Pays de Vaud.[16]

It is important to note that Neuchâtel's conversion to Protestantism countered the wishes of its sovereign, the countess Jeanne de Hochberg, who remained Roman Catholic. At the critical moment, she was in France at the court of Francis I, who refused to give her permission to go to Neuchâtel, leaving her helpless to prevent her subjects from adhering to the Reformed religion.[17] While she was in France, the tasks of governing were left to Georges de Rive, who served as governor and lieutenant general of Neuchâtel from 1529 until his death in 1552. He too was hostile to the new faith but, fearing Bern, wanted to avoid another occupation of the county. To safeguard the interests of the ruling family, Georges de Rive later allied with the Reformed faith after it had emerged victorious in French-speaking Switzerland.[18] With the exception of the period 1552–1574, the majority of the residents of Neuchâtel were to practice a different faith from that of their sovereign until the eighteenth century.[19]

To be sure, the new faith Bern promoted met some popular resistance, best seen in the seigneury of Valangin. At this time, Bern and its religious allies tended to apply a three-step method in spreading the faith among recalcitrant neighbors. First they threatened the rulers in question; then they called for a referendum when they deemed that a majority of the parishioners favored the Reformed faith; finally, when necessary, they resorted to force in the form of iconoclastic attacks or armed intervention. During the course of 1531, all three tactics were used against Valangin. First the Bernese magistrates wrote a letter in February to the countess of Valangin, beseeching her "no longer to molest or persecute those who wanted to return to the faith of Jesus Christ our Savior."[20] Such a policy ran contrary to the wishes of the bourgeoisie of Bern and tarnished its long-standing friendship with the House of Aarberg, the ruling family of Valangin. Evidence also indicates that

16. Montandon et al., *Neuchâtel et la Suisse*, p. 32; Comité Farel, *Guillaume Farel*, p. 229.
17. Courvoisier, *Panorama de l'histoire*, p. 68.
18. Comité Farel, *Guillaume Farel*, p. 212.
19. The exception was the reign of Léonor d'Orléans. A Protestant, he shared suzerainty over Neuchâtel with his cousin Jacques de Savoie until 1557 and ruled alone until 1573. Jean-Jacques de Bonstetten served as governor from 1552 to 1574, the only period in the sixteenth century, since the conversion to Protestantism, when the prince and his subjects practiced the same faith; Scheurer, *Pierre Chambrier*, p. 7.
20. Comité Farel, *Guillaume Farel*, pp. 246–247.

Bern sent two delegates to Valangin "with instructions to prohibit under menace of war all persecutions against honest people especially
against the evangelicals of [the village of] Boudevilliers, and to make
clear that Bern would not permit in Valangin or elsewhere the reestab-
lishment of the mass."[21] The next step was a referendum in the village
of Dombresson provoked by the city of Biel, an ally of Bern, which took
place on 19 February. Protestant parishioners filled the church and
voted for the acceptance of the Reformed confession. Catholic parishioners, who were the real majority, voted three days later in favor of
maintaining the mass. Finally, the use of force took place in June 1531,
as a group of Neuchâtelois mounted an iconoclastic attack on the
church at Valangin. In spite of this pressure, only in 1536 was the mass
abolished in Valangin. René de Challant, count of Valangin, had little
sympathy for his suzerain, Jeanne de Hochberg, and still less for the
bourgeoisie of Neuchâtel and was thus understandably reluctant to embrace this new faith. Bern's invasion of the Pays de Vaud in 1536 and de
Challant's weakening position—he was an officer in the service of the
defeated duke of Savoy—were important factors in the disappearance of
the mass in Valangin.[22]

If Protestantism was slow to take hold in Valangin, it was never to be
accepted in the *châtellenie* of Le Landeron and the neighboring parish
of Cressier, the only communities in the canton of Neuchâtel that have
remained Catholic to this day. Inhabitants of these communities persistently refused to be bullied into accepting the new faith. Their success in
withstanding the pressure to convert was in large part due to their close
ties with the Catholic city of Solothurn. Le Landeron and Solothurn
had enjoyed *combourgeoisie* since the fifteenth century, and even the
powerful Bern had to refrain from using force against Le Landeron to
avoid conflict with Solothurn.[23]

Much emphasis has been placed on the role of Bern in the Reformation at Neuchâtel. Historians have said this, for example: "It is
thanks to Bern that the French-speaking part of Switzerland became
and was converted to the Reformation. For a long time, the powerful
republic dreamed of extending its domain as far as the Jura and as far as

21. Jonas Boyve, *Annales historiques du comté de Neuchâtel et Valangin depuis Jules-César
jusqu'en 1722*, 5 vols. (Bern, 1854–1858), 2:314–315, cited in Comité Farel, *Guillaume Farel*,
p. 247.
22. Comité Farel, *Guillaume Farel*, pp. 249–250; Courvoisier, *Panorama de l'histoire*, p. 67.
23. Comité Farel, *Guillaume Farel*, p. 388.

Geneva, but it is the Reformation alone that permitted it to realize this dream."[24] And though the influence of Bern is undeniable, it must not be overstated.

> The external ferment was the active proselytism of the Biennois and the Bernese. . . . To say that the Neuchâtelois, reformed by their neighbors, had an exclusively passive role is no more realistic than the notion that they were the sole instigators of their religious evolution. In Chézard-Saint-Martin, in 1536, it was clearly a group of fifteen young people moved by religious enthusiasm who imposed the Reformation by means of sharing the property of the church and by undertaking to repair the chapel.[25]

Despite the influence of outside forces, there were surely plenty of inhabitants of Neuchâtel who eagerly accepted this new faith.

Politically speaking, the main benefactors of the conversion to Protestantism were members of Neuchâtel's bourgeoisie, whose power greatly increased at the expense of the seigneury. Jeanne de Hochberg's death in 1543 marked the end of a reign that was disastrous for the counts of Neuchâtel but decisive for their subjects' rights. Another group that obviously lost ground with the arrival of the Reformation was the clergy. Before the Reformation, clerics had played an important political role in Neuchâtel and were represented on the Conseil d'Etat and the Tribunal des Trois Etats. With the conversion to the Reformed religion, the clergy lost this political power while the bourgeoisie and nobility increased their political and judicial influence. The clergy's representatives on the Conseil d'Etat were replaced by four officials who served the count, usually the *châtelains* of Boudry, Le Landeron, Thielle and, Val-de-Travers. These officials typically were part of the ennobled bourgeoisie; the prince had ennobled these men of bourgeois origin out of recognition for their service to him. The new Protestant clergymen were represented on the consistories, but these legal organs were essentially lay courts. True, in the sixteenth and seventeenth centuries the Classe des Pasteurs did intervene whenever legislation appeared to infringe on their ecclesiastical domain. Be that as it may, the fact that Neuchâtel's magistrates mandated the conversion to Protestantism independently of reformers indicated that pastors would never be as

24. Ibid., p. 338.
25. Courvoisier, *Panorama de l'histoire*, p. 67.

prominent as in Calvin's Geneva. The fact that so many of the early pastors were French refugees with no ties to Neuchâtel's political structure contributed to the decline in power of the first estate.[26]

The ordinances that enjoined the conversion to Protestantism also called for a reform of morals. The first such laws were passed in 1536, 1539, and 1542 for Neuchâtel and in 1539 and 1541 for Valangin. At issue were questions directly related to the religious conflict between Protestants and Catholics; for example, a law declared that there were only two sacraments, baptism and the eucharist, thus rejecting five of the seven sacraments recognized by Rome.[27] Some questions treated in these ordinances had nothing to do with confessional debates. For example, magistrates passed laws against adultery, requiring that first offenders be sentenced to three days in prison on bread and water and fined five livres; the prison term and fine was to be doubled and tripled for second- and third-time offenders. Those guilty of adultery four or more times were to be punished further at the discretion of the authorities.[28] This cannot be said to be one of the controversial issues of the Reformation, since Protestants and Catholics alike opposed adulterous relationships. Among other laws passed were ordinances condemning gluttony, games, ruffians, usury (defined as receiving interest of 5 percent or higher), and the use of diviners; others required that the Sabbath be kept and that each household head say grace before and after every meal.[29]

Among the most significant ordinances passed were those pertaining to the institution of marriage. These various laws show that the magistrates of Neuchâtel and Valangin remained true to Protestant theories of marriage, changing the institution of marriage in three ways: they

26. Comité Farel, *Guillaume Farel*, p. 374; Courvoisier, *Panorama de l'histoire*, pp. 68–69; Favarger, "L'élaboration des lois," pp. 186–212; Henry, *Crime, justice et société*, pp. 77–79; Scheurer, *Pierre Chambrier*, pp. 10–11.

27. Dominique Favarger and Maurice de Tribolet, eds., *Les sources du droit du canton de Neuchâtel*, Les sources du droit suisse, no. 21 (Aarau, Switzerland, 1982), p. 175: "Ordonnances ecclésiastiques consécutives à la Réforme et concernant les sacrements et les moeurs, promulguées par René de Challant pour la seigneurie de Valangin," Valangin, 16 July 1539.

28. "Ordonnances sur les moeurs, la liturgie et les sacremens," Neuchâtel, 15 February 1542. Valangin ordered that those guilty of adultery or fornication for the first time be imprisoned for five days, ten days for the second offense, fifteen for the third. Fourth-time adulterers were to be banished from the country; ibid., pp. 176, 191. Ordinances in Neuchâtel and Valangin do not reveal a double standard. But in Calvin's Geneva, women guilty of adultery received harsher sentences than did men. The Petit Conseil of Geneva was known to banish adulterous women without regard to the number of times they had been guilty of infidelity; Cornelia Seeger, *Nullité de mariage, divorce et séparation de corps à Genève au temps de Calvin* (Lausanne, 1989), pp. 412–413.

29. Favarger and Tribolet, *Sources du droit du canton de Neuchâtel*, pp. 188–195.

abolished clandestine marriages, requiring that witnesses be present and that parental permission be given when marriages were contracted; they reduced the number of impediments to marriage; and divorce, as opposed to annulment or separation, and subsequent remarriage became possibilities. These three changes were in fact the most important practical ramifications to stem from the views on marriage of Luther, Calvin, and virtually all major reformers.

Condemning clandestine marriages, the ordinances laid down by René de Challant for Valangin in 1539 and by Georges de Rive for Neuchâtel in 1550 provided that those wishing to contract marriages were required to have as witnesses to their promises at least "two honest men."[30] To avoid unlawful marriages, the magistrates forbade marriage outside one's parish, subjecting offenders to fines of five livres, and required that ministers publicize the banns three times before consecrating marriages. The consent of parents or guardians was also required for those who were not at least, as the ordinances vaguely prescribed, nineteen or twenty years old. In the absence of such permission, marriages of minors would be null.[31] The ordinances, however, also forbade parents and guardians from forcing their children to marry, declaring invalid any such forced union. Still, if parents made several reasonable offers of marriage for their son or daughter, but he or she wanted nothing to do with these propositions, parents were no longer obligated to provide dowries.[32] These requirements echoed the criticism by Protestant reformers of the institution of clandestine marriages, which had been recognized as valid by canon law for centuries.

Roman Catholic doctrine on how one entered into marriage had been set in the twelfth century after debates between two conflicting theories. For Gratian, marriage was initiated by the consent of two individuals to marry but became indissoluble only with sexual consummation. A second theory, supported most notably by Peter Lombard, maintained that present consent, as opposed to future consent, alone sufficed to create an indissoluble marriage. Thus for Lombard consent, not coitus, made a marriage binding.[33] By contrast, future consent—agreeing to take one another as husband and wife at a later date—became a valid marriage only if consummation followed. The formula

---

30. Ibid., pp. 179, 205: "deux hommes de bien, honnestes et bien famez non suspectz"; "deux hommes de bien et d'honneur."
31. Ibid., pp. 180, 189, 205, 206. Those without parents or guardians could marry at fourteen for girls and at sixteen for boys.
32. Ibid., pp. 179–206.
33. Helmholz, *Marriage Litigation*, p. 26.

adopted by Pope Alexander III (1159–1181) fell somewhere between the two theories. According to this compromise, which became an integral part of canon law, marriage was theoretically indissoluble from the moment of consent but not perfected until sexual union. In extraordinary circumstances, unions could be dissolved in the absence of consummation. An important ramification of this theory was that valid marriage did not require a public ceremony. It was still a sin to marry without the publication of the banns or the benediction of a priest; but, though the offenders were subject to "the spiritual penalties of penance," the marriage nevertheless remained valid.[34] Furthermore, the age at which one could legally contract a marriage was fourteen for boys and twelve for girls.[35] Having attained these respective ages, adolescent boys and girls could contract binding marriages without the authorization of their parents.

Reformers criticized clandestine marriage for a variety of reasons. Luther and Erasmus attacked it because it circumvented the authority of parents. According to both the ex-monk from Wittenberg and the prince of the humanists, God's authority manifested itself through the will of the parents. Moreover, this doctrine of marriage could clearly be the source of legal complications. If mutual consent were the necessary and sufficient condition for contracting a binding marriage and no witnesses were required to such an engagement—in theory God alone sufficed as a witness—proving such a marriage could be very difficult. Having had only God as witness to her engagement to marry, a woman would indeed have trouble proving the validity of this marriage in court if her pretended husband refused to acknowledge such a commitment. If the publication of the banns were not required, there was also a strong possibility that bigamous unions would result. For example, a man might first marry one woman clandestinely and then another publicly. According to A. Esmein, if the first union could be proved only by the testimony of the couple involved, then the second marriage would be legal. But the church still considered the first one valid since canon law maintained that consent alone was needed to form a marriage. Therefore, the conscientious man should return to his first wife, and at the penitential tribunal the priest would tell him that he must not render the conjugal debt (the sexual relations that spouses owe one another) to

---

34. A. Esmein, *Le mariage en droit canonique*, 2 vols., 2d ed. (Paris, 1929), 1:100–101; Helmholz, *Marriage Litigation*, pp. 26–27.

35. Paul Viollet, *Histoire du droit civil français* (Paris, 1905), p. 445. These ages had been set by Roman law.

the second wife; but an ecclesiastical judge would order him to do just that and threaten him with excommunication if he did not. In other words, clandestine marriage would be responsible for producing a bigamous situation. Two marriages existed, both of which were valid in the eyes of the church—one for its *forum internum,* the other for its *forum externum.*[36] It was precisely such awkward situations that reformers sought to avoid.

In light of these criticisms, most Protestant magistrates throughout Europe passed laws against clandestine marriages, requiring publication of the banns and parental permission in the case of minors. In response to many attacks, Roman Catholics also ceased to recognize the validity of clandestine marriages. In 1563, the Council of Trent issued the decree *Tametsi,* which held that to form a valid marriage a couple must express their consent in the presence of witnesses, including a priest. It did not require, however, parental consent. In Catholic France, where Trent was not accepted, still stricter laws were passed. There, marriages had to be public, in the presence of the curé and four witnesses. A royal edict passed in 1556 and reconfirmed in 1579 required parental permission until the age of thirty for men and twenty-five for women.[37] Even after this age people were required to ask their parents' opinion, and parents had the right to disinherit children who married without their consent. By declaring null any marriage contracted by men and women under the age of nineteen or twenty years without parental consent, Neuchâtel's magistrates were in line with the views of Protestant and many Catholic reformers.[38]

36. Pierre Bels, *Le mariage des Protestants français jusqu'en 1685: Fondements doctrinaux et pratique juridique* (Paris, 1968), p. 65; Esmein, *Marriage en droit canonique,* 2:148–149.

37. French Protestants also required parental permission to marry up to age twenty-five for women and thirty for men; Raymond A. Mentzer, Jr., "Church Discipline and Communal Pressure and the French Protestants," paper delivered at the Sixteenth Century Studies Conference, St. Louis, Mo., 29 October 1988, p. 9.

38. Esmein, *Marriage en droit canonique,* 2: 204, 215; Flandrin, *Families in Former Times,* p. 131. The French ordinances of 1560 and 1579 went so far as to declare that anyone would be put to death who bribed a minor— male or female—to marry without the permission of the minor's parents, Paul Ourliac and J. de Malafosse, *Histoire du droit privé,* vol. 3: *Le droit familial* (Paris, 1968), pp. 205, 207–208; Viollet, *Histoire du droit civil français,* p. 447. Ironically, the only countries in which clandestine marriages were not eliminated during the Reformation were Protestant. In England, clandestine marriages remained valid until Lord Hardwicke's Marriage Act in 1753; Ingram, "Spousals Litigation," in *Marriage and Society,* ed. Outhwaite, p. 40. Still more surprising is that in Scotland consent continued to be the necessary and sufficient condition for forming a marriage in spite of the strong Calvinist influence there. Theoretically, Scots could still marry at the age of twelve for girls and fourteen for boys with no need of witnesses, parental permission, or an officiating clergyman. Scottish law continued to recognize the validity of clandestine marriage until 1940. Scotland became Prot-

Neuchâtel's legislation on impediments to marriage also reflected Protestant criticisms of canon law. Many reformers felt that Catholic impediments were too strict with respect to consanguinity and affinity. "Consanguinity" was defined as the tie that binds people descended from common ancestors, and "affinity" the relationship between two people one of whom is married to a relative of the other.[39] From the tenth to the twelfth century, the Roman Catholic church forbade marriage as far as the seventh degree of consanguinity and affinity, thereby condemning marriages between sixth cousins as incestuous.[40] Under Innocent III's leadership, the Fourth Lateran Council of 1215 reduced impediments from the seventh to the fourth degree, thus prohibiting marriages between third cousins.[41] Medieval canon law also forbade marriage in cases of premarital impotence, "spiritual affinity" resulting from godparentage, deception concerning one's status (e.g., a serf who

---

estant in 1560 and, according to T. C. Smout, the Scots did not reject clandestine marriage partly because they did not want to follow the directives of Trent. Moreover, the laity feared that requiring the presence of a pastor unnecessarily enhanced the power of the clergy; see Smout, "Scottish Marriage, Regular and Irregular, 1500–1940," in *Marriage and Society*, pp. 206, 212.

39. Viollet, *Histoire du droit civil français*, pp. 428–430.

40. Flandrin, *Families in Former Times*, p. 24. Such degrees were tabulated differently according to canon law and Roman law. In Roman law, one determines the degree of consanguinity between two people by counting generations, beginning with one of the two persons in question, ascending the family tree to the common ancestors, and then descending the family tree to the other relative examined. In this accounting, brothers and sisters are at the second degree of consanguinity. In canon law, the degrees are calculated by climbing the tree from one of the relatives to the common ancestors and stopping there. According to this method, siblings are at the first degree of consanguinity. If two relatives are of unequal distance from the common ancestors, one counts from the perspective of the person farther removed from the common ancestors. Thus a man and his brother's daughter are at the second degree of consanguinity, since one counts the number of generations the girl is removed from her grandparents. The degree of affinity is determined by the degree of consanguinity that unites one person with the spouse of another. A man whose wife has a cousin of the second degree is himself at the second degree of affinity with that cousin; Viollet, *Histoire du droit civil français*, pp. 428–430. When referring to these degrees, I use the canonical system, since Neuchâtel's courts used this method in determining the degree of *parenté*. Occasionally the *procès verbaux* reveal cases in which witnesses reconstructed a family tree to determine the degree of parentage between two people. For example, in 1586 Pierre Maridor and Jehanne de Salles appeared before the consistory of Valangin. Someone had halted the publication of their banns, saying that they were related by the third degree of consanguinity. Relatives appeared as witnesses and testified that the couple's maternal grandfathers were brothers. The courts accordingly denied them permission to marry because they were relatives of the third degree. Had the Roman system been applied they would have been relatives of the sixth degree; AEN, CSV2:292, 295–297.

41. Brundage, *Law, Sex, and Christian Society*, p. 356. The Roman Catholic church reduced impediments from the fourth to the second degree for Indians of South American origin in 1537, for Blacks in 1897, and for the whole world in 1917; Goody, *Development of the Family*, p. 144.

falsely claimed to be free), and sexual relations between a fiancé and a third party after betrothal. Fiancés who practiced different religions were also forbidden to marry.[42]

Reformers considered some of these impediments unwarranted. Among Protestants, Luther held an extreme position with regard to consanguinity and affinity. Citing the standards set in Leviticus 18, Luther argued that only twelve relationships precluded marriage: a man could not marry his mother, stepmother, sister, half-sister, granddaughter, aunt, daughter-in-law, brother's wife, wife's sister, stepdaughter, or uncle's wife. Moreover, he maintained that marriages were forbidden only to the second degree of consanguinity and to the first degree of affinity. In attacking Catholic impediments, Luther held that they were a ploy to bring in revenue by selling dispensations.[43] In the marriage laws he drafted for Geneva, Calvin noted that divine law and Roman law did not forbid marriages between first cousins. Nonetheless, because impediments to marry were so ingrained in European society, Calvin for the time being continued to prohibit marriages between first cousins, though he permitted unions between people more distantly related.[44] Magistrates in Neuchâtel and Valangin reflected reformers' criticisms by passing laws that modified impediments for consanguinity and affinity in a modest way: they allowed marriages between relatives of the fourth degree.[45] In Neuchâtel, as in Protestant areas in general, impediments based on spiritual affinity also disappeared. On the whole, however, the conversion to Protestantism did not effect dramatic changes in the area of impediments.

42. Ozment, *When Fathers Ruled*, pp. 44–45.

43. Ibid., pp. 45–46; Goody, *Development of the Family*, pp. 181–182. Luther was not altogether consistent on the question of impediments. On one occasion, he maintained that first cousins could marry and that a man could marry the sister of his deceased wife or fiancée; elsewhere, he declared these marriages prohibited. It is interesting to note that he did not say a man could not marry his grandmother.

44. *Ioannis Calvini Opera Quae Supersunt Omnia*, ed. Guilielmus Baum, Eduardus Cunitz, and Eduardus Reuss (Brunswick and Berlin, 1834–1968), X/a, 38, 109.

45. The laws dealing with degree of consanguinity between spouses were not completely consistent. Ordinances passed by René de Challant in Valangin in 1539 and 1550 forbade marriage between persons not beyond the third degree of consanguinity. In Neuchâtel, Georges de Rive, still Catholic at heart, promulgated an ordinance in 1550 that denied men and women the right to marry unless related beyond the fourth degree of consanguinity. The Tribunal des Trois Etats of Neuchâtel declared in 1559 that on the basis of Scripture it was permissible to marry relatives of the third degree, but in those neighboring areas where the Reformation had not firmly taken hold the limit would remain at the fourth degree. Thus, while in Valangin marriages were prohibited to the third degree, in Neuchâtel the ban vacillated between the second and fourth degrees; Favarger and Tribolet, *Sources du droit du canton de Neuchâtel*, pp. 179–180, 209, 220–221, 234.

A more important change in the institution of marriage was the introduction of divorce and subsequent remarriage, an issue closely tied to the question of whether marriage was a sacrament. Though the view that marriage was a sacrament became dogmatic truth only with the Council of Florence in 1438, the idea that marriage was indissoluble had a long history in Roman Catholic doctrine. Divorce had existed among the Romans, and two general theses developed among the early church fathers: divorce was permissible for reasons of adultery but only men could receive a divorce, or both men and women could divorce adulterous spouses.[46] Augustine opposed both these theories, claiming that marriage was indissoluble; in the twelfth century, Peter Lombard wrote of marriage as a sacrament. In the thirteenth century, Thomas Aquinas and others affirmed that marriage was a sacrament and that consent conferred grace just as the other sacraments did. The notion that marriage was a sacrament had thus been informally accepted well before the Council of Florence. And, if marriage is a sacrament, a vehicle of God's grace, it is understandable that theologians considered it indissoluble, since God does not err in bestowing his grace. As a result, the only type of divorce canon lawyers allowed was *divortium quoad torum et mensam,* which in reality was only a separation that did not permit remarriage. Three causes justified granting such a separation: adultery, the spiritual offenses of apostasy and heresy, and cruelty.[47]

Reformers disagreed with Catholic attitudes about separation and divorce, in part because they doubted that marriage should be considered a sacrament. Some Catholic reformers—most important, Erasmus—had questioned the sacramental nature of marriage. Erasmus examined the sources of the ideas of indissolubility and of the sacramental nature of marriage and concluded that these were historically determined and therefore varied according to the period. Consequently, the doctrine ought to change to accommodate contemporary conditions. Luther believed that marriage had considerable religious value; he denied that celibacy was a more noble state than married life. Nevertheless, he denied

46. Roman law had held that only married women could be guilty of adultery; by definition men could not commit adultery. Canon law eventually eliminated this double standard, holding that men as well as women were expected to remain faithful to their spouses; James A. Brundage, "Adultery and Fornication: A Study in Legal Theology," in *Sexual Practices and the Medieval Church,* ed. Vern L. Bullough and James Brundage (Buffalo, N.Y., 1982), p. 131, and Brundage, *Law, Sex, and Christian Society,* p. 247.

47. Brundage, *Law, Sex, and Christian Society,* pp. 146, 433; Esmein, *Mariage en droit canonique,* 2:56–57, 106; Helmholz, *Marriage Litigation,* p. 100; Phillips, *Putting Asunder: A History of Divorce in Western Society* (Cambridge, 1988), pp. 13–14.

that there was any scriptural basis for the idea that marriage was a sacrament. For him marriage was something of this world, just as women, houses, and courts were; like them, it was subject to the authority of the state. In effect, Luther was calling for the secularization of marriage. Calvin voiced similar criticisms against the sacramental nature of marriage. Marriage, as he saw it, was instituted by God but was not a sacrament. Agriculture, architecture, and shoemaking were also instituted by God, but they were not sacraments.[48]

If marriage was not a sacrament that conferred grace on participants, only a short step was needed to deny its indissolubility. It is therefore not surprising that all important reformers accepted the possibility of divorce and remarriage under certain circumstances. For Erasmus, as for many Protestant reformers, marriage was "a constant creation of the *affectus coniugalis* and divorce [was] inherent in this conception." Marriage was to enjoy all the richness of the intimate life coming from a faith genuinely felt, and external coercion should be eliminated.[49] Many Protestant reformers echoed Erasmus's claim that the *divortium* of the Catholics was unfair to the innocent party. A general theme among reformers was that divorce was possible only in cases of matrimonial fault—that is, when one of the spouses was a guilty party, and the other a victim. Divorce says Roderick Phillips, "was not thought of as a remedy for marriage breakdown as such but as a punishment for a matrimonial crime and as a relief for the victim of the crime (the innocent spouse)."[50] Protestants held that the *divortium* was a modern innovation not found in the early church and that a permanent separation was a travesty of marriage. Since the married state was appropriate for most people, the reformers deemed it immoral to subject individuals to indefinite separations without the possibility of remarriage. Separated couples remained married in a legal sense yet were not married in a social sense. Phillips notes:

> This ambiguity implied by separation *a mensa et thoro* struck the Reformers as being intolerable to the spouses concerned and as dangerous to society. . . . Recognizing that there would inevitably be sin, that some vices practiced within marriage were unredeemable, they

48. Bels, *Mariage des Protestants français*, p. 78; Esmein, *Mariage en droit canonique*, 2:144–145.
49. Bels, *Mariage des Protestants français*, pp. 74, 77.
50. Phillips, *Putting Asunder*, p. 90.

believed that the marriages made possible by divorce (remarriages) would contribute more to the totality of morality, just as enforced celibacy and separated men and women detracted from it.[51]

Under certain circumstances, Protestants therefore viewed divorce as an appropriate solution for marital dysfunction.

True to this tradition, magistrates passed ordinances in Neuchâtel that provided the possibility of divorce under certain conditions. Prominent among the grounds for which one could file for divorce was adultery, the only ground common to all divorce doctrines and legislation among continental Protestants. Protestant reformers gave far more importance to adultery as a ground for divorce than had Catholics as a reason for separation. For Catholics, adultery was simply one of several reasons for receiving a separation. The increased importance accorded it by Protestants was a result of their emphasis on the Bible as sole authority. Adultery was the only ground for divorce clearly and unequivocally mentioned in the Bible: "I tell you, then, that any man who divorces his wife for any cause other than her unfaithfulness, commits adultery if he marries some other woman" (Matthew 18:9). Neuchâtel's ordinances therefore held that, if a married person had been convicted beyond a reasonable doubt of infidelity and the innocent spouse refused to forgive the guilty party, a separation would be granted. After the separation, the innocent party had to wait at least six months and receive judicial permission before remarrying. The guilty spouse could never marry the party with whom he or she committed adultery, a barrier that had been erected by medieval canon lawyers.[52] To marry another person, he or she had to wait one year, remaining chaste during this time. After this year, if the party petitioned to remarry, the judges heard testimony on his or her behavior since the separation and granted or rejected the request accordingly. If offenders remarried without permission before the allotted waiting period had expired, such marriages were to be declared null and the offenders imprisoned and then banished for a year.[53]

---

51. Ibid., pp. 93–94.

52. According to James Brundage, the underlying theory behind this prohibition was that "sexual relations between two persons created a bond of legal affinity analogous to that created by the relationship between a baptismal sponsor and a godchild"; "Adultery and Fornication," p. 133.

53. Favarger and Tribolet, *Sources du droit du canton de Neuchâtel*, pp. 209–218: "Ordonnances matrimoniales promulguées par le gouverneur Georges de Rive," Neuchâtel, 21 March

Adultery was not the only ground for divorce recognized as valid by
Neuchâtel's magistrates. In cases of abandonment or desertion, if a person left the country without the consent of the other spouse, the abandoned spouse was to wait a year and a day before filing suit.[54] After this
delay, three announcements to inquire about the whereabouts of the absent spouse were to be made within a period of six weeks. If such inquiries proved fruitless, a divorce could be accorded. If, however, a
person departed with his or her spouse's consent, the other could not
remarry until sufficient testimony proved that the absent one was dead.
Various medical infirmities could also be the basis for terminating
a marriage. If there was a leprous spouse, the couple were to continue
living together for a year or a half year to see if there was any improvement. If not, and if it was dangerous for the other spouse to have sexual relations with the leper, then a separation could be granted, allowing the healthy one to remarry provided that he or she continued to
support the leprous spouse and that the latter concurred. Other possible
grounds for divorce were insanity and impotence, if the aid of physicians had been to no avail. Whatever the alleged reasons for requesting
a divorce, they were to be granted only when absolutely necessary.[55]

These guidelines for the dissolution of marriage were roughly consistent with the views of the most influential reformers. Luther considered adultery, desertion, and refusal to engage in sexual relations valid
reasons for divorce. Calvin took a more restrictive view of divorce,
claiming that the Bible clearly stated that the only justifiable reason for
terminating a marriage was adultery. He therefore denied that marriages could be terminated for leprosy or impotence. But, in spite of his
claims to the contrary, Calvin in effect also accepted desertion as a valid
ground for divorce. Like Luther, he maintained that abandonment was
a type of "aggravated adultery": the spouse who deserted the household

---

1550. Neuchâtel's laws made it easier to divorce an adulterous spouse than was the case in
Zurich immediately after the conversion to the Reformed faith. According to marriage laws
composed by Zwingli, before a divorce would be granted for adultery a couple first had to live
together for a year to see if they could work out their differences. If they failed to reconcile,
they could separate and remarry. Evidently the guilty party did not have to wait longer than
the innocent spouse before remarrying; Phillips, *Putting Asunder,* pp. 62–63. Quite different
were the practices in Geneva during the time of Calvin. Beginning in 1548, the Petit Conseil
of Geneva forbade adulterous women to remarry anyone in the seigneury. They did not, however, forbid men from remarrying, apart from the prohibition against marrying their paramours; Seeger, *Nullité de mariage,* p. 413.

54. As we see in Chapter 3, in practice abandoned spouses had to wait seven years before
receiving divorces for reasons of desertion.

55. Favarger and Tribolet, *Sources du droit du canton de Neuchâtel,* pp. 209–218.

most likely would have sexual relations with another person and therefore could be presumed guilty of infidelity. Zwingli went a bit further than either Luther or Calvin on the question of divorce, maintaining that the passage in Matthew simply indicated the least serious offense for which a marriage could be dissolved. Elsewhere in the Bible, other offenses appear worse than adultery—surely they too must be grounds for divorce. It is a far greater sin to be an unbeliever than an adulterer, Zwingli argued; therefore, someone married to an unbeliever should have the opportunity to terminate the marriage. Moreover, Zwingli held that the Apostle Paul's claim that it is better to marry than to burn underscores the importance of sexuality in marriage, justifying impotence as a ground for divorce.[56]

The reformer with the most radical views on divorce was Martin Bucer. In his *De Regno Christi* (1557), Bucer expressed libertarian views on marriage, anticipating divorce laws that would not prevail until the twentieth century. Bucer insisted that the purpose of marriage was not primarily procreation and the avoidance of nonmarital sex; rather, companionship was the most fundamental element of the Christian marriage, entailing fidelity, mutual love, and cohabitation. Consequently, Bucer not only recognized adultery and desertion as grounds for divorce but even approved of divorce by mutual consent and by repudiation by either spouse. That is not to say that Bucer took divorce lightly. He felt that divorce should be more difficult to attain if children were involved and that a person should be penalized financially for repudiating a spouse without due cause.[57] Though of great interest to the modern reader, Bucer's views on divorce were far ahead of their time.

It was Luther and Calvin who wrote the most influential divorce doctrines of the sixteenth century. Legislation based on their work was widespread throughout Europe, mainly in the Protestant states but also among Reformed populations within Roman Catholic states. Except in England, where the Reformation actually made dissolving a marriage more difficult, Protestants throughout Europe followed the lead of Luther and Calvin: laws in Württemberg, Augsburg, Nuremburg, Geneva, and many other Protestant cities and states allowed divorce for

---

56. Phillips, *Putting Asunder*, pp. 48, 53–57, 62–63.

57. According to Bucer, other grounds that merited divorce were witchcraft, "desecration of sepulchers, committing sacrilege, favoring thieves, the wife's feasting with strangers without her husband's knowledge or consent, the husband's frequenting lewd women within his wife's sight, and violence." These were all serious offenses that merited death, and there was no need to remain with a partner who committed such heinous acts; cited in Phillips, *Putting Asunder*, pp. 69–71.

reasons of adultery and willful desertion.[58] These were to be the most important grounds for divorce in Neuchâtel throughout the early modern period.

To handle matrimonial cases as well as various minor infractions, magistrates in both Neuchâtel and Valangin established consistories, a type of morals court. Wherever Reformed Christianity took hold, officials established similar institutions. Zurich's Ehegericht, founded by Huldreich Zwingli in 1525, was the first such institution and served as a model for courts established in St. Gall, Bern, Basel, and Schaffhausen.[59] Overseen by two clerical and four lay judges, the Ehegericht, as its name implies, dealt only with issues pertaining to marriage. In Geneva in 1541, John Calvin called for the formation of a consistory to enforce all aspects of Reformed morality. In establishing consistories, the magistrates of Neuchâtel and Valangin were following precedents set by other Reformed cities.

Throughout the Old Regime, Valangin maintained its own consistory.[60] Beginning in 1538, Bern strongly encouraged the countess of Valangin, herself still Catholic, to establish a consistory. She and her grandson eventually complied and founded a consistory originally formed exclusively of officials of the seigneury, thus excluding members of the clergy. In 1547 the local ministers complained and asked to be included as consistorial judges. This request was granted, and from this time the consistory that functioned for three hundred years had its origins. The composition of this tribunal varied, but in general the church was represented by two ministers—most often by those of Valangin, Fontaines, Cernier, or Dombresson—though at times only one member was a clergyman and at others as many as three or four pastors were present. Secular judges were more numerous. There were always at least two officeholders: one mayor—most often, the mayor of Valangin—and the *banneret*, another official. In addition, the bourgeoisie of Valangin was represented by from one to eight members. During its sessions the consistory heard cases involving moral infractions such as drunkenness, blasphemy, and fornication, as well as those involving marital disputes.[61]

58. Ibid., pp. 50, 62; Ingram, *Church Courts, Sex, and Marriage*, p. 147.
59. Phillips, *Putting Asunder*, pp. 62, 64.
60. Valangin's is the only *consistoire seigneurial* in the county of Neuchâtel whose records are largely extant, having been preserved with very few lacunae in eleven volumes, 1547–1848.
61. Berthoud, "Le consistoire seigneurial de Valangin." Michèle Robert has categorized the

At first the consistory was to have only four sessions per year, each held just before the various celebrations of the eucharist at Christmas, Easter, Pentecost, and Saint Michael's Day. The sessions were so timed because moral offenses were often punished by deprivation of the eucharist, but the meetings soon became more numerous and their dates seemingly arbitrary. The denial to partake of communion was not simply a religious question. In his work on church courts in Elizabethan and Stuart England, Martin Ingram notes that, since "the church was supposed to be coterminous with the whole society, excommunication could also involve civil disabilities. In fine, the church courts reflected the fact that in early modern England the notions of 'sin' and 'crime' were not clearly differentiated."[62] David Sabean views the relationship between the individual and the community as vitally important for the concept of communion in sixteenth-century Protestant areas. Of the duchy of Württemberg of the 1580s, he asserts that every member of the community had to be reconciled with all others before being allowed to partake of communion. These conclusions of Ingram and Sabean are certainly valid for the principality of Neuchâtel and Valangin. By denying delinquents the right to take communion and requiring them to do humiliating acts of public penance before readmitting them to full membership of the church and community, the consistories were imposing, according to Ingram, "a ritual of repentance and reconciliation, but equally a deeply humiliating experience designed to deter

---

various causes for which people were convoked before Valangin's consistory for the period 1590–1667. This tribunal summoned 2,355 persons for the following reasons: illegitimate births (362); scandals and dissolute lives (201); fornication and adultery (183); insults and disputes (178); drunkenness (119); dancing, illicit games, or music (101); blasphemy (89); refusal to appear before the parish court (84); work on Sunday (46); truancy from church (27); disobedience to parents (27); frequenting taverns at an improper hour (27); going to a Catholic church for a baptism, marriage, or other ceremony (21); suspicion of witchcraft (16); "Le consistoire: Inquisition des réformées?" *Musée neuchâtelois*, 1986, 14. Ray Mentzer, Jr. found a very different breakdown of offenses heard before Reformed consistories in southern French towns such as Nîmes. Half of all cases there involved disputes and quarrels, and one-third dealt with a return to "popery." Sex offenses, so numerous in Valangin, amounted to only 7.5 percent of all *délits* in southern France, where consistories convoked more people for dancing than for illicit sex; "Church Discipline," pp. 7–8, and "*Disciplina nervus ecclesiae:* The Calvinist Reform of Morals at Nîmes," *Sixteenth Century Journal* 18 (1987): 93, 103, 108–109. As for the Genevan consistory, the first volume of registers (1542–1544) shows people being convoked primarily for religious offenses such as truancy from church, prayers to the Virgin Mary, and fasting during Lent. In later volumes, such religious improprieties are rare, giving way to cases of marriage contract disputes, fornication, and insults; Archives de l'Etat de Genève, Consistoire de Genève, vols. 1–18. I assume that this change in the character of moral offenses means that Calvin and the other judges either gave up or, more likely, succeeded in routing out unacceptable religious practices.

62. Ingram, *Church Courts, Sex and, Marriage*, p. 3.

others and give satisfaction to the congregation for the affront of public sin."[63] Beyond censure and excommunication, the sentences the consistory could impose included fines, prison terms, the pillory, and banishment.[64] Stronger sentences could be levied only by a criminal court.

Insofar as it could impose secular punishments, the consistory of Valangin was different from almost all analogous institutions. In Calvin's Geneva, for example, the consistory had the right to excommunicate and censure delinquents as well as to refer them to secular courts. It could not, however, levy any secular punishments such as fines or prison sentences. Likewise, in southern France consistories established by Reformed churches in towns such as Nîmes rarely levied fines and could not imprison, banish, or impose corporal punishment. The effectiveness of the French consistories' sanctions against bad behavior ultimately depended on the good will of the local government; the consistories could do nothing but request secular officials to enforce Reformed morality.[65] Having broader punitive powers, Valangin's consistory distinguished itself from those of Geneva and Nîmes as well as virtually all others, despite the common label.

Valangin's consistory was in fact a legal tribunal; the others were essentially compulsory counseling services, resembling more Neuchâtel's *consistoires admonitifs* than Valangin's *consistoire seigneurial*. The former were consistories, which regrettably kept no records, established during the Reformation for each parish. Composed of the pastor and a few elders, the parish consistories, unlike the *consistoires seigneuriaux,* were exclusively ecclesiastical in nature and could not levy any secular sentences; the punishments they could inflict were limited to censures and suspensions of Holy Communion. Offenses requiring more serious action had to be referred to the seigneurial consistories, which, as noted above, could inflict certain secular punishments. In theory, the seigneurial consistories and the Justices matrimoniales, discussed below, heard only those cases referred to them by parish consistories.[66]

Valangin's consistory was different from those of Geneva and Nîmes in part as a result of differences in personnel. Geneva's consistory com-

63. Ibid.; David Warren Sabean, "Communion and Community: The Refusal to Attend the Lord's Supper in the Sixteenth Century," in *Power in the Blood: Popular Culture and Village Discourse in Early Modern Germany* (Cambridge, 1984), pp. 37–60.

64. Berthoud, "Le consistoire seigneurial de Valangin."

65. Mentzer, "Church Discipline," pp. 11–12; see also Mentzer, "*Disciplina nervus ecclesiae,*" pp. 89–115.

66. Henry, *Crime, justice, et société,* pp. 87–89.

prised clergymen and laymen in roughly equal numbers, whereas pastors were a small minority on Valangin's consistory. It could be argued that Valangin's consistory was empowered to pass secular sentences because it was essentially lay in nature. That, however, cannot explain why Valangin's consistory had powers that those of Nîmes and other communities of southern France did not enjoy; as in Valangin, the clergy, though represented on these consistories, was easily outnumbered by lay members.[67] The deciding factor was not the issue of lay members as opposed to pastors but rather that of civil as opposed to religious authorities. Valangin's lay judges were members of this court because they were officeholders serving the count or representatives of the bourgeoisie, not because they were elders of the church, as was the case in southern France. Consequently, the consistory of Valangin was dominated by people who already held influential positions; granting them authority to impose certain secular penalties posed no threat to those in power.

The consistorial system in the county of Neuchâtel proper was quite similar to that of Valangin, though there were some differences. Six *consistoires seigneuriaux* were established for the county as a whole: one for the city of Neuchâtel, one for the *mairie* of La Côte, and one each for the baronies and *châtellenies* of Val-de-Travers, Thielle, Le Landeron, and Boudry.[68] Like Valangin's consistory, each of these tribunals was concerned with controlling the moral behavior of its subjects and theoretically heard only cases referred by parish consistories. Matrimonial disputes, however, were handled by a special consistory, the Justice matrimoniale, which had exclusive jurisdiction over marital concerns everywhere in the principality except the seigneury of Valangin. In Valangin, a similar matrimonial court split off from the consistory only in the early eighteenth century. Like Valangin's consistory, Neuchâtel's Justice matrimoniale was originally composed exclusively of secular authorities, though it soon included clergymen among its ranks. In its mature form, the matrimonial court consisted of the mayor of Neuchâtel, the ministers of the city, two members of the Conseil d'Etat and four members of the city's Petit Conseil.[69]

Though the personnel of Neuchâtel's matrimonial court resembled that of Valangin's consistory, the matters over which they had jurisdic-

67. Robert M. Kingdon, "The Control of Morals in Calvin's Geneva," in *The Social History of the Reformation*, ed. Lawrence P. Buck and Jonathan W. Zophy (Columbus, Ohio, 1972), pp. 3–16; E. William Monter, "The Consistory of Geneva, 1559–1569," *Bibliothèque d'humanisme et renaissance* 38 (1976): 467–484; Mentzer, "Church Discipline," p. 1.

68. Favarger and Tribolet, *Sources du droit du canton de Neuchâtel*, pp. 218–219.

69. Ibid., p. 205; Henry, *Crime, justice, et société*, p. 89.

tion were not identical. Whereas the consistory had authority over all moral questions, including marital disputes, Neuchâtel's court had jurisdiction only over matrimonial concerns. On the basis of reports from parish consistories, the consistory habitually took the initiative in ordering delinquents to appear before it. Though it too could impose secular punishments such as jail sentences, the Justice matrimoniale generally did not actively seek out offenders to prosecute but rather heard only cases initiated by plaintiffs. Police actions against adulterers or brutal husbands would have been made by the county's *consistoires seigneuriaux*, which were similar to that of Valangin. But unlike Valangin's consistory, these consistories theoretically did not handle matrimonial cases such as divorces or contract disputes over which the Justice matrimoniale had exclusive jurisdiction.[70]

Though marital issues were ordinarily first heard in the consistory of Valangin or the Justice matrimoniale of Neuchâtel, appeals could be made to other institutions. The Conseil d'Etat, which served as the supreme administrator of justice, was often involved in marriage questions. Ordinarily, parties who were dissatisfied with the decisions made in the consistory or matrimonial court could appeal to the Tribunal des Trois Etats of Neuchâtel or Valangin. Appeals could also be made in both Valangin and Neuchâtel to the respective counts or their lieutenants, who always had the last word on such cases, leaving no opportunity for further appeal.[71] The cases most frequently heard by the counts, their lieutenants, and the Conseil d'Etat were petitions for dispensations to allow marriages between persons more closely related than the law permitted.

Occasionally there was some confusion as to which of these judicial bodies had jurisdiction over various types of litigation. During the sixteenth century, examples can be found of divorce cases being heard before the Conseil d'Etat or of marital cases appearing first before the Tribunal des Trois Etats and being sent from there to the Justice matrimoniale, the reverse order from what was prescribed. Nevertheless,

70. Very few records of these consistories are extant. The fate of the consistory of the city of Neuchâtel is one of the great mysteries in the history of Neuchâtel's legal institutions. Although the ordinance described above called for such a consistory, there is no indication that this tribunal ever actually functioned. Not a trace of a record has survived, and no mention is made of it in the records of other tribunals. No doubt those guilty of moral offenses in the city of Neuchâtel were punished by the city's government, that is, the mayor, the Petit Conseil, or the Quatre-Ministraux.

71. Berthoud, "Le consistoire seigneurial de Valangin," p. 14; Henry, *Crime, justice et société*, p. 765.

these deviations were exceptional; the vast majority of marriage-related cases appeared only before the matrimonial court of Neuchâtel or the consistory of Valangin, and it is the volumes of the records, or *procès verbaux*, of these two institutions that serve as the most important sources for this book.

Taken together, the various institutions that oversaw matrimonial issues indicate that Neuchâtel's conversion to Protestantism brought about the secularization of the control of marriage. Church courts ceased to exist, giving way to consistories and matrimonial courts in which secular officials predominated. Though clergymen were represented on these tribunals and no doubt exercised considerable influence on parish consistories, ultimate authority over matrimonial concerns passed from their hands into those of the politically powerful. When appealing a decision made by a consistory or matrimonial court, a litigant next appeared before the entirely secular Tribunal des Trois Etats. If two cousins wanted to marry, they petitioned the Conseil d'Etat, not the church, for a dispensation. In matrimonial questions, it was now the count or his lieutenant, not the Roman curia, who served as the court of last appeal.

Prior to the Reformation, the Roman Catholic church had enjoyed jurisdiction over marriage in large part because of the belief that marriage was a sacrament. With Protestantism's rejection of the sacramental nature of marriage and abolition of ecclesiastical courts, secularization of the control of marriage appeared, to varying degrees, in virtually all areas that converted to Protestantism.[72] On the one hand, Calvin dominated Geneva's consistory from its origins until his death in 1564, ensuring that the clergy would continue to have a strong influence over matrimonial concerns. In contrast, the power to control morality shifted entirely from the clergy to the city council in Reformation Augsburg.[73] Like most other Protestant states, Neuchâtel fell somewhere between these two extremes.

This secularization of the control of marriage did not, however, entail a radical change in the institution of marriage. Mary Ann Glendon observes that, as the Roman Catholic church lost jurisdiction over marriage in much of western Europe in the sixteenth century, the state in

---

72. Seeger, *Nullité de mariage*, p. 24.
73. Lyndal Roper has found that in Reformation Augsburg the secular authority was viewed as "the executor of God's commands" to such an extent that the clergy was to have no function in controlling morality; *Holy Household*, pp. 69–70.

effect assumed this jurisdiction by default, adopting to a large extent preexisting marriage rules from canon law. According to Glendon, it was only during the Enlightenment that legal attitudes toward marriage made a dramatic departure from Roman Catholic tradition.[74] As we see below, the court records from early modern Neuchâtel lead to similar conclusions.

74. Glendon, "Legal Concepts of Marriage and the Family," in *Loving, Parenting, and Dying*, ed. Fox and Quitt, pp. 103–104.

2

The Formation of Marriage, 1547–1706

MARRIAGE CONTRACT DISPUTES

In this chapter I examine three related types of legal action that preceded the formation of marriage: contract disputes, petitions to marry, and actions against illicit sexuality. Disputes over marriage contracts involve cases in which one party came before the court to attempt to prove—or occasionally to disprove—that he or she had a binding contract to marry another person. Also concerned with the formation of marriage were petitions filed by couples who needed special permission to marry because of certain impediments. In police actions against acts of impurity, the consistory itself, not a plaintiff, took the initiative, convoking delinquents for various moral infractions such as adultery, fornication, or scandalous *fréquentation*. Actions against these *délits* often converged with contract litigation, since premarital sexual relations could cause a pregnancy, perhaps leading the woman to file suit to require her seducer to marry her. Similarly, a divorcé who had been convicted of adultery had to petition for permission to remarry. Though actions against impure acts were technically not matrimonial cases, since they did not involve litigation between spouses or fiancés, they nevertheless were closely related to marital issues. One would expect cases of fornication and adultery to contribute directly to divorces and contract litigation. The records of these various cases provide insight into how marriages were formed and what criteria people used in choosing spouses. Did couples marry for sentiment, material motives,

TABLE I
Matrimonial litigation, 1547–1706

	Valangin	Neuchâtel	Gorgier	Total
Petitions	55	468[a]	2	525
Contract disputes	246	110	6	362
Divorce	78	53	0	131
Police actions	105	1	12	118
Miscellaneous	29	2	1	32
	513	634	21	1,168

[a]Of these 468 petitions, 449 were heard before the Conseil d'Etat and 19 before the Justice matrimoniale.

or a combination of both? The courts' handling of this litigation also sheds light on the impact of the Protestant Reformation on marriage and the status of women.

The litigation heard before the tribunals that clearly ought to be labeled matrimonial cases can be divided into three basic categories: disputes concerning marriage contracts, suits for divorce, and requests for permission to marry. These correspond to the three changes in the institution of marriage brought forth by the Reformation: the abolition of clandestine marriages, the introduction of divorce, and the reduction of impediments to marry. Also frequent in Valangin, though almost nonexistent in Neuchâtel, were police actions in which married people were ordered to appear before the consistory to account for the poor domestic life they led. In spite of the fact that reformers wrote so much about divorce, by far the most common cases heard before the consistories were disputes over alleged contracts of marriage. For the period 1547–1706, records have survived for 362 cases involving disputed marriage engagements (see Table 1): 246 for Valangin, 110 for Neuchâtel, and 6 for the consistory of Gorgier, thus far outnumbering requests for divorces (131: 53 in Neuchâtel and 78 in Valangin).[1]

Most other studies of marital litigation have also shown that contract disputes were the most common form of matrimonial suit. R. H. Helmholz found that of the litigation heard before church courts in England from the thirteenth to the end of the fifteenth century, the most common matrimonial suits were actions to enforce marriage contracts. These courts were not so much concerned with dissolving existing mar-

1. As Table 1 indicates, petitions to marry were more numerous than contract disputes if we include the requests for dispensations heard before the Conseil d'Etat. Only 76 of the 525 petitions were brought before the consistories and the *Justice matrimoniale*.

riages as with settling disputes over the formation of marriages. According to Helmholz, the prevalence of marital disputes was a ramification
of the absence of a required formula on which marriages were to be
contracted, the legal difficulties of interpreting the words used, and the
persistence of the view that marriage was a private act.[2] Similarly,
Thomas Max Safley notes that sixteenth-century marriage courts, in
both Catholic Constance and Protestant Basel, dealt above all with premarital litigation; and Ralph Houlbrooke has observed that in Tudor
England most plaintiffs to marital litigation sought the enforcement
rather than the dissolution of marriages.[3]

Not all research on court records has shown this predominance of
contract litigation. Lyndal Roper, for example, found that in Augsburg
in 1535–1536, just before its conversion to Protestantism, contract disputes made up 69 percent of marriage cases. Following the conversion,
however, they constituted only 25 percent of the litigation brought
before the Reformed civic marriage court from 1537 through 1546.[4]
Martin Ingram's evidence from the various English church courts
reveals an important change in litigation during the sixteenth and seventeenth centuries. Ingram found that, whereas contract disputes constituted the bulk of litigation in the fourteenth century, they became
much less common by the early Elizabethan period and were reduced to
"the merest trickle" during the period 1570–1640. This decline, Ingram maintains, resulted from the popular acceptance of the ecclesiastical requirement of the benediction of marriages in church, thus
causing a decline in the formation of binding spousals that preceded the
church wedding.[5] Neuchâtelois did not embrace church ideals to that
extent: marriage contract suits would remain a prominent form of matrimonial litigation throughout the early modern period. In spite of the
evidence of Roper and Ingram, the predominance of disputes over engagements to marry was typical of most sixteenth- and seventeenth-
century matrimonial courts.

In dealing with questions concerning promises of marriage, Neuchâtel's courts were on the whole consistent in enforcing the edicts

2. Helmholz, *Marriage Litigation*, p. 72. In Neuchâtel, contract disputes were the most
common form of litigation, notwithstanding the fact that the magistrates had passed a detailed
formula by which marriages were to be contracted.
3. Houlbrooke, *Church Courts and the People*, p. 83; Safley, *Let No Man Put Asunder*, pp.
170–173.
4. Roper, *Holy Household*, p. 158. For the same period, 29 percent of the cases before the
Reformed court were divorces.
5. Ingram, *Church Courts, Sex, and Marriage*, pp. 189, 192–193.

against clandestine marriages. They ordinarily declared invalid alleged promises that could not be proved by witnesses. The importance of the presence of witnesses at marriage engagements was strictly applied in the case of Jachaire Phillipin against Anthoina Petremond (1580/81). The latter had announced her intention to marry David Vatel, whereupon Phillipin intervened, claiming that Petremond and he were engaged and that he had given her a gold ring *en nom de mariage*. Among the witnesses produced was a young woman who had overheard Petremond admit that she had promised to marry Phillipin but wanted to return the ring he had given her in the name of marriage since she had decided to marry Vatel. Another witness claimed that Petremond had confided that only Phillipin and she were present when their promises were made—clearly a de facto confession that such an engagement existed. No witness, however, claimed to have been present when the alleged contract was made. Furthermore, Phillipin failed to prove that Petremond's father and grandfather had given him permission to marry her. The two men confessed to having discussed the matter with either Phillipin or his father, but both steadfastly denied having consented to such a match. As a result, the judges rejected Phillipin's suit and condemned him to pay all legal costs. In explaining their decision, the judges stated emphatically that marriage agreements had to be proved by two or three honest men, that the promises had to be made clearly and directly, and that the consent of close relatives had to be given. Witnesses here had spoken only from hearsay, and the relatives had not agreed to this match. The plaintiff therefore had no right to pretend to have a valid marriage contract.[6]

By requiring that there be witnesses to marriage promises, the consistories were explicitly denying the possibility that such promises be proven by oaths. During the Middle Ages, the oath was vital in daily life as well as in judicial procedures. For medieval minds, to take an oath was to take God as a witness, and therefore to lie under oath was tantamount to lying before God. It was often believed that, since God was the witness, it was impossible to lie under oath, and consequently that testimony made under oath could be accepted unequivocally as the truth.[7] According to Paolo Gallone, by the fourteenth century the ser-

6. AEN, JMN2:56v–63v, 66, 68r–v, 72–73, 74–76v, 77v–80, 83–88.

7. Paolo Gallone, *Organisation judiciaire et procédure devant les cours laïques du Pays de Vaud a l'époque savoyarde (XIIIe–XVIe siècle)* (Lausanne, 1972), p. 210. It was customary in courts of law that, before testifying, witnesses swore an oath to tell the truth. This was described as "a most solemn oath; witnesses get on their knees, placing their hands on the Holy Scriptures;

ment was no longer a viable mode of proof in the Pays de Vaud; rather, the oath was given to the defendant if his adversary had failed to prove the accusations. In these cases the *serment* was "destined to exculpate an accused vis-à-vis public opinion, which despite the failure to prove the charges continued to believe in his guilt if he did not swear by his own innocence."[8] To a large extent, this was also the case in sixteenth-century Neuchâtel. In disputes concerning promises to marry, the accuser—that is, the party who sought to prove that promises existed—could not prove that the marriage contract existed by swearing an oath that he or she had in fact promised to marry the defendant. But, if the plaintiff failed to show convincingly that real promises of marriage had been made, the defendant could exonerate himself and in effect disprove the alleged engagement by taking an oath and denying the promises. Hence in 1584, when Jacqua Grossiere of La Sagne claimed to have contracted marriage promises with her master, her request to take an oath to show that promises existed was denied. By contrast, Jehan Vuillame was able to bring an end to the process Guillama Vuillemin of Le Locle waged against him by swearing under oath that he had not made a marriage engagement with her.[9] Denying the right to demonstrate the existence of engagements through oaths was an effective check on clandestine marriages.

Closely related to the requirement of witnesses was the need for parental consent to marry, a prerequisite repeatedly acknowledged in the court records. In 1611, for example, David Le Maistre, pastor in Les Verrières, was the plaintiff against his son and Freny Aulbertier, his son's fiancée. The elder Le Maistre was protesting the fact that the two had promised to marry each other without his consent. Appearing before the matrimonial court of Neuchâtel, the father read some passages from the Bible and from "some good authors" in order "to show the authority fathers and mothers have over their children" and the respect children owe their parents. He expressed his disappointment that his son had disregarded this duty in contracting to marry Freny without his father's knowledge. The beginning of these "sinister promises" dated as far back as 1607, when the son was only seventeen or eighteen years old and therefore too young to become engaged without parental permission. The son and his fiancée, "on their knees, cried mercy to God

---

the windows are opened, and the president and judges stand while they administer the oath"; Boyve, *Annales historiques du comté de Neuchâtel*, 2:484.
    8. Gallone, *Organisation judiciare*, p. 210.
    9. AEN, CSV2:22, 262, 264, 265.

and to Mr. David [Le Maistre] for the fault they committed." The father in turn "condescended to pardon his son and the girl" and gave his consent so that the marriage could take place.[10] Evidently this pastor felt that the importance of paternal authority was so great that it merited taking his son and his future daughter-in-law to court even though he would later consent to their marriage. Moreover, at this time the son must have been twenty-one or twenty-two years old and therefore old enough to marry without parental permission. The fact that these promises dated from a time when the son was still a minor sufficed to give the father the right to exercise his authority.

In fact, paternal consent was often stressed even after the age of twenty.[11] For example, in 1604 Daniel Collin demanded that Bendichte Mathiez follow through with the promises they had made together. Several witnesses supported his claim that, in the presence of her mother, Mathiez had accepted Collin's offer to drink in the name of marriage. Her father protested that the engagement should be null because he had not been present, Bendichte had not asked his permission, and Collin had not been presented to him. Notwithstanding these claims, the Justice matrimoniale decided that since Bendichte was past twenty and had drunk in honor of marriage in the presence of others, including her mother, the marriage had to take place. But it was added that, for her contempt in not asking her father's permission to marry,

10. AEN, JMN2:242v–243.

11. At times it was difficult to determine the age of a person in order to judge whether he or she could contract engagements without parental permission. During most of this period, birth or baptism records virtually did not exist. Parish records, kept by pastors or regents, are extant for Cornaux from 1560 and for the city of Neuchâtel from 1590 (with a lacuna for 1611–1645). Travers's baptism records date from 1617, but it was not common to keep such records until the mid- to late-seventeenth century; see Léon Montandon, "Les registres d'état civil aux Archives de l'Etat de Neuchâtel," *Musée neuchâtelois*, 1938, 31–42. In the absence of such registers, witnesses were needed to determine the age of the interested party. This could cause complications if different witnesses did not agree. An example is that of Marie Courvoisier, who in 1612 did not want to execute her promises with Jonas Montandon, claiming that she was too young to have made a marriage contract without the consent of her father. The witnesses testified as follows: (1) Marie's maternal grandfather maintained that she could be from seventeen to eighteen years old; (2) Bartholomé Mathiex claimed that one of his daughters was baptized twenty-one years earlier and that one of the Courvoisier children, perhaps Marie, was baptized at the same moment; (3) Abraham Clement, Marie's uncle, and his wife said that she turned twenty-one between "calends and Saint Martin's Day";(4) Jacqua Clement believed that Marie was nineteen years old the previous Saint Martin's Day; (5) Guillama Calame thought that Marie was seventeen or eighteen years old. Thus, Marie was anywhere from seventeen to twenty-one. At any rate, these promises were declared invalid, but not because of lack of paternal consent; AEN, CSV3:187–191, 193–194. In an earlier case before the consistory of Valangin, the uncle of Andre Chollet failed to prove that Andre was too young to contract a marriage without his consent. In light of this fact and that he seemed mature enough, Andre was required to marry Huguenin Reymond; CSV2:78, 80–82, 84–85.

Mathiez would be subject to the punishment the seigneury deemed appropriate.[12] Sons and daughters over twenty could be punished for not conferring with their fathers over their marriage plans, but their engagements remained valid and binding.[13] These various cases demonstrate that on the whole the tribunals were consistent in combating clandestine marriages by requiring the presence of witnesses and reasserting the authority of parents, especially that of fathers, over their children's choice of spouses.

Parental authority, however, was not to be exercised arbitrarily. As the matrimonial ordinances enjoined, parents were not to force their children to marry against their will. In 1612, Valangin's consistory released the daughter of Pierre Morel, a minor, from her engagement with Huguenin Morelet because her parents had forced her into the match. One day, Morelet was working for Pierre Morel, and the latter said to him that

> he would like to have a worker as good as he in his household. And provided that he wanted to live in his house as his son-in-law, he would give him his daughter in marriage. Consequently, a few days later, at the instigation of Pierre Morelet [Huguenin's father], solemn promises were reciprocally made between Huguenin and the girl in the presence of people and with the consent of the father and mother of the girl. Since that time the girl backed down from the promises.[14]

Concluding that this so-called engagement had been frivolously made by the girl's parents, the consistory declared the engagement invalid and ordered Morel to pay the court costs and to return to Morelet the *ares,* or gifts received at the time of the *fiançailles.* Morel, his wife, and daughter all had to make *réparation,* a formality in which one publicly (usually in church) confessed one's wrongdoing and asked for forgiveness from God, the seigneury, and those one had wronged.[15]

By the same token, parents were not to hinder children in their marital pursuits if they had already reached the age of majority and dis-

12. AEN, JMN2:216–218v.
13. In Geneva as well, men and women were expected to confer with their fathers about their marriage plans even after reaching the age of majority. In the marriage laws Calvin drafted for Geneva, men and women needed parental permission to marry until the ages of twenty and eighteen, respectively; Calvin had originally recommended requiring paternal permission until twenty-four for men and twenty for women. After these ages, if fathers ignored their children's requests for assistance in forming marriages, sons and daughters were free to marry without paternal authorization; *Calvini Opera,* vol. X/a, 34, 105.
14. AEN, CSV3:186.
15. Ibid.

cussed the matter with their parents. In 1553, Parmenon Vuillie and Jehan Chastenetz confessed before the consistory that they had made mutual promises of marriage they both wanted to honor. Parmenon's father, however, was opposed to the match. Since Parmenon was old enough to marry without her father's permission, the consistory declared the marriage valid and required her father to give her the customary dowry. Various relatives and friends were to attempt to arrive at a mutually acceptable sum for the dowry. If they failed to reach an accord, the seigneury would undertake an investigation of Vuillie's property and the judges of the consistory would determine the dowry. In addition, the father was condemned to pay all court costs.[16] In effect, these limitations on paternal power over children's choices of fiancés was a reaffirmation of the importance of consent in forming marriages. Consent had been the necessary and sufficient condition for contracting marriages in canon law. Though the Reformation added the requirements of parental permission for minors and of the publication of the banns, reformers nevertheless viewed freely given consent to marry as a necessary prerequisite for contracting binding promises and required the presence of witnesses merely to ensure that consent had been given.

Because of this emphasis on freely choosing to marry, the tribunals adjudged promises made under duress invalid, as a case in 1697/98 aptly demonstrates. Eve Herguet, a Frenchwoman, filed suit against Josué Merveilleux, alleging that he had promised to marry her and that he was the father of her child. According to Merveilleux, while garrisoned as a soldier in France he had indeed paid to have sexual relations with this woman, whom he characterized as a prostitute. One day when Josué was ill in bed, Eve's sister entered his room and threatened to slit his throat if he did not agree to marry Eve. Having recovered his health, Josué heard nothing more of this affair until one day, while in Spain, two soldiers burst into his room and forced him to sign a promise to marry Eve. Later he encountered Eve and in her presence tore up the piece of paper that bore the written engagement. They then went their separate ways, and Merveilleux married another woman. After a fourteen-year silence, Eve wrote Josué asking him to come marry her or at least send money to support the child. Having received no recompense, she came to Neuchâtel and threatened to publicize that she had given birth to Josué's illegitimate child. To silence her, Josué paid her a sum of money, and he later consented to pay her a second time when she

16. AEN, CSV1:72r–v.

repeated the same threat. When she asked for money a third time, Josué, weary of these frequent forced donations, refused to give her anything, whereupon Eve filed suit. The *Justice matrimoniale* of Neuchâtel asked the opinion of the Compagnie des Pasteurs of Geneva, who rejected Eve's request on several grounds. The Genevan pastors noted, for example, that at the time of the promises Josué was still a minor and thus incapable of making an engagement without the consent of his father. Furthermore, the parties were of different religions, and the Reformed faith forbade mixed marriages under pain of excommunication. Also important was the difference in the status of the persons involved: the nobility of Merveilleux and the "poverty and baseness of a vile wash-woman" who worked in a tavern (even worse, according to the Genevan pastors the laws made no distinction between taverns and houses of prostitution). Most obvious of all, Josué had not freely agreed to the promises but rather had been constrained to sign them. What obligations Eve may have been owed by Josué were lost when she accepted money from him. And since the child could have been fathered by various other men, no one could be recognized as the father. It is not clear whether the judges of the tribunal agreed entirely with the reasoning of the Genevan clergymen, but in any event they declared the promises null in March 1698, twenty-one years after they had been contracted.[17]

In Neuchâtel, consent to marry could be expressed in various ways. It was not always necessary to express verbally one's acquiescence to marriage proposals; nonverbal forms of acceptance could be held in court as binding. In the absence of verbal consent, gifts men presented to women at the moment of engagement—a tradition that has its origins among the ancient Hebrews, was adopted by the Romans, and survives today in the form of engagement rings—often sufficed to show that real marriage promises existed between two people.[18] In Roman betrothals, the two families assembled and exchanged their pledges as well as *arrhae* (earnest money), the first financial contribution of each family to the new couple. The couple then kissed and a ring was given. In ancient Rome, the ring was viewed as an advance on the dowry; in early medieval Germany it became part of the ceremony that sealed a binding engagement. In late medieval Europe, the ring the man gave his bride had become a symbol of the dower, that property he designated to

17. AEN, JMN: *Annexes* 405.
18. Viollet, *Histoire du droit civil français,* pp. 459–460. In Hebrew tradition, a man gave a woman a coin or object, usually a ring, at the wedding ceremony itself. Roman men generally bestowed such gifts at the *fiançailles,* before the marriage.

support her should his death precede hers. Both the kiss and the ring assumed legal importance in betrothals and would continue to be important symbols of betrothals to the present.[19]

Such rituals are what anthropologist Arnold Van Gennep describes as "rites of incorporation" or "rites of union," ceremonies associated with marriage that are common to virtually all cultures. As a symbol of the union of husband and wife, different cultures have maintained rituals such as giving belts, bracelets, rings, or clothes; touching each other by joining hands, intertwining the fingers, kissing, or embracing; eating from the same dish or drinking from the same vessel. Such acts are basically rites of union, often serving as the first ritual in betrothal, and, as Van Gennep observes, the refusal to accept such gifts is generally tantamount to rejecting the proffered union.[20] Neuchâtel's court records reveal that gift giving and other popular rituals such as drinking in the name of marriage were commonly part of engagement ceremonies. Such rituals were in fact practiced throughout western Europe: couples could be found sharing a cup as a symbol of their union among the Huguenots of sixteenth-century Languedoc, the residents of late medieval Troyes, the urban classes of Reformation Germany, and the peasants of early modern England. In this custom of drinking in the name of marriage, the suitor offered a drink—sometimes wine but often simply water—to his prospective fiancée, saying "drink this in the name of marriage." In popular opinion, accepting the drink symbolized the acceptance of the marriage proposal. As Roper observes, it is not surprising that gifts and similar rituals were so common, since the wedding was in a way the "gift of bride and groom to each other. . . . Husband and wife drank from the same cup, ate from the same bowl, or joined hands to symbolize their union."[21]

19. The ring attained legal significance under late imperial law; Judith M. Bennett, *Women in the Medieval English Countryside: Gender and Household in Brigstock before the Plague* (Oxford, 1987), pp. 94–95; Christiane Klapisch-Zuber, "Zacharius, or the Ousted Father: Nuptial Rites in Tuscany between Giotto and the Council of Trent," in *Women, Family, and Ritual*, p. 196. David Herlihy notes the importance of the symbolic kiss: "If the engaged couple has exchanged a kiss, and if one subsequently died before the marriage, then the surviving spouse could keep one-half of the gifts received; if no kiss had been exchanged, all the gifts had to be returned"; *Medieval Households*, p. 7, n. 30.
20. Gennep, *The Rites of Passage*, trans. Monika B. Vizedom and Gabrielle L. Caffee (Chicago, 1960), pp. 132–133.
21. Roper, *Holy Household*, p. 133; Mentzer, "*Disciplina nervus ecclesiae*," p. 98; Phillips, *Putting Asunder*, p. 31; André Burguière, "Le ritual du mariage en France: Pratiques ecclésiastiques et pratiques populaires (XVIe–XVIIIe siècle)," *Annales; E.S.C.* 33 (1978): 642; Samuel Pyeatt Menefee, *Wives for Sale: An Ethnographic Study of British Popular Divorce* (New York, 1981), p. 29.

In Neuchâtel and elsewhere, gifts presented in the name of marriage could be rather modest. Roper has observed that, when sixteenth-century couples made clandestine promises without their parents' consent, the man might give the woman a coin, a ribbon, or a hairpin.[22] Concentrating on the rituals surrounding courtship, John Gillis notes that in early modern England the object given—popular gifts included hand-carved spoons or hair combs, knitting sheathes and garters—was not nearly as important as the intention of the giver:

> Gifts were believed to have a magic power, so that to deliver a lock of hair, articles of clothing, even a kiss to another was to place oneself in that person's possession. . . . The intention of the giver had much to do with whether a gift had binding powers. . . . The way a thing was given determined whether the parties were friends or lovers, whether a man was a vile seducer or true suitor, whether a woman was a potential wife or casual whore.[23]

In early modern Europe, symbolic gestures sometimes sufficed to convince judicial authorities that a binding contract existed. Flandrin found that in sixteenth-century France accepting a pin in the name of marriage was, in the eyes of judges, tantamount to consenting to a marriage proposal. Ralph Houlbrooke similarly discovered that in Tudor England gifts—most commonly gold or silver rings, though often coins or trinkets—could sometimes constitute conclusive evidence of matrimonial intention. In his work on matrimonial disputes in the sixteenth and seventeenth centuries, Martin Ingram discovered that spousals were characteristically sealed with the exchange of tokens, embraces, or sometimes a celebratory meal. Litigants cited such rituals as evidence of intent to marry, though gifts in particular usually did not hold up in court when defendants argued that they had not been given with marriage in mind.[24]

The members of Neuchâtel's consistories took very seriously gifts and drinks presented in the name of marriage. For example, in 1580 the Justice matrimoniale ruled in favor of Claude Borrel in his suit against Elise Simonin, even though Elise had expressed no verbal acceptance.

---

22. Roper, *Holy Household*, p. 1.
23. Gillis, *For Better, for Worse*, pp. 31–33.
24. Flandrin, *Amours paysannes*, p. 112; Houlbrooke, "Making of Marriage," p. 344; Ingram, *Church Courts, Sex, and Marriage*, pp. 196–198. Disagreeing, Stone holds that popular customs accompanying engagements, such as gifts, had little or no legal validity in early modern England; *Road to Divorce*, p. 74.

Several witnesses testified that Elise had drunk and accepted a leather belt from Claude in the name of marriage in the presence of her mother.[25] In the same manner, Claude Riaudet of Nyon won his case against Jehannette Droz in 1614 even though she had not uttered a syllable in response to his offer of marriage. Witnesses reported seeing the two touch hands and said that Riaudet had taken a pan and offered its contents to Droz to drink in the name of marriage. She in turn had accepted the pan and brought it to her mouth. Droz herself admitted as much, though she denied having actually taken a drink. Much to her dismay, various witnesses reported otherwise, and the consistory heeded this evidence. Its decision read that, in the presence of her mother and uncle (her father was deceased), "Claude and Jehannette touched one another and held hands as a symbol and promise of marriage. Furthermore, Claude took the pan on the table and drank in the name of marriage to Jehannette, who in turn willingly drank after Claude. All these things having been considered, the honorable judges . . . declare that the marriage must take place."[26] It is ironic that such nonverbal forms of acceptance were acknowledged as valid in Neuchâtel, for they had been officially condemned in Calvin's Geneva as frivolous.[27]

Though important popular rituals, the exchange of gifts or symbolic drinks were not necessary for making valid marriage contracts, as demonstrated by the case of Jehannette Vallin of Chesard in 1557. Jehannette had had a child with Jehan Vallet of the same village and claimed that Vallet had agreed to marry her. Various witnesses reported that Vallet had told Jehannette that he wanted to marry her but did not have any money to present her as a gift. One of the persons present offered to loan him five solz to give to Jehannette. Vallet replied that he was already willing to accept her as his wife in front of witnesses and that should suffice. The consistory agreed and ordered Vallet to marry Jehannette, condemning him to pay all legal costs.[28] What is most interesting about this case is not the decision but rather the fact that the people present at the *fiançailles* deemed it necessary to present a gift to

25. AEN, JMN2:67v–68, 69–71.
26. AEN, CSV3:213.
27. A Genevan ordinance enjoined that betrothals must be made "in the fear of God" and must not be made frivolously, "as in simply inviting each other to drink, without first having exchanged the proper words"; Emile Rivoire and Victor van Berchem, eds., *Les sources du droit du canton de Genève* (Aarau, Switzerland, 1933), 3:337, no. 1183: Ordonnances ecclésiastiques, CXXXII.
28. AEN, CSV1:102r–v.

the bride-to-be. If gift giving was not a legal requirement to marriage contracts, it was nevertheless clearly part of popular culture in Reformation Neuchâtel.

At times the consistories rejected claims to marriage even though gifts were exchanged because one of the parties did not appear to have freely given his or her consent. An excellent example is the suit that Jehan Jaques Navillot filed against Annellet Gicot in 1603. Working as a hired hand for Annellet's father, Navillot was present one day when Annellet and a female servant were making sausages. Annellet wanted to taste the meat to see if it had been salted enough. She therefore asked Navillot to put a piece of sausage in her mouth, since she was unable to do so herself because her hands were too messy. Navillot in turn cut a piece of meat and placed it in her mouth, telling her to eat it in the name of marriage. Annellet ate some of the sausage and let the rest drop to the table. In Navillot's opinion, the fact that she ate the meat in the name of marriage sufficed to form a binding marriage. Indignant, Annellet replied in court that this was no way to conclude promises of marriage since the sausages already belonged to her and therefore should not be presented to her as a gift. As might be expected, the judges declared this alleged marriage null, deeming the promises frivolous and sinister and condemning Navillot to pay all legal expenses.[29] Though this case certainly was not typical, it serves to show that the consistories showed a certain flexibility in determining whether valid promises existed, often using common sense to conclude whether the parties had freely consented to marriage.

Various other factors could also indicate whether one had freely agreed to marriage proposals. Occasionally, pretended engagements were annulled because one of the parties involved was not considered mentally competent to contract promises to marry. In 1590, for example, Catherine Vaterin filed suit to enforce a contract with Abraham Mathiez dict Junod of Le Locle. Jehan Junod, Abraham's brother, appeared as *tuteur* and *curateur* of Abraham, claiming that his brother was an idiot and legally incapable of undertaking any promises.[30] Furthermore, Jehan accused Catherine of having solicited his brother into making this engagement. The marriage was declared null, and Blaise

29. AEN, JMN2:211–214.
30. A *tuteur* is someone who exercises a certain authority over the property of another, most often a minor. A *curateur* has a *tutelle* over someone who is already an adult. A *curateur* is appointed to a person who suffers from insanity or prodigality, for example; Viollet, *Historie du droit civil français*, pp. 576, 596.

Huguenin Clerc was condemned to three days in prison and charged all court costs for having surreptitiously arranged this marriage between Abraham and Catherine.[31]

In another case, a multiparty suit in 1599/1600 involving Jehan Marchant, pastor at Les Brenets, shows that being drunk at the time of a proposal was not an adequate excuse to nullify marriage promises. Marchant was accused of first promising Jehanne Billon of Les Brenets and then proposing to a second woman, Susanne Gorgerat of Boudry. Convoked before the consistory of Valangin, Marchant confessed that during the course of one evening he drank excessively and, as his sister later told him, gave Jehanne a golden ring *en nom de mariage,* drank with her in the name of marriage, and kissed her repeatedly. Because of his inebriated state, he remembered none of these things, though he confessed they might well be true. Various persons who had participated in this soirée gave similar accounts of these events. In light of this proof, the consistory recognized the first promises with Jehanne as valid, declared void the second engagement with Susanne, and sentenced Marchant to prison for his scandalous behavior.[32] In striking contrast is a later judgment made by the same institution, the consistory of Valangin. Convoked in 1659 for having promised to marry Magdelaine Baroud, Jehan Lesplatinier asked for forgiveness, confessing that he had indeed jokingly asked the woman to marry him after having drunk wine excessively. The court decided that no real promises existed between them and that they were free to marry others. For holding the sacred state of marriage in derision and for being inebriated on the day of the Sabbath, Lesplatinier was to be subject to a suitable fine.[33] This case illustrates that seventeenth-century judges were somewhat more reluctant than their predecessors to enforce marriage contracts that only one of the parties recognized.

SENTIMENT AND PARENTAL INFLUENCE

Though they showed some flexibility in determining whether someone had freely consented to marry, judges of the Reformation period

31. AEN, CSV3:8, 10.
32. Marchant's troubles with women did not end here, however. Five months after this decision, Jehanne, the first fiancée, asked to be released from her engagement with Marchant since he had violated the faith of marriage in asking another woman to marry him while engaged to marry her. This request was granted, and Jehanne was free to contract marriage promises with another man; AEN, CSV3:67–69, 76–77.
33. AEN, CSV5:59.

were resolutely inflexible in dealing with cases in which the parties had clearly followed the ordinances in forming marriage contracts. If both parties were legally capable of contracting promises and had freely agreed to marry in the presence of others, then they were obligated to execute their engagements. We have already seen cases in which one of the parties did not want to go through with the marriage but was ordered to do so. By twentieth-century standards it seems cruel and imprudent to force a person to marry someone whom he or she no longer wants as a spouse. During this period, however, there were even cases in which neither party wanted to honor an engagement but were obliged to do so, since judges considered valid marriage contracts indissoluble. In 1618, Daniel Quarthier and Roze Milliods, both from the village of Les Brenets, were ordered to appear before the consistory of Valangin because there was a rumor that they had promised to marry each other. At first both denied the engagement. Roze had reportedly even said that, if forced to marry Daniel, she would leave the country; and Daniel had promised to marry another woman and had even made the first proclamation at church. When the pastor heard about the rumored engagement between Daniel and Roze, he suspended the second proclamation. As the case proceeded, however, Roze admitted having accepted Daniel's proposal by symbolically touching his hand and receiving from him a *teston,* a coin. Daniel too acknowledged these promises but had lost all interest in marrying Roze, having been totally disgusted with her statement that she would rather leave the country than be his wife. In the end, the court concluded that Daniel had strictly followed the proper procedure for contracting a marriage, that the promises had been reciprocally made in the presence of and with the consent of the closest relatives of both parties, and that both Daniel and Roze were old enough to make such an engagement. Therefore Daniel Quarthier and Roze Milliods must be husband and wife. Both were denied the right to partake of the eucharist, and the seigneury was to punish each as it saw fit for their wrongdoings—Roze for her imprecations and Daniel for his subsequent proposal to another woman.[34]

In the vast majority of cases involving questions over marriage contracts, one party was the plaintiff and the other the defendant. In this case, however, the consistory decided to prosecute through a police action. To protect public order, members of the consistory were willing to take the initiative in convoking those who violated the accepted moral

34. AEN, CSV3:268, 272, 274.

code. And among those norms to which they adhered tenaciously was the idea that marriage promises that had been properly formed had to be respected. A man and woman could not simply change their minds and not follow through with the marriage. It is not insignificant that, when someone wanted to be released from an engagement to marry, the tribunals referred to this process as petitioning for a divorce. Indeed, assuming that the contract had been properly made, the judges ordinarily granted permission not to consecrate a marriage only for the same reasons that they awarded divorces: infidelity, desertion, and so on.[35] During the first century of the courts' existence, not once did the consistory of Valangin or the Justice matrimoniale of Neuchâtel annul a marriage contract simply because a couple no longer wanted to marry.[36] As had been the case under canon law, marriage contracts were already binding from the moment of consent, not from the consecration of marriage in church.[37]

35. One notable difference was that abandoned fiancés were not required to wait seven years to be released from their engagements. No minimum period of absence was established. If a party could prove that he or she had been deserted by the other, the consistory might grant permission to marry someone else. Barbely Quinche succeeded in having her engagement with Pierre Morellet annulled in 1602, since he had left her to go to war as a mercenary. She was not asked to prove how long he had been absent, indicating that it was not necessary to wait seven years, the period an abandoned spouse had to wait before receiving a divorce; ibid., 93–94, 96–97. In Geneva as well, magistrates handled absent fiances differently from absent spouses. Whereas abandoned spouses might have to wait ten years to obtain a divorce, women whose fiancés left the country for legitimate reasons had to wait only one year to be freed from their engagements. There was no fixed delay for men whose fiancées had left the country for whatever reason, or for women whose fiancés had maliciously abandoned them before the wedding; *Calvini Opera*, X/a, 113.

36. Indeed, only once before the mid-seventeenth century did judges even mention the antipathy fiancés had for one another as a reason to annul a marriage engagement, and that was clearly not one of the main grounds for according this annulment. Jehan Jaques Hory and Marie Legoux had made an engagement clandestinely, on the condition that their parents agreed to the match. As it turned out, neither party's parents consented, and Marie was not old enough to contract a marriage without parental permission. The sentence rendered noted that neither party desired the marriage. But more important were the facts that the promises were conditional and to be binding an engagement must be unconditional, that this condition had not been fulfilled since the parents had not agreed to the match, and that this betrothal had been made clandestinely without the required two witnesses. It was above all for these reasons, not for the absence of mutual affection, that the contract was declared null. Each party was fined 5 livres for having disobeyed the ordinances in not asking their parents for permission; AEN, JMN2:160v–162, 10 April 1591.

37. The emphasis on consent can also be seen in various police actions the consistory of Valangin undertook against people who had married Catholics in other countries, usually France. Several men were also convoked for having allowed their daughters to be married in Catholic services in France. During the Reformation period, eleven cases of this nature occurred. The consistory usually required the offenders to make *réparation* in church and occasionally to pay fines or even pass a few days in jail. It is significant that the marriages, though contracted illegally, remained valid. This was a continuation of the doctrine of canon law that declared it illegal to contract a marriage with a heretic. If, however, one had formed such a marriage, the union remained binding and indissoluble.

In this regard, the consistories of the principality of Neuchâtel were stricter than many contemporary courts elsewhere in Europe. In France, for example, the Reformed church decided in 1612 that betrothal was not a binding marriage promise.[38] John Gillis observes that in early modern England betrothal was not viewed as an indissoluble contract either by judicial authorities or by popular opinion. According to Gillis, the most essential feature of the betrothal was that, having entered it, one could change one's mind without loss of status or honor.[39] Similarly, Simon Schama found that in seventeenth-century Reformed Holland, marriage betrothals, even those written and notarized, were not necessarily regarded as contractually binding; magistrates seemed reluctant to enforce them without the drastic element of sexual violation.[40] In Reformation Neuchâtel justices were actually less liberal in canceling betrothals than some late medieval Catholic courts had been when clandestine marriages were still considered valid. In late fourteenth-century Paris, for example, church courts granted virtually all requests to be released from engagements.[41] Similarly, in the second half of the fifteenth century the courts for the dioceses of Troyes and Châlons-sur-Marne in Champagne ordinarily released couples from engagements, be they formal *fiançailles* made in church or informal promises, and imposed a fine on one or both parties. The evidence from Neuchâtel certainly refutes the notion that the Reformation brought about the decline of betrothal as a legal category: breach-of-promise suits were to remain the most common form of matrimonial litigation until the eighteenth century.[42]

The court records provide important information on the role of sentiment in marriage from the viewpoints of both the judges and the

38. Mentzer, "Church Discipline," p. 9.
39. Gillis, *For Better, for Worse*, pp. 50–51. Gillis's argument concerning popular opinion on betrothals is not entirely convincing. He acknowledges that disputed betrothals made up much of the business of the church courts in the sixteenth and seventeenth centuries, which seems to undercut his theory of "the popular liminality of betrothal that allowed people to make and break relationships without unduly disrupting their own lives and the peace of the community." If indeed most Englishmen did not view betrothals as indissoluble, why did they bother trying to enforce these contracts?
40. Schama, *Embarrassment of Riches*, p. 445.
41. Phillips, *Putting Asunder*, pp. 11–12, citing Jean Philippe Lévy, "L'officialité de Paris et les questions familiales à la fin du XIVe siècle," in *Etudes d'histoire du droit canonique, dédiées à Gabriel Le Bras* (Paris, 1965), pp. 1272–1273.
42. Beatrice Gottlieb, "The Meaning of Clandestine Marriage," in *Family and Sexuality in French History*, ed. Robert Wheaton and Tamara K. Hareven (Philadelphia, 1980), pp. 63, 73. Gottlieb argues that beginning with the Reformation breach-of-promise suits were for damages (due to mental anguish and monetary expenditure), rather than for enforcement of the promises.

litigants. The question of affection among family members, though one of the more hotly debated themes in family history, is also one of the most problematic. Martine Segalen cogently sums up the difficulty of dealing with the issue of sentiment in family history:

> There is no more problematic area than that of the history of sensibility. We can draw up and study graphs showing the marriage rate, analyse the intervals between births or the geographic catchment area for marriage partners, but once we are dealing with the personal sphere of emotions and sexual relationships it is hard to find documentary evidence and even harder to interpret it. The vagueness of our vocabulary is just as much a hindrance. Do we all mean the same thing by love? The analyses we read are often highly subjective, the work of authors who interpret the available data in the light of their own philosophical, political or religious ideas, and men and women interpret the same facts in different ways. With regard to love and sexuality in past times, for which we will never have the equivalents of the Kinsey or Simon reports (though they too raise problems, of course), we can only suggest hypotheses.[43]

We must address the issue of marriage and sentiment, even though problematic, if we are to get a full appreciation of early modern family life.

We can certainly conclude that the consistories themselves placed little importance on the affection between fiancés. During the Reformation period, the judges' sole concern was to determine whether marriage engagements had been properly made. If so, the couple had to marry regardless of their current inclinations and of the wishes of their parents, if they were past the age of minority. The courts themselves clearly were not champions of marriages of sentiment.

Beginning in the mid-seventeenth century, however, the justices modified their position: in their decisions, they frequently took individuals' wishes into account in determining whether to require couples to go through with marriages. In 1661, Josué Barbe of Le Locle petitioned to be released from his marriage contract with Marie Jean Richard because she had confessed to stealing grapes and because her mother had been executed, evidently a hint that crime was in her blood. Though willing to marry Barbe, Marie Jean Richard declined to op-

---

43. Segalen, *Historical Anthropology of the Family,* trans. J. C. Whitehouse and Sarah Matthews (Cambridge, 1986), p. 128.

pose this action, most likely to avoid forcing him to marry her against his will. The consistory ruled that Barbe could not be forced to marry her and declared the engagement null "in order to avoid the unhappy life which they could have together." For having shown a lack of respect for the sacred state of marriage, Barbe was condemned to pay all court costs and to spend four days in prison.[44] The officials thus deemed liberating a man from a marriage contract on flimsy grounds preferable to condemning him and his fiancée to an unhappy married life together.

Similarly, in 1646 Pierre Carrel and Magdelayne Andrie of Cernier were convoked by their pastor for having made a marriage agreement. Pierre confessed to having promised to marry but maintained that his relatives were unaware of this engagement and subsequently expressed their disapproval. Magdelayne avowed that she was willing to go through with the marriage but did not wish to force Pierre to marry her. In bringing their verdict, the judges decided that the promises had not been made in the manner prescribed and could not subsist in light of the fact that the woman wished to be released from them; since Pierre had toyed with her emotions, he was ordered to pay her 55 livres in damages.[45]

Even when the consistories ordered a couple to honor a marriage contract, it was possible for one of the parties to appeal this decision successfully. For example, in 1702 Abraham Bedaux of Cormondrèche appealed a sentence of Neuchâtel's matrimonial court which had condemned him to honor his contract to marry Susanne Rebeur. The Tribunal des Trois Etats decided that to avoid a miserable marriage the parties were to be released from the contract; they also ordered Bedaux to pay his ex-fiancée 1,600 livres, a considerable sum.[46] In short, as far as disputes over marriage promises are concerned, justices of the mid-seventeenth century were clearly more receptive to the personal inclinations of the litigants than their predecessors had been. If they were not exactly servants of Cupid who advocated love matches, seventeenth-century judges at least deemed it prudent to avoid antipathetic matches.[47]

44. AEN, CSV5:88.
45. AEN, CSV4:169.
46. AEN, AGTE10:29v–30.
47. Though seventeenth-century consistories were more willing to release individuals from contracts than sixteenth-century courts had been, they nevertheless emphatically professed to have exclusive authority to dissolve such promises. They imposed severe financial penalties on anyone who married without first being released by the consistories from a previous contract. See the case below between Simeon Peter and Louise Prince.

In evaluating the significance of sentiment in betrothals, we must not limit ourselves to the decisions of judges. The fact that the courts were not the champions of sentiment does not necessarily mean that early modern Neuchâtelois themselves did not consider feelings important criteria in forming marriages. The consistories also deemed it unimportant to present gifts or to drink in the name of marriage at engagement ceremonies, but the records reveal that most people faithfully observed these practices. It is therefore worthwhile to look at the testimony of individuals involved in contract disputes to see if they put much emphasis on sentiment in choosing spouses. For the most part, the registers of the consistories shed relatively little light on the issue of sentiment for sixteenth-century fiancés and spouses. These records generally describe litigation in a matter-of-fact manner, seldom revealing the personal feelings of the parties. Furthermore, even when such personal information can be found, caution must be used in evaluating these sources since court records are skewed toward conflict. One who studies nothing but bitter disputes can easily be swayed into thinking that all marriages were loveless affairs entered for merely mercenary reasons.[48]

With this caveat in mind, we can nonetheless conclude, among other things, that early modern Neuchâtelois often entered into engagements quite quickly. For example, in 1601 Françoys Berssot was in the process of publicizing the banns of his upcoming marriage with Susanne Girardot when Françoys Jehannot opposed them, asserting that he too was engaged to marry Susanne. Jehannot was able to prove that the two of them had valid engagements and Susanne had to marry him. Four months later, in September, Berssot—obviously the same man since he was again identified as Françoys, son of the late Anthoyne—was again in court, this time trying to prove that there was no parentage to prevent his marriage to the daughter of the late Pierre Guynaud.[49] Making two marriage contracts within four months seems rather hasty. The fact that at times promises were contracted quite quickly with little fore-

48. There is, of course, more than one way to interpret evidence from court records. Discussing the manor of Brigstock in fourteenth-century England, Bennett concedes that peasants probably were not concerned with romantic love but contends that they "surely valued the companionable love of wife and husband." Among evidence of the importance of companionship, she asserts that personal incompatibility was a common reason for marital dissolution. But she cites only one case involving a married woman who had an adulterous affair. The woman was fined and forced to return to her husband. Nothing more was heard of this affair, and Bennett speculates that this woman may have run away with her adulterous lover; *Women in the Medieval English Countryside*, pp. 101–102. I fail to see how this case can be used to show the importance of companionship in marriage.

49. AEN, CSV3:82–83, 86.

thought is epitomized by the example of Jehan Meule in 1602. Meule first appeared in court in April of that year, attempting to enforce an alleged engagement with Guillama Berguerel. To counter this suit, Guillama sought to prove that Meule had since asked another woman to marry him. Jehan de Cour d'Arenze testified, indicating that Meule had asked if he could marry Elizabeth, a relative of de Cour. Another witness, Susanne Vaultravers, claimed that she too had received a proposal from Meule, though she had refused, saying that she was too young and would never marry without her parents' consent—and that she had heard that he had already proposed to marry Guillama. Another woman, Jehanne Bizard, reported that Meule had also discussed the possibility of marriage with her, without ever actually proposing. Two other women, Barbly Henry and Ysabel Hardi, claimed that Meule had given them a coin and a drink, respectively, in the name of marriage. Predictably, the consistory decided that there were no valid promises here.[50] Proposing to a half-dozen women in one year was certainly an aberration even in this period; nevertheless, this case reveals that often promises were made quickly without a lengthy courting period.

The fact that men and women often contracted marriages hurriedly without knowing each other well does not necessarily mean that these proposals were not based on sentiment. It is quite conceivable that such engagements could have been rushed into impetuously by lovesick young men and women. Tangential evidence, however, suggests that during this period people often were not very selective in choosing mates. For example, in 1586 Clement Gendre sought to prove that Magdaleine Vallet had agreed to marry him. A woman attested that she had asked Magdaleine in the presence of Clement if she were interested in marrying him. Magdaleine replied that she would take him as soon as another.[51] Although she did not exactly say that she would accept any man as a husband, her answer suggests that she took a rather nonchalant attitude toward choosing a husband, hinting that Clement, though a satisfactory candidate, had no special qualities to distinguish him from other potential suitors.

Evidence from court records reveals that men often made marriage proposals simply because they deemed it an appropriate time to marry and paid little attention to which woman was to be the bride. The *procès verbal* for David Collin's suit against Bendichte Mathiez describes a scene in which they were passing an evening with a group of other men

50. Ibid., 90–96, 98–101, 106.
51. AEN, CSV2:289.

and women in a neighbor's home. The discussion turned to the subject of marriage and Collin said to Bendichte's mother, "You must give me a girl." Madame Mathiez replied, "Take her [indicating Bendichte], if you can have her." He then offered Bendichte a drink in the name of marriage, which she accepted willingly, convincing the judges to rule in favor of Collin.[52] In discussing the subject, he did not ask Madame Mathiez to have her daughter's hand in marriage; he simply stated that she should give him a girl to be his bride, and she then proposed Bendichte. This is hardly a case of a man's pursuing the woman he loves. Apparently Collin had reached what he considered an appropriate moment to marry, and it just so happened that Bendichte was the woman at hand to be asked.

On another occasion, a man involved in a multiparty suit intimated that for him the degree of affection his fiancée had for him was relatively unimportant. In 1565, Blaise Jacquet filed suit before the consistory of Valangin to oppose the banns that Guillama Grandjehan Contesse and Huguenin Janeret had publicized, maintaining that he himself had an engagement to marry Guillama. She admitted having accepted proposals from both men but vowed that she wanted to honor the contract with Blaise, which was anterior to that made with Huguenin. As for the contract with Huguenin, she held that she had actually made no verbal agreement. Furthermore, she avowed that this contract had been made merely to appease her parents: she was afraid to disappoint her father, who was sick on his deathbed at the time, and her mother had vigorously solicited her agreement to this marriage. To this, Huguenin responded that Guillama was perhaps saying this simply because she preferred Blaise.[53] If in Huguenin's mind Guillama's testimony was not to be trusted since she might have favored Blaise, he obviously felt that one's personal preference for a spouse should not enter into a contract dispute. Evidently he also was not the least bit abashed that the woman he had asked to marry wanted to marry someone else.[54]

52. AEN, JMN2:216.

53. AEN, CSV2:60: "Ledict Huguenin a fait dire que ladicte Guillama peult dire ce qu'il luy plaist pour ce que peult estre l'ung luy plaist mieux que l'aultre."

54. In the end, the consistory ordered that the marriage between Blaise and Guillama take place. This decision, however, was made independently of Guillama's preference: the consistory gave *passement* to Blaise because he had proved that his engagement preceded that made with Huguenin. For having promised two men, Guillama was ordered to pay the court costs and to make *réparation* in church to Huguenin and his relatives the very day of the wedding; ibid., 59–60.

It must be noted, however, that cases can be found in which individuals did make reference to the affection, or more often the lack thereof, which they had for potential fiancés. For example, in 1589 Salomé Preudhom asked to be released from her marriage promises with Jehan Mieville, claiming that the promises had been conditional and that Mieville had subsequently been guilty of an act that made him unworthy of marriage. Evidence indicated that they had promised to marry each other provided that relatives of both parties concurred. Now Salomé said that she had had a change of heart and no longer felt as she once had. Relatives of Mieville, speaking on his behalf, asked that the two of them be released from this engagement in consideration of the fact that neither party wanted to follow through with the marriage.[55] This and a few other cases indicate that, if early modern people did not feel the need to be madly in love with their future spouses, they at least sought to avoid antipathetic relationships.

It is common, however, to find that material concerns, not an absence of affection, were the cause of a woman's refusal to marry a man. That memorable case in which Jehan Jacques Navillot tried to capture his employer's daughter with a piece of sausage aptly shows the role wealth could play in the making of marriage engagements. While Navillot obviously had material gains in mind in pursuing this cause, Annellet, the defendant, showed that material concerns were behind her refusal. She declared that if Navillot had really expected to marry her he would have had to offer her not a piece of sausage but 100 or 200 écus, a large sum of money.[56] The reason she opposed Navillot's alleged marriage contract was not because she had no feelings of love for him or considered him a conniving opportunist; at no time did the question of affection even enter the discussion of these so-called marriage promises. Rather, the woman felt that the gift offered was insufficient and indicated that if he had offered a considerable sum of money she would have accepted. If money could not buy love, it at least could buy a wife.

As noted earlier, this question of the relative importance of wealth and affection in choosing mates has provoked considerable debate. Some historians, including Lawrence Stone and more emphatically Edward Shorter, argue that sentiment and material concerns had to compete and that sentiment almost always lost until roughly the eighteenth century. Others, while acknowledging that wealth was the most important criterion in selecting spouses, see the relevance of affection well

55. This case was abandoned before a decision was reached; AEN, JMN2:154v–156v.
56. Ibid., 211–214.

before the Enlightenment and industrialization.[57] Still others reject altogether the dichotomy, arguing that sharing economic concerns could actually increase feelings among family members. According to David Sabean, "the way that property is held gives shape to feelings between family members, territorializes emotion, establishes goals and ambitions, and gives to each a sense of dependence."[58] It is no doubt true that common financial concerns are one of the ties that bind family members together. When we turn our attention to the process of choosing spouses, however, it is also clear that interest and emotion can compete in the weighing of merits of prospective mates. Simon Schama describes a perfect example of the way interest could conflict with emotion. Rejecting the notion that romantic love was an invention of eighteenth-century novelists, he refers to a seventeenth-century autobiographical verse memoir in which Jacob Cats described in melodramatic terms the feverish love he had for a young maiden when he was a young man. "But when he discovered that her father was a bankrupt," Schama says, "his ardor disappeared as abruptly as it had arrived, leaving him to ruminate on the sadness of life—and the suddenly deserted object of his attentions with rather more bitter conclusions!" Later, Cats married a woman who was closer to his ideal wife: "pious, learned, fair and rich."[59] Though this memoir shows that romantic love could be found in seventeenth-century Holland, it also proves that emotion at times gave way to financial concerns.

A most interesting case before the Justice matrimoniale in 1700 reveals that romantic love clearly existed at this time but that here, too, affection had to compete with material concerns. Simeon Peter filed against Louise Prince to receive damages for having forsaken their marriage contract by marrying another man. Endeavoring to prove their engagement, Simeon produced witnesses who described very strong feelings of love between them. Louise's cousin, Judith Marie Boyve, reported that Louise was very much in love with Simeon and was heartbroken when her father forbade her to see him, forcing her to meet Simeon secretly. Judith further reported this: "She showed me several letters which Simeon had written her with verses and even a song which she found so charming. Showing me these, she told me that she did not

57. Martin Ingram is a good example; see *Church Courts, Sex, and Marriage*, pp. 139–141, and "Spousals Litigation," in *Marriage and Society*, ed. Outhwaite, p. 50.
58. Sabean, "Young Bees," p. 171, and Medick and Sabean, "Interest and Emotion in Family and Kinship Studies: A Critique of Social History and Anthropology," pp. 9–27, both in *Interest and Emotion*, ed. Medick and Sabean.
59. Schama, *Embarrassment of Riches*, pp. 443–444.

want to marry anybody else, but that she would never marry him without the consent of her father. She would rather wait twenty years without marrying."[60] Louise had told Judith that her father had beaten her when he found her with Simeon in the vineyard, and threatened to take her before the matrimonial court. Louise responded that she would not go before the court and that she wanted no one else but Simeon. Later that same evening, Simeon came to see Louise at her home and professed to her that he could not live without her. A few months later, however, Louise told Judith that Simeon had been unfaithful and that she no longer loved him.[61]

Simeon's action was a result of Louise's marriage to Rodolphe Müsly, a bourgeois of Bern. According to Simeon, Louise had long been hopelessly in love with Simeon, and later he too had considerable affection for her. At first Louise's parents were very fond of Simeon, but then under a weak pretext they forbade him to see their daughter. Simeon claimed that he and Louise had made promises to marry, both oral and written, in the presence of others. The written promises, signed by both parties, read as follows:

> We the undersigned confess that, having invoked the name of God, we have pledged to each other the faith of marriage and have promised to get married in church after the publication of the banns, which will be done as soon as possible. This promise we have made reciprocally in good faith, taking as witness that which is most sacred in heaven that this promise is sincere and is never to be broken. Contracted at Saint-Blaise the seventh day of the month of September, sixteen hundred ninety-nine.[62]

Despite this agreement, Louise slipped away to the village of Maladière, where she married Müsly. Because of this affront and breach of contract, Simeon asked for half of Louise's property or that portion the tribunal judged appropriate. On the basis of the written promises and the testimony of witnesses to the engagement, the court granted Simeon's request, awarding him half Louise's property and requiring her to reimburse the costs of the trial.[63]

This case shows that romantic, even passionate, love was not unknown in late seventeenth-century Neuchâtel. The fact that this mad

60. AEN, JMN: *Annexes* 405.
61. Ibid.
62. Ibid.
63. Ibid.

love affair did not end in marriage does not necessarily mean this was a defeat for a marriage of sentiment. It may well have been that Louise was rather fickle and fell in and out of love quite easily, and that her feelings for Müsly were every bit as strong as those she had had for Simeon. At the same time, this case reveals that parents at times dissuaded their children from marrying certain individuals for economic reasons. In her testimony, Judith Marie Boyve reported that according to Louise's mother Simeon had a very nice personality and so it was a shame that he did not come from Saint-Blaise, the community where the Prince family lived.[64] In fact, Simeon was a bourgeois of Neuchâtel. Saint-Blaise is a village just a few kilometers from the city of Neuchâtel, and the two communities have no history of antagonism between them. Madame Prince's reticence was not due to a long-standing feud between the two communities. It is safe to assume that the reservation expressed by the mother pertained to finances. If the daughter married a bourgeois of Neuchâtel, she would no longer have any rights in her community of origin. The *commune d'origine,* an institution that still exists in Switzerland, refers as its name implies to that community from which one's family comes. Traditionally, individuals inherited their *commune* exclusively from their fathers. When women married, they lost their claims to their fathers' *communes* and became members of their husbands'. Marshal Berthier, who became the sovereign of Neuchâtel under Napoleon, noted the difference between the institution of the *commune* in Neuchâtel and in France:

> The communal regime in this principality has certain characteristics that distinguish it from that in France and several other countries. . . . In France, a community is composed of the sum total of the inhabitants of a city or a village. In Neuchâtel, a community's prerogatives, even its property, which is often considerable, have become the exclusive property of the descendants of families who had been granted these privileges in the past. These individuals have the exclusive right over these so-called communal advantages.[65]

Although this account was written in 1806, it was also true for the sixteenth and seventeenth centuries; the *communes d'origines* had already

64. Ibid.

65. AEN, fonds Berthier, "Essai sur l'état actuel de la principauté de Neuchâtel" (1806); cited in Pierre Caspard, "Une communauté rurale à l'épreuve de l'industrialisation: Cortaillod de 1750 à 1850," *Bulletin du Centre d'Histoire économique et sociale de la Region lyonnaise* 4 (1976): 10.

been established in the later Middle Ages. The *communiers,* those people with origins in a particular community, had the exclusive right to participate in the administration of the *commune,* to reap benefits of the communal lands and forests, to receive free education for their children in the village school, and to be eligible for financial assistance from the community if they ever found themselves destitute. People who were inhabitants of a village but had their origins elsewhere did not have these rights but did have to pay taxes.[66] In short, if a woman was a *communier* of a rather affluent village, financial concerns could serve as a disincentive to marrying someone whose family had its origin elsewhere. The reservations Louise's parents had toward Simeon were founded on the fact that he was not a *communier* of Saint-Blaise.

Nevertheless, the man Louise eventually married was also not a native of Saint-Blaise. Perhaps this bourgeois of Bern had in his favor more substantial property holdings. We can do nothing but speculate. It is also important to note that the testimony of Judith and of one other witness reveals that Louise, though amorous of Simeon, did not want to disobey her parents, despite her early clash with her father. Evidently many young people were willing to heed the advice of their parents on the matter of choosing mates.

The role parents played in forming their children's marriages is another issue that has been debated at length. Since the family economy prevailed and wealth was in land passed down from one generation to another, it is understandable that parents took a keen interest in their children's selection of marriage partners. Often historians have portrayed parents as virtually dictating whom their children were to marry, usually disregarding their wishes. According to Stone, in sixteenth- and seventeenth-century England sons and daughters had the power only to veto the mates their parents had chosen for them; only in the late seventeenth century did the tables begin to turn, as young people chose their own spouses and parents retained the veto power.[67] Just as some historians see sentiment and wealth as opposing criteria in choosing spouses, so various scholars see a division between the wishes of parents

66. Ibid.; Jean-Pierre Jelmini, "La vie publique dans les communautés rurales de Neuchâtel au XVIIIe siècle, établie d'après les documents de Dombresson et de Travers," *Musée neuchâtelois,* 1972, 158–163; Fernand Loew, "Les mariages au XVe siècle," *Musée neuchâtelois,* 1961, 59. Though communal schools existed in eighteenth-century villages, I am not sure that they were common in the seventeenth century. It should be noted that *communiers* did not have only privileges. They also had certain responsibilities to fulfill, such as the maintenance of communal roads and transportation of materials.
67. Stone, *Family, Sex, and Marriage,* p. 272.

and children. Jack Goody observes that, among young people in early modern Europe, love was "potentially a rebellious passion, running contrary to" the plans of their parents.[68]

Sundry studies of late medieval and early modern English families have failed to form a consensus on parental influence on the formation of marriages. R. H. Helmholz and Ralph Houlbrooke found evidence from the court records of late medieval and Reformation England of strong parental influence on the formation of marriages. At the same time, several scholars hold that common folk in late medieval and early modern England had greater freedom to marry than Stone and others have allowed.[69] Michael MacDonald who studied mental illness of the seventeenth century, asserts that young people generally took the initiative in courting and subsequently sought the approbation of their parents. He further observes that the frustrations of courtship and married life were the source of mental anguish for 40 percent of the people who sought professional pychological help. Their stories, says MacDonald, "make nonsense of historians' confident assertions that romantic love was rare in seventeenth-century England or that it was unimportant in choosing marital partners."[70] Even if most marriages were not arranged, it is nonetheless possible that parents, through their veto power, controlled their sons' and daughters' choice of spouses. The views of Stone and MacDonald are not necessarily irreconcilable. A possible explanation for MacDonald's evidence on depression caused by unfulfilled passions is that parents at times thwarted their children's romantic interests. As we have seen, Louise Prince wanted desperately to marry Simeon Peter but her parents forbade her to do so, apparently for material reasons. Even if young people initiated the courtship themselves, parents could still prevent these romances from ending in marriage.[71]

---

68. Goody, *Production and Reproduction: A Comparative Study of the Domestic Domain* (Cambridge, 1976), p. 17.

69. Bennett, *Women in the Medieval English Countryside*, pp. 95–96; Hanawalt, *Ties That Bound*, pp. 8–10, 188, 192–193, 200; Helmholz, *Marriage Litigation*, pp. 47–50; Houlbrooke, *Church Courts and the People*, pp. 62–64; Quaife, *Wanton Wenches*, p. 243; Sheehan, "Formation and Stability," p. 263.

70. MacDonald, *Mystical Bedlam*, pp. 88–94.

71. Gillis maintains that peers had a greater influence on the choice of spouse than did parents. According to Gillis, the closest relationships in early modern England were with one's friends, not with one's parents; *For Better, for Worse*, p. 39. The impression I get from the court records is that parents were much more decisive in forming marriages than were friends. Many Neuchâteloises accepted marriage proposals on the condition that their parents agreed; not once did I encounter an engagement made with the proviso that close friends concurred.

Various scholars have seen differing amounts of freedom in the formation of marriages on the continent as well. In Germany, Lyndal Roper finds at one extreme parents who arranged marriages without even consulting with their sons and daughters. Other parents allowed their children to take the initiative but reserved the right to veto their choice. Still other children completely ignored or even contradicted their parents' wishes. In their work on early modern French peasant life, Jean-Louis Flandrin and Jean-Marie Gouesse deny that parents generally arranged marriages for their sons and daughters. Both hold that young people enjoyed more freedom in choosing marriage partners than is commonly believed, though this freedom was closely circumscribed by various economic and social factors. Within these limits, however, French peasants could choose their mates, and love matches were more common than is often thought. Martine Segalen rightly asserts that the degree of freedom of choice varied according to region and to socioeconomic status, proposing that the more egalitarian groups had a greater degree of choice and consequently were more motivated by love in forming marriages.[72]

Indeed, several scholars have taken into account factors such as class and inheritance patterns when discussing parental influence on the formation of marriage. On the basis of marriage licenses for the period 1598–1619, Vivien Brodsky Elliott suggests that women who migrated to London, usually to find work as servants, enjoyed greater autonomy in choosing husbands than did the daughters of native Londoners, no doubt because the former received little or no financial assistance from their parents and had to build up their own dowries. One would expect the degree of influence parents had over a child's marriage to vary in proportion to their material contribution to the new couple. In fact, Flandrin notes that among French peasants parents controlled the eldest son's marriage more closely than those of younger sons, since he was the preferred heir who received the bulk of the family property.[73]

On the basis of sixteenth- and seventeenth-century court records, Martin Ingram finds that parents exerted considerable influence in Ely, Wiltshire, and parts of Salisbury, though they usually did not take the initiative in matchmaking, reserving rather the right to veto their

72. Roper, *Holy Household*, pp. 156–157; Flandrin, *Amours paysannes*, pp. 95–100; Gouesse, "Parents, famille et mariage en Normandie au XVIIe et XVIIIe siècles," *Annales; E.S.C.* 27 (1972): 1144; Segalen, *Historical Anthropology of the Family*, pp. 129–130.

73. Elliott, "Single Women in the London Marriage Market: Age, Status, and Mobility, 1598–1619," in *Marriage and Society*, ed. Outhwaite, pp. 89, 99–100; Flandrin, *Amours paysannes*, pp. 63–64, 243; Goody, *Production and Reproduction*, p. 63.

children's choice. In more than half the better-documented cases Ingram examined, contract disputes resulted from family opposition to individuals' choice of spouses. Ingram found that most often individuals themselves had initiated the choosing of mates. When, however, they reported to their families and friends of the prospective match, "they faced disapproval and opposition, and the match was broken off or thrown into jeopardy." Ingram further argues that the church courts' attempts to punish clandestine marriages tended to increase parental control over their children's choice of spouses and that familial opposition almost always was based on complaints that the other party was too poor or too lowly. Once again, conflicts arose from the conflicting concerns of wealth and "physical and emotional attachment; the importance of romantic love, with all its heartaches and inconstancies, emerges strongly from the depositions in contract suits, balancing the emphasis on financial prudence and family influence."[74]

Simon Schama has shown in a similar fashion that parents in seventeenth-century Holland had the power to veto but generally did not oppose suitable matches. Unsuitable marriages were those in which the social discrepancy between partners was considered too compromising. Schama recounts the story of the daughter of a Delft regent who fell in love with a predikant twenty-four years her senior. Her father denied her permission to marry this man, deeming him beneath them in status. At the age of twenty-five, she petitioned a provincial court to be allowed to marry the predikant, but the court ruled in favor of her father. She finally married him at thirty-three, only after her father's death. According to Schama, popular opinion was in favor of the daughter—her father was insulted on the streets of Delft—but the institutions were clearly on the side of paternal authority.[75] Simply put, interest and emotion did at times conflict.

The overall impression one gains from these various studies and from Neuchâtel's court records is that parents usually did not arrange marriages for their children but allowed them to do their own matchmaking as long as they chose partners of comparable wealth and status. When,

74. Ingram, *Church Courts, Sex, and Marriage*, pp. 200–201, 203–204, 210.

75. Schama, *Embarrassment of Riches*, pp. 441–442. Thomas Robisheaux sees growing parental influence in rural Germany: as part of a broader search for order, the Lutheran Reformation increased patriarchal control over the formation of marriage. In the sixteenth and seventeenth centuries, courts supported the heads of families who, in an effort to annul contracts their children made without their permission, were the most common plaintiffs to investigations concerning engagements; *Rural Society and the Search for Order in Early Modern Germany* (Cambridge, 1989), pp. 105–116.

however, a person became interested in someone who had nothing to offer but love, the parents pressured their son or daughter to find a more lucrative union. Nevertheless, the evidence from the consistorial records suggests for the most part that young people appreciated their parents' advice. Though there were examples of parents' trying to push their children into marriages they did not want, time and time again we encounter marriage promises made on the condition that parents agreed to the match. Perhaps sons and daughters felt that choosing a spouse was too burdensome to be made alone and therefore were relieved to hear their elders' opinion on these matters. Of course, it could be that they were merely afraid of the possible consequences if they did not ask their parents' permission, perhaps fearing disinheritance if they became engaged without consulting their elders. Whether the motivation was fear or, more likely, respect, promises made with such a reservation far outnumbered those cases in which young people were censured for not conferring with their parents before entering into engagements to marry. If the reinforcement of parental authority did not nurture marriages of sentiment, young men and women at least appeared quite willing to consult their elders on their choice of spouses.

WOMEN, ILLICIT SEX, AND CONTRACT LITIGATION

As noted above, there is disagreement about the status of women in the sixteenth and seventeenth centuries. On the one hand, even if they reject the stereotype of the Middle Ages as a golden age for women, most historians agree that there was a decline in economic opportunities for women during the early modern period.[76] As Sherrin Marshall notes, "the economic structure of European society became increasingly limiting for women. Work which previously had been open to women became closed; dependable opportunities for the economic autonomy of women through work became virtually nonexistent." Natalie Zemon

76. Judith Bennett does an excellent job of undercutting the myth that women enjoyed a golden age before the economic and commercial expansion of early modern Europe. In her work on pre-plague English peasants, she shows that lower-class women did not enjoy rough equality with men, as is so often believed. Women at all levels of the social scale had similar restrictions as far as public activities were concerned, and there was a definite sexual division of labor among peasants. Bennett concedes that in the early modern period the position of women probably deteriorated with the development of the commercial economy and the centralized state, but these changes were not necessary for the subordination of women; that subordination was rooted not in government or economy but in the household; *Women in the Medieval English Countryside*, pp. 4–6, 177–185, 198.

Davis views this decline as the result of the increasing patriarchal character of sixteenth-century society: magistrates put more emphasis on the male head of the household, and women's opportunities significantly diminished. Studying women and work in late medieval northern cities, Martha Howell asserts that it was possible for women to attain high-status labor—that is, work in which they oversaw production and the distribution of their products—as long as the home was the site of production. Beginning in the latter part of the fifteenth century, however, women lost access to high-status labor when work was shifted from family production units to larger structures that required political involvement. Given the patriarchal society they lived in, women could not participate in politics and saw their work increasingly taken over by men.[77]

Scholars do not agree, however, about the impact on women of the Reformation, be it Protestant or Catholic. Schama, like Steven Ozment, thinks that the Protestant Reformation had positive effects on women. Though acknowledging the patriarchal aspect of Protestantism, Schama nonetheless sees the Reformation as enhancing the status of women in the Netherlands, Germany, and Switzerland:

> There *was* a good deal of formal subjugation—women were excluded from all political offices—but within these limits they managed nonetheless to assert themselves, both individually and collectively, in public life. In particular they played an important role in charitable institutions as regents of orphanages, hospitals, old age homes and houses of correction. In these capacities they formed networks of family alliances and offices analogous to, but not necessarily identical with, the regent coalitions of their husbands.[78]

Other historians share this view that the growing importance of charitable institutions in Reformation Europe legitimized activist roles for both Protestant and Catholic women. Though often modeled on familial patterns, these roles enabled women to enter the public arena.[79]

77. Marshall, *Women in Reformation Europe*, p. 3; Davis, "Women in the Crafts in Sixteenth-Century Lyon," in *Women and Work in Preindustrial Europe*, ed. Barbara A. Hanawalt (Bloomington, Ind., 1986), pp. 167–197; Howell, *Women, Production, and Patriarchy in Late Medieval Cities* (Chicago, 1986).

78. Schama, *Embarrassment of Riches*, p. 404.

79. See, for example, the following articles in *Women in Reformation Europe:* Sherrill Cohen, "Asylums for Women in Counter-Reformation Italy," pp. 166–188; Sherrin Marshall, "Protestant, Catholic, and Jewish Women in the Early Modern Netherlands," pp. 120–139; Diane Willen, "Women and Religion in Early Modern England," pp. 140–165.

Contrary to these views, several specialists argue that the Reformation denigrated the status of women by, among other things, reducing the number of outlets for religious expression available to them. According to Merry Wiesner, both Protestant and Catholic reformers reduced opportunities to express female piety:

> Although the Protestant reformers did champion a woman's role as wife and mother by closing the convents and forbidding female lay confraternities, they cut off women's opportunities for expressing their spirituality in an all-female context. Catholic women could still enter convents, but those convents were increasingly cut off from society. By the mid-seventeenth century, religion for all women in Germany, whether lay or clerical, had become much more closely tied to a household.[80]

Grethe Jacobsen argues that, in Protestant Scandinavia as well, the Reformation offered fewer possibilities for expressions of female lay piety.[81]

For other historians, the Reformation not only reduced women's avenues for religious expression but also contributed to social and economic decline. Jacobsen, for example, views the new position of the minister's wife as potentially negative, perhaps undermining the acceptability of women working outside the family. She acknowledges that economic changes were important in reducing work opportunities for sixteenth-century women but also blames the new faith for relegating women to the role of wives and mothers.[82] Susan Karant-Nunn maintains that, because of the Lutheran conviction that a woman's place was in the home, women's work outside the home began to suggest financial need and was stigmatized accordingly.[83]

There is also no agreed-on analysis of the relationship of women to marriage courts in Reformation Europe. Thomas Safley sees an alliance between women and the courts in the German southwest, with women consistently outnumbering men as plaintiffs in matrimonial disputes.[84] Lyndal Roper, though conceding that the city council and matrimonial court of Reformation Augsburg defended the interests of women, holds

80. Wiesner, "Nuns, Wives, and Mothers," in *Women in Reformation Europe*, p. 26.
81. Jacobsen, "Nordic Women and the Reformation," in *Women in Reformation Europe*, p. 47.
82. Ibid., pp. 54, 57.
83. Karant-Nunn, "The Women of the Saxon Silver Mines," in *Women in Reformation Europe*, p. 43.
84. Safley, *Let No Man Put Asunder*, p. 173. For a later period, Sabean also found that, as far as marital disputes were concerned, Lutheran consistories were used primarily by women; *Property, Production, and Family in Neckarhausen.*

that they did so in a condescending manner that mirrored the real loss of status women suffered:

> If, as Ozment has argued, Reformation morality did not cast a wife as the "maid or common servant of her husband," its leading tone was hardly that which Ozment characterizes as invoking "the mother of the house," who enjoyed "a position of high authority and equal respect." . . . The Council's growing obsession with policing disorderly male behaviour did lead it to create a system which offered women far more recourse against violent husbands; but it did so in terms of the Council's duty to the weak, offering protection on the grounds of wifely subordination. That protection, however, depended on properly modest wifely behaviour.[85]

For Roper, the courts' attention vis-à-vis women was small recompense for their decline in social rank.

The evidence from Neuchâtel's courts can shed light on this debate. What, for example, was the impact on women of the new requirements concerning marriage contracts? At first glance, the abolition of clandestine marriages would seem to have both good and bad results for women. Since in theory marriage promises would not be recognized in court unless there were witnesses, perhaps some young women, having been seduced by vague promises of marriage made in private, were left without legal recourse. But it may well have been that previously, when clandestine marriages had been legal, seduced women were unable to prove the existence of binding promises since it was simply their word against their seducers'. Knowing that they must have witnesses to prove engagements, women might now be more prudent in dealing with suitors.

At any rate, women who had been seduced and had no witnesses to marriage proposals were not necessarily left defenseless. Laws passed in Neuchâtel and Valangin declared that a man who deflowered a virgin must give her a dowry and marry her. The problem, of course, was knowing which women were virgins. The formula for detecting virgins read as follows: "A girl will be considered a virgin if she has good morals and a good reputation without any suspicion, and if she does not give in to the will of a young man unless he has first promised her the faith of marriage in the presence of at least two honorable

85. Roper, *Holy Household*, p. 203, citing Ozment, *When Fathers Ruled*, p. 76.

men."[86] If these criteria were used, a man who had seduced a woman without having made marriage vows in the presence of others could not be convicted of having deflowered a virgin.

In practice, however, the consistory and the Justice matrimoniale showed a certain sympathy to women who appeared before them, usually pregnant or already the mothers of children born out of wedlock, with requests that their seducers be required to execute marriage promises. A few exceptional cases can be found in which men were actually forced to marry the women they had impregnated even though there were absolutely no witnesses to promises. Such a case took place in 1554 when a woman identified simply as Catherine petitioned that Jehan Humbert be ordered to marry her. She maintained that she gave in to him only after accepting a marriage proposal; Jehan, though admitting having had sexual relations with her, denied the engagement. The consistory ordered Jehan to marry Catherine, noting that Catherine was an honorable, upright girl (*une fille de bien et d'honneur*) and that she would not have abandoned herself to him unless he had promised to marry her. Furthermore, the judges observed that she came from a good home and that the two parties were of the same social status. They further warned against those who sought to deceive maidens with good reputations, emphasizing that those who deflowered virgins had to marry them. All this they decided even though no one had witnessed the alleged engagement. If the judges had strictly applied the letter of the law, they would have had to reject Catherine's request, since marriage agreements had to be made in the presence of at least two persons. Here the judges were essentially reasoning backward, maintaining that since Catherine's morals were praiseworthy Jehan must have proposed to her; otherwise, she surely would not have agreed to have sexual relations with him.[87]

Such decisions, however, were quite rare. The reasoning behind this judgment indicates that no general precedent was being set here for enforcing marriage contracts made clandestinely. In this case, the court was most likely accepting evidence of marriage by public repute. In a legal tradition that goes back to Roman law, a couple could be adjudged married simply by the way they acted in public and interacted in their

86. Favarger and Tribolet, *Sources du droit du canton de Neuchâtel*, pp. 183, 207: "Une fille sera tenue pour vierge, laquelle sera de bonnes meurs renommée et famée sans aulcung vitupere ny suspicion, et que ne consentira a la volonté du juvenceau sinon que premyerement il luy aye promis par devant deux hommes de bien pour le moings, et de main directement, la foy de mariage."
87. AEN, CSV1:60v–61.

daily lives. If a couple spent much time together and the man treated the woman as a man behaves toward his wife, courts in Neuchâtel and elsewhere might in exceptional cases recognize them as married even if they had not celebrated a wedding or betrothal. In England, Scotland, France, and other parts of late medieval and early modern Europe, courts took into consideration public repute or "common fame" to determine whether a couple ought to be considered husband and wife.[88] The decisive factors in this particular judgment were the woman's impeccable reputation and, more important, the comparable social standing of the two parties. Had there been disparity in social status, the judges would have been less sympathetic, fearing that Catherine was trying to trap a young man into marriage to climb a few rungs of the social ladder.

More common were decisions requiring seducers to pay some sort of indemnity to the women they seduced. In 1583, a woman identified only as Barbely declared that Pierre Jacobel had promised to marry her, though without witnesses. Jacobel replied that he had neither promised to marry her nor given her anything in the name of marriage. And if he had indeed approached her, he had done so only as one soliciting a prostitute. Since there were no witnesses to the alleged engagement, the judges held that there was no marriage contract. For having deflowered Barbely, Jacobel was required to pay her twenty livres and reimburse her expenses for the court appearance.[89] Similarly, in 1593 Jehanne Roullier failed in her quest to force Gerard Huguenaud to either marry her or pay her 500 livres. The Justice matrimoniale nevertheless required Huguenaud to pay Jehanne 30 livres for having deflowered her, rather meager recompense for the burden of an illegitimate child.[90]

88. Ingram, *Church Courts, Sex, and Marriage,* p. 197, and "Spousals Litigation," p. 51; Mitchison and Leneman, *Sexuality and Social Control,* p. 100; Phillips, *Putting Asunder,* p. 31; Segalen, *Amours et mariages de l'ancienne France* (Paris, 1981), p. 11. Roman proof of marriage included "*honor matrimonii,* or the decorum with which a husband treated his wife and the social dignity that he accorded her"; Brundage, *Law, Sex, and Christian Society,* p. 35.

89. AEN, JMN2:123v–124.

90. Ibid., 173, 174. Earlier in the Reformation period, the consistory was remarkably inconsistent in its treatment of mothers of illegitimate children who claimed to have a marriage contract but were unable to prove it. In 1554, a woman identified simply as Jehanne appeared before the consistory after having had a child out of wedlock and alleged that Claude Gaignot had promised to marry her. Claude recognized the child as his own but maintained that he had not asked her to marry him, given her money in the name of marriage, or had sexual relations with her in hopes of having her as his wife. Since there were no witnesses, the pretended marriage was declared null. Claude, however, was ordered to take custody of the child ("prendre l'enfant a sa charge"), to pay all court costs, and to pay Jehanne 10 livres since she had been without reproach before this affair. Three years later, the treatment Magdelaine Choppaudat received was far different from that shown to Jehanne. Magdelaine had had a child with

Among contract disputes, special treatment was given to servants seduced by their masters. Separated from the protection of their families,
female servants of the Old Regime were most vulnerable to seduction,
be it at the hands of their masters or of others. Often servants swelled
the ranks of unmarried mothers, representing perhaps 70 percent of the
mothers of illegitimate births in England in the 1580s[91] When a man
agreed to hire a woman and take her into his home as a servant, he had
to assume responsibilities toward her as if she were one of his own children. Consequently, the consistories were rather strict with masters who
abused servants. At times, unmarried masters were required to marry
servants they had impregnated even if the reputed promises were made
clandestinely. In 1576, Susanne Masson brought suit against Jacques
Poncier, her employer of three years, claiming that he had promised to
marry her and should be required to do so since he had deflowered her
while she was under his supervision (*en son pain et sel*). She admitted
that no one was present at the *fiançailles,* and Poncier produced witnesses who testified that Susanne had repeatedly denied being pregnant, saying she was still a virgin. Nevertheless other witnesses reported
that Poncier had said that he wanted to behave as an honorable man in
this affair. Furthermore, Poncier's mother reportedly avowed that she
would be happy if her son married Susanne. The judges decided that
"according to God and reason, even though no promise has been demonstrated, considering that she served him for about three years without being subject to any blame or dishonor," Poncier must take Susanne
as his wife, or if he refused to do so to pay her the sum of 200 livres.[92]
The fact that the judges appealed explicitly to reason underscores their
use of common sense when real evidence of marriage agreements did
not exist.

The matrimonial courts were also known to order the sons of masters
to marry servants they had seduced. Such a case took place in 1571

Nicholass Jehan Clement and vowed that he had promised to marry her. The consistory did
not even bother investigating this pretended engagement but simply sentenced her to three
days in prison on bread and water, after which time she was to make public *réparation* at
church. The first woman received compensation and, more important, was freed of the responsibility of raising the child; the second was simply punished as a fornicator. The blatant
discrepancy in these decisions can perhaps be attributed to the different reputations of these
women and their families. See AEN, CSV1:98v–99.

91. Ingram, *Church Courts, Sex, and Marriage,* p. 264. Though the records only rarely
mention the occupations of parties, the percentage of servants among women guilty of fornication appears to have been much lower in early modern Neuchâtel and Valangin.

92. AEN, JMN2:53–56.

when Magdeleine Chouz of Gorgier asked that her master, Jaques Henry, the mayor of the village of Cortaillod, give permission to his son to marry her or pay her a dowry of 600 livres. Describing herself as a poor, naive girl, Magdeleine avowed that the son, also named Jaques, had seduced her while she was employed in the service of his father. The son in turn complained that Magdeleine was one of those women who tried to coerce young men into marrying them. She claimed that he had proposed to her; he confessed to deflowering her but denied any contract to marry. Admitting so much, however, was enough to convince the judges to return a verdict in favor of Magdeleine: they ruled that Jaques and Magdeleine were to become husband and wife.[93]

Servants seduced by their masters or their masters' sons were treated rather liberally by Neuchâtel's matrimonial court, even when they appeared to have solicited proposals. A rather amusing case in 1580 involved Magdeleine Grandjehan and Jeremie, the grandson of Guillaume Phillipin, Magdeleine's master. Claiming that Jeremie had asked her to marry him and that she was now pregnant with his child, Magdeleine produced various witnesses during the first days of testimony who recalled seeing the couple promise to marry each other. Several were present in a vineyard two years before when Jeremie began kissing Magdeleine and poured wine into a goblet, beckoning her to drink *en nom de mariage*. Hesitating at first, Magdeleine finally gave in to his persistent requests and drank. Since there were a few drops of wine left in the goblet, Jeremie put a piece of bread into it to sop up the remaining drops and then ate the bread to confirm this agreement. While perusing this testimony, the reader cannot help but take the side of the woman. One envisions a well-to-do dandy taking advantage of a naive, poor servant girl. Only during the third day of testimony do we learn that at the time of their "engagement" the woman was thirty-five years old and her "seducer" but a lad of fourteen. Accordingly, the tribunal declared that Jeremie was too young to marry without the consent of his father and therefore proclaimed the promises null. Nonetheless, since Jeremie had sexual relations with her while she was under the charge of the family and since she clearly was relying on these promises when she gave in to Jeremie, Jeremie's father was ordered to provide her with a dowry of 100 livres and to pay all her legal expenses, plus 20 livres for the costs of childbearing.[94]

93. Ibid., 12v–13v, 17.
94. Ibid., 59, 61–65, 66v–67v.

This case is interesting for a variety of reasons. Most obvious, it seems quite unusual that a woman in her mid-thirties could actually be swept off her feet by an adolescent young enough to be her son. Notwithstanding the evidence of witnesses, one may well wonder whether a woman of that age was wholly passive in developing an amorous relationship with a teenager. Whether she actually was is of little importance. The fact remains that she was treated sympathetically by the tribunal as a woman seduced by a member of her master's family. This case also shows that familial responsibility extended from grandfather to grandson—Magdeleine was the servant of Jeremie's grandfather, not of his father.[95] Finally, this suit reveals that, even if masters or their sons were not required to marry the servants they seduced, they were generally ordered to provide them with a dowry, a sum that could be much greater than the amounts paid by men who deflowered virgins who were not their servants.[96]

Elsewhere in Europe, servants seduced by their masters were not always treated so sympathetically. True, in France a law of 1567 held that "any child of a female servant conceived while she was in her employer's household was automatically considered the offspring of the master unless he could prove otherwise." In practice, however, French tribunals may have been less sympathetic to the plight of pregnant servants.[97] In seventeenth-century Holland, popular literature portrayed female servants as scheming opportunists who tried to trap respectable men into

95. It appears that the three generations of Phillipins— the patriarch Guillaume, son Esaye, and grandson Jeremie lived in the same household, an indication that the extended household could be found in early modern Neuchâtel.

96. The size of the dowries awarded varied. In 1584 the Justice matrimoniale obliged Guillaume Tribolet to provide his servant, Isabel Rossel, with a dowry of 200 livres. In other cases, the consistory of Valangin allowed only 50 livres to Anthoina Grandjehan in 1556 and 30 livres to the daughter of Guillaume Moton in 1557. All three women had given birth to illegitimate children and claimed that their masters deflowered them after having promised to marry them. The circumstances of these three suits seem identical, but the latter two women were awarded only a fraction of what Rossel received. This discrepancy may reflect differences in the wealth of the masters' families. See AEN, CSV1:94, 98v; JMN2: 128r–v.

97. Cissie Fairchilds, *Domestic Enemies: Servants and Their Masters in Old Regime France* (Baltimore, 1984), p. 168. According to eighteenth-century French records, it was usually not masters or their male relatives who abused servants. As Sarah C. Maza notes, however, many such liaisons were unlikely to be recorded, since seducers of high social standing could hide pregnant women, bribe them, or terrorize them into lying. Maza also notices a decline in sympathy for servants vis-à-vis masters in the eighteenth century: "Originally a servant who accused her master was always believed, but by the eighteenth century this presumption in favor of the servant had been abandoned because, as legislators claimed, 'A master too often pays for the pleasures of a stableboy or a kitchen helper'"; see *Servants and Masters in Eighteenth-Century France: The Uses of Loyalty* (Princeton, 1983), pp. 90–91, citing Marie-Claude Phan, "Les Déclarations de Grossesse en France: Essai institutionnel," *Revue d'histoire moderne et contemporaine* 22 (1975): 82.

marrying them, though in fact they were much more likely to be victims of lecherous masters. Schama found only one case of a Dutch master who was forced to marry his servant, and that involved a man who had confessed to getting the woman pregnant. Schama speculates that, "for every case that came before the courts, there must have been scores in which the maids were far too intimidated to seek the help of the law."[98]

In dealing with cases of seduction, Neuchâtel's tribunals also gave special consideration to those suits filed by women who had been seduced by their fathers' male servants or apprentices. Here too the courts were more lenient toward women, sometimes requiring men to marry even if no one had witnessed a betrothal. Blaise Chollet appeared in court in 1573 complaining that his daughter Rose had been debauched by his apprentice, Pierre Collin, who was boarding in the Chollet household.[99] Chollet maintained that, according to the word of God, whoever deflowered a virgin had to marry her and that Collin should have behaved honestly while living under his roof. Admittedly unable to prove the engagement, Chollet nevertheless asked that Collin be enjoined to marry his daughter since he had been in service in his home. Collin denied the daughter's claims that he had promised to marry her but he admitted having sexual relations with her. In Collin's mind, since there were no witnesses to the pretended engagement, he could not be required to marry her. The judges pointed out that the law Collin was referring to had been passed because of the danger certain women posed: pretending to be virgins when they really were not, they sought to seduce young men from good homes and have them as husbands. According to the judges, this was not the case here. Rose had been a virgin until this affair, and even Collin conceded that she was an honorable person. Collin was thus not protected by the decree, since in effect it was he who was guilty of abuse. The court also took into account the fact that Collin's uncle and his minister both thought the two should marry and that Chollet was presenting "a marriage"—evidently they meant a dowry—of 500 livres, which was commensurate with Collin's social standing, insofar as he was "no longer of a great home."[100] All things considered, the Justice matrimoniale ordered Collin to marry Chollet.

98. Schama, *Embarrassment of Riches*, p. 459.
99. Collin's relationship to Chollet was described as being "a son service et pain"; AEN, JMN2:28.
100. Ibid., 28–30.

This case effectively shows the importance of wealth and social status in litigation concerning marriage contracts. In this case and the one against Jehan Humbert, pregnant women filed suit against seducers who confessed to sexual relations but denied any engagements to marry. Though no one had witnessed any betrothals, the courts ruled in favor of both women, in part because the parties enjoyed comparable social standing. For the judges, marriage was to be a union of equals, and they rejected those suits filed by plaintiffs who sought to use marriage as a means of climbing the social ladder. The washwoman who sought to marry the noble soldier, the hired hand who wooed his employer's daughter with a piece of sausage, and the servant woman who was "seduced" by her master's fourteen-year-old grandson all failed in their attempts to secure financially advantageous marriages. In short, the judges tried to ensure social equilibrium by avoiding egregious differences in social status between fiancés. These decisions lend support to Goody's contention that the control of marriage tends to lead toward homogamy, marriages between people of the same status.[101]

Judicial authorities throughout Europe shared this concern for the social background of parties to contract disputes. Schama has found that in early modern Holland a pregnant woman could sue her seducer to get him to marry her or, if already married, to provide her with a dowry, pay the costs of childbirth, and perhaps contribute to the long-term costs of raising the child. If the couple were of the same status, the woman had good chances of winning: in Leiden, close to three-fourths of the women who filed suit between 1671 and 1795 won their cases. A female servant debauched by her master, however, had virtually no chance of convincing the courts to order a marriage between two persons of disparate social classes; as in Neuchâtel, a servant had more realistic prospects of receiving some form of financial support. The size of dowries awarded under such circumstances depended on the backgrounds of the accused and the plaintiff.[102] Whereas Neuchâtel's courts showed a greater sympathy for servants seduced by masters, Schama's findings on the role social status played in deciding contract suits largely hold true for Neuchâtel. This effort to ensure that spouses were of comparable status was the continuation of a long tradition, the roots of which can be found in Roman law.[103]

101. Goody, *Production and Reproduction*, p. 14.
102. Schama, *Embarrassment of Riches.*, pp. 405–406.
103. In ancient Rome, a principal difference between wives and concubines was that concubines were usually of a lower status than that of their lovers. In fact, Roman law made

TABLE 2

Marriage contract disputes, 1547–1706

| | Outcome | | | |
Action	Contract binding	Contract null	Abandoned	Total
All disputes				
Valangin	41	120	84	246
Neuchâtel	20	59	29	108
Gorgier	0	5	1	6
	61	184	114	360[a]
Enforce contract				
Female plaintiff	21	48	53	122
Male Plaintiff	21	76	38	135
Annul or disprove contract				
Female plaintiff	2	29	4	35
Male plaintiff	2	12	3	17

[a]One decision provided that a man had either to marry or give a dowry to the woman he had deflowered. In two other cases, men filed before Neuchâtel's matrimonial court to sue for damages because their fiancées had illegally married other men, thus bringing the number of contract disputes to 362. Furthermore, 26 couples were convoked by the consistories; 4 couples mutually asked that their marriage contracts be recognized as valid; for 20 cases it is unclear who the actor was, and for another it is not clear whether a man sought to enforce or to annul a contract. These various cases are not computed under actions to enforce or to disprove or annul contracts in this table.

A look at the Neuchâtel statistics pertaining to marriage contract disputes in Table 2 provides some interesting results. Most important and most surprising is the fact that men slightly outnumbered women (135 to 122) among those who sought to enforce marriage promises. One might expect most plaintiffs to have been pregnant women who desperately sought to avoid being single mothers. Nevertheless more men than women sought to enforce marriage engagements with recalcitrant fiancés.

No pattern concerning the breakdown by gender of plaintiffs to contract disputes has emerged from European studies of this period. On the one hand, Safley has observed that women initiated over three-fourths of suits to enforce marriage agreements in both Basel and Constance. Likewise, women initiated over half the marriage contract suits in Reformation Augsburg and in seventeenth- and eighteenth-

marriage between parties of widely disparate social classes illegal; see James A. Brundage, "Concubinage and Marriage in Medieval Canon Law," in *Sexual Practices and the Medieval Church*, ed. Bullough and Brundage, p. 118.

century Scotland. Roper found that immediately after the conversion to Protestantism in Augsburg (1537–1546) women initiated 57 percent of all contract disputes while men were plaintiffs in only 9 percent of the cases; parental opposition was behind 22 percent of the suits, and it is unclear who the actor was in the remaining 12 percent. Diametrically opposed to these figures are those Houlbrooke found in sixteenth-century English court records, which show that twice as many men as women tried to enforce marriage engagements. In fifteenth-century Champagne, men outnumbered women as plaintiffs to breach-of-promise suits by almost three to one. Ingram found conflicting evidence on the gender of plaintiffs in his work on Tudor and early Stuart courts: in Ely men outnumbered women among those who tried to enforce marriage contracts by a two-to-one ratio in 1580, increasing to three to one in the early seventeenth century; in contrast, in early seventeenth-century Wiltshire about 60 percent of the plaintiffs were women. It is not clear why there was such a difference between contemporary Ely and Wiltshire.[104] With slightly more men than women initiating such suits, Neuchâtel stands between extremes in late medieval—early modern Europe.

A perplexing question is why the percentage of female plaintiffs in marriage contract disputes changed during the course of this period in Valangin. From 1547 to 1588, 47 women and 24 men requested that marriage promises be recognized as binding. In striking contrast to these figures are those for the period 1590–1618: 15 women and 40 men. Of these 15 women, only 3 alleged sexual consummation after the engagement, as opposed to 25 during the previous forty years. One might speculate that this indicates that young people were finally heeding the advice of the moralists and no longer indulging in premarital sex. But such a hypothesis looks weak when one considers the consistory's evidence of illegitimate births and fornication.[105]

As Table 3 indicates, the consistory of Valangin convoked over 900 people during this century and a half for fornication, adultery, or the suspicion of illicit sexuality. These police actions, however, were not spread out evenly throughout this period. Whereas only 21 women were summoned for fornication during the years 1547–1588, the next three decades saw 91 women accused of fornication, 84 of whom were

104. Safley, *Let No Man Put Asunder*, p. 173; Roper, *Holy Household*, p. 160; Mitchison and Leneman, *Sexuality and Social Control*, p. 89; Houlbrooke, "Making of Marriage," p. 342; Gottlieb, "Meaning of Clandestine Marriage, p. 64; Ingram, "Spousals Litigation," p. 45.

105. Such records exist only for Valangin. There are no such records for Neuchâtel.

TABLE 3
Illicit sexuality in Valangin, 1547–1706

	Women	Men	Total
1547–1588			
Fornication	21	41	62
Adultery	6	14	20
Fréquentation	21	22	43
	48	77	125
1590–1618			
Fornication	91	74	165
Adultery	14	21	35
Fréquentation	12	12	24
	117	107	222
1629–1706			
Fornication	266	168	434
Adultery	49	56	105
Fréquentation	18	18	36
	333	242	575
1547–1706, total			
Fornication	378	283	661
Adultery	69	91	160
Fréquentation	51	52	103
	498	426	924

convicted.[106] In spite of the low number of women alleging that sexual consumption had followed marriage promises, the records specifically mention 78 illegitimate births for this thirty-year period, compared to only 11 for the years 1547–1588 (see Table 4). Even more startling is that between 1629 and 1706 only 14 women tried to enforce marriage contracts and purported that sexual consumption had followed, even though the consistory censured 217 women during this same period for having given birth to illegitimate children.[107] For all three periods, these figures for illegitimate births exclude cases that explicitly involved adulterous affairs, since these latter would have no bearing on marriage contracts; as noted above, those who committed adultery together were never to marry one another. True, *paillardise,* the term normally used in convicting these women, was a rather ambiguous word and could conceivably have referred to fornication or adultery. But since there were

106. AEN, CSV1-3. Of these 84, 10 women were at least second-time offenders.
107. AEN, CSV4-7.

TABLE 4

Illegitimate births and deflowered plaintiffs in Valangin, 1547–1706

	1547–1588	1590–1618	1629–1706	Total
Women convoked[a]	11	78	217	306
Suits to enforce marriage[b]				
Contract Binding	4	1	0	5
Contract Null	12	1	3	16
Abandoned	9	1	11	21
	25	3	14	42

[a]Women convoked for fornication who had given birth to illegitimate children. These figures refer only to those women specifically said to be the mothers of illegitimate children. Most likely there were others punished for fornication for whom the clerk failed to record that they had borne children out of wedlock. Births resulting from adulterous affairs are excluded. My interest here is the contrast between the increase in illegitimate births and the contemporary decrease in the number of women alleging sexual consummation who asked that marriage contracts be enforced. Since marriages between adulterers were not possible, evidence concerning such births is not pertinent.
[b]Suits filed by women to enforce marriage contracts after defloration.

rulings that specifically condemned people for adultery, it is safe to say that the majority of cases of *paillardise* involved premarital relations, not extramarital affairs.

Why then was there a decrease in the number of female plaintiffs to marriage contracts and a contemporaneous increase in illegitimate births? Perhaps women simply saw little hope in successfully convincing members of the consistory that they had valid engagements. As Table 4 reveals, between 1590 and 1706 only one woman who alleged sexual consummation successfully enforced a marriage contract; and as we see later in this chapter, the consistories rejected the vast majority of suits to enforce marriage contracts filed by both men and women. Such a theory is problematic, however, in light of the increase in the number of men trying to execute marriage engagements in the late sixteenth and early seventeenth centuries.

Another theory is that men were voluntarily furnishing some sort of financial aid to the women they had seduced. Cases have been described in which women were awarded compensation for having been deflowered. Among the 78 cases involving illegitimate births between 1590 and 1618, only twice was such compensation granted.[108] Could it be

108. In 1595, Abraham Huguenin and Huguenette Gentil, both of Le Locle, were convoked for committing *paillardise* and having an illegitimate child together. Though no promises of marriage were alleged, Abraham was required to pay Huguenette 200 livres for the costs of rearing the child. In 1601, Anthoina Barbe demanded that David Montandon of Le Locle provide her with a dowry since he had deflowered her and fathered her child. The

that the other 76 women received absolutely nothing from the fathers of their children? These mothers must have lost their virginity at some time, so one would think they might have received some compensation for having been deflowered. Throughout the seventeenth century, court registers only rarely mentioned financial settlements over questions of paternity. The consistory of Gorgier recorded such an arrangement concerning the child of Barbelli Henri. In 1683, Barbelli gave birth to a child and avowed that Jean Marlby of Gorgier was the father. Jean was out of the country, and his father reached an agreement with Barbelli. Barbelli was to look after the child for the first six months during which time André Marlby, the child's paternal grandfather, was to pay her 30 livres for the costs of rearing the child. Thereafter the paternal grandparents were to take custody of the child.[109] It is important to stress that the consistory was not mandating this financial arrangement but simply reporting the agreement made by the interested parties. In all likelihood, many similar settlements were made but not recorded in the court registers.

Some sort of out-of-court agreement seems possible in light of the fact that early modern consistories had a fairly effective way of "proving" the identity of the father of children born out of wedlock. Such proof depended on oaths. In Neuchâtel, a practice was used until the eighteenth century to identify the fathers of illegitimate children—the oath given on the *petit lit*, the bed on which a woman gave birth. According to the custom of the county, two or more justices went to the home where an unmarried woman was going into labor. When she was at the height of the agony of childbirth, the justices administered to her the oath and ordered her to reveal the identity of the father.[110]

---

consistory ordered him to pay her 50 livres for rearing the child and for other expenses such as the costs of her assistants; and for having "deflowered" her, David had to pay Anthoina 120 livres; AEN, CSV3:41, 84–85.

109. AEN, CSG:83. This case and others from the records of the consistory of Gorgier show that grandparents, both maternal and paternal, could be considered legally responsible for their illegitimate grandchildren.

110. Similar oaths could be found elsewhere in Europe, though often it was the midwife herself, not a special inquisitor, who administered the oath. Stone notes that in seventeenth- and eighteenth-century England it was common for the midwife and other local women to interrogate the woman during labor, refusing to assist her until she identified the father. The midwives' oath of 1726 actually imposed this duty upon them. In the same manner, Protestants in Reformation Germany required midwives to ask mothers of illegitimate children the identity of the father when the pain of labor was most excruciating; *Family, Sex, and Marriage*, p. 635. See also Alan Macfarlane, "Illegitimacy and Illegitimates in English History," in *Bastardy and Its Comparative History*, ed. Peter Laslett, Karla Oosterveen, and Richard M. Smith (Cambridge, Mass. 1980), p. 73; Wiesner, "Nuns, Wives, and Mothers," pp. 24–25.

The notary Jean Roulet recorded an example of such a visit which must have been typical of the way this *serment* was administered. In February 1693, the mayor of Travers and three other justices went to the home of Jean Pellaton to administer the oath to his daughter, Judith. First, the mayor chastised her, saying that he was disappointed in her and that he had expected better conduct from her. Then he gave her the oath to swear by the name of God if someone had seduced her by promises or menaces. She had to tell the truth; doing otherwise would be "an unforgivable sin instead of simple fornication," which was pardonable. He warned her that she had to choose the road to heaven or to hell; she had to declare who had made her pregnant to pacify her soul. Judith asked for forgiveness and declared:

> I give this child to François DuBois, secretary, son of Jonas DuBois, juror, because it is his. In so doing, I do no wrong to him, nor to my conscience, because I have never had sexual relations with anyone else in the world except him and that this was by solicitation and by the faith of marriage which he had promised me. Already for a long time he had pursued me with that goal in mind, telling me that I had to believe him. I told him that I couldn't because I wasn't worthy of him, that he needed a girl of his status, that he had a certain amount of property and that I didn't have any.[111]

Judith also claimed that DuBois had frequently sworn that he would never dishonor her but would remain faithful until death. Finally, she swore that she would never have given in to him had he not employed force or oaths and promises; she now wished that she had never met him.[112] If a woman made such an oath on the *petit lit,* she was

111. AEN, Jean Roulet, Notaire, 1662–1697, p. 419.
112. Ibid., pp. 417–420. Sometimes more explicit information was provided about the actual seduction. For example, in 1720 Anne-Marie Sandoz of La Chaux-de-Fonds told the justices who administered the oath on the *petit lit* that the father of the child was Jean-Pierre Droz, a watchmaker who lived in her father's house. Under oath, she swore that one night he came to her room, blew out the candle, and threw her on the bed. Anne-Marie declared that at first she was stunned and did not believe that he wanted to abuse her. But "he got on top of her and she tried to resist, but he told her two or three times to be still. She said to him, 'You're disgusting! What do you think you're doing? You could get me pregnant.' He responded that she mustn't worry, that no harm would ever come to her. After he had had her company one time, he asked her if she was quite mad; to which she said, 'You disgusting man. I didn't think you were capable of this.'" After asking her not to tell anyone, Droz left. Anne-Marie further claimed that she never had such relations before or after, though he did try to seduce her again. See AEN, David, fils d'Huguenin Robert, Notaire, reg. 6:485–486, 18–19 June 1720.

commonly believed incapable of telling a lie in these circumstances, or, at least, she could do so only at the risk of the damnation of her soul. If an oath was sworn on the *petit lit,* the man accused of being the father virtually had to recognize the child as his own.

The only possible recourse a man had to deny paternity and disprove the woman's oath was to make the *clame forte,* a process whereby both the man and the woman voluntarily entered prison and were subjected to torture. Abolished in 1715, this procedure was used very rarely even before that date.[113] From 1547 to 1706, only on a few rare occasions did a man make the *clame forte* against the woman who accused him of being the father of her child.[114] Apart from these isolated incidents, men accused of fathering illegitimate children agreed, perhaps reluctantly, to recognize the children as their own.[115] For virtually all these cases no mention is made of any compensation or child support to be paid to the woman. We are therefore faced with the prospect of women who either were burdened entirely with the expenses of illegitimate children or perhaps received some sort of compensation out of court.

113. The *clame forte* was abrogated in September 1715 because it was considered barbaric and unjust. It tended to provoke false oaths, since two people were swearing contradictory statements, and it favored those who were physically strong and capable of enduring torture. The tradition of the oath on the *petit lit* continued for some time, though it was modified in 1755. At this time the Tribunal des Trois Etats passed thirteen articles on the problems of paternity surrounding illegitimate births. The *conseillers d'état* decided, among other things, that magistrates would ask the woman, when she was suffering the most acute pains of childbirth, who the father was. This, however, was no longer to be an oath but merely a question. See Georges-Auguste Matile, ed., *Travaux législatifs des plaits de mai, états et audiences* (Neuchâtel, 1837), pp. 272–274; Samuel Ostervald, *Les loix, us et coutumes de la souveraineté de Neuchâtel et Valangin* (Neuchâtel, 1785), pp. 64–67; William Pierrehumbert, *Dictionnaire historique du parler Neuchâtelois et Suisse-Romand* (Neuchâtel, 1926), s.v. "clame."

114. For example, Othenry Cosandier du Boz of La Chaux-de-Fonds refused to recognize Susanne Vefue's child as his. Claiming that Susanne shamelessly lied in naming him the father of her child, Othenry said that if she did not retract this accusation he would make the *clame forte* against Susanne. Both of them agreed to go to prison to "make the *clame forte* on the body of each other" to get to the truth of the matter. This appearance before the consistory was in August 1597. The next mention of this conflict was in March 1599, when Othenry appeared before the consistory to petition to receive the eucharist. The consistorial records indicate that Othenry continued to maintain, even under torture, that the child was not his. The judges decided that to be readmitted to communion, Othenry could make *réparation* in the presence of only the minister and the elders rather than the whole church; AEN, CSV3:55–56, 64.

115. In exceptional cases, men could discredit the oaths women made while in labor. In 1698, Françoise Matthey gave birth to a child. In the oath she made on the *petit lit,* Jeanne revealed that she was not sure who the father was, confessing that she had had carnal knowledge of two different men, Jean Jaques Sandoz and Josué Callame. In the eyes of the consistory, a woman who acknowledged having sexual relations with more than one man was not to be trusted. Denying these charges by oath, Sandoz was declared innocent. The fates of Matthey and Callame are unknown; AEN, CSV6:239–242.

Although there is no evidence to corroborate the latter theory, it is safe to assume that many of these women received some assistance from their seducers.[116]

Such unfortunate women existed throughout this long period, but it is clear that illegitimacy did not reach epidemic proportions; unwed mothers remained a marginal group. Nonetheless, one cannot help but conclude that beginning in the late sixteenth century there was a perceptible increase in illicit sexual relations, that is, those that took place completely independent of any *fiançailles*. One might argue that 300 illegitimate births spread out over a century in a seigneury of 3,000 people do not suffice to show a changing trend. But we know only of the women who were unlucky enough to get pregnant. These unfortunate young women were undoubtedly far outnumbered by those who indulged in illicit relations and avoided unwanted pregnancies.

During the period 1629–1706, the breakdown by gender of those convoked for illicit relations shifted. As Table 3 indicates, the consistory of Valangin convoked a total of 575 individuals, 333 (58 percent) of whom were women, to answer charges of fornication, adultery, or scandalous *fréquentation*—a police action against a man and a woman, usually one of whom was married, who were suspected of having an unwholesome relationship because they spent too much time together.[117] The disparity between the number of men and women

116. Ingram, pointing to the large percentage of contract disputes that were abandoned in seventeenth-century English litigation, also postulates that interested parties were reaching out-of-court settlements. By allowing these suits to be abandoned, says Ingram, courts helped undermine the credibility of extra-ecclesiastical marriage contracts; *Church Courts, Sex, and Marriage*, pp. 207–208.

117. As Table 3 indicates, the sizable majority of such offenses involved fornication. No doubt some of these people guilty of *paillardise* were adulterers, since it seems that often no distinction was made between fornicators and adulterers. Later, however, the consistory did distinguish them. In 1703 a married man and a single woman were condemned for having had illicit relations together. The man was convicted of adultery, his second such offense, and sentenced to twelve days in prison. The woman, a first-time offender, was sentenced to three days in prison as a *paillarde*, that is, fornicator; AEN, CSV7:3. Among those who had to answer charges of illicit relations was the mayor of Valangin, who also served as president of the consistory. In 1649, H. Tribollet Hardy, then mayor of Valangin, confessed to being the father of the illegitimate child Suzanne de Saulles had recently given birth to. The consistory, presided over by a *procureur* in Hardy's stead, was guilty of a double standard in rendering its decision: Suzanne was sentenced to be punished according to the decrees, including a prison term of a few days in addition to public *réparation;* Hardy was merely required to do public reparation; AEN, CSV4:193–194, 197. Not all early modern courts were so concerned with *fréquentation*. Though he does describe a few such cases, Ingram maintains that the church courts of England had little interest in extramarital sexual activities that fell short of full intercourse; *Church Courts, Sex, and Marriage*, p. 240. Still, in an effort to fight adultery, magistrates in Catholic Augsburg decreed in 1558 "that anyone found in a suspicious place or with suspicious people should be admonished." Recidivists had to swear an oath that they had

convicted of fornication may lead one to believe that the consistory used a double standard, punishing female offenders more avidly than males. Though canon law had eliminated a double standard with regard to adultery, the manner in which local courts punished illicit relations could vary greatly. Edward Britton found a blatant double standard in fourteenth-century rural England: only women were cited for premarital sex offenses; though married men and women were punished in the same manner for adultery, fornication was strictly a female crime. Church courts in fifteenth-century France, however, condemned men to heavier fines than women for fornication. After the arrival of Protestantism in Augsburg, men were in theory subject to the same penalties as women for fornication and adultery; in practice, however, men were punished less harshly, having prison sentences commuted to fines more often than did women. In Elizabethan England, as in Valangin, more women than men were cited for fornication. According to Ingram, this discrepancy was due in part to the greater difficulty of determining paternity, but it also reflected a double standard that accepted a man's extramarital or premarital affairs more readily than a woman's.[118]

Although many scholars argue that courts habitually practiced a double standard in punishing sex offenses, that does not appear to be the case in Valangin for the period 1547–1706. During the sixteenth and seventeenth centuries, the common punishment for first-time fornicators, both male and female, was three or five days in jail on bread and water, followed by public *réparation*. Certain cases of fornication, however, were punished more severely than others. If, for example, a master had sexual relations with a servant, the master was usually required to pay a fine as well. In 1657, Moyse Prevost and his servant, Magdelaine Prevost, were convoked for having produced an illegitimate child. Both were condemned according to the ordinances, and Moyse was also fined 5 livres for having debauched his servant.[119] The predominance of women among those condemned for fornication can best be attributed to the fact that women had a more difficult time hiding their transgres-

---

committed no dishonorable act and could be subjected to corporal punishment; see Roper, *Holy Household*, p. 64.

118. Britton, *The Community of the Vill: A Study in the History of the Family and Village Life in Fourteenth-Century England* (Toronto, 1977), pp. 52–54; Gottlieb, "Clandestine Marriage," p. 57; Roper, *Holy Household*, pp. 125–126; Ingram, *Church Courts, Sex, and Marriage*, pp. 260, 262.

119. AEN, CSV5:47–48.

sions than did men. The majority of female offenders—251 of 333—were explicitly said to be pregnant or already the mothers of illegitimate children; it may well be that most of the remaining 80 women accused of fornication were in the same condition. Illicit behavior often became publicly known only when a pregnancy outside of marriage was discovered. In an era of increased premarital sexual activity, it is understandable that women outnumbered men among those condemned for fornication.

One subtle change from the Reformation period was that, by the second half of the seventeenth century, people were punished more for having produced bastards than for fornicating. On at least one occasion the consistory expressed the opinion that fornication that produced a bastard was a greater evil than a liaison that bore no unwanted offspring, a notion absent from sixteenth-century registers. In 1669, Marie Jeanneret was convoked for having had illicit sexual relations with Esaye Vuagneux. The sentence ordered that she be punished according to the dictates of the ordinances; "nevertheless because of her frank confession, the extreme cold [it was December and the prison was no doubt quite cold], and the fact that she procreated no child, the customary prison term will be waived."[120] Though they still considered fornication a sin and a legal infraction, justices now looked on it less harshly if no illegitimate children were born.

One may wonder why there was a sudden increase in illicit relations in the late-sixteenth and early-seventeenth centuries. Could it be that after the Reformation had been firmly established Neuchâtelois followed a more relaxed code of morality, even though the consistory remained just as strict on such matters? Had women become more willing to indulge in sexual relations even when they received no marriage proposals? Change in morality could possibly have been significant, but economics almost certainly was a factor.

Several important demographic studies have documented contemporaneous increases in illegitimacy elsewhere in Europe. Some historians attribute this increase in bastardy to economic instability, pointing to an economic crisis throughout Europe in the seventeenth century—according to Peter Kriedte, "a reaction to the excessive population growth of the sixteenth which ended in deterioration of the overall economic situation."[121] The ratio of illegitimate children in England

120. AEN, CSV6:48.
121. Kriedte, *Peasants, Landlords, and Merchant Capitalists: Europe and the World Economy, 1500–1800*, trans. V. R. Berghahn (Cambridge, 1983), p. 63.

reached an unprecedented high between 1595 and 1610 then declined, and remained stable until the mid-eighteenth century. The cause of this increase can be traced to a series of bad harvests England and other parts of Europe suffered in the 1590s, the effects of which were still felt into the early seventeenth century. As a result of this agricultural crisis, many young people did not have the financial means to marry and form independent households. Nonetheless, popular courtship patterns had allowed young people more independence vis-à-vis their parents and greater sexual freedom than either church or magistrate would have liked. In these difficult times, fewer courtships culminated in marriage, as reflected in the increases in the average age at marriage and the number of illegitimate births, a phenomenon not limited to a "bastardy prone" subculture but permeated throughout the social scale. The illegitimacy rate declined after 1610 as a result of increased economic stability and stricter local control of marriage and courtship; local magistrates in England commonly forbade poor people to marry and undertook more aggressive prosecution of sex offenses, even introducing punishments for prenuptial conceptions that were discovered only after marriage. This effort to reduce illicit sexuality and limit marital opportunities—developed by the local yeoman elite, supported by the church courts, and imposed on the lower classes—helped modify behavior and contributed to the decline in bastardy.[122] As in England, various areas in France suffered an economic crisis in the last decade of the sixteenth century which caused a dramatic increase in illegitimate births.[123] This economic explanation may also hold true for Valangin, since the seventeenth century was generally a period of stagnation there as elsewhere.

122. David Levine and Keith Wrightson, "The Social Context of Illegitimacy in Early Modern England," in *Bastardy and Its Comparative History*, pp. 158–175; Wrightson, "The Nadir of English Illegitimacy in the Seventeenth Century," in *Bastardy and Its Comparative History*, p. 191; Wrightson and Levine, *Poverty and Piety in an English Village: Terling, 1525–1700* (New York, 1979), pp. 127, 132; Peter Laslett and Karla Oosterveen, "Long-Term Trends in Bastardy in England, 1561–1960," *Population Studies* 27 (1973): 256–257, 269, 282–284; Wrightson, *English Society*, pp. 145–146; Laslett, *Family Life and Illicit Love in Earlier Generations* (Cambridge, 1977), pp. 113–117, 125; Quaife, *Wanton Wenches*, pp. 56–57. Ingram found that most women fornicated out of prospects of marriage: in the 1580s and late 1610s, 30 to 40 percent of the female offenders in the better-recorded cases before the church court of Salisbury alleged some kind of marriage agreement; and the proportion is even higher if actions against married men are excluded; *Church Courts, Sex, and Marriage*, pp. 233–234, 267, 279, 281. As we have seen, the percentage was much lower in Valangin in the sixteenth and seventeenth centuries.

123. Jean Meyer, "Illegitimates and Foundlings in Pre-Industrial France," in *Bastardy and Its Comparative History*, pp. 249–250.

Economic stagnation may account for the increase in illegitimacy, but it does not explain the contemporary decline in female plaintiffs to contract disputes. Perhaps this decrease simply reflected a reluctance on the part of women to marry. Getting married at this time ordinarily involved the transfer of property, and women might hesitate to marry if they had to turn their holdings over to their husbands. The manner in which family property was transmitted to children varied considerably throughout Europe, and certain inheritance patterns could indeed have deterred women from marrying. If, for example, the dowry excluded one from further inheritance, then a woman might not be too enthusiastic about pursuing marriage. Exclusion was in fact the rule in many areas of Europe: in urban and rural areas of late medieval Italy, in early modern Haute Provence, and in most parts of fourteenth-century France, inheritance customs held that the dowries daughters received on marriage excluded them from further inheritance.[124] If a dowry precluded all future claims on family property, then a woman might have material reasons for not marrying, assuming that she had the right to consent to marriage, as canon law required. Beginning in the fifteenth and sixteenth centuries, however, practices concerning the impact of the dowry on inheritance began to change. In Paris and Orléans, for example, a new custom known as option and restoration appeared. In this procedure, a daughter or son who received property to set up a new household was not necessarily excluded from further inheritance; rather, he or she had the option of restoring the property to the family and thus becoming eligible to share with the other heirs in the division of property.[125]

In Neuchâtel, the role of the dowry also changed during the sixteenth century, though not as in Paris and Orléans; this modification, however, should not have deterred women from marrying. Beginning in the sixteenth century, the principle of exclusion, which had prevailed during the Middle Ages, began to weaken. In 1547, the Tribunal des

124. Brundage, *Law, Sex, and Christian Society,* p. 541; Collomp, "Tensions, Dissensions, and Ruptures," in *Interest and Emotion,* ed. Medick and Sabean, pp. 158–159; Christiane Klapisch-Zuber, "The Griselda Complex: Dowry and Marriage Gifts in the Quattrocento," in *Women, Family, and Ritual,* p. 216; Christiane Klapisch-Zuber and Michel Demonet, "*A uno pane e uno vino:* The Rural Tuscan Family at the Beginning of the Fifteenth Century," in *Women, Family, and Ritual,* p. 19; Jean Yver, *Egalité entre héritiers et exclusion des enfants dotés: Essai de géographie coutumière* (Paris, 1966), pp. 25–26.

125. Emmanuel Le Roy Ladurie, "Family Structures and Inheritance Customs in Sixteenth-Century France," in *Family and Inheritance,* ed. Goody, Thirsk, and Thompson, p. 48; Yver, *Egalité,* p. 88.

Trois Etats proclaimed that one could not disinherit children of their *légitime*—that portion of family holdings to which they had hereditary rights—either by marriage agreement or by testament, unless they were guilty of some crime or there were some other reason considered sufficient.[126] Women in Neuchâtel did not have to restore the dowry to the family to be eligible for further inheritance; rather, the dowry came to be viewed as simply an advance payment on inheritance, what Goody describes as a "pre-mortem inheritance."[127] Whereas hitherto the dowry had been the woman's only material contribution to marriage, it now became simply the first installment. Furthermore, according to Dominique Favarger, in the fifteenth century men rarely made donations akin to dowries at the time of their marriages, since they were usually still under paternal authority. Young married couples therefore generally lived with the husband's family until he received his inheritance. But in the sixteenth and seventeenth centuries an increasing number of young couples set up separate households, and men now brought *apports,* similar to dowries, into marriage. Basing his conclusion on notarial records, Favarger holds that this evolution had two principal effects: the weakening of the influence of the extended family and the "realization of a remarkable reciprocity of rights between husband and wife."[128] Since dowries no longer excluded them from inheritance, women need not lose any property in getting married. Indeed, the dowry now could be an incentive to marry: through the dowry, women immediately received a portion of their inheritance which they otherwise would receive only at the death of parents.

Even if the principle of exclusion did not apply, women might have been reluctant to marry if they had to turn their property over to their husbands. In late medieval England, for example, the husband controlled all the property belonging to him and his wife and had the right to alienate property as long as he did not deny his wife's right to claim dower lands to support her during her widowhood. A man had the right to sell his wife's property, though the sale would not endure after

---

126. Favarger and Tribolet, *Sources du droit du canton de Neuchâtel,* p. 199.
127. Goody, "Bridewealth and Dowry in Africa and Eurasia," in Jack Goody and S. J. Tambiah, *Bridewealth and Dowry* (Cambridge, 1973), p. 1. Jean Yver's comparison of French and Swiss inheritance patterns does not hold true for sixteenth-century Neuchâtel. He argues that the exclusion of "l'enfant établi" predominated in Switzerland and that the system of strict equality among heirs was unknown in Germany and Switzerland; Yver, *Egalité,* pp. 277–278.
128. Favarger, *Le régime matrimonial dans le comté de Neuchâtel du XVe au XIXe siècle* (Neuchâtel, 1970), pp. 67–69, 214–215.

the marriage unless she had agreed to it.[129] Under such circumstances, women might indeed have thought twice before marrying. A few legal studies, however, have painted a very different picture of the property rights of married women in Neuchâtel. Describing fifteenth-century marriages, Fernand Loew sees a wife as

> an influential member of the family, a collaborator whose approval the family head must have when he makes a decision concerning the commonly owned property. She is by no means the slave of her husband and possesses herself the property that she brought into marriage. This property is expressly reserved for her and for the family from which she came. The husband oversees it because he is believed to be more capable, but he cannot dispose of it at his pleasure. He receives family property for which he is responsible and which he may use, but he must never abuse it. The wife, his collaborator, may also use the family property—that of her husband and her own—but the property that she brought into the marriage bears the imprint of the family from which she came and will return to it if she has the misfortune of dying without children.[130]

In theory, the wife's consent was required throughout the Old Regime if dotal property was to be sold.[131] If this custom was strictly observed, it seems that women need not fear losing their property on marrying.

In addition, married women enjoyed increased property rights beginning in the sixteenth century. The husband alone had the authority to administer both his own property and the *acquêts,* property acquired by the couple after marriage; but, from the early sixteenth century on, women theoretically had the right to one-half the *acquêts,* the profits of their husbands' management. At the death of her husband, a woman received half the *acquêts,* the other half going to his heirs. Heretofore, a woman could make no claim on this acquired property, which belonged exclusively to the husband.[132] With this newly acquired privilege,

129. Bennett, *Women in the Medieval English Countryside,* p. 110.
130. Lowe, "Mariages au XVe siècle," pp. 58–59.
131. Favarger, *Régime matrimonial,* p. 90.
132. Ibid., pp. 19, 108, 111, 204. At least some women played an active role in the administration and aggrandizement of family property. In 1556, Blaise Pic filed suit before the Tribunal des Trois États on behalf of his wife, Huguenette, widow of Jean Villain, and asked for half the *acquêts* made during her marriage with Villain. Witnesses asserted that Huguenette had actively collaborated with Villain in their ventures and that the aggrandizement was due as much to her efforts as to his. The court accordingly granted the Pics' request; Maurice de Tribolet, "Un exemple de collaboration entre mari et femme au milieu du XVIe siècle,"

women would seemingly find marriage all the more attractive: not only did they retain their rights over dotal property, they also had the possibility of increasing their fortunes by means of sharing the wealth acquired after the marriage.[133]

It appears doubtful, then, that women's property rights can be used to explain why females constituted a much smaller percentage of plaintiffs to contract disputes in Neuchâtel than in nearby Basel and Constance. The only way property could have served as a disincentive for women to marry is if practice differed from theory. If in practice a man could coerce his wife into selling her property for his advantage, then a woman would surely have been reluctant to marry.

If property concerns do not provide the most convincing explanation for the larger number of men seeking to enforce marriage promises, the answer may be found in the patterns of courtship. Since it was traditionally the man who took the initiative by proposing to the woman, perhaps it should be no surprise that men made up the majority of those who sued to enforce disputed contracts. Furthermore, in this society in which wealth was in land, most men would have a greater need to marry than women. Once a man acquired or inherited enough wealth to leave his parents' authority, he would consider a wife an absolute prerequisite to setting up his own household. In towns as well, artisans needed wives to help run their shops.[134] Young women perhaps did not see an urgent need to leave their families' homes and therefore played a more passive role in courtship. Quite simply, wives were indispensable to most men; widowers generally remarried more quickly than widows, for example, simply because men found it difficult to get along without a woman to care for the house and children.

In any event, the low number of female plaintiffs to contract disputes and the high number of women punished for fornication together show that women did not view the consistories, the new judicial organs that

---

Musée neuchâtelois, 1982, 283–290. This communauté d'acquêts was common in many parts of France—in seventeenth-century Bordeaux, for example; Robert Wheaton, "Affinity and Descent in Seventeenth-Century Bordeaux," in Family and Sexuality, p. 121.

133. It must be noted, however, that women now shared the debts as well; Favarger, Régime matrimonial, p. 215. The property rights Simon Schama describes for women in seventeenth-century Holland are virtually identical to those outlined by Favarger for Neuchâtel; Schama, Embarrassment of Riches, pp. 404–405.

134. Roper has the following to say about guild masters and marriage: "Marriage marked the boundary between the guild of masters, who had to have wives, and the journeymen, who ought not to, and weddings enacted the rites of passage between these two states"; Holy Household, p. 136. I cannot explain, however, why women were in the majority of contract disputes in Augsburg.

enforced morals and upheld domestic stability, as the defenders of their rights. We have seen several cases in which masters were required to marry or give dowries to servant girls they seduced. Most unwed mothers, however, had not been impregnated by their masters. Considering changes in how one entered into marriage, perhaps we can say that the new matrimonial law was favorable to a small subgroup of women—those female servants who were seduced by their masters. The effects on women in general, however, cannot be said to have been progressive. The decline in the number of suits initiated by women to enforce marriage contracts and the concomitant increase in illegitimate births suggest general feelings of futility toward male deceit. Moreover, this evidence does not put Neuchâtel in a favorable light with respect to contemporary courts elsewhere. Though she claims that the position of women declined in Reformation Augsburg, Roper found that the city council there did a much better job than earlier church courts in ordering compensation to women for loss of virginity or for child support—almost all women who filed suit before the civic court received damages, whereas scarcely more than half those who petitioned the Catholic court succeeded.[135] Simply put, the evidence from Neuchâtel's contract litigation does not support the view that the conversion to Protestantism elevated the status of women.

A more obvious conclusion, already alluded to, is that the vast majority of plaintiffs, both male and female, failed in their suits to enforce marriage contracts in Neuchâtel and Valangin. Of those cases for which decisions were rendered, only one-fourth of the alleged contracts (61 of 245) were recognized as binding. For the period 1547–1706, the proportions of those plaintiffs who successfully proved reputed promises of marriage were virtually identical for Neuchâtel and Valangin: 25.3 and 25.5 percent, respectively. This low success rate was a reflection of the new and more strict requirements for proving marriage contracts. Beginning with the Reformation, if witnesses could not verify promises freely and directly made, chances were quite slim that the consistories would recognize such a contract.

Other studies have also shown that most plaintiffs failed to enforce disputed contracts. Houlbrooke, for example, found that only a small percentage of plaintiffs successfully proved alleged engagements. His findings show that decisions for defendants outnumbered those for plaintiffs by about four to one, mainly because most plaintiffs did not produce enough witnesses or sufficient evidence. Roper's study reveals

135. Ibid., pp. 161–162.

that, immediately before the Reformation in Augsburg, only 4 percent of contract suits were declared binding, and the rate increased to 20 percent under the Protestant marriage court of the 1530s and 1540s. Ingram also found a small percentage of successful suits to enforce contracts and noted a decline in the success rate from the late medieval into the early modern period. Of those cases for which decisions were given, fully 50 percent of plaintiffs won their contract suits in Ely in the 1370s and 1380s. Two hundred years later in the same diocese, however, only 20 percent of the decisions were in favor of the plaintiffs, and the success rate fell to less than 12 percent in seventeenth-century Ely and Wiltshire. Ingram maintains that the decline in the percentage of successful contract suits reflected changing attitudes among judges. The courts, he argues, had become more reluctant to recognize as binding disputed contracts because church lawyers eventually rejected the ancient law of spousals and began to treat unsolemnized unions, at least when disputed between the parties, as virtually unenforceable.[136] To a degree, his assessment holds true for Neuchâtel. As we have seen, seventeenth-century judges appeared more reluctant than their predecessors to recognize disputed engagements as binding. But it would be a misrepresentation to describe disputed marriage promises as virtually unenforceable. A significant number of plaintiffs won suits against alleged fiancés in the seventeenth century, and this percentage would actually increase in the eighteenth century. Moreover, those who did not succeed in their contract suits usually failed because they lacked sufficient proof, not because judges were reluctant to rule in their favor.

A high percentage of Neuchâtelois who wished to disprove promises were successful. Of the 45 such cases for which judgments were made, 41 succeeded in showing that there were no real engagements or that the other party had since broken the contract. These figures include a few cases in which a person sought an annulment of a marriage agreement because the other party had committed some sort of transgression. In 1575, for example, George Marin received an annulment of his contract with Clauda Rolland because she was guilty of fornication.[137]

Many such cases were those in which one party, usually the woman, demanded *réparation d'honneur* for another's unwarranted claims that the two had agreed to marry. In 1590, Perrenon, the daughter of Francey Robert, asked that Pierre Besancenet make reparation of honor

136. Houlbrooke, "Making of Marriage" p. 348; Roper, *Holy Household*, p. 160; Ingram, "Spousals Litigation," pp. 52–53, and *Church Courts, Sex and Marriage*, p. 366.
137. AEN, JMN2:44v–50.

for having boasted that he had a valid marriage engagement with her. According to witnesses, Perrenon and a few other young women were busy making *chappelets,* little hats, one Saturday evening when Pierre and two other young men arrived and started playing cards.[138] Though their parents were not present, Pierre interrupted his card playing to place a gold coin on the table, telling Perrenon to accept it in the name of marriage. Perrenon, however, did not pick up the coin, and it remained on the table until the following Monday. At that time a girl tried to return the coin to Pierre, who refused to accept it. Concluding that Perrenon had not given her consent, the judges declared that no marriage agreement existed. Pierre was ordered to get on his knees and "in the presence of the entire court ask for mercy from God, the seigneury, the honorable assistants, Francey Robert, his daughter and relatives and beg them for forgiveness." The father and relatives were ordered to forgive Pierre, who was also sentenced to three days in jail.[139] What cases of this genre and annulments have in common is that in both instances the consistories were asked to declare that valid marriage contracts did not exist.[140]

The gathering at which Pierre proposed to Perrenon, an example of the widespread custom of the spinning bee, would have been a scene familiar to most young people in early modern rural societies. Hans Medick has described the spinning bee, or *Spinnstube,* as a form of "work sociability." At these evening reunions of young people, women worked at some activity, usually spinning, knitting, or sewing, but of equal or even greater importance was the social aspect of the *Spinnstube.* These gatherings of young men and women offered them an opportunity to socialize and to court more or less free of parental supervision. These informal assemblies of young people served as a marriage market but also threatened parental control over their children's choice of spouses. Consequently, in sixteenth- and seventeenth-century Germany, magistrates passed ordinances against the *Spinnstube* that defended the interests of parents.[141] The events of the spinning bee that Pierre and

138. It is interesting that card playing, though censured in Geneva, was evidently tolerated in Neuchâtel.

139. AEN, JMN2:157–159.

140. Disputes of this nature resemble cases of sexual slander that were one of the most common types of litigation in English church courts of the late sixteenth and early seventeenth centuries. One's sexual reputation was especially important for women, and, though ecclesiastical courts could not award damages for sexual slander, they could force the guilty party to do public penance; Ingram, *Church Courts, Sex, and Marriage,* pp. 292, 294.

141. Medick, "Village Spinning Bees: Sexual Culture and Free Time among Rural Youth in Early Modern Germany," in *Interest and Emotion,* ed. Medick and Sabean, pp. 317–339.

Perrenon participated in seemed to justify parents' fears that these un-chaperoned soirées could lead to unwanted marriage proposals.

All in all, the registers of the consistory of Valangin and the Justice matrimoniale of Neuchâtel demonstrate that, as far as marriage con-tracts were concerned, the changes inspired by the Reformation were limited. Once contracted, promises could be dissolved only for the same reasons a marriage could be. Male plaintiffs outnumbered female plain-tiffs, and neither gender had a high success rate in proving marriage contracts since the courts strictly required that promises be observed by witnesses, that parental permission be granted (if one of the parties in-volved was a minor), and that both parties freely consent to the prom-ises without solicitation. The only exceptions to this rule occurred when pregnancies were involved. When masters or their sons seduced their servants or when the parties were of similar social standing, male de-fendants occasionally were obliged to marry the women they had im-pregnated even though no *fiançailles* had been proven.

PETITIONS TO MARRY

Petitions to marry were complementary to contract disputes. Whereas contract litigation ordinarily involved one party who asked an-other to honor an alleged engagement, petitions concerned couples who needed permission to marry because of various obstacles. Both contract litigation and requests for dispensations were legal actions per-taining to the formation of marriage. If we include the dispensations awarded by the Conseil d'Etat, petitions were the most common form of marital legal action in Neuchâtel during the sixteenth and seven-teenth centuries. From 1547 to 1706, Neuchâtel witnessed 525 requests for dispensations: the Justice matrimoniale of Neuchâtel and the con-sistories of Valangin and Gorgier heard 19, 55, and 2, respectively; the Conseil d'Etat heard 449.

The two most salient features of this form of litigation were the dra-matic increase in the number of petitions in the first half of the seven-teenth century and, contemporaneously, the clarification of jurisdiction over dispensations. During the years 1547–1621, petitions made before the Conseil d'Etat were only a little more than a third of all such re-quests. But, from 1622 to 1706, the Conseil heard 98 percent of all pe-titions, and the consistories virtually ceased to consider requests for dispensations. Moreover, the number of petitions filed for the years

1622–1706 soared, outnumbering those for the earlier decades by nearly four to one.

One drawback to studying the records of petitions is that the registers of the Conseil d'Etat are quite lacking in detail. These records often reveal little apart from the names of petitioners and the decisions. For example, of the 449 petitions made before the Conseil d'Etat, we know the motives of petitioners in only 59 cases. Of these, 57 were made by couples related by blood or affinity. It may well be that the grand majority of the cases whose motives are unknown were also made by people so related.

One thing we can certainly say is that petitioners enjoyed very good odds of success: for the period 1547–1706, the Conseil d'Etat granted 435 of the 449 petitions made before it. There were, however, certain changes in decisions rendered during this period. In the 1570s and early 1580s, the Conseil d'Etat was rather lenient in allowing relatives to marry, granting dispensations to several pairs of second cousins.[142] Evidently magistrates later regretted this liberalism; the Conseil passed laws in 1583 and 1597 forbidding marriages between relatives who were at the third and fourth degrees of consanguinity and affinity.[143] Since second cousins are at the third degree of consanguinity, this amounted to a tightening of the reins on dispensations for reasons of blood relationships. Though in the late sixteenth century it became more difficult for people related more closely than the fourth degree to marry, members of the Conseil d'Etat awarded dispensations much more readily in the seventeenth century, granting thirteen dispensations to couples who were explicitly said to be first cousins (i.e., of the second degree). In all probability, many other couples so related received such requests during the course of the century. In other words, by the 1600s the Conseillers d'etat were showing an unprecedented liberalism in granting marriage dispensations for reasons of consanguinity. Whereas canon law had once forbidden marriages between relatives of the seventh degree, seventeenth-century Neuchâtelois who were first cousins merely had to ask permission of the Conseil d'Etat, which almost automatically honored these requests. Of the 406 petitions made before the Conseil between 1622 and 1706, 398 were granted, only 3 rejected, and

142. They are described as "cousins issus de germains"; AEN, TMCE1:253.
143. In the registers of the various tribunals, reference is frequently made to people related "au tiers et quart degré." The third degree refers to second cousins and the fourth to third cousins. I imagine, therefore, that persons *au tiers et quart* are those who are separated by an unequal number of generations from the common ancestors. The common ancestors would be the great-grandparents of one of the parties and the great-great-grandparents of the other.

5 abandoned. Among the three petitions that were denied, we know the reason for the refusal for only one couple, a man and a woman who previously committed adultery together.[144] The registers for these eight decades do not reveal a single rejection of a request to marry because of consanguinity or affinity. For relatives who wished to marry in seventeenth-century Neuchâtel, filing for a dispensation was becoming a mere formality.

It is interesting to note that almost half the petitions filed during the period 1547–1706 before the Conseil d'Etat—217 of 449—were made during the three decades spanning 1622–1651. The largest number of petitions made in any one year was 25 in 1681, all of which were granted. Thereafter, there was a considerable decrease in the volume of these requests made: from 1682 until the end of this period, only 28 couples filed petitions to marry. Why this dramatic decrease in the number of petitions made before the Conseil d'Etat? Since the sixteenth century, there had been no statutory changes concerning the marriages of persons related by consanguinity or affinity. One may be tempted to think that this drastic decline in petitions to marry was a result of increased mobility. If people moved away from the villages where their families had their roots, they would be less surrounded by kin and accordingly less likely to find relatives among prospective fiancés. Such a theory falls apart, however, when one considers that dramatic demographic changes began in Neuchâtel only in the eighteenth century, particularly after 1750. Furthermore, in spite of increased mobility, the Conseil d'Etat of the late eighteenth century heard many petitions to marry, at a rate more reminiscent of the early seventeenth century than of the late.[145]

144. Among those petitions granted were three that were accorded by the prince, not the Conseil d'Etat. Furthermore, one of the so-called abandoned causes was a request that the Conseil referred to the prince, refusing to pass judgment itself. Although Ingram found that some English women who had affairs with married men later married their paramours after the deaths of their first wives, such remarriages were forbidden in Neuchâtel; *Church Courts, Sex, and Marriage*, p. 274.

145. In his work on Como and its environs, Raul Merzario found that the vast majority of the relatives who asked permission to marry came from small villages, not from the city of Como, and that there was a noticeable increase in the number of petitions during the period 1631–1655. In the previous decades (1563–1630), the most common reason for requesting dispensations (cited in 60 percent of all petitions) was economic; when upper and middle class women could not have a large dowry, they preferred marrying cousins to marrying men beneath them in status. Only 34 percent of the petitions were motivated by the paucity of available husbands. For 1631–1655, however, potential grooms were in short supply, since many men, though few women, emigrated from small villages; many village women were left with little choice but to marry cousins. Consequently, 84 percent of all petitions were the result of this limited marriage market, and economic motives virtually disappeared, representing only

Other hypotheses must therefore be proposed to explain why these decades witnessed almost no petitions to marry even though a large number of such requests were made in both the preceding and succeeding periods. One possible explanation is that, plain and simple, relatives were not marrying each other in the late seventeenth century. Such a theory, however, seems implausible vis-à-vis the large numbers of petitions both before and after this period. Perhaps, then, the Conseil was less strict in requiring that a person receive permission before marrying somebody related by consanguinity or affinity. Since virtually all petitions were granted, people might simply have stopped going through with the formality of asking permission to marry; perhaps only in the late eighteenth century did the Conseil d'Etat again require relatives to get its authorization to marry. This theory, however, is also problematic. As we see Chapter 4, in the early eighteenth century, when the number of petitions was still small, the Conseil d'Etat inflicted harsh penalties on cousins who married without first asking the Conseil's permission. The most feasible theory may be that the clerks were not very diligent in recording petitions to marry in the late seventeenth and early eighteenth centuries. In light of the sketchy nature of the Conseil's registers, we cannot be certain.

Though fewer in number, the petitions made before the consistories are described in much greater detail than those before the Conseil d'Etat. The consistorial registers reveal the change in jurisdiction with respect to dispensations. All but eight of the petitions heard by the consistories were made before 1622. Moreover, though before 1622 most of the petitions brought before the consistory of Valangin involved cases of consanguinity or affinity, petitions from relatives ceased thereafter. In the seventeenth century, jurisdiction over petitions became better defined: if relatives sought a dispensation in the principality of Neuchâtel and Valangin, they were expected to address the Conseil d'Etat.

Among those petitions the consistories heard in both the sixteenth and seventeenth centuries were those made by persons who sought to prove that their spouses were dead. This almost always involved a husband, often a soldier, who had been absent for years and whose death needed to be proved so that his widow might remarry. Of the 16 such

---

0.25 percent of all dispensations; see Raul Merzario, *Il Paese Stretto: Strategie matrimoniali nella diocesi di Como secoli XVI–XVIII* (Turin, 1981), pp. 11–12, 123. No evidence has suggested that Neuchâtel witnessed similar levels of emigration during the seventeenth century.

requests made during this period, 10 were granted, 2 rejected, and 4 abandoned. It is probably safe to say that the tribunals often made no distinction between this sort of case and divorce suits filed on the ground of extended absence (see Chapter 3). Here I have perhaps imposed a distinction that did not exist at the time. At any rate, I have labeled those cases "petitions" that either clearly demonstrated the death of the former spouse or were pursued by a couple and not simply the abandoned spouse. Obviously, if the absent spouse was proved dead, such litigation cannot be termed a divorce. Similarly, an action initiated by a couple requesting to marry is not a divorce; the fiancé of the abandoned spouse did not ordinarily enter into a divorce proceeding. Be that as it may, often the procedure followed was identical to that in divorce cases based on abandonment.

Ten other petitions concerned persons who had earlier committed some sort of moral transgression. Twice the guilty party of a divorce asked permission to remarry.[146] Huguette de Brot, for example, was divorced from her husband because of her adultery during his absence and received permission to remarry a year after the divorce. To receive such permission, she had to produce as witnesses neighbors who could vouch that she had led a morally upright life during the past year.[147] Eight times the courts heard petitions of couples who had earlier had illicit relations together and now sought to marry. In 1642, a couple asked for and received permission to marry despite the fact that they had previously had an illegitimate child together.[148] The court was not so benevolent toward Pierre Robert and Madelaine Lescurier, who had produced two illegitimate children; it refused in 1674 to allow them to marry. Unlike the other couple, however, they had had a child while Robert was still married to his first wife. Since they were guilty of adultery, the consistory turned down their petition.[149]

On the whole, however, the success rate for those who requested dispensations was quite high. The evidence from contract disputes and requests for dispensations shows that members of Neuchâtel's judicial institutions were much more likely to rule in favor of a marriage desired by both parties than a contract recognized by only one.

146. I am quite surprised at how low this figure is. The explanation, I assume, is that those who had been divorced and wanted to remarry had to petition the Conseil d'Etat.
147. AEN, JMN2:184, 184v.
148. AEN, CSV4:117.
149. AEN, CSV6:68.

3

The Breakdown of Marriage, 1547–1706

DIVORCE

In the long run, divorce was to be the most important innovation brought to the institution of marriage by the Reformation. For better or worse, marriage was no longer a union that invariably lasted until the death of one of the spouses. Nevertheless, the immediate impact of this modification to the institution was modest. Divorcés in Reformation Neuchâtel formed a marginal group, for divorces could be obtained only on a few specific grounds, primarily those of desertion and adultery. If the laws passed in Protestant areas in Reformation Europe set an important precedent in allowing divorce and subsequent remarriage, they did not lead to widespread instability in sixteenth-century households. Throughout the Protestant world, divorces remained rare in the sixteenth and seventeenth centuries, despite contemporary moralists' claims to the contrary.[1] Be that as it may, after marriage contract disputes, divorce was the most common type of marital litigation heard by Neuchâtel's consistories. For the period 1547–1706, records have survived for 131 divorce cases: 53 before the matrimonial court of Neuchâtel and 78 before the consistory of Valangin. Of these the tribunals

---

1. The Genevan consistory complained in the early seventeenth century that the Genevan church had a reputation of being lenient in dissolving marriages. In fact, divorces there probably numbered no more than one a year; Phillips, *Putting Asunder*, p. 58; E. William Monter, "Women in Calvinist Geneva (1550–1800)," *Signs* 6 (1980): 195.

awarded 93 divorces and rejected only 11; the remaining 27 were abandoned before a decision was given.

Desertion or the absence of a spouse was the most commonly alleged ground for divorce in this period and was cited far more often by female plaintiffs than by males: during the period 1547–1706, 47 women and 20 men sued for divorce because of desertion (see Table 5). The reasoning behind divorce on this ground was that after a certain period of time one could assume that the absent spouse was dead. As Roderick Phillips notes, divorce in cases of absence or desertion is more like a substitute death certificate for the missing spouse than a decision on the marriage's breakdown in a moral sense.[2] A person who received a divorce for reason of absence was therefore much like a widow or widower, though Neuchâtel's tribunals referred to this procedure as a divorce, not a declaration of widowhood. This manner of dissolving a marriage was not unknown before the Protestant Reformation. Centuries before, Roman Catholic canon lawyers had recognized the possibility of dissolving a marriage after a spouse's extended absence on the presumption of his or her death. Catholics, however, did not develop a coherent policy with respect to the abandoned spouse, and ecclesiastical courts were generally reluctant to permit remarriage without proof of the absent spouse's death. Nevertheless, because of precedents in canon law, some of the Neuchâtelois who obtained divorces for abandonment might have received permission to remarry even if the principality had remained Catholic, a further indication that the Protestants' introduction of divorce did not cause a revolution in the institution of marriage.[3]

Whether it was the willful desertion of one spouse by the other or the absence of a husband who had left the country to fight as a mercenary, Neuchâtel's courts had general procedures that had to be followed. To begin with, the tribunals ordinarily did not hear a case until the spouse had already been absent for seven years unless there was evidence that he or she was dead. In so doing, the consistories were continuing a tradition set by canon law in the High Middle Ages. Most canonists of this

---

2. Phillips, *Putting Asunder*, p. 91.

3. James Brundage finds evidence of divorce in pre-Reformation Europe, 1348–1517: "Divorce and separation . . . showed discrepancies between social reality and legal theory. The courts granted divorces with the right of remarriage when the law said they could not do so, they granted separations on grounds that the canons did not recognize, and conversely some of the grounds for separation that are most elaborately discussed in the commentaries appear very infrequent in practice"; *Law, Sex, and Christian Society*, p. 548. The fact that divorces were awarded occasionally in late medieval Catholic Europe further supports the view that Protestant divorce laws did not effect a radical change in marriage.

TABLE 5
Grounds cited in divorce suits, 1547–1706

	Absence/ desertion	Adultery	Sexual dysfunction	Female deceit	Illness	Spouse banished	Bigamy/ incest	Crime	Cruelty	Grounds unknown	Total[a]
Female plaintiffs											
Granted	38	12	2	NA	1	1	1	1	2	0	58
Rejected	0	0	3	NA	0	0	0	0	0	0	3
Abandoned	9	1	2	NA	0	0	0	0	0	2	14
	47	13	7		1	1	1	1	2	2	75
Male plaintiffs											
Granted	16	17	2	4	1	2	3	0	0	1	46
Rejected	2	3	1	1	2	0	0	0	0	0	9
Abandoned	2	5	0	1	0	1	1	1	0	2	13
	20	25	3	6	3	3	4	1	0	3	68
All plaintiffs											
Granted	54	29	4	4	2	3	4	1	2	1	93
Rejected	2	3	4	1	2	0	0	0	0	0	12
Abandoned	11	6	2	1	0	1	1	1	0	4	27
	67	38	10	6	4	4	5	2	2	5	143

[a]Nine plaintiffs, six men and three women, petitioned for divorce on two different grounds, and one woman filed for divorce on three grounds. One case involved a man and woman who sued each other for divorce on different grounds. Consequently, though 143 different grounds were cited for divorce, the court actually heard 131 cases.

123

period felt that it was legitimate under certain circumstances to allow remarriage on the basis of the presumption of death of absent spouses. Pope Alexander III (1159–1181) had issued a declaration allowing the dissolution of a marriage for the protracted absence of a spouse under circumstances in which the absent party's death might reasonably be presumed. Alexander set the waiting period at ten years; Celestine III (1191–1198) shortened it to seven years, and this remained the most commonly prescribed wait.[4]

In the absence of evidence of the spouse's death, Neuchâtel's courts strictly observed this long waiting period before granting divorces for desertion, generally requiring the same delay for both male and female petitioners during the Reformation period. This strictness can be seen in the case of Jaques Gorgerat dict Blanchet, who wanted to divorce his wife because she had abandoned him. First appearing before the Justice matrimoniale in February 1609, he claimed to have met and married his wife in France while he was serving as a mercenary there. She had then accompanied him to his home in Boudry, where they lived together for a few years. Two and a half years ago, however, using a pretext that her brother needed her services, she returned to France, saying that she would never return to Gorgerat. The court ordered him to try to find her and make her appear before the tribunal. If these efforts proved fruitless, he was to attempt to contact her closest relatives to learn of her whereabouts. If this too was to no avail, he had to produce an affidavit indicating that he had duly conducted this investigation. He next appeared in court nearly four years later, in January 1613, still seeking the divorce. This time, he was told that he had to wait until the seven-year period had expired. Accordingly, Gorgerat repeated his request in February of that year, maintaining that she had left him in February 1606. The judges pointed out, however, that the document that first recorded her absence was signed 17 September 1606. The fact that she had actually left him earlier was of no importance; he had to wait until seven years had passed since the signing of that document. Thus, only in December 1613, after having made three announcements in the church at

---

4. Ibid., pp. 334, 374. According to Natalie Davis, by the sixteenth century it was increasingly difficult for abandoned spouses to obtain permission to remarry under Catholic law: "Since the laxer days of Pope Alexander III in the twelfth century, the doctors had insisted that a wife was not free to remarry in the absence of the husband, no matter how many years had elapsed, unless she had certain proof of his death"; *The Return of Martin Guerre* (Cambridge, Mass., 1983), p. 33.

Boudry to see if anyone had any news of his wife, did Gorgerat finally receive the divorce he had been seeking for nearly five years.[5]

The Justice matrimoniale was even known to require spouses of banished criminals to wait seven years before awarding divorces. Such a case began in 1597 when Isabel Gallandre asked to be divorced from Jehan Bedaux, who had abandoned her and fled the country after having severely beaten his mother and left her for dead in September 1596. Isabel was ordered to try to discover where he was and, if necessary, to contact his closest relatives. Isabel produced affidavits of the sentence of banishment rendered against Bedaux and of her contact with him to inform him of her suit. Nevertheless, she was required to wait a year and a day before proceeding. In fact, she waited five years before appearing again in court, in December 1602. Even then the judges deemed it unwise to grant a divorce before the full seven years had expired. She therefore was required to wait another ten months; the divorce was granted only in October 1603.[6]

In light of the Protestant reformers' diatribes against the celibate life—they asserted that the majority of humans were incapable of following such rigorous abstinence—it seems cruel and inconsistent of them to force someone to live chastely for years and wait patiently to see if the absent spouse returned. This is particularly so in cases such as Isabel's, inasmuch as her husband's crime seems to the modern observer to be reason enough for a divorce. Rarely, however, did the courts make exceptions to the usual waiting period. In sixteenth-century Neuchâtel, practices concerning divorce for abandonment entailed both shorter and longer waiting periods than in contemporary Geneva, where desertion was also the most common ground cited in divorce litigation. Geneva's magistrates, unlike Neuchâtel's, distinguished between malicious desertion and the extended absence of someone who had left the country for legitimate reasons. According to Calvin's marriage laws, when a person left for legitimate purposes and no one knew what had become of him or her, then the other spouse had to wait ten years before being allowed to remarry. But, when a person maliciously deserted the household and proclamations turned up no information concerning the spouse's whereabouts, a woman could have a divorce after a one-year delay and a man did not have to wait even that long.[7]

5. AEN, JMN2: 229r–v, 245v–246, 249.
6. Ibid., 192v–193, 211, 215.
7. *Calvini Opera*, X/a, 111–112; Seeger, *Nullité de mariage*, p. 463.

In the mid-seventeenth century, Neuchâtel's judges were on occasion less strict. For example, Jaques Cuche, complaining that he could no longer live in continence and needed help in managing his household, filed for divorce against his wife, who had left him and their week-old child, taking with her Jaques's gold and silver as well as her finest clothes. Since her departure, he had received no news of her despite his consistent efforts to learn of her location. The court ordered that Cuche's wife be summoned three different Sundays, a fortnight between each, at all the churches in the seigneury of Valangin. Cuche also had to contact her closest relatives to see if they opposed his legal action. Because the announcements turned up no information about his absent wife, Cuche received his divorce in August 1649, roughly three and a half years after her departure.[8]

Such a decision, however, was clearly exceptional. During the entire period 1547–1706, the consistory apparently granted divorces for abandonment only three times without requiring the deserted spouse to wait seven years; perhaps not coincidentally, these three plaintiffs were all men.[9] This may reflect a certain sexism on the part of the judges, who may have believed that men simply could not remain continent for extended periods of time. In the case of Cuche, they may have felt that a man was simply incapable of taking care of a small child and therefore needed to remarry (though in other cases the courts showed no such bias). During this same period, no woman ever tried to file for divorce on the ground of abandonment before seven years had expired since her husband's departure. Perhaps the consistory's tradition of requiring a seven-year waiting period simply inhibited women from filing suit earlier. Or, perhaps the parish consistories refused to refer female plaintiffs to the higher tribunals if their husbands had been absent for less than seven years. But many of the suits women did file involved absences

8. AEN, CSV4: 188, 192–193, 199–201. The consistory further ordered that the woman's property be left in the hands of Cuche, later to be inherited by the child.

9. During the sixteenth and seventeenth centuries, a few other cases can be found in which a court accorded a divorce for reasons of desertion without requiring the innocent spouse to wait the usual seven years, but these involved extenuating circumstances. For example, in 1597 Abraham Herman of La Sagne appeared before the consistory of Valangin asking to be divorced from Susanne nee Bourquin, who had left him four years earlier to become Catholic. One appearance in court sufficed to attain his divorce; he was not even required to make any announcements. This quick decision was undoubtedly the result of Susanne's apostasy; AEN, CSV3: 57. There were a few cases in which a spouse sued for divorce because the other had both deserted the household and committed adultery. Under such circumstances, divorces were granted as a result of the adultery even if the absence was shorter than seven years. In 1703 there was yet another divorce granted after an absence of less than seven years, but this case was also grounded on cruelty; AEN, JMV1: 20v–25.

considerably longer than seven years: in the seventeenth century, ten women brought actions against their husbands only after absences of ten years or more. In short, many abandoned women appeared in no hurry to be divorced from their husbands.

Property could have deterred women from requesting divorces sooner. When spouses died, the property they had brought into marriage went to their heirs or returned to the family from which they came. In either case, a woman could lose the usufruct of her husband's property. A spouse who had been absent seven years could be presumed dead, and any property he had left behind would be treated as if he had died. In short, abandoned women would want to remarry quickly only if their husbands left behind no substantial property holdings. Otherwise, they might find it convenient to wait until their children came of age and received their *légitimes* before seeking a divorce in hopes of remarrying.

If patient enough to endure seven years of loneliness, however, one had very good odds of eventually receiving the divorce. Of the 67 cases in which the absence of a spouse was alleged as one of the grounds for divorce, only 2 requests were denied; these involved apparently short separations of women who had left their husbands but were known to be alive and well elsewhere. Eleven other cases were abandoned, but the remaining 54 requests for divorce were granted. Absence or desertion was the ground for divorce most frequently cited by female plaintiffs. Fully 38 of the 53 women who received divorces in Neuchâtel and Valangin during the sixteenth and seventeenth centuries alleged the absence of their husbands as a motive for their legal actions.

The prominence of abandoned women among plaintiffs to divorce cases is a direct result of the common practice among early modern Neuchâtelois of hiring themselves out as mercenaries, usually in France. Because of this practice, many men were absent for years and their wives did not know if they were still alive. The connection between warfare and the dissolution of marriage on the ground of absence is as old as divorce itself. The ancient Romans had allowed remarriage in cases of abandonment that usually involved men who did not return from war and were presumed dead. If the first husband later returned, his wife was not guilty of adultery—the second marriage having effectively ended the first.[10] In early modern Europe, it was common for soldiers to leave the country and not be heard from for years. The story of Martin Guerre, a man who left his family in southern France and became a

---

10. Brundage, *Law, Sex, and Christian Society,* p. 38.

soldier for the king of Spain, recently caught the imagination of historians and the general public, thanks to Natalie Zemon Davis's book and a French film that brilliantly captures the popular culture of early modern peasantry. Having quarreled with his father, Martin left his village of Artigat in 1548 and headed for Spain, expecting never to return. Eight years after his departure, a man claiming to be Martin appeared in Artigat and eventually convinced everyone that he was the long-absent soldier. In fact, this man was an impostor, a man named Arnaud du Tilh, who pretended to be Martin for several years. In the film, the impostor's motivation in posing as Martin is his affection for Martin's wife, Bertrande. Though that makes a nice love story, he no doubt was also attracted to Martin's extensive property holdings. In any event, the impersonator came into conflict with Martin's uncle over the question of property. Suspecting all along that this man was not really his nephew, the uncle pressed charges of fraud against the false Martin. The case went to the Parlement of Toulouse in 1560, where the judges were about to acquit the impostor when the real Martin Guerre arrived. Bertrande and other witnesses acknowledged that the new arrival was the real husband, and the Parlement accordingly condemned the false Martin to death for his fraud.[11] Though Neuchâtel's court records do not reveal any men who audaciously tried to act the part of someone else, there were many women who could have identified with the plight of Bertrande, the abandoned, long-suffering wife.

After abandonment, the most commonly alleged reason for divorce was adultery. Of the 38 divorce cases in which infidelity was an issue, the courts awarded 29 divorces and rejected only 3; 6 cases were abandoned.[12] Among those suits that were rejected were cases of people who

11. Davis, *Martin Guerre.*
12. One unusual affair that did not lead to a final decision demonstrates that one had to be present to petition for a divorce. Christoff Harttman committed homicide in Germany and was condemned to be executed, though this sentence was commuted to confinement for an indefinite duration "in a certain place belonging to the emperor on the boundaries of the Turk where he would be exposed to all sorts of dangers." In what appeared to be a rather magnanimous gesture, Harttman asked in 1600 that his wife be given a divorce, seeing that she was young and needed someone to care for her and their children. His wife, Barbely, however, claimed that she did not want to be divorced despite the fact that her exiled husband could not fulfill his conjugal responsibilities. The tribunal concluded that there was no basis for giving a divorce and "enjoined the woman to bear patiently the accident and pray to God." Five years later, Christoff sent a messenger to the Justice matrimoniale with a request for a divorce on the grounds of adultery. Through the messenger, Harttman conveyed that he had learned that Barbely was pregnant and that he could not possibly be the father of the child. The tribunal, however, refused to hear the case, declaring that Harttman had to appear personally, not through a messenger, to file suit; AEN, JMN2: 199v–200, 218v–219.

had unwittingly forgiven their spouse's infidelity; borrowing a notion from canon law, the courts held that, if a person had sexual relations with one's spouse though knowing that he or she had committed adultery, the coition was viewed as a sign of forgiveness and the innocent party no longer had grounds for divorce.[13] Apart from such rare cases, however, if there was ample proof that a person had committed adultery and the innocent spouse refused to forgive this infidelity, the latter almost surely could have a divorce.

The proof of adultery could take various forms. Occasionally a person's confession of adultery sufficed to verify one's guilt. This was the case in 1607 when Jehan Massonde sued his wife, Eve, for divorce, basing his claim on the reports of various witnesses that she had committed adultery with David Huguenan. Eve had told several people that she had had sexual relations with Huguenan after he had asked her to eat apples laced with a sort of aphrodisiac. According to the story, after eating the apples she started to tremble, and he threw himself on her, gagging her with a handkerchief to keep her from screaming. The aphrodisiac may seem rather dubious, and at first glance this case appears to be one of rape. Some witnesses, however, claimed that Eve had confessed that Huguenan and she had exchanged gifts, and one even reported that Eve had confided that her youngest child was not Massonde's. Further testimony revealed that Eve had confessed to two ministers that she had indeed committed adultery with Huguenan several times after first having been seduced by him. Taken as a whole, the evidence indicated that she had committed impure acts, whether willingly or unwillingly at first, with Huguenan. And this was enough to convince the judges to award Massonde his divorce and to punish Eve with a sentence of three days and nights in jail for her infidelity. Since there was no witness to an adulterous act, this decision rested solely on her confession.[14]

Ordinarily, though, the proof of adultery lay not in the confession of the guilty party but in the birth of an illegitimate child. In 1593, Pierre Paillaux returned to the area after having been away at war, only to find

13. In Geneva, the consistory used the same practice, even though the marriage laws made no mention of it. In any event, the consistory often asked plaintiffs whether they had had sexual relations with their spouses since learning of their adultery. Female plaintiffs were asked this question more often than males, an indication that Calvin and other members of the consistory considered a woman's infidelity a greater evil than a man's; Seeger, *Nullité de mariage*, pp. 423–424.

14. AEN, JMN2: 220–224v, 225v, 230–233, 235. It is somewhat ironic that this confession sufficed for a divorce. As we see below, in the mid-seventeenth century the consistory of Valangin, fearing collusion, rejected a husband's divorce suit since his claim was based solely on the confession of the wife.

that during his absence his wife had given birth to a child that could not possibly be his. Irate, he filed for divorce. Confessing her sin, his wife begged for mercy, pointing out that Paillaux had been away at war for four of the five years of their marriage, leaving her without aid or comfort. She defended herself by saying that he had not cared for her as a husband should and that she had even heard rumors that he was dead. Left to her own resources, she was forced to work as a servant in Bern, which was the source of her misfortune. Paillaux retorted that he had left her enough assets to support herself and their child, since deceased. Considering that the adultery was undeniable and that Paillaux refused to be reconciled with his wife, the judges accorded him the divorce and ordered his wife to be imprisoned for three days for her fault. Neither party, however, was to remarry without the permission of the Justice matrimoniale.[15]

Similarly, divorces granted to women on the ground of adultery virtually always resulted from the fact that their husbands' mistresses had become mothers. For example, Jehannette, wife of Guillaume Jehan Richard dict Maullon, filed suit against her husband, who had begotten two illegitimate children during their twenty-six years of marriage. She asked for a divorce from Richard as well as the restitution of her property and the usufruct of his property for the remainder of her life. His sin was obvious, and the judges accordingly granted Jehannette's request in its entirety in April 1610.[16]

Although this case shows that women occasionally received very favorable divorce settlements against adulterous husbands, the nature of the proof of adultery entailed that it was more often cited against wayward wives than unfaithful husbands in divorce cases. If the concrete products of adulterous affairs were illegitimate children, then a woman whose husband was absent for a lengthy period would have a difficult time concealing a pregnancy. If an unfaithful husband did not actually

15. Ibid., 175. It is interesting that the tribunal granted this divorce in only one court appearance. Often plaintiffs for divorce for reasons of adultery had to wait several weeks or even months before receiving a divorce.

16. AEN, CSV3: 173. Not all women in early modern Europe enjoyed the same property rights. Indeed, Lawrence Stone argues that until the end of the seventeenth century English women had no property rights whatsoever. Men had the authority to seize their wives' property at any time, though the wealthiest women may have made provisions in their contracts to maintain certain rights over their property. The power most men had over their wives' property, however, strongly deterred English women from filing for separations. In Scotland, there was also a double standard governing property. Married women guilty of adultery generally lost their tochers, whereas adulterous men were usually able to keep their property; *Road to Divorce*, pp. 4, 12; see also Mitchison and Leneman, *Sexuality and Social Control*, p. 86.

get caught in the act of coitus, he ran the risk of being discovered only if his partner revealed his name. It is therefore not surprising that among those plaintiffs who sought divorces for reasons of adultery, males (25) easily outnumbered females (13). Caution, of course, must be used in dealing with figures so small. Thirty-eight cases do not suffice as a basis for broad statistical analysis. With this caveat in mind, it is nevertheless worthwhile to compare the findings in Neuchâtel with those in other areas. In Zurich from 1525 to 1531, men initiated close to 60 percent of divorce cases based on adultery, and more than twice as many men as women were plaintiffs to such suits in Augsburg during the period 1537–1547. In early modern Geneva, as in Neuchâtel, adultery was the ground generally cited by male plaintiffs, while desertion more often than not was alleged by female plaintiffs. During the time of Calvin, men outnumbered women by more than two to one among those who filed for divorce against adulterous spouses, and they enjoyed much better odds of winning their suits. In Basel from 1529 to 1550, men were the plaintiffs in about 60 percent of all divorce cases; from 1550 to 1590, women initiated a slight majority of all divorce cases.[17] Although it is not clear if in Basel adultery cases followed this pattern of divorce suits in general, no evidence has been given to the contrary. Thus, with the possible exception of late sixteenth-century Basel, neighboring Reformed areas, like Neuchâtel, witnessed a majority of men as plaintiffs to divorces for reasons of adultery.

When a sentence of divorce was passed against an adulterous woman, she could be subject to rather severe financial penalties. Although for most cases the consistorial registers say nothing about financial settlements that might accompany divorces, occasionally we do find evidence on such matters. In 1593, Jaques de Brot returned from foreign military service to discover that Huguette, his wife, had committed adultery and given birth to a bastard in his absence. Confessing her sin, Huguette begged forgiveness, asking Jaques not to forget the five children and

17. Köhler, *Zürcher Ehegericht*, p. 109; E. William Monter, "Women in Calvinist Geneva," p. 195; Thérèse Pittard, *Femmes de Genève aux jours d'autrefois* (Geneva, 1946), pp. 31–34; Roper, *Holy Household*, p. 198; Safley, *Let No Man Put Asunder*, p. 175, and "Protestantism, Divorce, and the Breaking of the Modern Family," in *Pietas et Societas*, ed. Sessions and Bebb, p. 55; Staehelin, *Einführung*, pp. 181–198. Cornelia Seeger notes that from 1541 to 1564 only six women, as opposed to a score of men, received divorces from adulterous spouses. She found evidence that a women's infidelity was viewed as a greater sin than her husband's. In divorce cases based on adultery, the consistory and Petit Conseil consistently exhorted female plaintiffs to forgive their husbands for their foibles. Men who were seeking divorces from unfaithful wives did not always hear the same admonitions; *Nullité de mariage*, pp. 403–404, 417.

many years they had had together. Admonishing him to forgive his wife, the judges ordered a delay of seven weeks before proceeding any further, hoping that Jaques would have a change of heart. He, however, obstinately persisted and in June of that year the Justice matrimoniale awarded him a separation of bed and table (*du lict et de la table*). The sentence added: "In the same manner, we adjudge to Jaques all the property of his wife which he is to use in caring for and feeding the five children which God has given them during their marriage. Jaques will be responsible for caring for these children. Huguette will be punished with a prison sentence as an example to others."[18] At this point, the judges did not yet give Jaques permission to remarry, still hoping that he would deign to forgive Huguette. In the end, he received his divorce and permission to remarry.[19] This case reveals the custom of the courts in early modern Neuchâtel to award the custody of the children to the innocent party in divorce cases based on adultery, whether it be the father or the mother. Gender roles were not as stereotyped as we often think; in Neuchâtel and elsewhere it clearly was not deemed unnatural for a man to be in charge of raising children.[20]

What is more surprising about this case is the court's adjudging all the woman's property to her husband to help pay for the costs of the child. This is particularly unexpected since throughout the proceeding the judges showed a certain sympathy toward the woman. They delayed the final verdict and admonished the plaintiff throughout the proceeding to forgive his wife. Despite this sympathy, the court could have not been more stringent toward Huguette in mandating this early modern version of child support.

An adulterous wife might suffer similar financial penalties even after receiving a divorce for abandonment, if by chance her absent husband suddenly reappeared. In 1605, Jacqua, wife of Guillaume Rossel, sued for divorce from a husband who had deserted her twelve years earlier to go off to war in a foreign land. Left without aid or comfort, she had received no news from him since his departure. After the usual three

---

18. AEN, JMN2: 176v.

19. Ibid., 175v, 176v, 183, 184.

20. Records from fourteenth-century Ghent concerning judicial separations show that there was no notion that the woman was better suited to care for the children than the man; Nicholas, *Domestic Life*, p. 46. In cases of judicial separation, early modern English courts awarded custody of the children to the father even when he was the guilty party. During the separation, a man could even forbid his wife from ever seeing their children again—a strong deterrent to separating from wayward husbands. During the Victorian period, the right to have custody of the children shifted from the father to the mother, unless she was an adulteress; Stone, *Road to Divorce*, pp. 5, 180.

announcements had been made in church without turning up any news of the missing Guillaume, the consistory awarded her the divorce in January 1606, though it declared that she was to be punished as the governor saw fit for having committed *paillardise,* producing her second illegitimate child.[21] She soon remarried, but shortly thereafter Guillaume returned to Dombresson and himself filed for divorce on the ground of adultery. He further demanded that she make *réparation* and that all her property be adjudged to him, including any that was rightfully hers but possessed by her father at the moment. Jacqua countered that, since she was already divorced from him, his action was null. Unfortunately for her, the consistory did not accept this argument; it awarded Guillaume the divorce as well as Jacqua's property and ordered her to make *réparation.* As for any property that her father might have, the court ordered that the affair be heard before the appropriate civil jurisdiction.[22] No mention was made of the validity of Jacqua's second marriage.

This decision is quite perplexing. In effect, the consistory granted the same divorce twice, first to Jacqua and then to Guillaume. And since Guillaume had been away for twelve years without providing his wife any financial assistance and had not responded to Jacqua's announcements, one might well have thought that he would no longer have any rights over her. This case reveals that adultery was considered a greater evil than deserting and neglecting one's spouse for over a decade. To the Reformed consistory, a woman mercilessly abandoned by her husband was expected to remain chaste indefinitely, and any violation of this imposed abstinence could result in the forfeiture of all her wealth.

Closely related to, though nevertheless distinct from, adultery was female deceit. Such a case arose when a man married a woman he thought was a virgin when in fact she had already had sexual relations with another man. Appearing only six times in the *procès verbaux* during the sixteenth and seventeenth centuries, such litigation usually involved a newlywed man who desired a divorce after discovering that his wife was pregnant by another at the time of marriage. Occasionally the decisions rendered against women guilty of deceit were every bit as harsh as those against adulterous wives. For example, in 1600/1, Zacharie Blanc, a deacon in Neuchâtel, filed suit against his wife, Susanne nee Jaquemet,

21. It is surprising that the consistory awarded this divorce. Ordinarily one had to live chastely during the spouse's absence to be eligible for a divorce for desertion.
22. AEN, CSV3: 127–128, 133–134, 136–137.

because she had given birth to a child that she acknowledged was not his. Thinking that he had married a virgin, Blanc was quite disappointed and felt compelled to sue for divorce because of the moral obligations the office of deacon entailed. In light of her great wrong and of the high costs of their wedding, Blanc further sought all her assets. Relatives of Susanne begged Blanc to forgive her, but he replied that he had two wives, "one was the church and the other Susanne. The latter had deceived him and he did not want to take her back lest he forsake his spiritual wife."[23] Her relatives pointed out that, since discovering his wife's sin, he had said that he was willing to stay with her provided that it would not prejudice his ecclesiastical charge. Admitting having uttered these words, Blanc now stated quite pompously that "having since considered the deed which affects his charge and his honor," he felt compelled to file suit for divorce "both for the aforementioned reasons and for the fact that a short time ago lesser personages had received sentences of divorce" for the same motive. In the end, members of the court awarded Blanc the divorce as well as all his wife's assets.[24] Whereas Jaques de Brot had received all his adulterous wife's property to defray the costs of raising children, here the man received his wife's assets as damages for the affront to his honor.[25]

Of the cases of deceit for which sentences were given—one case was abandoned—all but one of the actors received divorces. The exception was Guillaume Frollet of La Sagne, who in 1560 filed suit for a divorce because his wife, Collette, had committed fornication before marriage and had subsequently acknowledged that the child's father was Claude Choppardet. She admitted her past foibles but asserted that her conduct had been irreproachable following the marriage. For better or worse, the judges of the consistory accepted this argument and ordered the two of them to return together and live as husband and wife.[26] This is one of the flagrant examples of how over the course of time the consistories could render contradictory decisions for strikingly similar cases. The different judgments may well be attributed to changes in judicial per-

23. AEN, JMN2: 200v.
24. Ibid., 201. Later Blanc had a change of heart, but the Classe des Pasteurs did not allow him to take back his ex-wife unless he left the deaconry; Boyve, *Annales historiques,* 3: 358.
25. This judgment is similar to the custom in late medieval Italian towns of awarding all or part of an adulterous woman's dowry to her husband as compensation; Brundage, *Law, Sex, and Christian Society,* p. 541. In Calvin's Geneva, however, a divorced woman always had the right to recover her dowry, even when she was the guilty party; Seeger, *Nullité de mariage,* pp. 413–416.
26. AEN, CSV2: 9. For her offense Collette was to be punished by the governor as he saw fit.

sonnel: as new judges arrived and old ones left, alterations in their judgments are understandable.

Another cause for divorce closely related to adultery was bigamy. Appearing only three times in divorce litigation, bigamy was cited when one spouse abandoned the other, left the country, and married another in a foreign land. No doubt bigamy was rarely alleged because it was so hard to prove. It was rather unlikely that witnesses could be produced in Neuchâtel to verify that the defendant had married in a foreign country. If a person deserted the household and remarried illegally on foreign soil, the odds were that the abandoned spouse would have to wait seven years to receive a divorce for reasons of desertion.

Other complaints occasionally alleged as grounds for divorce were illness and sexual dysfunction. Terminating a marriage because of impotence was nothing new. Since canon lawyers had put so much emphasis on the sexual aspect of marriage, it is not surprising that they denied the right to marry to those incapable of having sexual relations. Consequently, Pope Gregory IX (1227–1241) declared that impotence was an impediment to marriage and that any marriage an impotent person contracted would be null.[27]

Pierre Darmon has written an interesting work on impotence cases in early modern France. Although his research uncovered only a few dozen cases, Darmon maintains that actions to annul marriages on the ground of impotence were quite common in early modern France, suggesting that the extant cases represent only the tip of the iceberg. He is led to believe that this litigation was common by the abundant literature penned by moralists complaining about couples who dissolved their marriages through such suits.[28] Though it is undoubtedly true that many judicial records from early modern France have been lost, it is dangerous to give too much credence to the literature of moralists, who tended to exaggerate the evils in their society. Moreover, the evidence from Neuchâtel's courts does not corroborate Darmon's view. Rarely was impotence cited in divorce cases, and plaintiffs who did seek divorces for sexual dysfunction had little chance of success. As we have seen, virtually all the plaintiffs who filed for divorce because of the infidelity or prolonged absence of their spouses were successful in their suits. At the same time, for the ten cases brought forth because of various physical infirmities, the courts awarded only four divorces—two to

27. Pierre Darmon, *Le tribunal de l'impuissance: Virilité et défaillances conjugales dans l'ancienne France* (Paris, 1979), p. 91.
28. Ibid., pp. 94, 99.

men and two to women—and these generally involved marriages that had not been consummated after several years of cohabitation.[29]

A suit filed in 1590 reveals that sexual dysfunction ceased to be a ground for divorce once the marriage had been consummated. Nicollas Grandjehan filed for divorce from Anthoina, his wife of eight years, claiming that she was incapable of having conjugal relations. [30] To these charges, Anthoina responded that she was old and that illness had left her physically unfit for sexual relations. If Grandjehan wanted the separation, she would not object, provided that he return the property he and his mother had taken from her and give her some of his own assets. Nicholas and Anthoina affirmed that they had had carnal knowledge of one another both before and after the wedding and that it was only during the previous five or six years that illness had left Anthoina sexually dysfunctional. As a result of this testimony, the members of the court concluded that there was no valid ground for a separation and ordered the couple to return together and fulfill the vows they had made when they were married in church. Like others, this decision seems terribly inconsistent with Protestant preaching against the celibate life, especially since the afflicted person agreed to the divorce, provided that she receive material support. Nonetheless, this decision was consistent with those Darmon describes for early modern France: impotence was a ground for an annulment only if it had existed before the marriage.[31]

In addition to cases of impotence, a few other cases were initiated for medical reasons. Here again, the courts clearly hesitated before granting divorces because of illness. For example, in 1552 a man sought a divorce from his leprous wife. Despite the fact that she had been sick for seven years and showed no hope for recovery, the judges declared that the man was "still to live for a while abstaining from marriage, judging that he must not receive a marriage separation until God calls his wife to Him."[32] For this couple, marriage was to endure in sickness and in health until death did them part. The only action in which a plaintiff received a divorce from a leprous spouse was one in which the latter agreed to the separation. In accordance with the ordinances cited ear-

29. AEN, CSV1: 103r–v; CSV2: 276–277; CSV4: 2–3, 15–16; CSV6: 82–85.

30. This was an unusual action in that suits based on sexual dysfunction against women were rare, representing only about 5 percent of the cases Darmon studied in France; *Tribunal de l'impuissance*, p. 49. In Geneva during the time of Calvin, five-sixths of the cases involving sexual dysfunction were initiated by women against impotent husbands; Seeger, *Nullité de mariage*, p. 353.

31. AEN, JMN2: 159v; Darmon, *Tribunal de l'impuissance*, p. 29.

32. AEN, CSV1: 46.

lier, Pierre Guillemet was granted a divorce from his leprous wife, who had agreed to an arrangement whereby he continued to support her.[33] All in all, the scanty number of suits brought forth against ill spouses indicates that the judges were quite reluctant to award divorces on such bases. Too few to build meaningful statistical analyses, these suits show that, notwithstanding Darmon's contentions, neither impotence nor illness was an important basis for ending a marriage in early modern Neuchâtel.

Neuchâtel had its version of the witchcraft craze that afflicted so much of Europe during the late sixteenth and early seventeenth centuries, and sorcery was a factor in a handful of divorce cases. In Neuchâtel, witches were evidently a bigger problem than warlocks, since all plaintiffs who cited witchcraft in divorce proceedings were men. In 1599, Guillaume Jecquier of Fleurier filed for divorce from a wife who had fled after being accused of witchcraft. He desired to remarry and asked for pity on account of the four small children he was burdened with. Jecquier was ordered to make the usual three announcements, enjoining his wife (or someone representing her) to respond to this suit. In July, just two months after his first appearance in court, the tribunal awarded him the divorce and permission to remarry in view of the fact that no opposition was made and that his wife was currently a fugitive fleeing the charges of witchcraft. At no time was Jecquier required to prove how long she had been away, a clear indication that there was no prescribed minimum waiting period.[34]

A few years earlier, however, Jehan Baptiste Bergier and Anserme Henry had encountered much more difficulty in obtaining divorces on similar grounds. In March 1592, Bergier filed suit against Lucya Paris, who had been detained five months earlier at Colombier for the evil spells (*mallefices*) she cast and for charges of witchcraft, an accusation based on other witches' denunciations. On 12 November 1591, she was banished for life from the principality of Neuchâtel and Valangin. The same day Bergier appeared in court, Henry requested a divorce from Jehannata Allemand, who had been banished along with Lucya on similar accusations. Both men were ordered to wait a year and six weeks from the date of the banishment before filing suit.[35] Bergier repeated his request in May 1593 and the judges ordered:

33. AEN, JMN1: 31.
34. AEN, JMN2: 197r–v.
35. Henry, who had already promised to marry another woman and had made the first two announcements without the permission of the seigneury or of the matrimonial court, was

In order to take nothing too lightly, *Messieurs*, having received the advice of the Compagnie des Pasteurs and Professors of Geneva, dated 9 March 1593, deem it prudent that Bergier make inquiries as to where his wife could be and what has become of her. They want to see the records of the proceedings against those women who accused her as well as the sentence of banishment. If he cannot obtain any news of her, he is to notify her closest relatives.[36]

In his next court appearance in August of that year, Bergier was censured for not following the court's directives insofar as he had not produced an affidavit showing that proper inquiries had been made concerning his wife's fate. A week later, Bergier presented to the tribunal an attestation to his investigation and to the notification of his wife's relatives. Having seen this affidavit, the judges awarded him the divorce in light of the fact that he was totally innocent, that she alone was guilty, and that "he is a young man who does not have the gift of continence and would fall into the sin of fornication if we were to deny him the right to marry." To avoid a greater evil, then, the court awarded Bergier a divorce and permission to remarry.[37] Though less richly documented, Henry's case followed a similar pattern, and he too eventually received a divorce and the right to remarry.[38]

These latter two cases are interesting for several reasons. The twentieth-century observer may have trouble appreciating the early modern fear of witchcraft. But, given the fact that these women were condemned for witchcraft and banished from the county, it is hard to understand why their husbands were still required to investigate their whereabouts. Permanently forbidden to reenter the principality, the women obviously could not return to their households. The court's actions reflected a serious reluctance to grant divorces under such circumstances.[39] Though the tribunal in these cases was quite rigorous

---

ordered to be punished as the seigneury saw fit and the third announcement was stopped; ibid., 163v.

36. Ibid., 176. From 1547 until 1806, this is one of only two cases in which the courts of Neuchâtel and Valangin say that they consulted Geneva's Compagnie des Pasteurs.

37. Ibid., 163v, 172v, 176, 177v. The evidence against the woman was that she had been found "at the synagogue" and that she had made another person deathly sick. This is the first time either tribunal included among its principal reasons for granting a divorce the fact that the party was incapable of abstaining from sex. Their reluctance to give divorces for sexual dysfunction shows that the tribunals were not at all consistent in this regard.

38. Ibid., 178, 179v.

39. It was even harder to get a divorce for witchcraft in Geneva under Theodore Beza. In 1572, Jacques Quiblet petitioned to remarry since the previous year his wife had been accused

vis-à-vis the plaintiffs, the judges nonetheless did in the end award divorces less than two years after the witches' flight. These men undoubtedly received divorces more because of the crime of witchcraft than because of abandonment.[40]

In the discussion so far I have concentrated on those reasons for which the courts awarded divorces. But it is important to mention that, throughout the sixteenth and seventeenth centuries, cruelty was not recognized as grounds for divorce. A case brought before Valangin's consistory demonstrates graphically that at this time violent behavior did not suffice for even a separation, let alone a divorce. In 1649/50, Pierre Perret Gentil filed for divorce against his wife, Suzanne, who had confessed to her pastor and others that she had committed adultery with Moyse Jacob Juré. When they first appeared in court, Suzanne admitted her sin and begged her husband for forgiveness. Seeing her genuine repentance, the judges passed an unprecedented sentence in ordering Pierre to forgive her and take her back. This, however, was by no means the end of the case. A couple weeks later, in March 1649, Pierre persisted in asking for a divorce because of his wife's infidelity. Suzanne now denied that she had committed adultery and claimed that she was suffering from a troubled spirit when she had confessed to being unfaithful. Appearing again in December 1649, Pierre denied that Suzanne was out of her senses when she made this confession—which she even repeated in the presence of Moyse, who did not deny the transgression.[41]

At yet another appearance, in 1650, the two parties now began accusing each other of poor behavior and negligence toward domestic

of witchcraft and banished for life under pain of death if she returned. The city council, however, rejected this request, saying that he could remarry only if he proved that his wife was dead. In spite of this ruling, Quiblet made a new marriage engagement, which the council declared null; it also condemned Quiblet and his fiancée to six and three days of prison, respectively. Quiblet then petitioned the consistory, noting that Martin Bucer had approved of divorce for the "practical effects of witchcraft," such as life banishment. Beza, however, responded that adultery was the only ground for divorce; Phillips, *Putting Asunder*, p. 59, n. 73, citing *Registres de la Compagnie des Pasteurs au temps de Calvin*, 5 vols., ed. Robert M. Kingdon and J.-F. Bergier (Geneva, 1962), 3: 91–92. During the time of Calvin, banishment alone was never recognized as a ground for divorce. As in cases of desertion, those whose spouses were banished had to make public announcements to locate their absent husbands or wives; Seeger, *Nullité de mariage*, p. 433.

40. Only one other case of this genre was heard by either court, an action dating from 1620. Because of the lacuna in the records, we do not know the outcome of this case; AEN, JMN2: 260r–v.
41. AEN, CSV4: 190–192, 202, 205–206.

duties. Suzanne claimed that Pierre had on many occasions brutally beaten her and further alleged that one day he flavored her soup with *pousset,* an evil powder that the devil gave to witches. According to Suzanne, ever since that day she suffered from a troubled spirit.[42] For his part, Pierre confessed to having beaten his wife to make her attentive to her domestic duties, but he vowed that she had given him good reason to do so. As for her mental stability, Pierre held that she was not mad at the time of their marriage but had later become so by a just judgment of God.[43]

Various witnesses attested to the poor domestic life the Perret Gentils led. Daniel Matthey testified that one day at the Perret Gentil home Pierre offered him some dessert. When he opened the pantry door to fetch some, Pierre discovered Suzanne inside. As she came out, Pierre ran after her and they began beating each other. When the punching stopped, Daniel noticed that Suzanne had suffered what appeared to be a knife wound, though he did not know how she had acquired it. While Suzanne continued to pull his hair, Pierre yelled at her, complaining about her misbehavior. Daniel also reported from hearsay that Suzanne later said that, if she had known that it was her husband who was opening the pantry door, she would have cut his hand. On another occasion, Daniel saw Pierre chasing Suzanne down the road. When he caught her, he threw her down in the middle of the road, though she immediately escaped and continued running away from him. Daniel further added that it seemed to him that Suzanne did not keep very good house, since their home was very dirty and disorderly.[44]

Other witness also characterized the Perret Gentil household as enjoying something less than marital bliss. Daniel Grandjehen saw and heard the two of them fighting on several occasions both in their home and in the street, though he was unable to discern who was beating whom. Others saw Pierre on one or more occasions chasing Suzanne down the road. Watching from his window one day, Josué Matthey saw Pierre pursuing Suzanne. When he caught up with her, they began "punching and beating each other so that they both fell to the ground. He saw that Pierre was holding her by the hair and was taking her back home in such a fashion. And when [bystanders] thought about sepa-

42. Ibid., 218. *Pousset* is described as a "poisonous and magical powder that the devil supposedly gave to witches to work their evil spells"; Pierrehumbert, *Dictionnaire historique,* s.v. "pousset."
43. AEN, CSV4: 218–220.
44. Ibid., 221.

rating the two of them, Suzanne cried, 'Let him alone! He's not hurting me.' Josué believed that she could not even feel the punches."[45] Evidence thus indicates that extremely violent behavior was routine in the Perret Gentil household.

A decision was finally given 16 July 1650, a year and a half after the opening of the case. The judges noted that there had not been a single witness who could attest to Suzanne's adultery. This accusation rested solely on her own confession, and it was not clear if she was in her good senses when she admitted to being unfaithful. According to the judges, the dignity of the institution of marriage required that it be dissolved only when unquestionable grounds justified it. Mere conjecture did not suffice. The members of the consistory further conceived that there were two types of confession: "solitary" and "social" confessions. The solitary confession could be trusted, since the only interested party was the person who was confessing. Judgments could not, however, be based on social confessions, since a third party was involved. Because Suzanne's confession implicated a lover, a third party was concerned and her confession was not to be trusted.[46]

In further discussing the role confessions could play in such divorce cases, the judges launched into a lengthy and unusually philosophical examination of this question:

> We must also consider the opinions of the ancient and modern Doctors of the Church who, in treating the subject of divorce, maintained that judgments must not be based on the confession of that spouse who should avow his own turpitude or villainy because of the dangerous consequences that could follow. For it could happen that a husband or wife, dissatisfied with his or her marriage—whether it be for poor behavior, brutality, disputes, a poorly run household, mental or physical infirmities of one or the other spouse—should accuse himself of adultery in order to escape from such an unhappy marriage. Such an individual may deem it worthwhile to get out of a marriage at the price of a *réparation* or of a prison sentence . . . of short duration in order to free himself of perpetual turmoil and aggravation. By the same token, one could accuse oneself of a moral offense of which one was innocent in hopes of receiving a divorce and of then remarrying—a second marriage that is premeditated even before the divorce—either with the goal of personal wealth in mind or of other

45. Ibid., 221–222.
46. Ibid., 241–242.

mundane considerations. This could cause an infinite number of suits, broken marriages, and unrest that would be all too frequent, abusing the Savior's dictate that permits divorce only in the case of adultery, which must be manifest.[47]

The judges also feared collusion between spouses, believing that a husband and wife might agree that one would confess to adultery so that they could both be free of their union. Finally, the tribunal held that to award a divorce for reasons of adultery "one can base a judgment only on the reports of at least two good, solid witnesses."[48] Accordingly, the court rejected Pierre's request for a divorce and ordered that the two be reconciled. Notwithstanding the "temerarious confession" of Suzanne, the honor of Pierre and his relatives was to remain untarnished. As for the costs of this long trial, because of Suzanne's recklessness in making this rash confession Pierre received permission to take 1,000 livres from her assets as compensation.[49]

This case provides many insights to seventeenth-century mentality. To begin with, the judges' discussion on adultery and proofs thereof is quite surprising. Never before had a tribunal in Neuchâtel proclaimed that adultery had to be attested by at least two witnesses to serve as a ground for divorce. It seems rather preposterous to require two eyewitnesses to an adulterous act. Even in this age of rather limited privacy, such intimate relations were not ordinarily performed in front of an audience. Furthermore, among the numerous divorces already awarded on the ground of adultery, only a few times had people witnessed acts of infidelity. More important, in the sixteenth century the courts more than once had granted divorces based solely on individuals' confessions of infidelity. It seems rather strange to maintain that confessions of adultery were not to be trusted since they could be a mere pretext for dissolving an unhappy marriage. This attitude could seemingly be a stimulus for actually committing adultery. If a confession of adultery did not suffice to receive a divorce, one could simply go one step farther and actually find a willing adulterous partner (along with two witnesses).[50] Furthermore, this is the only occasion during the

---

47. Ibid., 242.
48. Ibid., 243.
49. Ibid., 243–244.
50. A trial that took place a few years later is a case in point. In 1656, Saara, wife of Jacques Ducommun, claimed to the consistory that she had committed adultery with Moyse du Bois. Moyse, however, completely denied this accusation. Since she accused Moyse of having debauched her without producing any proof thereof, Saara was condemned to three days in

period 1547–1806 that a tribunal mentioned the statement of Jesus on divorce. Although Jesus limited divorce to cases of adultery, earlier consistories had not done so. As we have seen, divorces for desertion outnumbered those for adultery, and divorces had also been granted for impotence and other physical infirmities. Most likely, in the judges' minds these dissolutions were distinct from those stemming from infidelity. Divorce for abandonment was based on the presumption of the absent spouse's death, and the deserted spouse was thus more akin to a widow or widower than to a divorcé or divorcée. Perhaps the judges also viewed impotence more as a ground for annulment than for divorce. Nevertheless, the consistories cannot be said to have consistently followed the rigid standards set by the New Testament. The tribunals had already awarded divorces because of witchcraft and illness incurred after marriage, grounds with no scriptural basis. Notwithstanding certain inconsistencies, this case reveals the consistories' strong reluctance to award divorces.

But what this case shows above all is that at this time cruelty and incompatibility were by no means grounds for divorce. After hearing testimony concerning the animosity between the Perret Gentils, the modern observer might immediately think that the woman—perhaps also the man—should have been able to sue for divorce because of cruelty. By modern standards, either Pierre or Suzanne or both together ought to be able to sue for divorce on the basis of incompatibility. It certainly seems imprudent to force a couple to remain together despite the fact that they frequently beat each other and in one case perhaps even stabbed each other. But cruelty was not even mentioned as a motive for divorce. In fact, in no extant case before 1700 was cruelty clearly cited as a ground for divorce.[51] Suzanne was the defendant despite the

---

prison. A year later, in May 1657, Jacques Ducommun was convoked for refusing to live with his wife. Since Saara's self-accusations were without proof, Jacques had no valid reason for being separated and was ordered to return to Saara. Four years later, Jacques received a divorce because Saara had deserted him and married another in Burgundy; AEN, CSV5: 29, 31–34, 46, 75–76, 78. Thus, if Saara's goal in voluntarily confessing to adultery was to be divorced from her husband, she attained this end only when she actually did violate the faith of marriage.

51. There was, however, one case brought before the matrimonial court of Neuchâtel that may have been based in part on cruelty and violence. The sketchy *Annexes* of this court describe a jurisdiction that was both criminal and matrimonial. Isaac Merveilleux had stolen papers from a home and had attempted to poison his wife. Furthermore, he had impregnated a woman to whom he gave some "medicine," which may have been the cause of the death of the child shortly thereafter. The divorce apparently was granted in 1672. It is unclear if this divorce was granted because of his crimes or his infidelity. In 1690, Merveilleux asked permis-

fact that she was apparently more often than not the victim of the beat-ings. Had it not been for her spurious confession, this case would not have even have been heard in court. Most shocking is that the judges uttered not a word of reproach concerning the vicious discord that reigned between the Perret Gentils. Although several people saw Pierre beat Suzanne on more than one occasion, the court did not censure Pierre to treat her better. True, the consistory often did use police ac-tions to admonish cruel husbands. In the Perret Gentil case, however, the judges declared that, despite his violence, the husband's honor was not to be impugned by the rash avowal of his wife. Although, as we have seen, the consistory of seventeenth-century Valangin at times viewed antipathy between fiancés as sufficient grounds for annulling marriage contracts, mutual hostility was no ground at all for dissolving the union after the consecration of marriage. Indeed, several decades would pass before the consistory agreed even to hear a divorce suit based on cruelty or incompatibility.

A most perplexing question is why the woman here opposed her husband's action for a divorce. Most likely, when she made this dubious confession of adultery to her pastor, she wanted to be released from her volatile marriage. Why, then, did she change her mind? After hearing of their violent disputes, one wonders if indeed she was not out of her senses when she denied, rather than when she made, the confession. Or perhaps this reflects a phenomenon Johann Huizinga described years ago in analyzing the predominant mentality of the late Middle Ages. According to Huizinga, people of the fifteenth century were prone to emotional extremes, easily switching from feelings of tender affection to violent discord.[52] We noted that Suzanne told bystanders not to inter-vene as her husband beat her, assuring them that he was not hurting her; this too could be an example of a woman capable of having the most extreme emotions toward her husband. Though subjected to her husband's brutal beatings, she nevertheless did not want to see him re-

---

sion to marry the woman with whom he had committed fornication and produced an illegitimate child, claiming that this sin was committed after the divorce and thus was not adultery. The registers suggest that his cruelty may have been a factor in the divorce; AEN, JMN: *Annexes* 405.

52. Huizinga describes late medieval feelings as follows: "So violent and motley was life, that it bore the mixed smell of blood and of roses. The men of that time always oscillate be-tween the fear of hell and the most naïve joy, between cruelty and tenderness, between harsh asceticism and insane attachment to the delights of this world, between hatred and goodness, always running to extremes"; *The Waning of the Middle Ages: A Study of the Forms of Life, Thought and Art in France and the Netherlands in the XIVth and XVth Centuries* (New York, 1954), p. 27.

proached. Although one such example does not suffice to show a general trend, it is at least feasible that Huizinga's theory is applicable to seventeenth-century Neuchâtel.

A more likely explanation for Suzanne reneging on her confession involves property concerns. Knowing that people guilty of adultery had lost all their property to their spouses, Suzanne would be prudent to have second thoughts about admitting infidelity. Moreover, though the large fine she was charged indicates that the Perret Gentils were not poverty stricken, many women must have felt economically vulnerable when faced with the prospect of living without their husbands. A police action before the consistory of Geneva during the time of Calvin provides palpable evidence to this effect. In August 1542, the Genevan consistory convoked the butcher Claude Soutiez and his wife, Martinaz, because of their domestic turmoil. Four months previous to their appearance in court, Claude had beaten Martinaz so severely that she lost one of her eyes. Martinaz, however, had not wanted to appeal to the authorities lest Claude become angry and abandon her and their children. In the end, the consistory censured Claude for his behavior, calling him to promise henceforth not to irritate (*corroser*) his mate, a promise that Martinaz also had to make. Because of her fear that he would leave, Martinaz requested that Claude receive no punishment. The consistory did refer him to the Petit Conseil, which did not, however, impose any additional penalty. To remind her of her proper place in the family, the consistory ordered Martinaz to obey her husband and live peacefully with him.[53] Genevan women would have to wait longer than their Neuchâtel counterparts before they could file for divorce on the ground of violent behavior.

Though cruelty was not significant in the Perret Gentil decision, it was a factor in later divorce litigation. In 1703, Madelaine Droz sued for divorce from her husband, Abram, on the combined grounds of cruelty and desertion. Abram abandoned her four and a half years earlier and had been so physically abusive that her life was in danger on several occasions. Customary announcements were made, without any success, to try to discern the whereabouts of Droz. In its sentence the consistory proclaimed, "considering the malicious desertion of Abram Droz dit Busset, the cruel and violent treatment which he used toward his wife, making several attempts on her life," Madelaine was to be divorced from

---

53. Archives de l'Etat de Genève, Registres du Consistoire de Genève, 1: 51v–52; Registres du Conseil, 36: 99v.

Abram and could remarry nine months after the opening of the trial, that is, seven and a half months after this judgment.[54] This decision can be said to be progressive in two respects: the deserted spouse was not required to wait seven years before filing for divorce, and cruelty was for the first time a factor in awarding a divorce in early modern Valangin. As we see in Chapter 5, cruelty as well as incompatibility were much more important in divorce proceedings in the following century.

Closely related to divorce was a solution to conjugal disputes which first appeared in Neuchâtel in the early eighteenth century: the separation of body and property.[55] The first such separation in Valangin took place in 1705 when Jean Perret dit Barba requested that the court force his wife, Marie, to return to the household. Marie claimed that she had left him—as everybody, including members of the consistory, knew—because when "the vapors would invade his brain" Jean became frenetic and furious, making it exceedingly dangerous to live with him. Furthermore, her husband was so avaricious that he denied her not only the provisions necessary for life but often even the shelter of their home, obliging her to seek refuge elsewhere during the night. As a result of this cruel behavior, she requested a separation of property and domicile. Responding to this action, the consistory declared that, in consideration of Jean's notorious, incurable physical and mental infirmities and of the futility of the previous exhortations to lead a better life together, the couple was to receive a separation of bed and table for a period of three years. During this time, the two were to attempt to rekindle the warmth that a husband and wife were supposed to have for one another.[56] This form of separation was to become quite common during the next hundred years.

54. AEN, CSV4: 25. Women often had to wait longer than men before remarrying after a divorce. For example, when Jaques Sagne received a divorce on the ground of desertion—his wife had left him and gone to Burgundy, where she converted to Catholicism—he was required to wait only six weeks before remarrying; CSV5: 38. This longer waiting period for women reveals a fear of granting divorces to those guilty of adultery; women were ordinarily required to wait a period of several months to make sure that they were not pregnant at the time they received the divorce.

55. The consistory of Valangin had awarded a separation in 1587 to a man whose wife was violently insane. In that case, however, the plaintiff did not petition for a separation but merely requested advice. Inasmuch as the wife's son-in-law agreed to take her in and oversee her care, the judges allowed her to leave her husband and live with her daughter and son-in-law. This separation is distinct from later ones in that the plaintiff was not actively seeking a separation but rather merely asking for directions on what he should do to cope with his wife's insanity; AEN, CSV2: 306–307.

56. AEN, JMV2: 21–24.

The introduction of the legal separation, commonly referred to as the separation of body and property (*séparation de corps et de biens*), was both a precedent for future litigation and a throwback to past judicial practices. Today it may seem a matter of common sense to allow a separation from a violent spouse. But this sort of separation also strikingly resembles the *divortium ad torum et mensam* of the Middle Ages, a Catholic tradition that reformers vigorously criticized since they believed that most people were unable to pass long stretches of time in abstinence. Had they been alive in the early eighteenth century, Calvin and Farel would have disapproved of this decision; Calvin after all had been the most prominent member of the Genevan consistory that ordered a woman to obey her husband even though he had brutally put out one of her eyes. In the absence of sufficient grounds for divorce, Calvin and other reformers would have ordered the couple to remain together. Be that as it may, the introduction of the separation of body and property should be viewed as a logical step in the evolution of divorce. If originally divorces were granted in Neuchâtel primarily for adultery and desertion, a fundamental change in mentality was needed before cruelty and incompatibility could also be considered grounds for divorce. Before marriages could be terminated for such reasons, it is not surprising that the consistories first awarded temporary separations, distinct from the earlier *divortia*, which were normally for an indefinite term. Whereas sixteenth-century reformers had not been capable of accepting such separations, eighteenth-century judges, faced with the practical exigencies of married persons, were willing to introduce these separations in cases of violent cruelty that endangered life.[57]

In general, the evidence on divorce in sixteenth- and seventeenth-century Neuchâtel indicates that this was a society in which married couples stayed together. In a principality whose population peaked at about 28,000 during this period, records show fewer than a hundred marriages ending in divorce during one and a half centuries. Even when we consider the lacunae in the records, the fact remains that divorce was quite rare, just as judicial separations had been infrequent in late medieval Europe.[58] Though, to be sure, divorce and subsequent remarriage

57. In early modern England, the most common ground for judicial separation was cruelty, a motive alleged by women only (the only other possible ground was adultery). But, as Martin Ingram notes, " since in common law a husband had the right to beat his spouse, the church courts had perforce to interpret cruelty in a strict sense; and plaintiffs normally claimed that they had suffered abuse sufficient to endanger their well-being or even their life"; *Church Courts, Sex, and Marriage*, pp. 181–183.

58. Nicholas, *Domestic Life*, pp. 34–37; Phillips, *Putting Asunder*, pp. 13–14.

were important innovations, they did not immediately provoke a revolution in the institution of marriage or upset domestic stability. The judges of the consistories were willing to award divorces only on certain grounds, primarily adultery and the prolonged absence of a spouse. During the first century and a half of the Protestant courts' existence, suits filed on the grounds of adultery and desertion together accounted for about 76 percent of all such legal actions.[59] Of the 93 divorces actually granted during the years 1547–1706, 79 (85 percent) were awarded because of the infidelity or absence of a spouse.

Perhaps the most surprising revelation of the court records is the high success rate of plaintiffs seeking divorces. In light of the fact that the ordinances themselves had emphasized that divorces were to be given only as a last resort, one would think that the courts would have rejected most suits. The success rate in divorce suits was low in sixteenth-century Zurich and Basel, for example: in Zurich from 1525 to 1531, only 28 of 80 plaintiffs received divorces, and Basel's Ehegericht granted 125 divorces in the 226 cases it heard for the period 1550–1592.[60] In Neuchâtel, in contrast, of those proceedings for which judgments were rendered, successful divorce claims outnumbered rejections 93 to 12. This could reflect a certain prudence among the early modern inhabitants to Neuchâtel—perhaps they initiated such actions only if they had genuine grounds to warrant such procedures. More likely, it represents an effective screening of plaintiffs: the parish consistories simply did not refer to the higher tribunals parties who lacked the recognized grounds for divorce. Undoubtedly, the 132 plaintiffs to divorce cases were not the only individuals in Neuchâtel who would have liked to dissolve their marriages. In spite of the introduction of divorce, the Reformation was a time when married couples could generally expect to stay together until separated by death.

POLICE ACTIONS AGAINST MARRIED PERSONS

Other matrimonial disputes that involved spouses rather than fiancés were police actions in which the consistories convoked married people

59. If we include those who filed for divorce because their spouses were banished for crime under the general rubric of desertion and those suits based on bigamy under adultery, the proportion jumps to 82.5 percent.
60. Phillips, *Putting Asunder,* p. 92, n. 177; Safley, "To Preserve the Marital State: The Basler Ehegericht," *Journal of Family History* 7 (1982): 172–173.

to account for their poor domestic life. This genre of legal action is found almost exclusively in the registers of the consistories of Valangin and Gorgier. During the period 1547–1706, only once did Neuchâtel's Justice matrimoniale convoke a couple for domestic discord. In this same period, the consistories of Valangin and Gorgier took respectively 105 and 12 police actions against married persons—either couples or only one of the spouses—to admonish them to lead a more wholesome married life.

That police actions can be found often in the *procès verbaux* of the consistory of Valangin but almost never in those of the Justice matrimoniale of Neuchâtel reflects the fact that the consistory had jurisdiction over a much broader range of affairs than did the matrimonial court. Whereas the latter generally limited itself to divorce cases and disputes over promises of marriage, actions initiated by plaintiffs, the consistory, as the instrument to uphold the moral code espoused by reformers, often was itself the actor against subjects who violated matrimonial mores.

Among those whom the consistory targeted through its police actions were couples who had entered into marriage in a scandalous fashion. Seven times consistories convened couples for allegedly having fornicated before the wedding. In 1550, for example, Valangin's court convoked Huguenin Nicod and his wife, Henriette, on such charges. During the hearing, Huguenin confessed that earlier he had perceived that other men showed an interest in Henriette. To discourage them, he told them that she was his fiancée and intimated that they were having sexual relations. In court, however, Henriette and Huguenin swore by oath that they had not known each other carnally before the betrothal, though they had done so between the engagement and the wedding. For his mischievous words, Huguenin was condemned to five days in prison and ordered to do *réparation* at church. Henriette also had to do *réparation* for having consented to sexual relations before the wedding.[61] Falsely saying that one had sexual relations before the betrothal was deemed a greater sin than actually having them between the *fiançailles* and the wedding in church.

These actions against couples who had sex before the wedding demonstrate that moral misdemeanors were not to go unpunished. One might think that, even if a couple had fornicated before marriage, the act of getting married would have made the prior offense irrelevant.

61. AEN, CSV1: 41v–42v.

The consistory obviously viewed its objective as guiding people to follow the straight and narrow path toward righteousness. With this goal in mind, the judges considered it necessary that individuals atone for every moral transgression, even if they had since forsworn sinful ways. The prosecution of those who had initiated their marriage in scandal represented, however, a small minority of police actions against married people; and these seven couples were surely not the only Valanginois to have sexual relations before marriage during this century and a half. Contrary to what researchers have found for contemporary England, these actions did not increase along with the illegitimacy rate, nor did Neuchâtel's consistories increase the penalties against newlyweds who consummated their relationships before the wedding in order to deter premarital sex.[62]

More common were police actions against domestic misconduct. Throughout the sixteenth and seventeenth centuries, these efforts to maintain stability within the home were the only legal actions pertaining to marriage that were first and foremost for the benefit of women. Of the 118 total police actions, only 7 were taken against women alone, 52 against men, and 59 times the courts convoked both husband and wife (see Table 6). Frequently men were censured for dissipating the family's assets—often because they spent too much time and money in the taverns—and for their poor behavior toward their wives.

The records for Valangin indicate that police actions against delinquent husbands peaked in the late sixteenth and early seventeenth centuries. Only 11 men were convened individually from 1547–1588, whereas the consistory took action against 26 men for the years 1590–1618. In addition, though through the 1580s the consistory limited itself to merely exhorting delinquent husbands to treat their wives better, from 1590 on it often took more severe action against such offenders. Though the most common punishment remained verbal admonishments, seven times the court condemned men to prison terms of three or five days for mistreating or neglecting their wives or families, and one woman received such a prison sentence during the same three decades. On occasion, the consistory could even take more drastic measures, as seen in the case of David Tissot Robert, convened in 1604 for his "scandalous" dissipation of the assets of his wife and small children. Since he had already been censured without showing any improvement, the judges ordered that he be imprisoned for three days and also im-

62. Levine and Wrightson, "Social Context of Illegitimacy," in *Bastardy and Its History*, ed. Laslett, Oosterveen, and Smith, p. 174.

TABLE 6

Police actions against married persons, 1547–1706

Action	Convoked			
	Wife	Husband	Both	Total
1547–1588				
Illegal separation	0	1	6	7
Domestic misconduct	0	9	6	15
Marriage initiated in scandal	0	1	3	4
	0	11	15	26
1590–1618				
Illegal separation	1	1	2	4
Domestic misconduct	2	25	1	28
Marriage initiated in scandal	0	0	0	0
	3	26	3	32
1629–1706				
Illegal separation	4	6	21	31
Domestic misconduct	0	7	19	26
Marriage initiated in scandal	0	2	4	6
	4	15	44	63
1547–1706				
Illegal separation	5	8	29	42
Domestic misconduct	2	41	26	69
Marriage initiated in scandal	0	3	4	7
	7	52	59	118

posed a form of ostracism on him: "On his dismissal from prison, it is to be made known that no one is to do business with him in any manner whatsoever, and tavern owners are not to serve him anything to drink or eat and anyone who does so will be punished."[63]

In a case involving Blaise Petterman of Le Locle in 1606, the consistory of Valangin indicated that it could also protect a woman from her in-laws. In this instance, Petterman was cited for the second time for the harsh treatment he used toward his wife, so extreme that she was compelled to leave home and take refuge elsewhere. The consistory also censured him for flagrantly disobeying an order issued in 1598 to separate from his mother. The judges had given this order because his mother tormented her daughter-in-law, tearing hair from her head and committing other intolerable acts. After having been "exhorted in a Christian manner," Petterman again promised to separate from his mother and to

63. AEN, CSV3: 118.

live peacefully with his wife, showing her the treatment she deserved. The mother was to be imprisoned twenty-four hours for having cruelly beaten her daughter-in-law.[64] Valangin's tribunal made it clear that the conjugal bond was to take precedence over the maternal tie.

From the 1620s until the end of this period, the consistories directed police actions more against couples than individuals. For the years 1622–1706, the consistories made a total of 63 police actions, about two-thirds of which were made against couples. Some of these couples were convoked for the scandalous domestic lives they led together. In 1658, for example, Valangin's consistory summoned Abraham Hergaux and his wife to account for an unusual *ménage à trois*. The woman was censured for having consented to her husband's adulterous affair with Barbelie Mathie, evidently their servant. According to the accusation, this "abominable cohabitation" went so far as to see Hergaux sharing the same bed with his wife and his mistress. Madame Hergaux apologized for her wrong but claimed that she was at first unaware of this liaison and later chased Barbelie from their home. Having been admonished, Hergaux's wife was permitted to go free. Hergaux himself confessed to having committed adultery but claimed that Barbelie had instigated the affair. Regardless of who initiated this liaison, the court ordered that Hergaux and Barbelie be punished according to the ordinances, forbidding them to see each other.[65]

More common, however, were police actions against couples who were illegally separated, an offense that was prosecuted much more frequently after 1622. Normally couples so separated were summarily exhorted to live in harmony and ordered to return together with threats of imprisonment if they failed to do so. In 1691, for example, the consistory convoked Isaac Bornel and his wife because of their unauthorized separation of three years. Although the wife complained that Bornel had badly mistreated her and had even wanted to kill her, they were ordered to reunite or be subject to prison sentences.[66]

When the consistory summoned a separated couple, occasionally one of the parties had a specific complaint which the judges ordered the other to remedy. When in December 1692 Isaac Bornel and his wife again appeared before the consistory for still being separated, Bornel claimed that he wanted his wife to return to his household. She,

64. Ibid., 145.
65. AEN, CSV5: 55.
66. AEN, CSV6: 159.

however, complained that his house had nothing but the four walls and feared that she and her child might freeze to death. Heeding this grievance, the justices ordered Bornel to "cover" his house by the following Easter or face imprisonment.[67] The consistories willingly ordered people to take measures to ensure the well-being and health of their spouses.

Still, the consistories were not always sympathetic to couples who maintained that their separation was for reasons of health, as the case of Jean and Marie Perret dit Barbe aptly illustrates. When they were convoked in 1700 for illegal separation, Jean explained that he was quite ill and regularly had "attacks"—evidently seizures—four or five times a day. According to Jean, Marie, who was not present at the hearing, was so stricken with fear to see him in such a state that she could no longer bear to live with him. As the judges were in the process of delivering the sentence, Jean, as if on cue, fell to the floor, the victim of yet another attack. The judges were not altogether convinced that this seizure was genuine and wrote a letter to his pastor, requesting that he investigate this alleged illness. Both Jean and Marie were forbidden to take the sacrament and ordered to reappear before the consistory during its next session if they failed to reunite.[68]

Equally amusing was the third appearance in court of Isaac Bornel and his wife, who had separated again. Though Bornel expressed anew his willingness to reunite, she complained that "it was impossible for her to live with him because of his foul odor and filth and his debauchery."[69] In response, the judges denied that her husband's poor personal hygiene justified her departure from the household. Accordingly, she was enjoined a third time to return to Bornel lest she be punished rigorously. The consistory admonished Bornel to pay more attention to his personal cleanliness, not to indulge in debauchery, and not to mistreat his wife. Even after this third appearance, their union was still something less than marital bliss: Bornel's wife appeared before the consistory in 1706, this time to ask for a divorce. The judges replied that she could not initiate such an action since her husband was not present and since they were not convened for matrimonial justice, but

---

67. Ibid., 166.

68. Their marital problems did not end here. Two and a half years later, the consistory again summoned them for living separately. Because of this repeated offense, Jean Perret was fined 20 livres. The consistory further declared that if this scandalous behavior persisted they would be vigorously punished and the guilty party imprisoned; ibid., 275–276, 316–317.

69. AEN, CSV7: 6v.

rather for the ordinary responsibilities of the consistory.[70] This is the last recorded mention of the Bornels.

As the Bornel case indicates, the consistories did not have overwhelming success in combatting illegal separations. Some couples apparently paid little attention to orders to reunite. Though the tribunals of this period introduced the separation of body and property, the judges for the most part remained dedicated to the idea that married couples were to live together. The evidence from police actions and divorce litigation shows that seventeenth-century judges remained quite strict in requiring couples to stay together after the consecration of the marriage, even though they were becoming more flexible in dealing with fiancés. If they did not always succeed in bringing couples back together, the consistories for the most part still ruled that, in the absence of infidelity, sexual dysfunction, or desertion, married couples were expected to live under the same roof.

Like the consistories' police actions, other miscellaneous cases show concern for couples who separated illegally. In 1700, Valangin's consistory wrote a letter to a certain pastor because there were four married couples in his parish who were no longer living together. The judges sought to probe the pastor for further information about these unauthorized separations.[71] A few years earlier, in 1696, another pastor wrote the members to ask "advice concerning notaries who, through the acts which they receive, favor voluntary divorces and separations of body and property." In response to this letter, the mayor of Valangin was to ask the governor to take action against these notaries.[72] This correspondence shows the conservative nature of the consistory, which obstinately refused to part with tradition on the question of separations. Faced with popular pressure to allow separations or even divorces on the ground of incompatibility, the consistory consistently resisted such measures throughout the seventeenth century. Those avant-garde notaries who favored so-called voluntary divorces—evidently, divorces by mutual consent—anticipated an idea that would later become axiomatic in most Western countries: the right to divorce based on nothing other than incompatibility. There was, in short, a gap between the values of the justices and those of the population at large. Describing the relationship between church courts and popular values in sixteenth- and

70 Ibid., 24v–25. In 1700 the consistory instituted special sessions devoted exclusively to matrimonial justice.

71. AEN, CSV6: 278.

72. Ibid., 227.

seventeenth-century England, Martin Ingram says this: "In offering only limited grounds for separation and annulment, and in pursing at least the more 'offensive' cases of unlawful separation, the church courts were simply reinforcing these features of early modern English society in a way which most people regarded perfectly acceptable."[73] The same cannot be said for Neuchâtel's courts. Faced with changing popular values, the consistories significantly modified their stance only in the late eighteenth century.

WOMEN AND SENTIMENT IN MARRIAGE

The evidence from Neuchâtel's divorce litigation and police actions can shed light on currently debated topics such as the status of women and the affective ties between spouses in early modern Europe. The introduction of divorce can be said to have benefited women in a limited manner. Women were able to separate from adulterous husbands and remarry. But how great a gain was this? As we have seen, adultery as a ground for divorce was used much more frequently against women than by them. Wives divorced for adultery could be subject to severe financial penalties, at times forfeiting all their property to their husbands. The mere fact that suits against adulterous husbands were so rare shows that women rarely viewed divorce as a viable means of escaping an unhappy marriage. From 1547 to 1706, only 9 women in Valangin filed for divorce against adulterous husbands, while during the same period 88 men were convicted of adultery. Not an unusual phenomenon for the early modern period, this gap between the number of adulterers and the number of divorces based on adultery could have meant that most women did not care if their husbands were faithful, accepting their extramarital affairs with a nonchalant shrug of the shoulder.[74] Indeed, on the basis of his research on early modern Somerset, G. R. Quaife argues that peasants were largely amoral with regard to extramarital sex, showing indifference toward the affairs of both husbands and wives as long

73. Ingram, *Church Courts, Sex, and Marriage*, p. 188.
74. A similar discrepancy between the number of adulterers and the number of divorces based on adultery can be found in seventeenth-century Massachusetts, for example: 81 men and 66 women were convicted of adultery, but only 11 women and 4 men received divorces for adultery. In Connecticut of the same period, 56 men and women were condemned for adultery, but courts awarded only 12 divorces for infidelity; Phillips, *Putting Asunder,* p. 147, citing Lyle S. Koehler, *A Search For Power: The "Weaker Sex" in Seventeenth-Century New England* (Urbana, Ill., 1980), pp. 149, 453–458.

as they did not disrupt the peace of the community or cause economic burdens, as when poor people produced bastards.[75] Or perhaps this gap between the number of adulterers and the frequency of divorce suits against them is a reflection of very forgiving wives; though hurt and dismayed by their husbands' foibles, they forgave them in order to save their marriages. Or perhaps they feared the economic consequences that might result if they suddenly found themselves without a male head of the household. In support of this last hypothesis, it is important to note that rarely do the registers indicate how the divorced woman was to be supported henceforth. The silence of most cases on the question of financial settlements accompanying divorces provides a clue that there may have been strong economic incentives to remain married. Most likely, the majority of women could not afford to separate from their husbands.

A theory stressing the importance of economic concerns fits comfortably with the fact that abandonment was the most common ground for divorce cited by women. Most often these women complained that their husbands had left them with no financial support. If their husbands had left behind little or no property, clearly there were no economic interests to discourage divorces. Their sole financial hope was to remarry. And this is one way women clearly did make some social progress. Though canon law had set precedents for allowing abandoned spouses to remarry, Catholic courts did not grant such dissolutions systematically and were increasingly reluctant to do so in the sixteenth century. [76] In Neuchâtel abandoned women were no longer forced to wait indefinitely for the return of husbands who had deserted them. But the price to be paid was quite high: they were to wait patiently and live honestly and chastely for seven years. If they led irreproachable lives during this time, then and only then were they entitled to divorces and the right to remarry. At the very least, then, we can say that abandoned women who remained faithful during their husbands' absence benefited from the

75. Quaife, *Wanton Wenches*, pp. 124–142, 179, 247. Few scholars have supported Quaife's views. Ingram accuses Quaife of using impressionistic evidence, paying too much attention to the most sensational cases, and erroneously assuming that the libido could not have been "contained within the patterns of late marriages"; *Church Courts, Sex, and Marriage*, pp. 159–160.

76. Natalie Davis maintains that, like canon law, the civil law tradition that prevailed in southern France and elsewhere forbade an abandoned spouse to remarry barring proof of the other's death. In judging a case in 1557, the Parlement of Toulouse stated: "During the absence of the husband, the wife cannot remarry unless she has proof of his death . . . not even when he has been absent twenty years or more. . . . And the death must be proven by witnesses, who give sure depositions, or by great and manifest presumptions"; *Martin Guerre*, pp. 33–34, citing Bernard de La Roche-Flavin, *Arrests notables du Parlement de Tolose* (Lyon, 1619), pp. 601–602.

conversion to Protestantism. Those who did not remain celibate during these seven years, however, ran the risk of being sued for divorce on the basis of adultery when their husbands returned and of losing all their assets to their cuckolded spouses.

The most obvious indication that the introduction of divorce brought only limited social gains to women is the fact that cruelty was not recognized as a ground for divorce. The evidence from police actions indicates that there were plenty of cruel husbands at this time, yet not once did the courts deign to hear a divorce suit based on cruelty. We have seen cases in which women simply left their husbands to avoid their misbehavior. But if there were no other possible charges—such as infidelity or impotence—the woman was left with no valid basis for a divorce and was ordered to return to her husband.

That cruelty did not suffice for a divorce is no surprise in that the reformers, with the exception of Martin Bucer, generally ignored the question of cruelty in their divorce doctrines. Moreover, Protestant reformers accepted the inferiority of women, recognized the duty of women to obey their husbands, and tolerated the corporal punishment of wives if used in moderation. Notwithstanding his overall opposition to the *divortium quoad torum et mensam*, Luther favored separation rather than divorce in cases of cruelty. And Calvin went so far as to say that a Protestant wife must not leave her physically abusive Catholic husband unless her life was actually in danger.[77] To be sure, as Roderick Phillips observes, "discord and violence within marriage were deplored, and attempts were made to correct them, but their presence did not affect the essence of matrimony as it was understood by the Reformers. The existence of adultery and, less unambiguously, desertion, did affect marriage significantly. Hence their status as grounds for divorce in Protestant doctrines."[78] Unlike cruelty, adultery justified divorce because Protestants continued to identify the ends of marriage with sexuality—that is, with procreation and the quenching of the sexual impulse through monogamous intercourse.[79] Consequently, while Protestants in such diverse areas as Scotland, Languedoc, Switzerland, and free imperial cities generally permitted divorce for adultery

77. Phillips, *Putting Asunder*, p. 55, citing Charmarie Jenkins Blaisdell, "Calvin's Letters to Women: The Courting of Ladies in High Places," *Sixteenth Century Journal* 13 (1982): 71; see also Brundage, *Law, Sex, and Christian Society*, p. 559.
78. Phillips, *Putting Asunder*, p. 90.
79. Ibid., pp. 87, 89–90. The marriage court in Reformation Ausburg did hear five divorce cases based on cruelty, though none of these requests was granted; Roper, *Holy Household*, p. 188.

and desertion, rarely did anyone grant divorces for cruelty.[80] In this regard, Neuchâtel was typical of states that converted to Protestantism.

Records show that during the first 150 years of the tribunals' hearings, only 53 women received divorces—most for reasons of desertion or adultery—indicating that the introduction of divorce in Neuchâtel did not provide an important safety valve for women who sought to escape miserable marriages. Only at the end of this period do we begin to see the glimmerings of important social change; as a result no doubt of changes in personnel, by the early eighteenth century the consistory was ready to allow couples to separate in order to avoid chronic and sometimes violent incompatibility. In introducing the separation of body and property and accepting cruelty as a possible motive for divorce, the consistory was taking a significant step in the history of divorce in Neuchâtel. Women were to take advantage of these changes much more frequently than men, since husbands more often abused wives than vice versa. From 1547 to 1706, however, the number of women who benefited from these innovations could be counted on one hand. The manner in which the consistory treated these particular women's cases was important because it set precedents that anticipated future trends in marital disputes. It did not alter radically the institution of marriage at this time; rather, it was the blossom of social change that reached full fruition only later in the eighteenth century.

Consistorial records demonstrate, however, that, even if women could not dissolve marriages on the basis of cruelty, they nevertheless could find sympathy and protection among the judges of the consistory. Through its police actions, the consistory convoked married men who frequented the taverns too often, dissipated the family fortune, or badly mistreated their wives. The judges censured this behavior, warned the men to forswear their decadent ways, and inflicted punishments that ran the gamut from public *réparation* to ostracism. In short, the police actions of the consistory undeniably show that a woman's welfare did not depend solely on the whims of her husband. No doubt similar protection had not been unknown when Neuchâtel was still Catholic. It is unlikely that in Catholic Neuchâtel women could receive no comfort vis-à-vis brutal husbands. But the support priests may have shown

80. Mentzer, "Church Discipline," p. 10; Monter, "Women in Calvinist Geneva," p. 195; Phillips, *Putting Asunder*, p. 61; Roper, *Holy Household*, p. 167. Safley found that in sixteenth-century Basel physical abuse was cited in 19 divorce cases. Among those examples he provides, however, the Ehegericht awarded divorces only when abuse was accompanied by adultery; *Let No Man Put Asunder*, pp. 137–139, 142. My guess is that infidelity was more important than abuse in such decisions.

through the confession box—so important for medieval women, in Stone's view—most likely did not measure up to the protection the consistory later provided. Just as the city council and discipline courts of Reformation Augsburg greatly facilitated prosecuting violent husbands,[81] so Neuchâtel's consistories offered a greater degree of protection to women.

All told, the evidence from matrimonial litigation on the impact of the Reformation on women is mixed. One cannot say unequivocally that the status of women was either exalted or degraded with the conversion to the new faith. At best can we discern a small step forward; at worst, a limited setback. In considering the effects of the Reformation on women in Neuchâtel, it is prudent to follow the advice of Diane Willen: "It is futile to debate whether the legacy of the Reformation was a negative or positive influence in the lives of these women. The religious changes of the sixteenth century were linked to a variety of intellectual, social, political, and economic forces, each complex, ambiguous, even contradictory. They affected individual lives in a variety of ways that transcend any single, simple set of criteria."[82]

We have already seen that in choosing spouses men and women of Reformation Neuchâtel paid much more attention to status and wealth than to affective ties.[83] Unfortunately, little information can be gleaned from the court records to determine how sixteenth- and seventeenth-century couples normally felt toward each other after the wedding. Ordinarily, only those married couples who had problems appeared before consistories. How can these show what typical marriages were like? The

---

81. Roper, *Holy Household*, p. 191.

82 Willen, "Women and Religion," in *Women in Reformation Europe*, ed. Marshall, p. 158.

83. Jean-Louis Flandrin notes that a high percentage of widows and widowers remarried within six months of a spouse's death in sixteenth- and seventeenth-century France. From this finding he concludes that at this time "affective unfeelingness" reigned in the "brutality of marital relationships"; *Families in Former Times*, pp. 115–116. Steven Ozment questions this reasoning, claiming that this phenomenon merely reflects that the companionship of marriage was held in high regard; *When Fathers Ruled*, pp. 229–230, n. 125. I agree that it is an exaggeration to speak of the "brutality of marital relationships." I am not sure, however, that people quickly remarried because the companionship of marriage was highly regarded. Often it seemed that a woman sought to remarry because she needed the financial support of a husband. Similarly, men often petitioned to remarry in order to have someone to look after the household chores. For example, in 1599 Guillaume Jecquier petitioned to remarry after his wife fled following an accusation of witchcraft. The reason he gave for initiating this action was not that he needed the emotional support only a wife could provide but rather that he was burdened with four small children. In this case and others, the primary motivating factors in seeking to remarry were the practical demands of managing a household; AEN, JMN2: 197r–v.

records of police actions can show what excesses were to be avoided in marriages, but the consistories sought only to maintain order. Mere domestic tranquility and absence of serious discord do not necessarily indicate that couples had genuine feelings of affection for each other.

Nevertheless, the records do occasionally provide glimpses of the feelings married men and women shared. In 1665, for example, Estienne Breguet, a deacon of the church at Le Locle, allegedly tried to rape a married woman and was caught in the act by the woman's husband. The jealousy the husband, Jacques Vuillemin, showed this would-be rapist was not the reaction of a man indifferent to his wife. According to Madame Vuillemin, she was working in the garden when Breguet came and asked for some wine. She went upstairs to fetch some, and when she returned,

> he took her by force and threw her on a bed to rape her, holding her hands with one of his own and putting his elbow on her stomach which caused her considerable pain. He pulled up her skirt and forced her thighs apart with his knees. . . . She screamed for help, "You bad man! Is this how you want to treat me! God help me! You're disgusting—instead of correcting others, you try to rape me!" Just when she could no longer defend herself, her husband arrived and grabbed Breguet by the hair and beat him severely, screaming, "You bastard! Bad man! So you think it's okay to rape my wife! You're not worthy of being a minister! You should be arrested!" Whereupon Breguet fell to his knees and begged the husband for mercy. Going downstairs with [Breguet], [Vuillemin] took a hatchet and would have bashed his head in had [his wife] and his servant not held him back. Even so, [Breguet] was slightly wounded by a blow to the hand.[84]

Although it is understandable for a man to react with force to defend his wife against a rapist, Vuillemin's reaction was that of an extremely

84. AEN, CSV6: 5. Vuillemin reported roughly the same story, adding that Breguet threw him a *louis d'or* to bribe him to keep quiet. He further added that later Breguet's two brothers also tried to bribe him not to tell anyone about this incident. Breguet, however, entirely denied these charges, claiming that it was she who had invited him to drink a glass of wine. Later, her husband found them in the room upstairs together and accused him of misbehavior. Since this case involved a serious crime over which the consistory had no jurisdiction, the judges referred it to the governor; ibid., 4–7. This case shows that there was clearly a legal difference between rape and simple fornication, a distinction that had not always been made in medieval Europe. Parenthetically, deacons were not supposed to "correct others"; that, rather, was the responsibility of elders. Deacons, as defined by Calvin in his *Institutes* (4.3. 9), were more akin to social workers; their duties were to care for the poor and sick and to administer alms; *The Oxford Dictionary of the Christian Church*, 2d ed., s.v. "Deacon."

jealous husband. Attempting to kill the would-be rapist with a hatchet was a rather drastic response. It has been argued that such jealousy is understandable only if a man was particularly fond of his wife. David Nicholas presents such a view, observing that when a woman was attacked or her reputation impugned in late medieval Europe her husband often beat the offender, reflecting the importance of marital affection and the conviction that the wife must be defended.[85] According to this line of reasoning, if their marriage were nothing more than a pragmatic relationship for mutual domestic advantages, Vuillemin's response would have been less dramatic.

Vuillemin's violent reaction could certainly have been motivated more by the affront to his honor than by feelings for his wife. In early modern Europe, "cuckold" was the worst insult a man could suffer; it caused most of the defamation suits brought by men before church courts in England. Moreover, it was the cuckolded husband, not the unfaithful wife, who was the victim of charivaris, public acts of humiliation that were part of early modern popular culture. These rowdy events, perpetrated by young unmarried men in rural areas, were, according to Natalie Zemon Davis, "in the service of the community, dramatizing the differences between different stages of life, clarifying the responsibilities that the youth would have when they were married men and fathers, helping to maintain proper order within marriage and to sustain the biological continuity of the village."[86] It was a man's responsibility to ensure that his wife remained faithful, and failing to do so impugned his reputation and his virility. Regardless of whether Vuillemin reacted to the attempted rape as a threat to his masculinity or an attack on the one he loved, his response was in marked contrast to the supposed indifference husbands had toward their wives' infidelity in other regions of seventeenth-century Europe.

In spite of the paucity of evidence concerning affection between husbands and wives, I imagine that sentiment appeared in marriages in Neuchâtel much as it did, according to Edmund Morgan, among New England Puritans: love was more the product than the cause of marriage.[87] Though the court records do not indicate that romantic love was important in forming marriages, it is nevertheless possible, even

85. Nicholas, *Domestic Life*, p. 34.
86. Davis, "The Reasons of Misrule," in *Society and Culture in Early Modern Europe*, pp. 100, 107; Gillis, *For Better, for Worse*, p. 79.
87. Morgan, *The Puritan Family: Religion and Domestic Relations in Seventeenth-Century New England* (New York, 1966), pp. 47–55.

probable, that genuine if not passionate love developed after marriage. The companionship found in sharing the same household, in working and having children together, may well have nurtured feelings of love between spouses. But such love developed from relationships that were more often than not formed for the practical mutual benefits married life provided, not because the man and woman were madly in love.

PART II

THE PRUSSIAN ERA

4

The Formation of Marriage, 1707–1806

POLITICAL, ECONOMIC, AND
DEMOGRAPHIC CHANGES

The principality of Neuchâtel and Valangin underwent a significant political change as the direct line of the Orléans-Longueville dynasty came to an end in 1707, and Neuchâtel's magistrates prudently proceeded to find a successor. Louis XIV pressured his tiny neighbor to recognize as its sovereign one of several French candidates, who were in fact the closest relatives to the defunct Longuevilles. Wary of the influence of the Sun King, members of the Tribunal des Trois Etats proved themselves unusually independent in this age of absolutism, conferring the sovereignty of the principality on the king of Prussia 3 November 1707. Even though other candidates had more convincing dynastic claims, members of the house of Hohenzollern were to remain the official sovereigns of Neuchâtel until they ceded the principality to Napoleon in 1806.

Although theoretically under the suzerainty of Prussia, Neuchâtel enjoyed considerable independence; separated from this small principality by hundreds of miles, Prussian monarchs paid little attention to Neuchâtel and generally allowed it to govern itself. The Prussians had to pledge to uphold the customary rights of Neuchâtelois and introduced only a few minor changes in local legal practices—most notably in abolishing the oath on the *petit lit* and public *réparation*.[1] At no point during these one hundred years did a Prussian king even set foot in Neuchâtel.[2] As before, the prince was represented by a governor, usually appointed for life, who was the only official who did not have to be a native of the county. Defending the interests of the monarch, the governor continued to preside over the Conseil d'Etat and the Tribunal des Trois Etats and served as commander of the county's militia. The governor also had the power to grant pardons and direct judicial pursuits. In practice, however, he shared these various powers with the Conseil d'Etat, which at times prevailed over him and could meet and make decisions without him.[3]

The year 1707 also marked a turning point in the religious life of Neuchâtel. Like the residents of Neuchâtel, the Prussians were of the Reformed faith. Heretofore the ruling sovereigns of Neuchâtel had virtually all remained Catholic even though the vast majority of their subjects were Protestant. Moreover, the city of Neuchâtel, unlike Bern, was not powerful enough to subordinate the church, meaning that Neuchâtel would not have a state church or a form of cesaro-papalism similar to Bern's. This situation had nurtured a certain separation of church and state which in turn allowed the development of independent ecclesiastical institutions, leaving the Classe des Pasteurs as the supreme authority of the Reformed church in Neuchâtel. With the arrival of the Reformed Prussians, however, the Classe des Pasteurs began to see its power whittled away by the state, a trend that culminated in 1848 when the state abolished the Classe and established a democratic church structure.[4]

The eighteenth century was also a vitally important period for the economic and demographic expansion of the principality. Hitherto Neuchâtel had remained firmly tied to a simple peasant economy, based primarily on agriculture and wine production. Now the principality, like many other parts of eighteenth-century Europe, experienced

1. The governor, acting in the name of the prince, had to pledge publicly "that His Majesty will preserve for all subjects according to their quality and condition, their franchises, liberties, and constitutions along with their good ancient customs, both written and unwritten"; AEN, Pledge of le Gouverneur de Béville, in the name of Frederick William II, to the community of Saint-Blaise.

2. The first Prussian monarch to visit Neuchâtel was Frederic William III in 1814, after the principality was restored to the house of Prussia following the fall of Napoleon; Favarger, "L'élaboration des lois," p. 186.

3. Henry, *Crime, justice et société*, p. 51.

4. François Clerc, "Survivance et transformation des institutions canoniques après la Réforme dans le pays de Neuchâtel," *Mémoires de la Société pour l'histoire du droit et des institutions des anciens pays bourguignons* 24 (1963): 308.

the growth of protoindustrial activities.[5] According to Hans Medick, protoindustry, like the peasant economy, was based on the family economy, since the household often remained the unit of production. Nonetheless, households engaged in protoindustry differed in important ways from those of peasants. Peasants remained firmly tied to the rules and regulations of the village community, with family property directing the social processes of peasant societies "in such a way that the distribution and redistribution of resources remained tied to the nexus given by the family cycle, by kinship relations, as well as by marriage and inheritance strategies." Family controls were closely intertwined with the controls established by manorial customs. In protoindustry, however, people went outside the traditional influences of family and manorial custom. The peasant household aimed mainly at subsistence, but the protoindustrial household, though tied to the traditional structure of family economy, saw its production and consumption determined by the market.[6] As a result of various forms of protoindustrial activities, increasingly many people became involved in wage labor, their wealth being in wages rather than land.

In the eighteenth century, many Neuchâtelois found employment in various forms of cottage industry, activities in which people worked at home to manufacture products for the market. The watchmaking industry, a trade that has remained important to the region's economy to the present day, was one form of production that often took place in the home; it first appeared in the communities of Neuchâtel and La Chaux-de-Fonds in the late seventeenth century. The most dramatic economic changes, however, took place in the second half of the eighteenth century as increasing numbers of people were involved in wage labor. After 1750 there was considerable growth in lacemaking, a form of cottage industry which had existed in Neuchâtel since the early seventeenth century but which received a real boost with the arrival of Huguenot refugees after the revocation of the Edict of Nantes in 1685.[7]

5. According to Peter Kriedte, protoindustry, which preceded industrialization, is "the development of rural regions in which a large part of the population lived entirely or to a considerable extent from industrial mass production for interregional and international markets"; Kriedte, Medick, and Schlumbohm, *Industrialization before Industrialization*, p. 6.
6. Medick, "Proto-Industrial Family Economy," in ibid., pp. 38–41. See also Kriedte, *Peasants, Landlords, and Merchant Capitalists*, p. 137.
7. Sylvia Robert, "L'industrie dentellière dans les Montagnes neuchâteloises aux XVIIIe et XIXe siècles; La comptabilité d'un négociant en dentelles de Couvet: Le major Daniel-Henri Dubied," *Musée neuchâtelois*, 1988, 70; Jean-Marc Barrelet, ed., "La situation économique dans les Montagnes neuchâteloises vers 1836: Un document inédit d'Henri Houriet, du Locle," *Musée neuchâtelois*, 1987, 239. Studying the principality's census of 1750, Béatrice

Protoindustrial production took place not only in the homes of eighteenth-century Neuchâtelois but also in workshops. Though more people worked at home through the putting-out system, the development of workshops nevertheless marked the beginning of the end of the household as a productive unit.[8] Workshops were established for watchmaking and for the production of a new product: *indiennes,* cotton fabrics printed with colorful floral designs made by pressing cloth between engraved blocks of wood. The manufacture of *indiennes,* so called because they were inspired by cotton products of India, was the one area of the textile industry in which continental Europe outproduced England during the Industrial Revolution. The manufacture of cotton fabrics, which had been rather insignificant in Europe until the second half of the eighteenth century, became particularly important in England, but it also flourished in Saxony, Catalonia, and parts of France and Switzerland, employing more than 100,000 people throughout Europe by the end of the century. While the English were mass producing inexpensive textiles, continental Europeans were making luxury fabrics; *indiennes* were expensive cotton products that replaced silks, linens, and batistes in the homes of eighteenth-century high society. Thanks in part to Huguenot entrepreneurs seeking refuge, the principality of Neuchâtel became one of the most important centers for the printed-cloth industry in Europe. In 1761, there were twenty-one workshops for the production of *indiennes* in all of France, seven in Geneva, fifteen in Mulhouse, and nine in Neuchâtel.[9] In fact, all three of Neuchâtel's major protoindustrial activities—watchmaking, lacemaking, and the printed-cloth industry—involved luxury goods. Very labor intensive, these forms of production opened up new opportunities to inhabitants of a region poor in natural resources, initiating the move away from a predominantly rural subsistence economy in Neuchâtel.

As may be expected, these economic developments affected different villages in different ways. The changes were most dramatic in the

Miéville-Sorgesa observes that in the town of Le Locle almost all females over the age of five or six as well as many boys were employed in lacemaking; "Premier recensement de la population neuchâteloise (1750) ou 'Denombrement des peuples, des pauvres et autres,'" *Musée neuchâtelois,* 1988, 195–208.

8. Kriedte also found that, though centralized enterprises (*Manufakturen*) existed in early modern Europe, especially for preparatory and finishing-work processes, more people worked in the putting-out system than in workshops; *Peasants, Landlords, and Merchant Capitalists,* p. 139.

9. Ibid., pp. 132, 140; Pierre Chaunu, *La civilisation de l'Europe classique* (Paris, 1966), p. 340.

mountains, where previously inhabitants had often been forced to go elsewhere to find seasonal work; forms of cottage industry obviated such seasonal emigration, bringing general prosperity to the region.[10] Dombresson, Savagnier, and Les Lignières all remained almost exclusively agricultural throughout the eighteenth century. In contrast, from the beginning of the century Le Locle was a center of the watchmaking industry, and Travers and Noiraigue developed watchmaking and especially lacemaking industries. Boudry, Bevaix, and Cortaillod were three communities that after 1760 had large proportions of their populations involved in the manufacture of *indiennes*.[11] Cortaillod exemplified the magnitude of the rapid demographic changes that accompanied the growth in wage labor and protoindustrialization. In 1750 this village numbered 600 inhabitants, the vast majority of whom were farmers; only 69 persons were employed in the production of printed cloth. In 1752, Claude-Abram Dupasquier founded the Fabrique-Neuve, which quickly became one of the most important producers of *indiennes* in all Europe. This factory boasted 110 workers in 1754, 203 in 1759, 455 in 1765; after that time, the number of its employees oscillated from 400 to 700 until 1820.[12]

Contemporaneous to these changes in employment patterns was a considerable expansion in the population of the principality. In 1780, less than thirty years after the founding of the Fabrique-Neuve, 905 people dwelled in Cortaillod—an increase of 50 percent in three decades. By the end of the century, the population had jumped to 1,000.[13] Population figures indicate an equally impressive increase for the county as a whole. The population of the principality of Neuchâtel and Valangin has been estimated at roughly 28,600 in 1712, and it had probably remained more or less stagnant since the middle of the previous century. By contrast, the county numbered 32,300 souls in 1752 and 48,700 at the time of the cession to Napoleon.[14]

Placed in a broader context, Neuchâtel's demographic growth mirrors population trends for early modern Europe in general: steady

10. Courvoisier, *Panorama de l'histoire*, pp. 95–97; Henry, *Crime, justice et société*, p. 113; *Le Refuge Huguenot en Suisse* (Lausanne, 1985), pp. 161–184; Barrelet, "Situation économique dans les Montagnes," pp. 239–240.

11. In a similar manner, David Sabean has found that with the growth in wage labor entire villages became specialized in eighteenth-century Württemberg; *Power in the Blood*, p. 10.

12. Pierre Caspard, "Conceptions prénuptiales et développement du capitalisme dans la principauté de Neuchâtel (1678–1820)," *Annales: E.S.C.* 4 (1974): 991, n. 4; see also AEN, Fonds de la Fabrique-Neuve de Cortaillod (1754–1820).

13. Caspard, "Conceptions prénuptiales," pp. 990–993.

14. Henry, *Crime, justice et société*, pp. 92–102.

growth in the sixteenth century, stagnation in the seventeenth, and a demographic explosion in the eighteenth. Historians agree that the number of Europeans greatly increased after 1700: the population of some areas in Germany more than doubled and the number of Swedes increased by two-thirds during the course of the eighteenth century; for the same period, England's population grew by 70 to 80 percent, increasing by one-third in the last quarter of the century alone; and the French population grew by one-third from 1750 to 1800. Scholars have not reached a consensus, however, on what caused this population expansion. Pierre Guillaume and Jean-Pierre Poussou believe that this growth resulted from the decline in mortality, that is, the decline of plague, famine, and war in Europe during the years 1715–1789.[15] Other historians, most notably the English scholars E. A. Wrigley and R. S. Schofield, hold that England's population growth during the Industrial Revolution was due primarily to an increase in the birthrate. They argue that declining mortality was responsible for no more than one-fourth of the population increase and that, contrary to the views of Guillaume and Poussou, England's growth rate was considerably higher than any found in continental Europe. Pierre Chaunu also stresses increasing natality over declining mortality and observes throughout eighteenth-century Europe rising birthrates, decreasing intervals between births, and reductions in the age at marriage with a corresponding increase in the number of years of sexual activity among married couples.[16]

If indeed natality was greater in Europe, one may wonder what caused this growth. Could industrialization and protoindustrialization have been factors in the population expansion? Even Guillaume and Poussou acknowledge that the birthrate tended to be higher in industrialized areas than in agricultural regions. They deny, however, that the overall population increase was due to industrialization, claiming, for example, that the growth rate in agricultural Germany surpassed that of industrial England. In effect, these French scholars hold that industrialization could accelerate population expansion by expanding the horizons of work and stimulating immigration.[17]

15. Guillaume and Poussou, *Démographie historique* (Paris, 1970), pp. 118–120, 153–154.

16. Wrigley, "Marriage, Fertility, and Population Growth in Eighteenth Century England," in *Marriage and Society*, ed. Outhwaite, p. 171, and "The Growth of Population of Eighteenth-Century England: A Conundrum Resolved," *Past and Present* 98 (1983): 134, Wrigley and Schofield, *Population History of England, 1541–1871* (London, 1981); Chaunu, *Civilisation de l'Europe*, pp. 238–240; David Levine, *Reproducing Families: The Political Economy of English Population History* (Cambridge, 1987), p. 116.

17. Guillaume and Poussou, *Démographie historique*, p. 155.

Other historians go much farther, holding that economic changes altered family strategy in a way that stimulated population growth. Several have suggested that protoindustrial families tended to be larger than their peasant predecessors because people married younger. Even with no increase in life expectancy, earlier marriages meant longer marriages with more childbearing years; if large numbers of people followed this pattern, the population would likely increase. Hans Medick and David Levine argue that, whereas peasant marriages often had to be delayed until a couple had access to land, inherited property no longer determined family formation for those engaged in wage labor. With the decline in the importance of property, people enjoyed greater freedom from parental control in contracting marriages and had more opportunities to leave and form new households. Couples also had an incentive to have many children, since children were a source of labor. According to Medick, Levine, and others, protoindustrialization was thus in an important way responsible for the population increase in eighteenth-century Europe.[18]

Gay Gullickson, however, has shown that protoindustry affected different areas in different ways. She found that the Pays de Caux and the village of Auffay in Normandy did not undergo significant demographic changes for the period 1750–1850 even though a large percentage of the population was employed in the putting-out system as spinners and weavers of cotton cloth. On the basis of tax records, censuses, and other sources, Gullickson shows that late marriages remained the norm throughout this century. She suggests that the effects of protoindustrialization in the Pays de Caux differed from those in other areas because of a sexual division of labor.[19] Franklin Mendels (who

18. Levine, "Production, Reproduction, and the Proletarian Family in England, 1500–1851," in *Proletarianization and Family History*, ed. David Levine (Orlando, Fla., 1984), pp. 97–99, 109–110, "Proto-Industrialization and Demographic Upheaval," in *Essays on the Family and Historical Change*, ed. Leslie Page Moch and Gary D. Stark (College Station, Tex., 1983), p. 29, and *Reproducing Families*, pp. 121–122; Medick, "Proto-Industrial Family Economy," pp. 54–63; John R. Gillis, "Peasant, Plebeian, and Proletarian Marriage," in *Proletarianization and Family History*, pp. 138, 141, and *For Better, for Worse*, p. 119.

19. Gullickson found that from 1750 until the mechanization of spinning in the early nineteenth century the mean age at first marriage for the population as a whole was 28.9 for men and 26.0 for women. The mean ages for spinners and weavers were virtually identical to those for men and women—28.7 and 26.3, respectively. Gullickson does not, however, provide evidence for the age at marriage before protoindustry. She assumes that it was not much, if any, higher before 1750, since these mean marriage ages "are on the high side not only for Normandy but also for men and women throughout Western Europe in the eighteenth century"; *Spinners and Weavers of Auffay: Rural Industry and the Sexual Division of Labor in a French Village, 1750–1850* (Cambridge, 1986), p. 138.

coined the term "protoindustrialization"), Rudolf Braun, and Levine all studied cottage industries that evidently employed entire families: the linen industry in Flanders, the cotton industry in Zurich, and the knitting industry in Leicestershire. Medick has further argued that cottage industry effected the breakdown of the sexual division of labor, not only in protoindustrial activities but in all household tasks.[20] Gullickson found that in the Pays de Caux it was quite rare for entire families to be engaged in the putting-out system and that, whereas men worked as farmers, merchants, and artisans, it was primarily women—first as spinners, then as weavers—who were employed in protoindustry. This division of labor according to gender was the major factor behind late marriages: "Any tendency for full employment in cottage industry to lower female marriage ages could be and was offset by conditions and wages in the male occupations, which experienced few changes during the protoindustrial period." Had men as well as women been employed in large numbers in protoindustry, then the Pays de Caux might well have seen social and demographic changes similar to those found elsewhere.[21]

Neuchâtel's population increase can best be explained by a combination of factors. It no doubt is true that Neuchâtelois enjoyed greater longevity in the eighteenth century as a result of declines in plague and famine. There was also, however, a dramatic increase in the percentage of residents engaged in wage labor which clearly had a profound impact on Neuchâtel's population. In 1752 the principality had 464 people employed in watchmaking, 399 in the production of *indiennes*, and 2,793 in lacemaking. A half-century later, these figures had jumped to 3,939, 1,270, and 4,532, respectively. These latter figures, taken from an of-

20. Mendels, "Proto-Industrialization: The First Phase of Industrialization," *Journal of Economic History* 32 (1972): 241–261; Braun, *Industrialisation and Everyday Life;* Levine, *Family Formation,* pp. 127–145; Medick, "Proto-Industrial Family Economy," pp. 61–63.

21. Gullickson, *Spinners and Weavers,* pp. 108–109, 133, 139, 142–144; quotation from pp. 143–144. Others have cast doubt on the connection between protoindustry and changing marriage patterns. Myron Gutmann and René Leboutte show that in various Belgian protoindustrial villages the marriage age remained high and stable throughout the eighteenth and early nineteenth centuries; "Rethinking Protoindustrialization and the Family," *Journal of Interdisciplinary History* 14 (1984): 595. Similarly, James Lehning maintains that in the department of the Loire protoindustrialization did not necessarily lead to an increase in nuptiality and a decrease in marriage age; "Nuptiality and Rural Industry: Families and Labor in the French Countryside," *Journal of Family History* 8 (1983): 333–345. Rab Houston and K. D. M. Snell also question the link between protoindustry and marriage ages. They found the mean marriage age for women dropping in some eighteenth-century villages that did not experience protoindustrial developments; "Proto-Industrialization? Cottage Industry, Social Change, and Industrial Revolution," *Historical Journal* 27 (1984): 482. All cited in Gullickson, *Spinners and Weavers,* pp. 132–133.

ficial census, are probably lower than the actual numbers employed in these fields, since many people engaged in cottage industries also owned land and worked in agriculture.[22] Census data also indicate that the proportion of the active population engaged in these three forms of wage labor rose in fifty years from just over 25 to nearly 40 percent.[23] Unlike the spinners and weavers of Auffay, wage laborers in Neuchâtel were not exclusively women. Though lacemaking was primarily a female occupation, men predominated in the production of watches and printed cloth. Moreover, the opportunities for employment in the manufacture of *indiennes*, watches, and lace helped promote population growth by stimulating immigration. There was a significant increase in the proportion of foreigners living in the principality. From 1752 to 1756, 86.3 percent of the population were natives of Neuchâtel and only 13.7 percent were of foreign origin. For the period 1802–1806, however, Neuchâtelois numbered only 73.5 percent, while foreigners constituted 26.5 percent of the population. The proportion of the population that was foreign had thus doubled in a half century, an indication of an unprecedented dynamism in Neuchâtel's economy which stimulated immigration and emigration. In this regard, Neuchâtel resembled many other areas of Europe.[24] All things considered, Neuchâtel underwent considerable economic and demographic changes as protoindustrialization took root and thrived in the second half of the eighteenth century.[25]

22. Caspard, "Communauté rurale," p. 2, and *La Fabrique-Neuve de Cortaillod: Entreprise et profit pendant la Révolution industrielle, 1752–1854* (Paris, 1979), p. 11; Alphonse Petitpierre, *Un demi-siècle de l'histoire économique de Neuchâtel, 1791–1848* (Neuchâtel, 1871), p. 211; Barrelet, "Situation économique dans les Montagnes," pp. 245.
23. Census figures indicate that in 1752, out of a population of 32,335, 14,747 people were employed in all professions. In 1799, 25,154 of Neuchâtel's 46,934 inhabitants were active. I believe that the earlier figures underreport the percentage of the population that was active. Local officials at times were not very precise in reporting the number of people employed in various professions. Filling in the table that had been sent to him, the châtelain of Boudry reported in 1750 that there were "many seamstresses and washerwomen" and "an *indienne* factory that employs many people"; AEN, Série de Recensement, dossiers 25 and 30. Pierre Caspard goes so far as to say that by 1760 the majority of the population of the principality were engaged in wage labor, "as a result of either the immigration of laborers who came to work in the printed-cloth factories or the proletarianization—either total or partial— of some of the former small property owners." Caspard, however, has not provided much evidence to prove that the eighteenth century witnessed the appearance of "un prolétariat agricole" whose behavior paralleled that of the "prolétariat de fabrique." It may well be true that for the first time most agricultural work was performed by wage laborers, but Caspard has not provided adequate proof thereof; see "Conceptions prénuptiales," pp. 1007–1008.
24. Guillaume and Poussou, *Démographie historique*, p. 205.
25. Caspard, "Les ouvriers en indiennes au XVIIIe siècle," *Musée neuchâtelois*, 1974, 166–167; Henry, *Crime, justice et société*, pp. 101–104. Raoul Cop aptly contrasts the backward

TABLE 7
Matrimonial litigation, 1707–1806

	D	P	CD	S	PA	L	Misc.	Total
1707–1716	15	2	8	1	12	2	1	41
1717–1726	12	2	14	0	6	1	0	35
1727–1736	10	2	22	2	6	2	1	45
1737–1746	24	4	18	2	6	1	0	55
1747–1756	17	8	15	2	5	2	2	51
1757–1766	35	12	14	6	14	4	1	86
1767–1776	54	15	25	14	18	1	5	132
1777–1786	54	38	20	23	16	2	2	155
1787–1796	77	82	37	42	22	7	16	283
1797–1806	128	116	45	70	29	11	15	414
	426	281	218	162	134	33	43	1,297

Abbreviations: D, divorce; P, petitions; CD, contract disputes; S, separations; PA, police actions; L, legitimation; Misc., miscellaneous.

As one may expect, these economic and demographic innovations influenced the institutions of marriage and the family, a fact reflected in the marital litigation of the period. With the dramatic population growth, there was understandably a concomitant increase in the quantity of cases heard before the matrimonial courts. The increase in the volume of this litigation was, however, at a rate that far exceeded the population expansion (see Table 7). During the years 1707–1756, the courts heard a total of 227 marital questions, whereas these same tribunals heard 1,070 matrimonial disputes in the second half-century.[26] The second half of this century thus had almost five times the litigation of the preceding fifty years. The contrast is even more striking if we

nature of Neuchâtel's economy of the early eighteenth century with the later economic and demographic changes: "unlike later censuses, that of 1712 reveals a traditional economy that has not experienced the boom of either watchmaking or lacemaking and that apparently offered few opportunities for young people. In effect, the late marriages, the small numbers of children, the double current of permanent and seasonal emigration, and the almost total absence of immigration . . . could be interpreted as effects of a saturated economy"; "Un recensement de la population et des familles des Montagnes en 1712," *Musée neuchâtelois*, 1986, 136.

26. I have arrived at these figures by counting only cases heard before tribunals that were not serving as appellate courts. The vast majority of these cases took place before the Justices matrimoniales of Neuchâtel and Valangin. A few suits, however, were heard before the consistory of Valangin, a clear indication that the courts were not entirely systematic in separating the affairs of the consistories from those of the matrimonial courts. Furthermore, I found 8 pertinent cases in the records of the consistory of Travers, another *consistoire seigneurial*. More important, these figures include 160 petitions to marry made before the Conseil d'Etat and 60 pertinent cases heard before the Quatre-Ministraux. I have not included, however, the 733 police actions against illicit sexuality, since such actions were not, strictly speaking, marital disputes.

compare the marital litigation of the first decade of Prussian sovereignty with that of the last decade of this period. The tribunals heard only 41 cases from 1707 to 1716; they considered a total of 414 cases during the decade 1797–1806. In other words, whereas the population had increased by 70 percent over the course of the century, the volume of matrimonial litigation had increased tenfold. In short, the population growth alone cannot account for the increase in the volume of marital disputes. With these figures in mind, one may be tempted to conclude that the rapid social change caused by protoindustrialization wreaked havoc in households, driving husbands and wives apart in unparalleled numbers. As we see below, while marriage did undergo important modifications, it nevertheless remained a relatively stable institution.

Eighteenth-century judges introduced a minor change, already alluded to in the Introduction, in the way they handled litigation. During the previous century and a half, plaintiffs to matrimonial disputes often included people of humble origin, a clear indication that the court costs were not too burdensome. In the second half of the eighteenth century, the judges eliminated the last economic barrier to litigation by introducing *la loi des pauvres*, whereby poor people could ask the tribunal to hear their cases without imposing the usual court costs. Plaintiffs might be required to provide proof of their poverty, but more often than not the judges agreed to such requests. Thus, when Madelaine nee Dagon asked to be separated from her husband, Daniel Roullet in 1785, the parties were allowed to pursue this dispute *à la loi des pauvres* because of their indigence. By the end of the eighteenth century, legal expenses should not have inhibited anyone from filing suit.[27]

PETITIONS

As in the previous 150 years, petitions to marry represented an important form of litigation concerning the formation of marriage.

27. AEN, JMN6: 755–756, 759–760. In any event, legal expenses were quite low. Writing in 1836, Henri Houriet of Le Locle said that it was common for a court of eight to twelve members to work an entire day without receiving any recompense. Moreover, the total costs of litigation usually came to about 7 francs. Civil suits involving sums up to 24 francs were handled without charging anything except the costs of the bailiff's services; litigants disputing amounts between 24 and 60 francs were charged only 1.10 additional francs. To put these figures in their historical context, the annual salary for most watchmakers would have been about 1,000–1,500 francs. Few laborers would have made more than 20 francs a day on a regular basis. The costs of matrimonial courts clearly should not have been a deterrent to litigation; Barrelet, "Situation économique dans les Montagnes," pp. 244, 246.

Throughout the century, 281 such petitions were made, the vast majority of which were filed before the Conseil d'Etat. For their part, the matrimonial courts heard 48 petitions, 44 of which dealt with divorcés who needed permission to remarry, most often because they had been guilty of adultery. Of the remaining four petitions made before the Justices matrimoniales, three were made by women who needed to show that their husbands were deceased, and the motive for the fourth is unknown. As far as petitions were concerned, the marriage courts were thus concerned only with requests to remarry and rejected only one during the eighteenth century, a request made by a couple that had previously committed adultery together.[28] Whether they were divorcés who needed the court's permission to remarry or widows who had to prove their husbands' deaths, these parties needed the virtually automatic approval of the court to enter a subsequent marriage.

The petitions made before the Conseil d'Etat, in contrast, generally involved couples, not individual parties, who jointly asked for dispensations for impediments to their marriages. Of the 234 petitions heard before the Conseil d'Etat, 97 were made by couples related by consanguinity or affinity, and it may well be that most of the 87 petitions the motives of which we do not know were also filed by couples related by blood or marriage. In dealing with questions of consanguinity, the Conseil d'Etat proved itself to be quite liberal even by today's standards. Of the eighty couples who were first cousins, only one was denied the right to marry, though ten others abandoned their cases before a decision was reached. Even three uncles and nieces were allowed to marry, though three other such couples, including a man and his grandniece, were denied permission to wed. Only eight cases of affinity were mentioned, usually between brothers- and sisters-in-law. Seven of these were successful in their demands; only one man and his sister-in-law were forbidden to marry. Excluding those requests made by couples of mixed religions, we find that the overwhelming majority of petitions were granted: 133 petitions were awarded, only 5 denied, and 24 abandoned.[29]

Though the Conseil d'Etat was quite willing to allow first cousins to marry, it adamantly opposed marriages between Protestants and Catholics. Never before had a significant number of fiancés of mixed faiths petitioned to marry. During the century of Prussian rule, 74 such couples asked permission to marry. With the demographic changes that

28. AEN, JMV4:351–352.
29. AEN, TMCE6–16.

broughts large number of immigrants into Neuchâtel, many of whom were evidently Catholic, it is understandable that couples of different faiths became more common. Of these 74 couples, however, the Conseil allowed only 3 to marry in the principality of Neuchâtel, rejected 7 outright, and permitted 48 to marry in a foreign country.[30] The magistrates of Neuchâtel evidently turned a deaf ear to the pleas for religious toleration from their contemporaries, the philosophes, a fact that is underscored by the expulsion of Jews from Neuchâtel in 1790.[31] Nevertheless, allowing Protestants and Catholics to marry in a foreign country was progressive; heretofore, Neuchâtel's courts had forbidden the consecration of marriages with Catholics under pain of excommunication.

As in the previous period, the analysis of petitions by decade is rather perplexing. As noted above, in the late seventeenth century there was a dramatic reduction in the number of petitions, a trend that continued into the first half of the eighteenth century. From 1707 to 1756, the Conseil d'Etat heard only 6 petitions. By contrast, the three decades spanning 1777–1806 saw 210 petitions, 90 percent of those made for the entire century. Since there was no substantial change in laws on consanguinity and affinity, one possible explanation for the decrease in petitions in the late seventeenth and early eighteenth centuries is that the Conseil was simply being less strict in requiring that all cousins receive dispensations before marrying. A few cases from the early eighteenth century show, however, that though the Conseil d'Etat almost invariably granted petitions made by cousins it took harsh measures against those who married without its permission. In 1724, it convoked François-Rodolph Baillod and his wife, who was also his first cousin, for having married without permission in France. Since the marriage had already been consummated, the magistrates decided that it could not be dissolved. Lest they escape unpunished, however, the couple was to spend six days in jail and be exiled for two years.[32] Ten years later, the punishment was less severe: in 1733, David Maumary was fined 200 livres for marrying his first cousin, and another man merely had to

---

30. AEN, TMCE13–16. Sixteen petitions were abandoned.

31. The Quatre-Ministraux decreed in September 1790 that Jews were henceforth forbidden to stay in the city or *le pays* of Neuchâtel because of "the dangers to which public safety is exposed by the tolerance that has been shown to Jews in this state." After a similar action in Bern in December 1787, magistrates forbade Jews to do any business whatsoever in Neuchâtel, claiming: "This expulsion from the principal states of Switzerland of a people whose principal resource is deceit will help reassure inhabitants and spread the proper security that the vigilant eye of the police ensures"; AVN, QMN8:103.

32. AEN, MCE68:305–306.

TABLE 8

Illicit sexuality in Valangin, 1707–1806

	Fornication		Adultery		
	Women	Men	Women	Men	Total
1707–1716	37	13	2	11	63
1717–1726	36	6	2	7	51
1727–1736	39	4	3	6	52
1737–1746	35	5	2	6	48
1747–1756	39	7	4	8	58
1757–1766	45	6	2	6	59
1767–1776	39	3	5	4	51
1777–1786	39	2	3	2	46
1787–1796	37	3	0	2	42
1797–1806	56	7	3	3	69
	402	56	26	55	539

spend three days in jail for the same deed.[33] Regardless of the penalties it inflicted, and Conseil was consistent in defending its exclusive right to award dispensations to relatives who wished to marry. The possibly harsh consequences served as a deterrent to marrying relatives without authorization.

ILLICIT SEXUALITY

Sexual relations among unmarried couples tell us much about courtship patterns and the formation of marriage, indicating the degree of freedom young people enjoyed and the criteria they followed in choosing mates. Police actions against illicit sexuality were indeed the most common case heard before Valangin's consistory in the eighteenth century (see Table 8). For the century, the consistory subpoenaed 539 persons for having committed adultery or fornication. Accusations of fornication continued to be far more numerous than those of adultery: 458 to 81. In the city of Neuchâtel, the registers of the Quatre-Ministraux, extant from 1715, reveal 194 actions against people who were at least suspected of illicit sexuality (see Table 9).[34]

33. AEN, MCE77:148–149, 150–151.
34. This figure underreports the number of delinquents in the city of Neuchâtel, since at times the records are vague about how many people were involved. In 1717 "some" bourgeois men who had fathered illegitimate children were fined and sentenced to three days in prison; in the 1790s, the Quatre-Ministraux twice investigated groups of "several" women who were

Illicit sexuality in the city of Neuchâtel, 1707–1806

	Illicit sexuality		Fréquentation/ vie suspecte		Total	
	Women	Men	Women	Men	Women	Men
1707–1716	0	0	0	0	0	0
1717–1726	0	2	0	0	0	2
1727–1736	3	2	3	0	6	2
1737–1746	1	1	0	0	1	1
1747–1756	1	0	0	0	1	0
1757–1766	2	0	1	0	3	0
1767–1776	3	0	2	2	5	2
1777–1786	15	2	10	0	25	2
1787–1796	30	5	17	5	47	10
1797–1806	69	7	11	2	80	9
	124	19	44	9	166	28

That examples of *paillardise* were common is not surprising since, according to contemporaries, young people in eighteenth-century Neuchâtel had plenty of opportunities to associate with members of the opposite sex. Two customs facilitated such encounters: the *veillée* and the *Kiltgang*.

Like the aforementioned spinning bee, the *veillée* was a custom in which a group of young people of courting age met, usually at the home of a girl or a widow. Such get-togethers could take the form of balls, and no less a personage than Jean-Jacques Rousseau commented on them.[35] According to some contemporaries, *veillées* were not always innocent affairs. Pastor Peter, minister at the village of Les Ponts, said that they were a source of scandalous liberties for the young people.[36] Elsewhere in Europe, social activities resembling the *veillée* existed and, as noted above, were often criticized because they enabled young people to avoid parental supervision. Both in urban Holland and in

---

apparently working as prostitutes. Moreover, twelve women, two men, and one couple were convoked for poor behavior (*inconduite*). Though they are not counted in this table, it is likely that some of these, particularly the women, were presumed guilty of sexual misconduct; AEN, QMN1–11.

35. While staying at Môtiers in the county of Neuchâtel, Rousseau wrote that "young girls have a lot of freedom and take advantage of it. They often get together in groups to eat, chat, and attract young people as much as possible"; *Correspondance générale*, ed. Théophile Dufour (Paris, 1928), 9:16, cited in Caspard, "Conceptions prénuptiales," p. 994.

36. Samuel de Chambrier, *Description topographique de la paroisse et du vallon des Ponts* (Neuchâtel, 1806), pp. 35ff., cited in Caspard, "Conceptions prénuptiales," p. 994.

rural Germany, young people socialized often in groups, unattended by parents, to the dismay of many elders.[37]

Whereas the *veillée* was a form of group activity, the *Kiltgang* (Swiss-German, "nocturnal rendezvous") provided more intimate encounters between a young man and a young woman. This custom—variously known as bundling, night courting, and night-visiting—was found in the Netherlands, Germany, and England, and it even survived until recently among the Amish of America.[38] Arnold Van Gennep describes this custom of popular culture:

> This custom, openly approved of both by the youth of the village and by the families concerned, consists in a girl's receiving in turn various suitors by the window or door to her bedroom . . . on certain evenings, usually Saturdays. The boy who is chosen for a particular night gets in bed with her, staying completely dressed or disrobing only partially, without in principle going so far as making love. They spend the night together talking about recent events in the village, sleeping in each other's arms until dawn. Then the boy returns to his home or goes to work. It is the girl who decides which suitors she will receive successively in her bed, and her future fiancé will not necessarily be one of these suitors. The *Kiltgang* is not an experiment in love making, nor does the suitor receive any guarantee toward marriage. In addition, only young men and women of the same village take part in it.[39]

The *Kiltgang* existed in the French-Swiss cantons of Vaud, Fribourg, and the Valais under the name *aberdzi*. Rudolf Braun found that in Zurich and its environs bundling had existed in preindustrial times but became much more common in the eighteenth century with the growth in cottage industry and wage labor, which allowed young people greater freedom of courtship than ever before.[40] In the area around Neuchâtel, customs similar to the *Kiltgang* existed. According to Samuel de Chambrier, in Valangin when a man promised to marry a woman she was free

37. Medick, "Village Spinning Bees," in *Interest and Emotion*, ed. Medick and Sabean, p. 324; Schama, *Embarrassment of Riches*, pp. 439–440.
38. Gillis, *For Better, for Worse*, p. 31; Sabean, *Property, Production, and Family in Neckarhausen*, pp. 330–334; Schama, *Embarrassment of Riches*, p. 402.
39. Gennep, *Manuel de folklore français contemporain* (Paris, 1943–1946), 1.1:260–261, cited in Caspard, "Conceptions prénuptiales," pp. 994–995.
40. Braun, *Industrialisation and Everyday Life*, p. 44.

to receive him in her room at night.[41] This is a variation on the *Kilt-gang*, since it involves only couples who are engaged. At any rate, whether they met in groups or in the more intimate nocturnal rendez-vous of couples, young Neuchâtelois were relatively free to meet. And one may well be led to wonder whether such liberty could have con-tributed to the illicit acts that magistrates actively punished.

A closer look at those charged with sins of impurity reveals a most interesting analysis by gender. In the previous period men had slightly outnumbered women among those accused of adultery in Valangin, but they now did so by a two-to-one margin: 55 to 26. If this change is noteworthy, the alteration in the analysis by gender of fornicators is nothing short of amazing. Since the late sixteenth century, women had consistently outnumbered men among those convicted of fornication. For the period 1622–1706, for example, females constituted just over 60 percent of the people accused of fornication. This pattern was ac-centuated to an extreme in the eighteenth century, when women out-numbered men among those condemned for fornication by over seven to one: 402 to 56. Thus, whereas the number of women in Valangin accused of *paillardise* had increased by 51 percent over those convoked during the years 1622–1706, the number of men so accused had de-creased by 150 percent. In the city of Neuchâtel, actions against illicit sexuality showed an even more lopsided analysis by gender. Though they generally did not distinguish between adultery and fornication, the Quatre-Ministraux took 124 actions against women and only 19 against men on charges of illicit sexuality and illegitimate births. In the same manner, while 44 accusations of scandalous frequentation or *vie suspecte* were made against women, the Quatre-Ministraux convoked only 9 men on the same charges.

These figures are problematic to say the least. How is one to account for the fact that, in eighteenth-century Neuchâtel, 594 women were brought to court on charges related to illicit sexuality while the same charges were brought against only 139 men? If these women were in-deed guilty of illicit sexual relations, they obviously needed some comrades in crime. One may be tempted to suggest that the 139 men accused of sexual misconduct each had, on the average, illicit sexual re-lations with four women. Such a dubious theory is quickly dismissed,

41. De Chambrier, *Description topographique de Valangin*, pp. 103ff., cited in Caspard, "Conceptions prénuptiales," p. 995.

since the sentences reveal that only three men were punished for second offenses and no man was punished more than twice for adultery or fornication.

In attacking illicit sexuality, the Quatre-Ministraux of the city of Neu-châtel were clearly guilty of a double standard, viewing women as almost solely responsible for acts of fornication and adultery. Unlike the consistory of Valangin, the Quatre-Ministraux could be very harsh, deporting from the city 95 women—as opposed to only 9 men—for having produced bastards, practicing prostitution, or simply acting in a suspicious way, such as walking the streets or frequenting taverns at night.[42] Banished women who illegally returned to Neuchâtel could be subjected to brief prison sentences, public whippings (five occasions), and the humiliation of being paraded through the city's streets with bells around their necks (eleven occasions). In controlling sexuality, the municipal authorities were quite concerned with eliminating prostitution and generally reserved these most extreme sentences for women suspected of being prostitutes. But, though they sought to eliminate commercial sex, the Quatre-Ministraux showed little interest in punishing the customers of prostitutes. In 1804 the magistrates imprisoned two women, banishing one of them, for having illicit sexual liaisons in a tavern, but they did not even convoke the men named as their paramours.[43]

In cases of illicit sexuality in which prostitution was not presumed, the Quatre-Ministraux were less concerned with morality than with the economic burden illegitimate children could pose. Of the 166 women convoked for illicit sexuality and *vie suspecte*, 98 were explicitly said to be pregnant or the mothers of children born out of wedlock. The women who were liable to be deported were those who were not originally from the city and whose children appeared likely to need charitable assistance. Though we do not know the hometowns of most unwed mothers, 30 of them were clearly from outside the principality of Neuchâtel. These tended to be women who had come to the city seeking work; though occupations are almost never listed, 13 women were said to be servants or employees in taverns, very humble lines of work. Women whose *commune d'origine* was Neuchâtel were never banished for illicit sexuality and had access to the city's charitable institutions. Moreover, women who were from elsewhere in the principality were likely to be

---

42. Thirteen other women were told that they had to leave unless they could convince the magistrates that their children would not need charity.
43. AVN, QMN10:183–184, 536.

treated more sympathetically than those who were complete foreigners. When in 1775 police raided the bar Le Petit Pontarlier where young men and women were carousing in a scandalous way, they found Charlotte Petremand of Le Locle there. Since she was a "bourgeoise" of Valangin, the Quatre-Ministraux limited themselves to admonitions and threatened to punish her severely if they ever found her again in such a place.[44] Even foreign women who could convince the magistrates that they and their children would not be a burden to the city were allowed to stay, at least temporarily.

It should be noted that banishment was not a penalty reserved for unwed mothers. Entire families of "foreigners" were asked to leave if they were indigent or in some way disturbed the peace. When the wife of Guillot Maçon committed adultery in 1793, not only she but also her husband had to leave, though the magistrates generously offered to write a certificate attesting to his good behavior. In 1771 a German soldier was deported for having knowingly bought cheap bread intended for the poor. Another man was forced to leave the same year after saying unflattering words about the city's magistrates.[45] Thus, the Quatre-Ministraux's actions against illicit sexuality appear to be part of a broader effort to rid the city of unproductive residents. Magistrates viewed the city of Neuchâtel as a magnet that attracted all sorts of poor people in search of a living. Only those who were *originaires* of Neuchâtel or had purchased membership in the bourgeoisie automatically had the right to reside in the city.[46] To avoid possible financial burdens, the Quatre-Ministraux on five occasions intervened to discourage marriages between poor people, an action that no consistory took throughout the early modern period, and they forbade innkeepers to give rooms to people for more than three days without permission.[47] Since the Quatre-Ministraux were more concerned with illegitimate children than with sexual purity, and since women invariably predominated on poor relief rolls, it is not surprising that actions against illicit sexuality were directed more against women than men. Nevertheless, the harsh

44. AVN, QMN5:400.
45. AVN, QMN5:133, 155; QMN8:413.
46. Those whose *commune d'origine* was Boudry, Valangin, or the city of Neuchâtel were automatically members of the respective bourgeoisies of those communities. In addition, people who were *communiers* of other villages in the county could purchase membership in the bourgeoisie of any of these three towns and receive all the legal or financial advantages associated with that title. The cost of buying into these bourgeoisies varied but was generally too expensive for all but a small group of wealthy people; Caspard, "Conceptions prénuptiales," p. 1004, n. 52.
47. See, for example, AVN, QMN5:271–272; QMN10:453.

sentences against illegitimate births in the city of Neuchâtel were certainly detrimental to foreign women. They manifested a blatant double standard when compared with the Quatre-Ministraux's judgment on the only case of rape they heard during this period. In 1800, Christ Schmid was condemned for having raped a young German woman; though he denied the charge, he was later caught in her room, which he had entered by placing a ladder under her window. This same institution that banished women simply for walking around town late at night sentenced Schmid to three days in jail.[48]

One may wonder whether severe sentences could be behind the discrepancy between the numbers of male and female fornicators in Valangin. Fearing punishment, perhaps many men fled the country after seducing young women. In Valangin, however, such widespread desertion was unlikely, since the penalties inflicted were hardly excessive. For first offenses, the courts imposed prison sentences of three days for fornication and six days for adultery. During the first half of the century, persons guilty of illicit sex also had to endure humiliating public censures or public penance. In 1755, Frederick the Great, in a piece of enlightened legislation, abolished such humiliating practices. Henceforth, offenders were to do penance only before the consistory rather than publicly in church.[49] The most humiliating punishment of all, the *carcan*, or pillory, was inflicted only three times during the eighteenth century, once in 1745 and twice in 1766. The two women and one man put in the stocks received this punishment as a supplement to more conventional prison sentences because they had committed second and in one case third offenses. In short, Valangin's eighteenth-century magistrates were very much enlightened in allowing the most humiliating forms of punishment to fall into disuse.[50] This kinder, gentler treatment of acts

48. AVN, QMN10:183–184.
49. This act is recorded in the *procès verbal* of the consistory of Valangin. The Conseil d'Etat had instructed the mayor of Valangin to convey this decree to the consistory so that it might conform to the new practice: "His Majesty, having expressly ordered the abolition of public penance for acts of impurity and of public censures for those who anticipate marriage, mandates that all judicial officials of this sovereignty inform the consistories established in their jurisdictions that they must conform to the wishes of His Majesty. Instead of public penance, acts of penitence will be performed only in consistory; the sentence will remain 3 days and 3 nights or 6 days and 6 nights of prison as prescribed by our laws, depending on whether it is a question of fornication or adultery. In no case can these penalties be converted to monetary fines. . . . Given in council held at the castle of Neuchâtel, 13 August 1755"; AEN, CSV8:53r–v. Pressure to abolish these practices had come from the bourgeoisie and the Tribunal des Trois Etats; Courvoisier, *Panorama de l'histoire*, p. 89.
50. AEN, CSV8:11v, 95, 97, 115v. Stone also found that humiliating punishments became quite rare in eighteenth-century England; *Family, Sex, and Marriage*, p. 633.

of impurity contrasts markedly with the whippings and public mockery to which the Quatre-Ministraux occasionally subjected female offenders; this disparity can be explained at least in part by the fact that the Quatre-Ministraux used such harsh measures to punish prostitution rather than simple fornication. In Valangin it was even possible to be exempted from the usual prison term, and such grace was reserved almost exclusively for women. Of the 19 individuals whose prison sentences were waived during the eighteenth century, 18 were women, 11 of whom had been seduced by men who promised to marry them and then left the country.[51]

Another possible reason for the gap between the numbers of male and female offenders is that the consistory, unlike in earlier periods, resembled more a confessional than a court that determined an accused's guilt or innocence. On at least one occasion the consistory refused to pass sentence on a man's alleged fornication because he had not confessed his sin and therefore was not repentant. In that case in 1799, the president declared that the consistory was to deal only with those cases in which persons admitted their guilt and expressed remorse for the wrongs they had done.[52] Often, in fact, cases involving fornication do not seem to be police actions but rather initiatives on the part of the delinquent to make peace with the church. In 1761, for example, Judith Ducommun, who had committed a crime of impurity and had long been forbidden to take communion, asked to be readmitted to participate in the eucharist. Because she showed signs of sincere repentance, her wish was granted and she was sentenced to spend three days in prison and to ask for forgiveness on her knees before the consistory.[53] In short, if cases of fornication and adultery were essentially requests for forgiveness made by penitent believers, perhaps women simply were more interested in their spiritual salvation than were men. Theoretically, a few hundred men could have been excommunicated in eighteenth-century Valangin and never bothered to make peace with the church.

51. AEN, CSV7–9.

52. AEN, CSV8:179v–180. Lyndal Roper found that in Reformation Augsburg the city council, which had jurisdiction over moral offenses, resembled a confessor in that "it saw its task as being to extract a full confession of all the misdeeds an individual had committed, and to bring him or her to a sense of sinfulness"; *Holy Household*, p. 68.

53. AEN, CSV8:77r–v. This particular case took on larger proportions because of the rights of the *consistoire seigneurial* vis-à-vis those of the *consistoires admonitifs*. In his letter of *renvoi*, the pastor of La Chaux-de-Fonds reported that his parish's consistory had decided to grant Judith's request to be readmitted to holy communion. To conform to custom, he deemed it necessary to send her before the *consistoire seigneurial* of Valangin to receive the civil punishments necessary to be fully reconciled with the church. In the curt reply, the consistory of Valangin insisted that it alone had the authority to readmit such persons to communion.

Such a hypothesis is hard to defend, however, since many cases can be found of individuals who were accused of crimes of impurity but not condemned for them. In such cases the consistory resembled more a court than a confessional. Moreover, the consistory did not hear only contrite parties during the course of the eighteenth century. In 1758, for example, Jean-Pierre Droz was brought before the consistory because of his fornication with Jeanne-Marie Sandoz thirty-eight years earlier. Having been condemned by the Tribunal des Trois Etats Droz continued to profess his innocence. Despite his plea, the judges declared him guilty, though the president waived the prison sentence.[54] In other words, the disparity between the numbers of male and female fornicators cannot be totally explained by a greater desire on the part of women to be reconciled with the community and the church.

Two other explanations can be offered for the huge gap between the numbers of male and female delinquents in Valangin. First, the consistory, like the Quatre-Ministraux, might simply have been guilty of a double standard in pursuing those suspected of illicit intercourse. Though the sentences rendered were the same for male and female delinquents, the predominance of women suggests that the consistory might have prosecuted female offenders much more avidly than males. This double standard would have been an ironic innovation in the Age of Reason, contrasting with actions against *paillardise* from earlier centuries and with contemporary contract disputes in which, as we see below, unwed mothers received special attention. Another possibility is that many women, perhaps for reasons of loyalty, did not identify their seducers. To a certain extent, the prevalence of female delinquents stemmed from the fact that women could not conceal their transgressions easily. As mothers of illegitimate children, women's illicit sexual activity was manifest, whereas men's generally went unnoticed unless their lovers revealed their identity. Since the oath on the *petit lit* had been abolished, a concomitant decrease in the number of male delinquents is not surprising. Be that as it may, the extent of the gap between the number of males and females punished for fornication is quite perplexing.

Though the Quatre-Ministraux's prosecutions of illicit sexuality increased toward the end of the century, Valangin's actions against adultery and fornication did not in any way reflect the contemporary

54. Ibid., 62. Droz was the only male recorded to receive such grace for an act of impurity during the eighteenth century. Among all the court records I consulted, this represents the longest lapse of time between the moment of transgression and the appearance in court.

demographic shift. Despite dramatic population growth in the eighteenth century, males convicted in Valangin of fornication or adultery were more numerous in the first decade than in any other, numbering 13 and 11, respectively. More men were charged with acts of impurity during the first half-century than during the second (73 to 38), and female adulterers were exactly as numerous before 1757 as after. Most interesting, however, are the figures representing women accused of *paillardise*. Here the number of cases per decade is so consistent that one is tempted to think that judges had to fill a quota of female fornicators. For every decade except two, the number of women accused of fornication holds steady between 35 and 39. Only in 1757–1766 (45 women) and in 1797–1806 (56 women) do the figures deviate from this norm. While the population of the principality increased by 70 percent during the course of the century, the number of women faced with charges of fornication remained remarkably stable, increasing noticeably only during the last decade before Napoleonic rule.

In his work on the printed-cloth industry, Pierre Caspard found that the number of illegitimate births remained quite low in certain villages in the principality of Neuchâtel. For the village of Cortaillod, the proportion of illegitimate births was 0.9 percent for 1678–1720, 1.3 percent for 1721–1760, 1.1 percent for 1761–1790, and 1 percent for 1791–1820. In spite of the significant contemporary economic changes, Caspard found that illegitimacy was a marginal phenomenon, normally affecting women of the lower social ranks, such as servants, who frequently were outsiders to a particular parish or even to the principality as a whole—a characterization that holds true for the unwed mothers convoked before the Quatre-Ministraux. In short, though the city of Neuchâtel had a noticeable increase in illegitimate births, the county as a whole did not undergo significant growth in bastardy toward the end of the eighteenth century.[55]

This evidence on Neuchâtel's illegitimate births differs with the findings of many historians who assert that there was a pronounced growth in bastardy in late eighteenth-century Europe. Edward Shorter observes a striking increase in illegitimate births and prenuptial conceptions in the second half of the eighteenth and the early nineteenth centuries, primarily among the lower classes, and he argues that these

55. Caspard, "Conceptions prénuptiales," pp. 989–990, 1001–1002. Elsewhere, as well, domestic servants were among the most likely to become unwed mothers. In the eighteenth century, domestic workers made up at least 40 percent of the mothers of illegitimate children in Nantes, 50–70 percent in Aix, and 90 percent in Marseille; Maza, *Servants and Masters*, p. 89.

demographic changes were the result of a sexual revolution that began about 1750. He holds that women who found employment outside the home in protoindustrial and early industrial domains were being freed from the traditional constraints of family and community. Industrial activity liberated these women by providing them with economic independence. They could now indulge in sexual relations without regard to financial gain, as indicated by the fact that the vast majority of these women's lovers were not their employers but rather men of the same social status. Women were not having sexual relations out of hopes of getting married but simply for personal fulfillment, a change in mentality that amounted to a sexual revolution.[56]

Though almost all historians agree that the number of children conceived outside marriage increased in the late eighteenth century, Shorter's provocative thesis has found few supporters.[57] Some scholars deny that there was a general increase in the number of women working outside the home. Moreover, even when women did find outside employment, they generally were not involved in early industrial work. Louise Tilly, Joan Scott, and Miriam Cohen effectively argue that, even though beginning in 1750 more women were leaving their rural homes for cities, their work did not change. In urban settings, women were still employed primarily in domestic service, garment making, and textiles, which traditionally had been the most common forms of nonagricultural work for women. Industrial capitalism did not provide many new opportunities for women; the number of female workers in factories re-

56. Shorter, "Female Emancipation, Birth Control, and Fertility in European History," *American Historical Review* 78 (1973): 605–640, "Illegitimacy, Sexual Revolution, and Social Change in Modern Europe," *Journal of Interdisciplinary History* 2 (1971): 261–269, and *Making of the Modern Family*, chap. 3, "The Two Sexual Revolutions," pp. 79–119.

57. One person whose findings agree with the views of Shorter is Jacques Depauw. Studying the declarations of illegitimate pregnancies in Nantes, Depauw found that illegitimate births made up 3.1 percent of all births at the beginning of the eighteenth century but rose to 10.1 percent by the end of the century. Though most illegitimate children were the products of master-servant relationships in the early eighteenth century, by the end of the century most of the fathers as well as the mothers of illegitimate children were of the lower class. The fact that women were mating with their social equals represented, according to Depauw, a threefold emancipation for women: they were emancipated from the traditional hierarchy by which servants had been exploited by their masters; they had freed themselves of traditional religious morality, rejecting the necessity of a marriage ceremony; and finally, they were liberated from parental authority; "Illicit Sexual Activity and Society in Eighteenth-Century Nantes," in *Family and Society: Selections from the "Annales: Economies, Sociétés, Civilisations,"* ed. Robert Forster and Orest Ranum, trans. Elborg Forster and Patricia M. Ranum (Baltimore, 1976), pp. 189–190. Notwithstanding Depauw's argument, these women, who were burdened with children and abandoned by their lovers, almost certainly did not consider themselves emancipated.

mained low even at the end of the nineteenth century.[58] Women who emigrated to work in cities remained tied to the family economy, often being sent there by their families, and they generally used their wages to supplement their families' income (which was one of the reasons they were poorly paid). Urban working women were no longer protected by traditional constraints—family, community, and church—which could have coerced young men to marry women they had impregnated. Illegitimacy increased during the period 1750–1850 because people had moved out of traditional social contexts, not because they were undergoing a change in mentality or celebrating a sexual revolution. Though scholars generally agree with Shorter that couples who produced bastards were of the same socioeconomic status, they assert that most mothers of illegitimate children had engaged in sexual relations with the expectation of marrying their suitors. Thus, in the words of John Rule, women had become, "not more emancipated, but more vulnerable, as lack of money, unemployment and opportunities for work far afield all kept men from fulfilling promises in conditions where there was no power of enforcing them." As David Levine notes, the increase in illegitimacy in the late eighteenth century was the result of "marriage frustrated," not of "promiscuity rampant."[59]

Though she too disagrees with Shorter, Cissie Fairchilds provides an alternative explanation for growing numbers of illegitimate births. Fairchilds studied the *déclarations de grossesse* that unmarried pregnant women were required to make in France, usually in the seventh or eighth month of their pregnancy, indicating where, when, and under what circumstances they had gotten pregnant. Studying the years

58. Tilly and Scott, *Women, Work, and Family* (New York, 1978), pp. 116–123; Tilly, Scott, and Cohen, "Women's Work and European Fertility Patterns," *Journal of Interdisciplinary History* 6 (1976): 447–476; Theresa M. McBride has found that during the first phase of industrialization—that is, through the 1880s—far more women were involved in domestic service than in factory work. Indeed, she argues that women preferred servanthood to the factory, viewing employment in industry as impersonal work that attracted bad company; "The Long Road Home: Women's Work and Industrialization," in *Becoming Visible: Women in European History*, ed. Renate Bridenthal and Claudia Koonz (Boston, 1977), p. 290. Similarly, Mary Lynn McDougall found that industrialization had little impact on most women, its most important effect being the removal of most married women from the labor force; "Working Class Women during the Industrial Revolution, 1780–1914," in *Becoming Visible*, p. 275.

59. Rule, *The Labouring Classes in Early Industrial England, 1750–1850* (London, 1986), pp. 181, 200, quotation from p. 203; Levine, *Family Formation*, chap. 9, "Illegitimacy: Marriage Frustrated, Not Promiscuity Rampant," pp. 127–145; see also Maza, *Servants and Masters*, p. 70; John W. Shaffer, "Family, Class, and Young Women: Occupational Expectations in Nineteenth-Century Paris," in *Family and Sexuality in French History*, ed. Wheaton and Hareven, pp. 195–196.

1727–1789, Fairchilds finds Aix-en-Provence suffered a noticeable increase in illegitimate births even though it remained an economic backwater without urbanization and modernization. Fairchilds observes a decline in the proportion of illegitimate births resulting from master-servant relationships after 1750, and, more surprising, a decrease in illegitimate births to women who emigrated from the countryside to the city.[60] The increase in illegitimacy was to be found among women who remained in the countryside, a finding clearly at odds with Shorter's thesis and not completely consistent with the views of Tilly, Scott, and Cohen. Fairchilds therefore suggests that illegitimate births grew more numerous not because of changing attitudes toward sex among women, nor because of economic modernization, but simply because of economic hard times.[61]

More detailed quantitative studies have lent some support to this view. Peter Laslett and others have shown that for Europe in general there was a dramatic increase in illegitimate births and prenuptial conceptions beginning in the mid- to late eighteenth century, though the relationship of the increase in bastardy to urbanization and industrialization is ambiguous. England, the first country to industrialize and to increase urbanization, was also the first with substantial growth in bastardy. Be that as it may, Laslett rejects a simple causal connection since even countries that were slow to industrialize had growing rates of illegitimacy: in Sweden illegitimate births sharply increased in the 1770s and 1780s, surpassing the rate in England even though Sweden was scarcely affected at all by industrialization and urbanization. Indeed, Laslett holds that industrialization and urbanization began to affect most western European countries only in the 1880s, precisely when the illegitimacy rate began to fall. He further argues that the large numbers of illegitimate births were not simply the result of the "European marriage pattern" described by John Hajnal whereby couples married late,

60. Maza, too, has observed a decrease in the number of liaisons between masters and servants in eighteenth-century France and attributes this decrease to the nuclear family's growing need for privacy from servants. Agreeing with Lawrence Stone, she argues that this new desire for privacy "can be linked to the emergence in the eighteenth century of a more intimate and affectionate style of domestic life, one which tended to exclude foreign elements from the midst of the new 'companionate' family"; *Servants and Masters*, pp. 258–259, 266.

61. Fairchilds, "Female Sexual Attitudes and the Rise of Illegitimacy: A Case Study," *Journal of Interdisciplinary History* 8 (1978): 163–203. In similar fashion, Gullickson finds that the increase in illegitimacy, which was especially noticeable in Auffay after 1800, was the result of economic difficulties. Unlike Fairchilds, however, Gullickson asserts that, although illegitimate births were increasing, the number of pregnant brides declined, leading her to believe that the number of women "conceiving out of wedlock was not changing much, but their fate was"; *Spinners and Weavers*, pp. 179–187.

several years after reaching sexual maturity. Although one might expect large numbers of illegitimate children when many years passed between sexual maturity and marriage, Laslett maintains that there was no direct connection. More important, Laslett, E. A. Wrigley, and, as we have seen, many others have found that the age at marriage for both men and women was actually declining in late eighteenth-century Europe when bastardy rates were high.[62]

Even if there was no causal relationship between industrialization and bastardy, economic factors could still have been fundamentally important in the increasing numbers of illegitimate births. Several historians point to changes in courtship practices in the eighteenth century, alterations tied to the growth in wage labor. Many areas of Europe grew in wage labor in the eighteenth century even though they did not industrialize until later. Rudolf Braun found that, with the development of wage labor in the cotton and printing industries, the Zurich Oberland saw a significant increase in illegitimate births and prenuptial conceptions in the eighteenth century. Changes in birth patterns were directly related to new courtship practices made possible by the expansion of wage labor. Braun found that in traditional peasant society personal inclinations had to yield to property concerns in forming marriages. Among wage earners, however, young people enjoyed more freedom from parental influence in choosing mates. This greater liberty in courting was the cause of the increasing numbers of pregnant brides and illegitimate children. Similarly, John Gillis holds that the growth in wage labor in late eighteenth-century England meant that courtship practices became more direct, that go-betweens played less of a role in forming matches, and that betrothal agreements between families decreased. Betrothals and weddings themselves became more private affairs, resulting in fewer traditional weddings in which entire peasant communities participated.[63]

62. Laslett, Introduction to *Bastardy and Its Comparative History*, ed. Laslett, Oosterveen, and Smith , pp. 17–41, 59; Wrigley, "Marriage, Fertility, and Population Growth," pp. 145–146. See Hajnal, "European Marriage Patterns in Perspective," in *Population in History: Essays in Historical Demography*, ed. D. V. Glass and D. E. C. Eversley (London, 1965), pp. 101–143.

63. Braun, *Industrialisation and Everyday Life*, pp. 38–46; Gillis, *For Better, for Worse*, pp. 110, 136–137, and "Peasant, Plebeian, and Proletarian Marriage," pp. 138–145. See also Smout, "Scottish Marriage," in *Marriage and Society*, ed. Outhwaite, p. 234. Flandrin suggests that the increase in illegitimacy in France after 1750 resulted in part from unsupervised socializing between the sexes, which was replacing traditional chaperoned customs of courtship; "Repression and Change in the Sexual Life of Young People in Medieval and Early Modern Times," in *Family and Sexuality*, ed. Wheaton and Hareven, pp. 38–39. Rosalind Mitchison and Leah Leneman, however, question the connection between protoindustry and illegitimacy. In Scotland, only in the southwest did bastardy rates begin to rise about 1750, even

One point on which virtually all historians agree is that illegitimacy and prenuptial conception increased in late eighteenth-century Europe. Numerous studies of England, France, and even America suggest that increasing numbers of bastards and pregnant brides coincided.[64] Yet, as Martine Segalen notes,

> the distinction between premarital pregnancies and illegitimate births is an important one. One can see the former as a way of forcing a family's hand and making them consent to a marriage. It is also possible to assume—and this is perhaps more probable—that once the family and the young couple had agreed, the latter saw themselves as virtually married and anticipated their conjugal rights; in short, the church's attempt to clarify the situation of young betrothed couples and to abolish trial marriages without cohabitation had failed by the second half of the eighteenth century.[65]

Evidence from Neuchâtel of illicit sexuality gives us good reason to distinguish prenuptial conceptions from illegitimate births. In his study on prenuptial conceptions in the area around Cortaillod, Caspard found that, whereas illegitimate children were rare, pregnant brides became quite common during the course of the eighteenth century. Caspard discovered that before 1760 the rate of premarital conception—defined as births that took place less than eight months after marriage—oscillated between zero and 20 percent of all married couples' first births.

---

though the southwest was less affected than other areas of the country by protoindustry. Contrary to Laslett, they hold that illegitimacy rates increased significantly in Scotland only with the advent of the agricultural and industrial revolutions, *Sexuality and Social Control*, pp. 145–156.

64. That is not to say that prenuptial conceptions rose at the same level throughout Europe. Though in 1800 as many as 40 percent of first babies were born within eight months after marriage in England, in contemporary France the proportion of pregnant brides rose more modestly, reaching 12.4 percent by 1800. Wrigley postulates that the higher rate in England may have resulted from the more widespread wage labor there; "Marriage, Fertility, and Population Growth," pp. 178–183. In spite of the geographic and linguistic proximity of France, Neuchâtel's demographic patterns were closer to those of England. Gullickson, on the contrary, found that prenuptial conceptions were no more common among those employed in protoindustry than among the population at large; *Spinners and Weavers*, pp. 152–153. See also J. D. Chambers, "The Age at Marriage in England and Its Implications," in *Loving, Parenting, and Dying*, ed. Fox and Quitt, pp. 126–132; Flandrin, "Repression and Change," pp. 38–39; P. E. H. Hair, "Bridal Pregnancy in Rural England," in *Loving, Parenting, and Dying*, pp. 233–241; Laslett, *World We Have Lost*, pp. 135–155; Daniel Scott Smith and Michael S. Hindus, "Premarital Pregnancy in America 1640–1971: An Overview and Interpretation," in *Marriage and Fertility: Studies in Interdisciplinary History*, ed. Robert I. Rotberg and Theodore K. Rabb (Princeton, 1980), p. 341.

65. Segalen, *Historical Anthropology of the Family*, p. 131.

Beginning in 1760, however, the rate increased dramatically, attaining in just three decades a level of over 50 percent of first births. Contemporary to the spread of wage labor, this increase in antenuptial conceptions shows that, in spite of the views of pastors and moralists, eighteenth-century Neuchâtelois condoned sexual relations between fiancés.[66]

Caspard concludes that this pronounced increase in prenuptial conception was the result of new matrimonial strategy in the eighteenth century, at least among the nonpropertied classes. For the late eighteenth century, he observes a large gap between the rates of prenuptial conception among the wealthy propertied classes, on the one hand, and the rest of the population, on the other. Only about one-fourth of the wealthy's first children were born within eight months of marriage, a rate 32 percent lower than that for married people in general. Contraception was probably not the cause of this lower rate, since the interval between births was more or less the same for notables as for others. The difference must therefore be due to the fact that premarital sexual relations were less frequent among the propertied classes than among non-notables. The two groups had different levels of premarital sexual activity because, Caspard argues, they no longer shared the same matrimonial strategies. Up until the mid-eighteenth century, most workers possessed at least a part of their means of production—land and the capital needed to exploit it. As a result, most marriages posed problems of dowries and inheritances for the transmission of this property. By 1760, however, a large percentage of the population was involved in wage labor. Like Braun, Caspard believes that for wage laborers marriage was now becoming less a material venture and more a "union in which instinct and sentiment intervened." It was this new attitude toward marriage that was behind the remarkable increase in premarital relations. Economic concerns in choosing spouses had not disappeared but were now based less on one's property holdings and more on one's professional prospects. At the same time, the sons and daughters of notables remained tied to the traditional material concerns in forming marriages, since their wealth was still in property.[67] This is not to say that there was a causal connection between protoindustrialization and the marriage of sentiment; rather, the opportunity of working for

66. Caspard, "Conceptions prénuptiales," pp. 989–990.
67. Ibid., pp. 1006–1007. Flandrin also holds that, since wage laborers, unlike peasants and artisans, did not possess or even hope to possess their means of production, they began to consider marriage as primarily a love match; *Amours paysannes*, p. 74. See also Olwen H. Hufton, "Women, Work, and Marriage in Eighteenth-Century France," in *Becoming Visible*, pp. 198–199.

wages simply provided the material means for loosening family ties, allowing one to individualize courtship and marriage.[68]

The question remains why, apart from the city, the county of Neuchâtel differed from other parts of Europe in experiencing an increase in premarital conceptions but not in illegitimate births.[69] The most likely explanation can be found in the types of protoindustry available in Neuchâtel. The vast majority of women involved in wage labor were employed in lacemaking. Since the production of lace was a form of cottage industry, women did not have to leave their homes and families to participate. Moreover, whereas the printed-cloth and watchmaking industries would have stimulated the immigration of single men, couples, and families, Neuchâtel's protoindustrial opportunities would not have attracted large numbers of single female immigrants. Consequently, Neuchâtel's female wage earners had the material means of courting free from parental control, but they remained in familiar rural settings, closely tied to their families, who could offer them protection should they become pregnant. The evidence from the Quatre-Ministraux suggests that the foreign women who got pregnant outside marriage were generally not engaged in new forms of wage labor; rather, they worked at traditional vocations as servants and, if we are to believe the magistrates, as prostitutes.

LEGITIMATION

Since fiancés commonly indulged in sexual relations, there were predictably some couples who produced children but were never married. In such cases, the matrimonial courts were often asked to rule on the

68. Braun, *Industrialisation and Everyday Life*, pp. 38–46. Writing well before the other authors, Braun refers to the growth of cottage industry as "industrialization," though "protoindustrialization" more appropriately distinguishes this form of rural industry from the later system of factory production. As far as sentiment is concerned, even Friedrich Engels believed that because of the decline of property considerations, love under capitalism was really possible only among the proletariat; Rule, *Labouring Classes*, p. 191. Most historians also believe that homogamy was more prevalent before the economic expansion of the eighteenth and nineteenth centuries. David Sabean found, however, that in the seventeenth and early eighteenth centuries it was quite common for wealthy people to marry poor people. But in the late eighteenth century spouses were bringing about the same amount of wealth into marriage, even though the village of Neckarhausen's economy was expanding and diversifying; *Property, Production, and Family in Neckarhausen*, pp. 225–246.

69. In contrast, Mitchison and Leneman found that prenuptial conceptions remained low in eighteenth-century Scotland, even in those areas where bastardy was rather high. The low number of pregnant brides indicates, they hold, that the Scots adhered faithfully to Calvinist morality and frowned on sexual relations before marriage; *Sexuality and Social Control*, pp. 78, 159, 182.

legitimacy of individuals. Most of the 33 legitimation cases brought before the marriage courts were uncontested suits filed by women on behalf of their children. Often this involved a woman who had agreed to marry a certain man, had sexual relations with him, but was unable to celebrate the wedding because of the absence or death of the fiancé. Since it was still common for Neuchâtelois to seek employment as mercenaries in foreign countries, it is understandable that some of them left behind pregnant fiancées and never returned to Neuchâtel. The courts recognized the legitimacy of the great majority (25 of 33) of the persons in question. Of the remaining cases, 6 were abandoned and only 2 outright rejected.

Other legitimation cases dealt with persons born of allegedly adulterous affairs. Opposition to such litigation most often came from communities that might have to support these individuals if they were legitimate, as aptly demonstrated by the suit Etienne Desplan filed in 1801 against his mother, Marianne Desplan, the wife or widow of Guillaume Martin. Etienne initiated this unusual affair because Marianne now admitted to giving a false declaration on the *petit lit* when Etienne was born in 1782. According to Marianne, at her husband's insistence she had sworn that the child was the fruit of an adulterous liaison with an unknown man from the canton of Schaffhausen. Now she maintained that oath was a fabrication, incited by her husband's fear of being discovered by military recruiters if she were to announce that the child was Martin's. Marianne now affirmed that Etienne was her husband's son and that the two of them had raised him together until Martin's departure fifteen years earlier. (She did not know what had become of her husband, though French newspapers announced that a certain Guillaume Martin, born in Switzerland, had been guillotined in Paris at the time of the Terror.) Marianne's and Martin's three legitimate children supported Etienne, bringing no opposition to his suit. But the bourgeoisie of Neuchâtel and the community of Peseux both opposed Desplan's petition; they had an interest in this case because Martin's *commune d'origine* was Peseux, and he evidently was also a member of the city of Neuchâtel's bourgeoisie, a title that carried certain political and financial benefits. A lawyer representing Neuchâtel and four representatives of Peseux together opposed Desplan's suit on moral grounds; he was the fruit of his mother's adultery and therefore must not be regarded as legitimate. At the time of her pregnancy, Marianne did not even think of saying that the child had been fathered by her husband, who was absent at the time and never acknowledged his paternity. Moreover, if there had been real grounds for legitimacy,

Etienne should have acted while Martin was still alive rather than waiting twenty years before filing this petition. The city and village officials
further speculated that in denying her earlier oath Marianne was motivated by maternal love and that Etienne's siblings did not object simply because the family had no rich legacy they would have to share with
Etienne. Etienne's legitimacy would simply be a means of taking advantage of the city and the community.[70]

Etienne retorted that a bastard is someone born out of wedlock. Even
if his mother had committed adultery, one could not be sure that his
father was the adulterous lover rather that Martin. Appealing to a divorce case heard before the matrimonial court of Valangin, Etienne
noted that a woman had consented to a divorce on the ground of her
adultery, provided that her child be recognized as legitimate. In that
case, her lawyer argued this:

> The civil laws all agree that children born during a marriage are to be
> attributed to the husband. The adultery of the wife, even if acknowl-
> edged by her, cannot prejudice the legitimacy of the children born
> during the marriage, considering that they could be the fruit of con-
> jugal sexuality just as easily as that of adultery. In such uncertainty the
> law always rules in favor of legitimacy.[71]

Etienne further asserted that the officials had in no way proved that
Martin was absent at the time of conception and noted that the oath on
the *petit lit* was very vague: she had said that the father was a German
from Schaffhausen whose name she had forgotten. As a counterattack,
Etienne suggested that his poverty was at the heart of the officials' opposition to his legitimacy:

> As for those who oppose my demand for so-called religious reasons,
> don't they know that our religion requires that the poor be treated no
> differently than the rich? Could it be because that Barbe Kreps's chil-
> dren, born illegitimate, were rich that the Noble and Virtuous Bour-
> geoisie did not oppose their legitimation by the subsequent marriage
> with Mister Jean Pierre Varnod . . . ? One would be tempted to think
> so since previous to this marriage their mother had made an engage-
> ment to marry Gaspard Oxbein . . . , the announcements of which had

70. AEN, JMN7:775–780, 807–808.
71. Ibid., 817.

been publicized. Oxbein could have been the father of the children just as easily as Varnod.[72]

Eventually the city of Neuchâtel and community of Peseux withdrew their opposition. The court essentially agreed with Etienne's arguments, declared that he did indeed have the right to legitimate status, and condemned the city and community to all costs incurred from the moment of their opposition.[73] Notwithstanding the officials' contention that they opposed Etienne's demand for moral reasons, their opposition undoubtedly was based on the fear that he might become a financial burden.

There were, of course, some people who clearly were illegitimate. In such cases, however, it was still possible to petition the prince, who had the authority to legitimate anyone he pleased. Though the records of the chancellery are incomplete, there was a perceptible increase in the number of legitimation cases in the late seventeenth and early eighteenth centuries. The extant chancellery records indicate that princes legitimated only 5 individuals—3 men and 2 women—in the sixteenth and early seventeenth centuries. Records reveal that, from 1622 to 1706, 30 men and 8 women received the legitimate status, and in the period 1707–1760 princes legitimated 93 people—63 men, 29 women, and one unborn child. No records of the chancellery exist for the following decades.[74]

These records reveal a growing concern in the late seventeenth and eighteenth centuries in limiting the number of illegitimate persons. In legitimating people, princes no doubt were inspired in part by humanitarian concerns. Like eighteenth-century consistorial judges, princes probably were more interested in finding equitable solutions to such problems than their predecessors had been. But it was also in the best interests of the prince, if not of communities, to minimize the number of illegitimate persons in the principality. Medieval canon law had held that one must be legitimate to inherit, and illegitimate children continued to be slighted vis-à-vis legitimate offspring in questions of inheritance.[75] In the principality of Neuchâtel, membership in a *com-*

72. Ibid., 819.
73. Ibid., 849.
74. AEN, Actes de Chancellerie, vols. 1–6b, 11–16, 18–19bis, 23–26. It makes sense that men were in the majority, since women attained many of the advantages of legitimacy, such as membership in a *commune d'origine*, simply by marrying men who were legitimate.
75. Goody, *Development of the Family,* p. 205. See also Nicholas, *Domestic Life,* pp. 154, 157, 168.

mune d'origine was restricted to people who were legitimate. Communities were responsible only for the legitimate children of their members, as aptly demonstrated by a case before the Quatre-Ministraux in 1792. The administrator of the city of Neuchâtel's hospital—as much a poorhouse as a place for caring for the sick—received a request from his counterpart in Yverdon in the Pays de Vaud for assistance in supporting the abandoned illegitimate daughter of Alexandre Sinnet, a resident of Bern but a bourgeois of Neuchâtel. The Quatre-Ministraux responded that the hospital's funds were intended to support only the legitimate children of Neuchâtel's bourgeoisie.[76] A town or village had to provide poor relief only to its *communiers*. In the city of Neuchâtel, only members of its bourgeoisie—that is, those whose *commune d'origine* was Neuchâtel or who had origins elsewhere in the principality and had purchased membership in the bourgeoisie—could expect municipal help in case of indigence. Whereas various communities would have opposed legitimating poorer people lest they become a burden, the prince would have preferred that all his subjects belong to some community. From the prince's point of view, membership in a particular *commune* provided a safety net that could reduce the number of vagabonds roaming from town to town looking for handouts. Limiting the number of people tainted with the stigma of bastardy might therefore help nurture social stability throughout the principality. All told, plaintiffs to legitimation cases were motivated primarily by material concerns. The plaintiffs' main objective was to assure the legitimacy of persons born in questionable circumstances or of those whose parents had never consecrated their wedding engagements. This concern over legitimacy was above all a reflection of the material benefits—the right to a portion of the father's property and to membership in his *commune d'origine*—that this status provided.

MARRIAGE CONTRACT DISPUTES

Disputes over alleged marriage contracts were related in an important way to the questions of illicit sexuality and legitimacy. As we see

76. AVN, QMN8:257. A woman automatically became a member of her husband's *commune d'origine* and retained membership in that community even after a divorce. Thus, in 1800 the Quatre-Ministraux ruled that the ex-wife of Henri Couvert was eligible for charity since she had not lost the membership in Neuchâtel's bourgeoisie she had attained through marriage. Two years later, however, the magistrates ruled that it was possible for a woman to lose her status as bourgeoise if the divorce was her fault; QMN10:222, 314.

later in this chapter, in the eighteenth century both the plaintiffs' motives in trying to enforce alleged contracts and the judges' criteria in deciding which engagements must be honored were tied much more than before to pregnancies conceived outside marriage.

The most obvious change in eighteenth-century contract litigation, however, was its decline vis-à-vis other forms of matrimonial litigation, a trend that was not unique to Neuchâtel.[77] During the previous one hundred fifty years, questions over contracts to marry were the most common marital dispute heard before the consistories. During the eighteenth century, however, cases involving disputed promises to marry were far outnumbered by divorce proceedings, 426 to 218.

In handling contract litigation, the courts in many ways simply continued practices set during the Reformation period. Judges continued to regard consent as a condition sine qua non for forming a valid marriage agreement. Minors still needed parental consent to marry. In one sense, parents' control over their children's marriages actually increased in the eighteenth century: the Tribunal des Trois Etats passed a law in 1748 that increased the age at which one could marry without parental permission from nineteen or twenty to twenty-two years.[78] The matrimonial courts also continued to exercise the exclusive right to dissolve marriage engagements that had been made and publicized.

In spite of these continuities, contract litigation took on a strikingly different complexion in the eighteenth century. During the preceding one hundred fifty years, suits to annual marriage contracts made up only 14.4 percent of contract litigation; for the period 1707–1806, 34 percent of all contract disputes were initiated by people who wanted either to disprove alleged contracts or to be released from engagements. With this increase in plaintiffs who sought to annul contracts one would expect the proportion of contracts judged binding to diminish. That,

77. Stone found that disputes concerning the formation of marriage were more common than those involving marital breakdown in the seventeenth century but that the situation was reversed in the eighteenth century; after 1700, the Court of Arches began to hear fewer contract disputes than separation and nullity cases. Unlike Neuchâtel's courts, however, the Court of Arches saw an overall decline in litigation in the eighteenth century; *Road to Divorce*, pp. 35–40.

78. In May 1748, the Tribunal des Trois Etats passed the following law to raise the age of majority: "Since we have experienced several legal disputes and family disorders resulting from the weaknesses of children of both sexes who, reaching the age of majority at 19 years, become masters of themselves and their property and often enter poorly matched marriage agreements. To improve this situation as much as possible, we increase the age of majority for marriage to 22 years both for girls and boys, though the age of majority will remain as before for all other purposes"; Favarger and Tribolet, *Sources du droit du canton de Neuchâtel*, pp. 353–354.

however, was not the case. If abandoned cases are included in the calculations, only 17 percent of disputed engagements were adjudged valid for the previous century and a half. In contrast, eighteenth-century courts ruled that one-fourth of such disputed promises to marry (55 of 218) were binding and required the parties to honor them.

The explanation for this increase in the proportion of disputed contracts ruled binding can be seen in an analysis of litigants to contract disputes (see Table 10). The most striking contrast between eighteenth-century litigation and that of the previous period is the remarkable increase in the proportion of female plaintiffs. Throughout the sixteenth and seventeenth centuries, men slightly outnumbered women among plaintiffs who sought to enforce contracts. In the eighteenth century, however, women were an unambiguous majority, outnumbering men 112 to 27. Of those suits to annul promises to marry, 38 cases were initiated by female plaintiffs, 12 by men, and 24 by both parties. If these figures are noteworthy, even more astonishing is the fact that, of the 55 marriage contracts recognized as binding, 50 were filed by female plaintiffs. Only once during the entire hundred-year period did a man successfully file a suit to enforce a marriage engagement.[79] The overwhelming percentage of women among those plaintiffs who successfully enforced marriage contracts suggests a certain bias or sympathy for women.

A closer look at the details indicates that this sympathy was primarily directed toward a particular subgroup of women—those who were pregnant or had already given birth to children. As we have seen, in the sixteenth and seventeenth centuries only a handful of pregnant women endeavored to execute marriage contracts, alleging that sexual consummation had followed proposals. Of these women, very few were successful in their suits. But, during the century of Prussian rule, 88 contract suits were filed by women who were explicitly said to be pregnant or already mothers of children born out of wedlock.[80] Of these, 44, exactly half, were successful in their legal actions. In other words, 80 percent of the marriage contracts the courts recognized as binding

79. Another contract that was declared binding dealt with a couple who had mutually asked to be released from their engagement. They were ordered to go through with the marriage because they had had a child together; see below.

80. Stone found an exactly opposite pattern in the London consistory court. In the seventeenth century, women constituted 60 percent of the plaintiffs to all cases heard before the consistory, but they were in the minority in the eighteenth century. Stone maintains that this change resulted in part from the decline in the number of women, usually pregnant, who tried to enforce alleged contracts; *Road to Divorce*, pp. 186–187.

TABLE 10

Marriage contract disputes, 1707–1806

Action	Jurisdiction				Total
	JMN	JMV	CSV	CST	
All disputes					
Contract binding	39	16	0	0	55
Contract null	58	39	1	1	99
Abandoned	43	17	2	0	62
	141	73	3	1	218[a]
Enforce contracts					
Female plaintiffs					
Contract binding	35	15	0		50
Contract null	17	6	0		23
Abandoned	30	8	1		39
	82	29	1		112
Male plaintiffs					
Contract binding	1	0	0		1
Contract null	10	1	1		12
Abandoned	7	6	1		14
	18	7	2		27
Disprove or annul contracts					
Female plaintiffs					
Contract binding	0	0			0
Contract null	14	20			34
Abandoned	3	1			4
	17	21			38
Male plaintiffs					
Contract binding	2	1		0	3
Contract null	2	2		1	5
Abandoned	3	1		0	4
	7	4		1	12
Mutual requests					
Contract binding	1	0			1
Contract null	15	8			23
Abandoned	0	0			0
	16	8			24

[a]Judgments for two cases cannot be said to have declared the contracts either binding or null. For three other cases, it is unclear who initiated the trial.

involved women who were faced with the prospect of raising children without the support of a husband.

As before, a woman who was pregnant and claimed to have a valid marriage contract ordinarily could prove such an engagement only by the written promises themselves or by the testimony of witnesses to an oral agreement. Otherwise, the man in question would not be required to marry since the woman could not be considered to have been a virgin at the time she was seduced.[81] In practice, however, the courts continued to be less rigid, often taking into account public repute. If evidence suggested that a man had been courting the woman, for example, the tribunals might order the marriage even if no direct evidence of promises could be produced. The chronicler J. F. Boyve recounts that

> if the parties are of the same age and of similar social status, . . . and if the girl is of good moral standing and leads a wholesome life and can prove that the young man consistently pursued her or produce some letters that show tender feelings between them from which one can conclude that the young man had led her to anticipate marriage, then in such cases it is not the custom to disappoint the families and the judges will order that the marriage take place.[82]

In making their decisions, the judges thus considered the opinions of neighbors in determining whether there appeared to be an engagement between the couple in question. If the alleged seducer had in some way acted as a fiancé should act—caressing the woman, spending considerable time with her—then the judges might very well conclude that *fiançailles* existed even if no direct proof thereof could be produced. Moreover, a woman could be further safeguarded if she was pregnant. In 1799 a lawyer representing a pregnant woman in a contract dispute argued that "when, besides the contract itself—that is, the civil prom-

---

81. Caspard, "Conceptions prénuptiales," pp. 996–997.

82. Boyve, *Coutumier de Neuchâtel* (end of the eighteenth century), 1:147ff., Bibliothèque Publique et Universitaire de Neuchâtel, Ms A519, cited in Caspard, "Conceptions prénuptiales," p. 997, n. 31. At times it was not even necessary that the woman lead an irreproachable life. In 1776, Jean-Pierre Eckart filed suit against Catherine Greff for liberation from the marriage contract with her on the grounds that she was a prostitute. Called to testify, her former master said that he had fired her because he had found her "on the stairs, holding in her hands an unknown man's member, which was sticking out of his breeches." According to the judges, however, Eckart knew of this behavior when he proposed to Greff. As a result, they rejected his request and ordered him to go through with the marriage. In general then, if a woman had behaved well since the time of the promises, her fiancé could be forced to marry her; AEN, JMN6:302–323, 337–347, 349–357; Caspard, "Conceptions prénuptiales," p. 998.

ise—there is carnal knowledge and pregnancy, the fruit of the contract and of the subsequent carnal knowledge, then the marriage itself has already been contracted and the only element lacking is the solemnization which takes place with the nuptials."[83] Simply put, lacking definite proof of marriage promises, a woman was now much more likely to enforce a marriage contract if she was pregnant.

Elisabeth Gretillat's suit against Abram Magnin clearly shows that a woman who had given birth to a child might be able to enforce a contract even without direct proof of the engagement. First appearing before the Justice matrimoniale of Valangin in March 1745, two months before the birth of her child, Elisabeth claimed that she had had sexual relations with Abram only after accepting his marriage proposal. Abram consistently denied both the engagement and his paternity, and the *procès verbal* makes no mention of a written contract or of witnesses to oral promises. Most likely there was some evidence of *fiançailles,* because on June 24 Elisabeth was permitted to make a *serment suplétoire,* an oath that was ordinarily used to complement evidence that alone could not provide proof beyond a shadow of a doubt:

> On her knees, her hands on the Bible, the doors and windows open, she solemnized the *serment suplétoire* that had been granted her to support her cause and declared that what she had heretofore maintained was true, that Magnin was the father of the child she had given birth to on May 18 and that she had had sexual relations with him after he had promised to marry her.[84]

Having heard this oath, the judges passed sentence in favor of Elisabeth, assuring the child's legitimacy since he was conceived following promises of marriage and authorizing her to publicize the banns the following Sunday.[85] In effect, then, Elisabeth had "proved" the promises by swearing the oath, a practice expressly forbidden since the Reformation. Had there been no child involved, the court undoubtedly would not have allowed her to take the oath. In this case, the birth of a child was clearly used as an important piece of evidence. Essentially, the judges were reasoning backward: Magnin must have asked Elisabeth to marry him; otherwise she would not have given in to his desires. Though this

---

83. AEN, JMN: 24 October 1799, cited in Caspard, "Conceptions prénuptiales," pp. 997–998.
84. AEN, JMV3:103.
85. Ibid.

reasoning was not unknown to earlier periods, eighteenth-century judges appeared much more concerned about such births than had their predecessors.

Other suits further illustrate the important role played by pregnancies and illegitimate births in contract disputes. In 1792, Marie Madelaine Sandoz affirmed to the Justice matrimoniale of Valangin that André Mosset had asked her to marry him in the presence of witnesses and that it was he who had gotten her pregnant. Mosset denied all allegations. Swayed by Sandoz's evidence, the tribunal granted her request, ordering Mosset to respect the marriage contract. Two and a half months later, however, the parties again appeared in court; in the weeks that had passed, the child who had been the cause of this trial had died, rendering irrelevant the question of the baby's legitimacy. Both parties considered it prudent to avoid an unhappy, forced marriage and accordingly asked to be released from the contract. As a result, they had made a written agreement to back down from this engagement and humbly asked the tribunal to recognize this accord. The court accepted this request and released the parties from their *fiançailles*.[86] In the same manner, a woman who had won her contract suit in 1724 against the man who had fathered her twins was released from the engagement when the twins died.[87] In 1768 yet another woman withdrew her suit when, following a midwife's examination, she learned that she was not pregnant as she had thought. She convinced the judges to release her from the engagement since her sole intention had been to assure the legitimate status of the child with whom she thought she was pregnant.[88] This was, no doubt, the primary objective of most pregnant women who filed suits in hopes of forcing men to honor marriage contracts. The courts' willingness to release parties from contracts when children were no longer a question underscores the fact that judges were most concerned with the legitimacy of children conceived after marriage engagements.

At times women who had already given birth to children sought to prove that they had valid marriage contracts even though their fiancés were out of the country, another indication that they were more interested in procuring the legitimate status for their children than in forcing men to marry them. In 1764, Madelaine Louise Petitpierre brought

86. AEN, JMV5:188–190, 201–202, 218–219.
87. AEN, JMN3:229–230, 232–240.
88. Ibid., 925–949, 955–957; *Annexes* 416.

suit against Abram Barbezat, who was out of the country, claiming that he was the father of her son. To prove that Barbezat had proposed to her, Madelaine produced a letter he had written to her father asking for her hand in marriage. The customary three announcements were made without uncovering any information on the whereabouts of Abram, and the court recognized the engagement as valid and the child as legitimate.[89] Since her fiancé was out of the country and did not reply to the summons, the plaintiff did not really expect her seducer to share a domicile with her and join her in raising a family; rather, she simply wanted to assure the legitimacy of her son. But to what end? Even if the child was recognized as legitimate, Madelaine would still be a single parent; the family structure would appear no different from that of a woman living with an illegitimate child. Her motive may have been strictly a moral one. Having conceived a child after accepting a marriage proposal, she perhaps wanted to vindicate herself in the eyes of public opinion. More likely, she was seeking some sort of financial recompense. If her son was legitimate, he would have rights to any property his father might have left behind and to membership in his father's *commune d'origine*.

Material concerns were explicitly cited in a contract suit involving Lidie Huguelet, who held that Jean Pierre Prince of Neuchâtel was the father of her children. This case from 1790/91 was unique in that the plaintiff was not Lidie but rather the mayor, who happened to be her father, and a deputy of her home town of Woflin. These officials demanded that Prince go through with the marriage and that the children be recognized as legitimate, bluntly declaring that under no circumstances should the responsibility of supporting these children fall to the community of Woflin. Several witnesses testified that Prince had admitted to proposing to Lidie, though later he changed his mind and no longer wanted to marry her. Prince did not appear in court, and the Justice matrimoniale therefore passed judgment in favor of Lidie. In such fashion, the contract was binding, the children were legitimate, and the community of Woflin was apparently freed from the costs of raising these children. Claims could now be made on Prince's holdings to go toward the expenses of raising the children.[90]

89. AEN, JMN5:756–761, 764–769, 786–791. Among the evidence produced were some interesting love letters that Barbezat had written to Madelaine; see below.
90. AEN, JMN6:1265–1267, 1271–1296, 1300–1303, 1311–1313. On occasion the judges ordered the absent fiancé to pay a certain sum to support the abandoned woman and child. Elisabeth Madelaine Joux, for example, brought suit against Henry Guynand in 1729/

These suits to enforce marriage contracts on behalf of pregnant women or single mothers were closely related to legitimation cases. Both types of case were motivated primarily by material concerns, aiming to establish the child's legitimacy in order to assure rights to a portion of the father's property and membership in his *commune d'origine*.

When no pregnancy was involved, the judges applied different standards to determine whether a couple had to honor a disputed contract. When Jean Ozelie tried to force Susanne Henriette Ferrier to honor their contract in 1801, Susanne did not deny the engagement but bluntly expressed a repugnance for Ozelie and a desire to avoid a marriage with him at all costs. In dealing with this suit, Neuchâtel's matrimonial court noted the following:

> We must consider the repugnance manifested by the defendant toward fulfilling the promises and the all too remote hope that she could live with Ozelie in an edifying manner if she were forced to marry him. We must further take into account the fact that no question of pregnancy has been articulated, in which case the Venerable Chamber would not be able to refrain from forcing the parties to fulfill their engagement.[91]

The judges consequently declared the promises null, with the reservation that if the defendant was indeed pregnant the marriage would have to take place; otherwise, both parties were free to make engagements with others in four months, and Susanne was ordered to pay Ozelie 7 louis d'or in damages.[92]

Several other cases serve to show that when no child was involved the courts generally did not force couples to marry if one or both parties opposed the match. In 1732, David-François Huber and Marie Morel appeared before the tribunal of Valangin a few months after the publication of the banns. Now, they both wished to be released from their contract. Noting that the two of them agreed, the justices released them from the contract and condemned Huber to pay half the costs of the

---

30, asking that he execute their marriage contract and that the court recognize their child as legitimate. She further requested that Guynand provide material aid for both the child and her since her father was no longer able to support them. Considering that Guynand never appeared to respond to this suit, the court decreed that he had to honor the promises and provide a sum determined by *les assesseurs* to support his wife and child; AEN, JMN3:307–314, 321–337.

91. AEN, JMN7:766.

92. Ibid., 765–767.

court session (i.e., 25 livres), charitably exempting him from paying the rest.[93] Had they lived during the Reformation period, the consistory would have forced them to marry. By the mid-seventeenth century, they probably would have been released, though at the price of a serious censure and possibly stiff fines and even a few days' imprisonment. In this case, however, the judges did not utter a word of reproach; apart from the usual court costs, half of which were waived, no fine was imposed.

Similarly, the courts often canceled marriage contracts based on one party's refusal to go through with the marriage, provided that that party paid damages to the other.[94] In so doing, eighteenth-century courts continued the tradition, initiated in the preceding century, of not obliging couples to execute marriage contracts when it was clear that unhappy marriages would follow. If the tribunals did not require fiancés to be madly in love, they at least deemed it wise to avoid antipathetic matches. On occasion this pragmatic stand was taken even when children were involved, as seen in a case in 1733 involving David Gaberel. Gaberel was engaged to marry two women—Marie DeSaulles, who was pregnant at the time of the trial, and Judith Aubert, who apparently was not. Though it is unclear which engagement was made first, ordinarily a contract that produced children had priority over one that had not, even if the former was made later.[95] At first Marie wanted David to honor the engagement, but she changed her mind during the course of the trial. Disappointed with the light manner in which David entered into marriage agreements, Marie noted that he had openly stated his preference for Judith. Marie therefore agreed to dissolve their promises to marry on the condition that David recognize his paternity, provide financial support for the child, and pay her an appropriate sum in damages. Faced with this agreement, the judges agreed to cancel David and Marie's engagement, allowed him to marry Judith, and later recognized the legitimacy of Marie's child.[96]

By the early nineteenth century, however, Neuchâtel's matrimonial court—more so than Valangin's—expressed concern over the growing

93. AEN, JMV2:275–276.
94. Some marriage contracts established a sum to be paid if one party broke the engagement unilaterally. This was the case when Marie Madelaine Favre filed suit against David Barbier in 1743, asking him either to marry her or to pay her 1,000 francs as the contract specified. The court held in favor of Marie; AEN, JMN5:5–9; *Annexes* 410.
95. Samuel Ostervald, president of the Conseil d'Etat and one of Neuchâtel's most important eighteenth-century legal commentators, wrote that if a woman was pregnant her promise, though conditional and posterior, prevailed over another anterior, direct promise; *Loix, us et coutumes*, p. 20.
96. AEN, JMV2:335–356, 358–363; JMV3:1–2.

number of people who contracted marriage, produced children together, and then wished to be released from their engagements while maintaining their children's legitimacy. In 1802 judges expressed alarm in their sentence for the suit Marianne Benoit filed against Louis Frédéric Courvoisier. Having given birth a few months earlier, Marianne asked that Louis give full effect to their wedding engagement. The defendant, however, now had a strong aversion toward her and desperately wanted to avoid marrying her. Marianne replied that she was mainly concerned with the status of the child and would willingly drop the suit concerning the contract if the Justice matrimoniale recognized the child's legitimacy. Notwithstanding this agreement, the judges proclaimed:

> We must take into account the vital importance, especially in a time of decadent morals, of avoiding all confusion between the status of legitimate children and that of bastards, a distinction which the conclusions of the parties would tend, if not to eradicate, at least to weaken. Finally, we must consider that the institution of marriage and the promises that lead to it would become mere games taken lightly, ruled only by the libertinage of the parties, if we were to diminish the rigor of the laws already established and followed for such a long time. For these reasons, the tribunal refuses to acquiesce to the agreement proposed by the two parties . . . and orders them to proceed immediately with the publication of their marriage announcements followed without delay by the benediction of their marriage. Nevertheless, in light of the particular circumstances, the court deems it appropriate to allow this couple, after celebrating the marriage, to live separately during the period of six months. After this term, if they are unable to reunite . . . , they will have to appear once again before the *consistoire admonitif* of the church of Les Ponts, which in turn will refer them to this tribunal. At that time the court will decide what action must be taken: whether the marriage is to be dissolved or its effects suspended.[97]

Even though this decision required the couple to marry despite the defendant's repugnance for his would-be wife, this cannot be said to be a throwback to the Reformation, when antipathetic couples were not infrequently forced to honor their engagements to marry. Unlike these earlier cases, this decision foresaw that an actual union might not be

97. AEN, JMN7:866.

possible and allowed the parties to have future recourse to the matrimonial court if indeed they could not unite.

When it was obvious that forcing a couple to marry would produce unhappy, perhaps dangerous consequences, even Neuchâtel's Justice matrimoniale was willing to dissolve promises of fiancés who had produced children. Neuchâtel's judges showed a certain leniency in dealing with the suit involving Louise Vouga and Jean Henry Droz in 1797, a moment when the tribunal was least likely to dissolve contracts of couples who had children together. According to Louise, the plaintiff, when Droz had asked for her hand in marriage her father replied that she was only fourteen years old and had no fortune. But the reluctant father agreed to the match when Droz reportedly responded that he was rich enough for both of them. As a result of this relationship Louise now found herself pregnant, but Droz refused to marry her and, if forced to do so, threatened to beat her every hour, twenty-four times a day. Because of these menacing words, Louise sought to be released from the agreement to avoid a life of torment and asked for an appropriate sum in damages. The court accordingly canceled the contract and sentenced Droz to pay her 50 louis d'or.[98] In so doing, it again showed that in passing sentence it was willing to take into account the antipathy that reigned between fiancés. Neuchâtel's consistories were not the only courts to begin to pay more attention to affection in the eighteenth century when ruling on the formation of marriage.[99]

During these one hundred years, the courts were not altogether consistent in dealing with contract litigation. This inconsistency can undoubtedly be attributed to changes in the personnel of the tribunals; as old judges left, it is understandable that the new ones brought with them their own opinions concerning fiancés who had produced children together. Nevertheless, certain general trends can be discerned. In deciding whether to enforce disputed marriage contracts, judges proceeded in a very different manner from their predecessors. In Reformation Neuchâtel, the justices' only concern was to determine whether promises of marriage had been properly made: in the sixteenth century, if two people who were at least twenty years old agreed to marry in the presence of two or more witnesses, then the courts invariably ruled that the couple had to marry. In the eighteenth century, the justices showed

98. AEN, JMN7:294–305.
99. In the diocese of Montauban in southern France, the church was more willing to accept sentiment as a ground for granting dispensations to couples related within the prohibited degrees; Margaret Darrow, "Popular Concepts of Marital Choice in Eighteenth Century France," *Journal of Social History* 19 (1985): 261–272.

two overriding concerns that were not directly related to proving the existence of marriage engagements: illegitimate children and antipathetic marriages. Ideally, they would have preferred avoiding both. But attempting to minimize the number of children born out of wedlock meant at times requiring recalcitrant fiancés to go through with the consecration of the marriage. When the objectives of limiting both illegitimate children and unhappy marriages clashed, the courts generally gave more weight to the former. When a child was involved and evidence indicated that a contract existed, the couple ordinarily had to marry even if one party had an aversion to the union.

In the absence of a pregnancy, the tribunals almost never enforced a contract, deeming it a lesser evil to annul an engagement than to force an unwilling person into a marriage. Before the eighteenth century, most plaintiffs failed to enforce disputed contracts because they did not satisfactorily prove the existence of bona fide promises. After 1700, it became much more common for judges not to require couples to marry because of the unhappy marriage that would follow even though engagements had been properly made.

Parallel to this evolution in the attitudes of judges were similar changes among litigants. In the sixteenth and seventeenth centuries, it was not uncommon to find plaintiffs to contract disputes who blatantly tried to use marriage as a springboard to material wealth. The wage earner who used a piece of sausage to seal a promise of marriage with his employer's daughter and the washerwoman who vowed that a young noble soldier had agreed to marry her are cases in point. In the eighteenth century, cases in which people blatantly sought to capture wealthy spouses, often through deception, were much less common. No doubt material interests were still important to someone choosing a spouse in that century; the evidence from the court records indicates, however, that attempts to use marriage as a means of making dramatic ascents on the social ladder were much less common than they had been before.

Marriage contract disputes also reveal that at least some eighteenth-century Neuchâtelois discovered the love match. Some litigants expressed strong feelings of love for their fiancés, as seen in the aforementioned case of Madelaine Louise Petitpierre and Abram Barbezat. Madelaine gave birth to a child in 1761 and filed suit in 1764 to force Barbezat, the alleged father, to honor their engagement. The daughter of a Neuchâtel shoemaker, Madelaine had met Barbezat at

Caen in Normandy in 1760. Originally from Les Verrières in the county of Neuchâtel, Barbezat was a simple soldier in the French army stationed at Caen during the Seven Years' War. The defendant, like the plaintiff, belonged to the upper fringe of the working class; though he earned very little as a soldier, he possessed property in Neuchâtel worth several thousand livres. Despite the state of war, the troops at Caen were not under attack and had plenty of leisure time, providing Barbezat with ample opportunity to court Madelaine with the knowledge and evidently the consent of her uncle. The child was conceived in January 1761, but later that month Barbezat had to leave Caen to help defend Le Havre from the English. Thereafter, Madelaine saw Barbezat but one time, when he came to Caen for one week in March of the same year. In June she returned to Neuchâtel, where she gave birth to a son who was baptized 6 October 1761.[100]

Appearing before Neuchâtel's matrimonial court in June 1764, Madelaine asked that Barbezat honor their marriage agreement. Since he was still out of the country, Madelaine was instructed to contact his closest relatives and to post her demands at the county's boundaries. In support of her case, she produced twenty-five letters Barbezat had written between 1761 and 1763, twenty-four to her and one to her father. In these letters, as described by Caspard, Barbezat attested to the strongest feelings of love for Madelaine:

> The sentiment of love that Abram Barbezat expresses in his letters is characterized above all by its vehemence: the torrents of tears, oaths to the death, invocations to God or the gods, all of which were part of the contemporary romanesque literature with which Barbezat may have been familiar. Moreover, if the evocation of carnal love is almost totally absent, Barbezat clearly suffered no pangs of conscience concerning the sexual relations he had had a short time ago with his fiancée. He was shocked and indignant about the sanctions the church was taking against her—he seems rather far removed from the "official" morality, expressed in the legal or religious interdicts of the period, whose effect on the daily life of the people we have no doubt overestimated. Furthermore, Barbezat openly avowed his paternity,

100. Pierre Caspard, "L'amour et la guerre: Lettres d'un soldat neuchâtelois à sa fiancée pendant la guerre de Sept Ans," *Musée neuchâtelois*, 1979, 72–74; AEN, JMN5:756–758. The baptism was unusual in that the child was baptized as the legitimate son of Barbezat even though the trial before the Justice matrimoniale had not yet taken place.

expressly asking his fiancée to make it known around her. The tone with which he evoked "his fatherly compassion" or "the cries of his dear child" are perhaps also the expression of the sensitivity in regard to childhood which appeared in the course of the eighteenth century.[101]

The theme of the war appeared only as a counterpoint to that of love. In describing his duties as a soldier, Barbezat spoke above all about getting time off to visit Madelaine and eventually being discharged so that he could marry her.[102]

From the first letter to the last, Barbezat never wavered in assuring his affection and devotion:

> How happy I would be if I could be united with the object so dear to me. I repeat to you again that I don't know what in my soul makes me so joyful reading this letter [that you sent me], a letter that gives me so much pleasure. Never do I read it just once per day—as long as there is daylight, never does it leave my hands. I did all I could to come see you again, but they wanted to give me just ten days. How sad for me it would be to have to leave after just ten days, which would be like minutes for me, being close to you. I therefore postponed my visit until the first of next month, when I'll be able to stay with you longer.[103]

In his third letter, dated 17 February 1761, Barbezat wrote, "You alone can bring me happiness, and at the same time you alone, being separated from me, are the cause of my unhappiness." Drawing two interlaced hearts at the bottom of this letter, he proclaimed, "When two hearts are united, they make a paradise." In the eighth letter, written in May of the same year, Barbezat declared that he was devastated by his officers' refusal to give him leave. Sketching teardrops at the bottom of the page, he wrote, "I'll shed tears until I have my felicity."[104]

As the pregnancy progressed, Madelaine evidently grew exceedingly upset with her situation, but Barbezat did not once indicate that he had anything less than adoration for her. Writing in late July 1761, he consoled Madelaine:

---

101. Caspard, "L'amour et la guerre," pp. 74–75. In his last sentence, Caspard is supporting Ariès's thesis that the modern concept of childhood was born in the eighteenth century.

102. Ibid., p. 75.

103. Ibid., p. 76; AEN, JMN: *Annexes* 415.

104. Caspard, "L'amour et la guerre," pp. 77, 79–80; AEN, JMN: *Annexes* 415.

I join my chagrin with your tears, and the most tender feeling grows stronger in my heart from day to day. Yes, I dare repeat to you that this most sincere love will end only with my death. Because I recognize in you the greatest qualities, a spirit who deigns to love me. In a word, I can find nothing great enough with which to praise you. Oh, how happy am I to be loved by the most lovable woman of the century—I who am nothing. . . . Yes, I am favored by the gods. They use their intrigues between you and me, for one cannot find two lovers so tender.[105]

Barbezat had written Madelaine's father in April 1761 to ask for his daughter's hand in marriage, a request that Abram Petitpierre, as yet unaware of Madelaine's pregnancy, at first rejected. When Petitpierre later consented to their union, Barbezat expressed his joy to Madelaine in the following fashion:

How happy I was to be your servant and to offer my care and to pass moments obeying you. But now my state is so much sweeter since I have the name of husband that you now deign to accord me. Until now my heart was always pining, but this word "husband" makes it the happiest of hearts, most content with the choice that has been given it. . . . Yes, my love is still the same and nothing can change it.[106]

After the birth of the child, Barbezat showed a real interest in the child and continued to profess his love for Madelaine. In March 1762, he expressed his joy in learning that the young son, who had been ailing, was now enjoying good health. He confided to Madelaine that he dreamed about her every night and swore that "as long as God gives me life, I will never abandon you." Distraught, he added: "I am surprised that they refuse to let you take communion. I don't know the reason for this refusal. If you had a child, it was not a bastard. I recognize him as my own and you may show by the letters that I've written you and signed with my hand . . . that I recognize the child as mine, provided that I marry you, which I desire with all my heart."[107]

As the war waged on, Barbezat found himself forced to go first to Canada, where he was stationed at Saint-Jean Island (known today as

105. Caspard, "L'amour et la guerre," p. 82; AEN, JMN: *Annexes* 415.
106. Caspard, "L'amour et la guerre," p. 83; AEN, JMN: *Annexes* 415.
107. Caspard, "L'amour et la guerre," p. 85; AEN, JMN: *Annexes* 415.

Prince Edward Island), and then to Port Louis in Guadeloupe. His letters continued to arrive periodically, still professing the same feelings. In September 1763, Barbezat, now back in France, wrote his last letter to Madelaine. Signing this missive as "your dear and faithful husband," Barbezat composed a brief verse in which he assured her of his devotion despite the long absence.[108]

Notwithstanding his repeated claims to the contrary, we may wonder whether Barbezat was sincere in saying that he could not get leave to come to Neuchâtel to marry Madelaine. In the trial, Madelaine avowed that he was merely inventing pretexts to avoid marrying her. Nevertheless, at this time soldiers were often not even sure they would be liberated at the end of their enlistment period, especially in times of war. The fact that Barbezat had formally written Petitpierre in April 1761 for permission to marry Madelaine seems to indicate that, at least at that time, he sincerely wanted to marry. Since he abruptly broke off correspondence in September 1763, however, it may well be that he was having second thoughts.[109]

In light of the overwhelming evidence that they had been engaged, Madelaine won her case, but this love story did not have a happy ending. Though she was recognized as Barbezat's wife and her son as his legitimate child, they obviously would never live together in connubial bliss. Nevertheless, these letters are most valuable in providing a window on romantic love in the eighteenth century. Edward Shorter has asked how, even if we could get hold of a group of love letters of popular origin, we could know that the feelings expressed therein were typical of a class or group.[110] That, of course, cannot be known. The reason these letters are extant, however, is precisely because this story did not end happily. Had Barbezat returned to Neuchâtel to marry Madelaine, there would have been no suit and the letters would not have found their way into the records of Neuchâtel's Justice matrimoniale. Although there is no other contemporary collection of letters in Neuchâtel to provide a comparison, the romantic love of Barbezat almost certainly was not unique. These letters are an important piece of evidence that suggests that the role of sentiment in choosing spouses was increasing in the eighteenth century.

---

108. Caspard, "L'amour et la guerre," pp. 74, 89; AEN, JMN: *Annexes* 415. The verse read as follows: "Compatissé à la peine / De celuy qui vous aime / Jammais le longt temps ny l'absence / Ne changera pas ma constance."
109. Caspard, "L'amour et la guerre," p. 75.
110. Ibid., 75–76; Shorter, *Making of the Modern Family,* p. 18.

Aside from Barbezat's intimate letters, we have autobiographical material describing how Abraham Louis Sandoz, an eighteenth-century notary, chose his wife. Sandoz was a justiciary in La Chaux-de-Fonds and clearly a devout Reformed Protestant. On 15 April 1756, he described his courting period as a young man. Hoping that he would soon decide to marry, his parents had not interfered in his social life as long as he avoided bad company. During one year, however, he led a rather hedonistic lifestyle with "loud company," but he soon grew weary of this superficial atmosphere. He then began looking for a wife, associating only with those people with whom he could be completely open. Among potential candidates was a woman who openly professed an interest in marrying Sandoz, taking him somewhat by surprise since he did not expect someone as wealthy as she to be interested in him. Though he found this woman agreeable, Sandoz had stronger feelings for another with whom he had not yet broached the subject. Not wanting to reject the wealthy woman's offer quite yet, Sandoz first said that he was indeed honored that she had such feelings for him but needed some time to think it over. She replied, however, that she had brought up the subject of marriage so abruptly because another man—a wealthy man, as a matter of fact—had energetically solicited her hand in marriage. Before responding to this offer, she wanted to tell Sandoz how she felt about him. Surprised and flattered by this revelation, Sandoz was momentarily at a loss for words, but he managed to tell her that she might be wise to direct her affection toward the well-to-do suitor, pointing out the advantages the other man had to offer.[111]

Sandoz then spoke about his marriage prospects with his parents and indicated his preference for Anne Marie Robert, a former member of his confirmation class of 1727. They seemed pleased with his choice of Anne Marie, the daughter of the late Abram Robert. His father noted that in choosing a wife one must not put as much emphasis on wealth as on character. Though young and inexperienced, Anne Marie was deemed capable of making a good living. She was sweet and hardworking, and she came from a good family that was thrifty and had acquired through its labors some property that could be transmitted to their posterity. Their opinion was enough to convince Sandoz to speak to Anne Marie about the possibility of marriage.[112]

111. La Chaux-de-Fonds, Switzerland, Bibliothèque de la Ville, *Journal d'Abraham Louis Sandoz,* 3:14–15.
112. Ibid., pp. 13, 15.

Meanwhile, Sandoz had not seen the other woman since the day she had in effect proposed to him. She now wrote him a letter, begging him not to delay any longer in responding to her inquiry. Sandoz was becoming disenchanted with this woman's aggressiveness and accordingly wrote her a letter in which he politely told her that, though honored by her offer, he could not at that time make a decision. Not wanting to be an obstacle to her fortune, he mentioned the good qualities of the wealthier man who had proposed to her and recommended that she accept his offer. Sandoz never again spoke about the subject of marriage with this woman and did not know how this letter was received.[113]

Sandoz then proceeded to discuss the matter of marriage with Anne Marie. She graciously heard his proposal but, wise young woman that she was, refused to make a decision without first conferring with her uncle, who had assumed the authority of her late parents over her. Sandoz then spent a few anxious days waiting for her reply. So nervous was he that his teacher asked him what was wrong. He confided to her what was happening in his life, bemused at the "strange mystery" his feelings could cause him. After a few days, he returned to Anne Marie's abode for their rendezvous, whereupon she accepted the proposal and they touched hands as a symbol of their union. They wrote the announcements in August 1730, and everyone in both families was happy about the match, especially Sandoz himself, who had won the bride he desired. On 11 November 1730, the eighteen-year-old Sandoz went alone to fetch Anne Marie at her home, and together they walked to church where they were wed. The ceremony was followed by a big family supper at his father's home.[114]

Sandoz's narrative is interesting in showing that in early eighteenth-century courtship sentiment could outweigh wealth. Both he and the unnamed woman who proposed to him were willing to turn down offers from wealthier people in favor of partners for whom they had stronger feelings. Even though this narrative has no trace of the melodramatic romance that inspired Barbezat, Sandoz, writing a quarter-

113. Ibid., pp. 15–16.
114. Ibid., p. 16. Such early marriages were rare in Neuchâtel and elsewhere at this time. Studying Neuchâtel census of 1712, Raoul Cop has discovered that marriages in general were late. Men probably married at about thirty years; in the mountainous area around the town of La Chaux-de-Fonds, only 5 of 28 men between the ages of twenty and twenty-four were married. Wives were on average 3.75 years younger than their husbands. Because of these late marriages, families tended to be small, averaging fewer than three children per household; "Recensement," p. 134.

century after his wedding, nonetheless showed a genuine interest in Anne Marie. While awaiting her response, he suffered a few painful days in which his mood shifted from hope and joy to fear and uncertainty. And when she accepted his proposal, he was thrilled to have won her over. Though flattered that the wealthier woman was interested in him, Sandoz never hinted that he would forswear Anne Marie for her. The frank and earnest inquiries of the woman reveal that she deemed her affection for Sandoz far more important than the riches of her suitor. In short, both Sandoz and this woman were quite ready to trade wealth for affection.

Parents involved in this affair were passive advisers. Unlike some parents from earlier centuries, they did not actively solicit husbands and wives for their children; rather, they let the young people take the initiative themselves and then gave their approval or disapproval. Sandoz's parents, though hoping their son would soon marry, did not push him toward a particular woman. It was Abraham Louis Sandoz himself who first thought of Anne Marie as a potential wife and then asked his parents' opinion. Anne Marie's uncle did not actively seek an advantageous marriage for his niece but simply gave his approval when she received an offer that pleased her. Likewise, the more aggressive woman acted on her own initiative independent of her parents when she revealed her feelings to Sandoz. From all sides, this affair supports the view that young people were able to pursue marriages relatively independent of parental pressure in the eighteenth century.

Like their sons and daughters, parents also valued sentiment more than wealth in the process of choosing spouses. Though noting that Anne Marie's hard-working family had acquired some property, Sandoz's father explicitly recommended character over wealth. He was quite content with his son's choice and did not in any way try to pressure him into accepting the more financially attractive offer. For the previous one hundred fifty years, numerous instances can be found in which parents vigorously encouraged their children to marry certain individuals for financial reasons. In contrast to such practices—clearly exceptional even in the sixteenth and seventeenth centuries—more eighteenth-century parents simply advised, rather than directed, their sons and daughters in choosing spouses. Even though the young people of Neuchâtel could not marry without parental consent until the age of twenty-two, mothers and fathers who served as matchmakers were rarer than before; the vast majority of parents, like Sandoz's, allowed their children freer rein in choosing mates.

The various changes in the formation of marriage and the control of sexuality from earlier times to the Prussian period were all related. The increase in premarital sexuality, the growing number of female plaintiffs to contract disputes, and the more aggressive prosecution of female fornicators were tied to changing mores and economic developments. As more people became wage earners, the ownership of property became less important for financial status and thus declined as a factor in spousal choice. Since a couple's financial well-being depended less on the transfer of family property, parents accorded their children greater freedom in selecting mates. Consequently, young people were able to place greater emphasis on romantic love in forming marriages, and fewer people used matrimony as a means of ascending the social ladder. Popular mores began to condone sexual relations among couples who were engaged to marry, but some young people went beyond this newly acquired liberty and indulged in sexual relations even when they did not have marriage in mind. Magistrates generally tolerated the growing number of pregnant brides, but not the illegitimate births. Judicial authorities tacitly accepted sexual relations that were literally premarital and did everything to protect the interests of women who got pregnant after accepting marriage proposals. At the same time, magistrates, particularly in the city of Neuchâtel, were obsessed with eliminating prostitution and minimizing illegitimate births in the late eighteenth century.

5

The Breakdown of Marriage, 1707–1806

DIVORCE

During the course of the eighteenth century, the most dramatic changes in matrimonial disputes took place in the area of divorce. Whereas at the beginning of the century judges for the first time recognized cruelty as a viable ground for dissolving marriages, cruel misconduct was not commonly cited in divorce cases until the late eighteenth century. Toward the end of the century of Prussian rule, the justices further promoted companionate marriages by taking the unprecedented step of accepting incompatibility as sufficient grounds for divorce. These innovations promoted domestic harmony and served the interests of women more than men.

While divorce cases changed qualitatively, their numbers also increased dramatically vis-à-vis other forms of litigation. For the first time in the history of these courts, divorce suits displaced contract disputes as the most common type of marital dispute. The increase in the quantity of divorce suits is remarkable, far surpassing the rate of the contemporary population increase. The consistory of Valangin had heard a scanty 41 divorce cases for the years 1622–1706; a total of 426 requests for divorces were made during the eighteenth century: 227 in Neuchâtel and 199 in Valangin. Of these, only 78 suits were heard during the first fifty years of this period; 348 such cases were heard from 1757 to 1806. If we compare the statistics for the first and last decades of this century, the increase in court activity is still more dramatic: only 15 persons

219

petitioned for divorce in Neuchâtel and Valangin from 1707 to 1716, whereas Neuchâtelois filed 128 divorce suits from 1797 to 1806. Over all, while the population of the principality increased by 70 percent during this century, the volume of divorce cases heard in the same period increased by roughly 750 percent.

Several factors account for this increase in divorces. To a certain extent, the increase in marital breakdown was likely due to a greater emphasis on emotion and sentiment in marriage. As Lawrence Stone suggests, the more marriage is based on sentiment, the more common marital breakdown becomes. As love matches became more common in eighteenth-century England, Stone argues, women grew less tolerant of their husbands' infidelity and increasingly asked and received judicial separations.[1] Eighteenth-century French novelists and pamphleteers strongly advocated the love match as opposed to the marriage of convenience, and they eloquently argued in favor of divorce in order to maintain happy, loving marriages.[2] Residents of Neuchâtel may have been influenced by this literature; at any rate, eighteenth-century jurists and litigants put, as we see below, more importance on the personal compatibility of spouses than had Neuchâtelois of earlier centuries.

Another possible contributing factor to the expanding number of divorces was the growing secularization of society. Influenced by the pens of Voltaire, Montesquieu, and other philosophes, some western Europeans moved away from certain religious traditions. In Enlightenment Neuchâtel, perhaps religious motives were no longer such a strong deterrent to divorce. Moreover, various scholars have suggested that the control of marriage had become fully secularized by the eighteenth century. Roderick Phillips, for example, argues that matrimonial courts established during the Reformation were becoming secularized; mixed courts comprising both secular and ecclesiastical authorities became less common, giving way to completely secular tribunals. William Monter has found that even in late sixteenth-century Geneva the mixed courts lost jurisdiction over the control of marriage and morality to secular authorities.[3] Citing examples from eighteenth-century Scandinavia, Germany, Austria, Scotland, and England, Phillips attests to secularization at several levels.

1. Stone, "Broken Lives: Marital Separation and Divorce in England, 1660–1860," Merle Curti Lecture Series, Madison, Wis., 28–30 October 1986.
2. Traer, *Marriage and the Family,* p. 106.
3. Phillips, *Putting Asunder,* p. 203; Monter, "Women in Calvinist Geneva," p. 207.

One was the intervention of secular institutions such as Parliament or the monarchy in both legislation and jurisdiction; legislative, executive, and judicial functions often mingled happily in these cases. Second, the role of the church courts in dealing with the dissolution of marriage curtailed. Third, the content of divorce policies was extended beyond the grounds theologically approved in the sixteenth century to include circumstances and offenses justified by essentially secular notions of contract law, natural law, and equity.[4]

Of these examples of secularization, only the third held true in Neuchâtel. Although jurisdictional changes evidently took place in neighboring Geneva and elsewhere, Neuchâtel's tribunals in the eighteenth century were no different in structure from those of the sixteenth century. Church courts per se had never existed in Protestant Neuchâtel; throughout the 1700s, the consistories and Justices matrimoniales, which continued to oversee the control of marriage and morality, included two pastors among their members.

Economic changes indubitably played an important role in augmenting the number of divorces. As more people earned wages by working in protoindustrial activities, the economic bonds within households were loosening. The most important protoindustrial activities in Neuchâtel—the production of watches, lace, and *indiennes*—depended less on the cooperative efforts of all family members than had traditional agricultural endeavors, thereby reducing the household's importance as a productive unit. Consequently, husbands and wives who worked for wages would have felt less compelled to remain together for economic reasons than had their peasant counterparts. In his work on Rouen, Phillips uncovered some interesting information on the occupations of litigants to divorce cases under the very liberal divorce laws of the revolutionary period. From 1792 to 1816, 72 percent of the women who filed for divorce were "working women," engaged especially in the textile industry. Of the men who petitioned for divorce, 69 percent were "working men"; though many of them were also employed in the textile industry, male plaintiffs were engaged in a rather broad range of manual labor. Phillips has the impression that men seeking divorce in Rouen had broadly the same socioeconomic profile as married men who did not divorce, whereas more women seeking divorce were from

4. Phillips, however, further notes that the industrialization, urbanization, revolutionary sentiment, and international warfare of the eighteenth century also must have contributed to increased marital instability; *Putting Asunder*, pp. 204, 225.

the middle class and above, probably because they had the financial independence to remain unmarried after a divorce. Rudolf Braun maintains that, as the households of wage earners were losing their importance as centers of production, divorce became much more common in the Zurich Oberland. The economic bonds that had held peasant households together were coming undone.[5] We cannot know for certain how many Neuchâtelois wage laborers were involved in divorces, since the records of Neuchâtel's matrimonial courts almost never mention the litigants' occupations. Since a large percentage of the active population was involved in wage labor, it is reasonable to assume that a good proportion of the litigants were employed in protoindustry.

Demographic factors also could have been significant in the increasing number of divorces in the eighteenth century. As we have seen, wage labor tended to foster earlier marriages. Just as youthful marriages are associated with high divorce rates in modern times, so they contributed to marital breakdown in early modern Europe.[6] Moreover, spared the harsh bouts with famine and epidemics that had plagued their forefathers, eighteenth-century Europeans enjoyed unprecedented longevity. In his study of French parish registers, André Armengaud has found that in Beauvaisis only 28–40 percent of the people lived beyond the age of sixty in the seventeenth century; from 1771 to 1790, however, 43–61 percent survived to such an advanced age. If less dramatic, the figures for Saumur nevertheless reveal a palpable increase in longevity: whereas 35–38 percent of its population lived to the age of sixty in the 1600s, 47 percent did so in the following century.[7] This greater life span, coupled with younger brides and grooms, obviously meant that

5. Ibid., pp. 268–270; Braun, *Industrialisation and Everyday Life,* pp. 46–47. Even in areas that remained closely tied to agriculture and animal husbandry, economic changes could cause instability in marriages. David Sabean found that, with the introduction of root crops and the increase in animal husbandry in the late eighteenth century, women in Neckarhausen assumed several new productive tasks, including the gathering of fodder, the stall feeding of cows and oxen, the hoeing of fields, and the preparation of flax and hemp. This new sexual division of labor caused tensions in marriages, resulting in a significant increase in divorces during the period 1800–1840. Women sought the majority of these divorces, often complaining about their husbands' verbal and physical abuse or drunkenness—a fault viewed as a threat to a woman's property. This crisis in marriages subsided and the number of divorces fell off in the 1840s, reflecting a certain accommodation between husbands and wives with regard to the sexual division of labor; *Property, Production, and Family in Neckarhausen,* pp. 124–162.

6. Phillips discovered that 40 percent of the women who got divorced in revolutionary Rouen had married before the age of twenty-one, whereas the average age at marriage was between twenty-four and twenty-seven; *Putting Asunder,* p. 271.

7. Armengaud, *La famille et l'enfant en France et en Angleterre du XVIe au XVIIIe siècle: Aspects démographiques* (Paris, 1975), p. 78; see also Jacques DuPâquier, *La population française aux XVIIe et XVIIIe siècles* (Paris, 1979).

TABLE II
Divorce cases, by gender of plaintiff, 1707–1806

| | Plaintiff | | |
	Women (%)	Men (%)	Joint (%)
All Cases	246 (58)	175 (41)	5 (1)
Grounds			
Absence/desertion	140 (62)	87 (38)	0
Adultery	44 (41)	62 (59)	0
Cruelty/misconduct	48 (74)	17 (26)	0
Crime	25 (80.6)	6 (19.4)	0
Incompatibility	7 (39)	8 (44.4)	3 (16.6)

marriages lasted longer. Micheline Baulant found that "scattered families," which include children from previous marriages or adopted or-
phans, were common in the seventeenth century when mortality was
quite high but were much rarer after 1730 when death rates and remarriages declined—evidence that indicates marriages were lasting longer.[8]
In earlier centuries, divorces might have been unnecessary simply because marriages were ended so frequently by the death of one of the
spouses. Stone has found that, in spite of high divorce rates, marriages
tend to last longer in twentieth-century America than they did in early
modern England. In 1955 the average marriage in the United States
lasted thirty-one years, whereas in seventeenth- and eighteenth-century
England the average length was probably seventeen to twenty years.[9]
Because of our longevity today, divorce more than ever before has come
to replace the death of a spouse as the means of ending a marriage. In
a more modest way, the increased life expectancy of the eighteenth century likely contributed to the growing number of divorces.

Regardless of the causes, this increase in divorces is undeniable. In
analyzing plaintiffs to divorce litigation as a group, we find that women
constituted a sizable majority (see Table 11). Of the 426 cases, women
initiated 246 (58 percent), men filed 175 suits (41 percent), and 5 (1
percent) were brought jointly. In some ways the results of this litigation
resemble those for the earlier periods in that the vast majority of these

8. Baulant, "The Scattered Family: Another Aspect of Seventeenth-Century Demography,"
in *Family and Society*, ed. Forster and Ranum, pp. 114–115.
9. Stone, *Family, Sex, and Marriage*, p. 55. In the same manner, Peter Laslett has found
that, notwithstanding the great concern shown today for children growing up in single-parent
households, families in which one or both parents were absent were as common or more common in early modern England as in contemporary society; *Family Life and Illicit Love*, pp.
160–173.

requests were granted. Plaintiffs, be they male or female, enjoyed high odds of receiving divorces. Excluding the 42 suits that were abandoned, we find that 86 percent of the decisions rendered (330 of 384) accorded divorces. Only 16 such actions (4 percent) were rejected, and 38 parties (10 percent) received separations that allowed husband and wife to live apart for a specified period of time in hopes of an eventual reconciliation. This does not mean that the courts had become lenient in dissolving marriages. As before, parties who sought divorces still had to be referred to the court by their pastors or the *consistoires admonitifs,* a process that effectively screened those without plausible grounds for divorce. A comparison with contemporary English statistics, however, yields some striking results. From 1670 to 1857, when divorce was possible only by act of Parliament, only 325 people, 4 of whom were women, received divorces in England, a country with a population of several million.[10] In other words, the principality of Neuchâtel, which numbered 48,000 people at its peak, had more divorces in one century than did all of England in two; and the large majority of Neuchâtel's divorces went to women.

As in the previous period, the most commonly cited ground for divorce was desertion or the simple absence of a spouse (see Table 12).[11] Women continued to make up the large majority of those plaintiffs who cited abandonment as a motive for divorce: 140 women (62 percent) as opposed to 87 men (38 percent). In many ways, eighteenth-century tribunals resembled earlier courts in the manner in which they handled suits based on desertion. On the whole, if a spouse was absent without the consent of the other for a certain period of time, the other could file for divorce and would most likely succeed in his or her suit. Only when it appeared that the husband and wife colluded to separate, or that the abandoned spouse was not worthy of receiving a divorce, did the courts refuse to grant a divorce or at least a separation. In 1802, for example, Marie Madelaine Bergenat asked to be divorced from her husband, Olivier, on the grounds of incompatibility and desertion, based on his stubborn refusal to live with her. When the judges ordered her to declare by oath whether there was any collusion between them, Marie seemed to be on the verge of receiving her divorce. She dutifully swore that there was no collusion between them; then, in an incredible act of bungling self-contradiction, she produced a transaction that she and her

10. Phillips, *Putting Asunder,* p. 279.
11. It was not uncommon that more than one motive was given in divorce cases.

TABLE 12
Grounds cited in divorce suits, 1707–1806

	Absence/ desertion	Adultery	Cruelty/ misconduct	Crime	Incompati- bility	Impotence	Illness	Bigamy	Misc.	Grounds unknown
Times cited										
1707–1716	3	7	1	2	0	1	0	1	0	0
1717–1726	8	7	1	0	0	0	0	1	0	0
1727–1736	4	6	1	1	0	0	0	0	0	1
1737–1746	12	10	0	1	0	1	0	0	0	0
1747–1756	9	5	2	2	0	2	0	0	1	0
1757–1766	21	10	3	1	0	1	1	3	0	0
1767–1776	35	13	7	1	2	1	1	2	2	0
1777–1786	29	7	8	7	1	4	2	0	3	2
1787–1796	45	22	15	5	1	0	2	0	1	1
1797–1806	61	19	27	11	14	1	2	1	5	4
	227	106	65	31	18	11	8	8	12	8
Percentage[a]										
1707–1806	53	25	15.3	7.3	4.2	2.6	1.9	1.9	2.6	1.9
1797–1806	47.7	14.8	21	8.6	11.0	0.8	1.6	0.8	4.0	3.1

[a]Percentage of divorce cases in which grounds were cited.

225

husband had signed whereby they agreed to the divorce. Indignant, the judges viewed this convention, which blatantly contradicted her suit and her oath, as scandalous and dismissed the case.[12] Such cases, however, were exceptional; ordinarily, if a spouse had been abandoned and had behaved in an upright manner during the separation, then he or she would receive the dissolution.

One notable change in the eighteenth century is that abandoned spouses were no longer required to wait so long before receiving divorces. Even in the seventeenth century the courts had occasionally granted divorces after absences of less than seven years, the traditional waiting period. This tendency, however, was taken much farther during the eighteenth century. By the end of the century, abandoned spouses, usually wives, were often able to obtain divorces quite quickly. This is aptly seen in the case Susanne nee Richard brought against her husband, Jean Daniel Digdos, in Valangin in 1786. Complaining about her husband's behavior, Susanne filed for divorce only two months after Digdos had deserted the household. Susanne made the usual three announcements, but Digdos failed to appear. His father came in his stead, saying that he had no idea where his son was and protesting that an abandoned spouse had to wait at least one year and six weeks before filing for divorce. The elder Digdos asked for a delay of six months so that his son could be informed of the suit. But, rejecting this request, the judges awarded Susanne a divorce in August 1786, only three months after the case opened, and they granted her the right to remarry seven months after the decision.[13] Similarly, in 1793 Jean Jacob Beittler received a divorce even though his wife had abandoned him and their three children just months before the case opened. A rather poor man, Beittler made the customary three announcements and also produced witnesses who testified to his wife's desertion and intimated that she might have committed adultery. The judges awarded the divorce in October 1793, three months after Beittler's first appearance in

12. AEN, JMN7:857, 859, 861–865. In cases in which the abandoned spouse may have agreed in a less conspicuous manner to the departure of the other, the court might accord a separation instead of a divorce. This was the sentence rendered when Henriette, wife of Daniel Henry Matthey, filed for divorce on the ground of desertion. In explaining their decision, the judges noted that the husband's absence did not appear to be "malicious desertion" and they therefore could not grant the divorce. Nevertheless, because of Matthey's "criminal negligence" of his duties toward his children, Henriette was awarded a separation of body and property for four years, during which time Matthey was ordered to pay her 1 écu per month in child support; ibid., 407–409, 416–418.
13. AEN, JMV4:441–448.

court. Beittler was also given permission to remarry in three months, during which time his wife could still appear to oppose the *passement* her husband had received.[14]

Since the above two cases had accusations of misconduct and adultery along with those of desertion, one may be led to believe that the rapidity with which these divorces were accorded was a result of the other grounds. Such a conclusion, however, is tenuous at best. If Beittler had received the divorce on the ground of adultery instead of desertion, he would not have been required to wait three months to remarry; had unequivocal proof been produced of his wife's infidelity, she would not have had the opportunity of later overturning the decision against her. By the same token, it is clear that Susanne Digdos received a divorce because of her husband's absence, not his mistreatment. Had it been the latter, she would have had to produce witnesses who could attest to his misbehavior. Furthermore, in yet another case, Marianne Grezer was granted a divorce in a similarly short period of time though absolutely no motive other than desertion was mentioned. Her husband, Philippe Grezer, deserted the household in July 1805, and Marianne filed suit for divorce in January of the following year. Marianne made the three announcements in church and posted notices of her action at the boundaries of the county, but Grezer did not respond to this suit. Accordingly, in March 1806 the court awarded Marianne her divorce with permission to remarry after a three-month wait.[15] In other words, Marianne could have remarried in June 1806, less than one year after her husband's departure. This and the previous cases indicate that by the end of the eighteenth century the requirements for receiving a divorce on the basis of desertion were a far cry from the standard seven-year wait of the sixteenth and seventeenth centuries. Eighteenth-century judges, in brief, paid considerably more attention to the rights and needs of abandoned spouses than had their predecessors.

Eighteenth-century judges also rejected the traditional view that desertion was a valid ground for divorce only if the absent spouse could safely be presumed dead. In Enlightenment Neuchâtel, judicial authorities were known to award divorces when a person was alive and well in the county but refused to live with his or her spouse. Typically, such cases involved women who had left their households, often citing their husbands' misbehavior as the reason for living apart. At times the courts deemed such separations unwarranted and awarded divorces to the

14. AEN, JMN7:1–8.
15. AEN, JMN8:130–133.

plaintiffs, often imposing fines on the absent women.[16] In other cases, judges showed sympathy toward the spouse who had left, at times indicating that the departure was justified. In 1800, for example, the Justice matrimoniale of Valangin delivered a sentence in favor of Rose Guinand, who refused to return to her husband, Moyse. Following a four-year judicial separation, Moyse filed for divorce on the ground of desertion, since Rose refused to live with him. To this demand, Rose responded that Moyse's poor treatment of her had been the original cause of the separation, that she was the innocent party, and that, already advanced in age, she wished to pass the rest of her days peacefully, a wish that would not be fulfilled if she were forced to live with Guinand. Interestingly enough, though Moyse had filed the suit, the tribunal granted the divorce to Rose, holding both parties accountable for their own expenses and for half the court costs.[17] In 1733, Anne Marie nee Sandoz received a similarly favorable decision against Fredrich Perret Gentil, who had deserted the household and had provided no support for his wife and their five children during his twelve-year absence. Returning to the county, Perret Gentil now wished to live with his wife, but Anne Marie wanted no such reunion. She claimed that in five years they had been together Fredrich had dissipated the family fortune of 5,000 écus; and if that was bad, his subsequent desertion of twelve years was worse. Considering that Perret Gentil had deserted his wife for twelve years and showed no improvement in behavior, the judges awarded Anne Marie a divorce and permission to remarry.[18]

These and other cases show that judicial standards had changed dramatically from the days when divorces for desertion were granted only after long absences—usually seven years—when it appeared likely that the absent spouse was deceased. And it is significant that all parties in such cases who persistently refused to return to their spouses were women. Whether they viewed this refusal sympathetically or disapprovingly, the judges granted divorces in these circumstances. Even if the woman was ordered to pay a certain sum in damages, she nevertheless was eventually freed from an insufferable marriage. In such cases, the courts were in a way granting a divorce more for incompatibility than for desertion. Unable to force women physically to return to their hus-

16. AEN, JMN6:549–555, 561–566, 571–609, 760–764, 766–770; JMN7:271–272, 274–281, 284–289.
17. AEN, JMV6:120–124.
18. AEN, JMV4:121–126, 128–132.

bands, the courts eventually awarded divorces that both parties wanted. The male plaintiffs desired divorces because their wives would not live with them; the female defendants sought the same outcome to avoid their husbands' excesses or misbehavior.

Many suits founded on desertion were thus closely related to those based on the grounds of cruelty or misbehavior. Women, however, did not have to wait for their husbands to sue for desertion to counter with a suit grounded on cruelty. Records reveal only one divorce being granted for cruelty in the previous period, but the courts heard 65 cases in which cruelty was cited as a motive for divorce during the Prussian era. As one may expect, women made up the overwhelming majority of plaintiffs citing cruelty or misconduct as grounds for divorce: 48 of 65 (74 percent). When staying with one's spouse could put one's life in jeopardy, the courts willingly granted a divorce to the innocent party, as seen in Judith Grenier's suit in 1773. Witnesses testified that on several occasions her husband threatened Judith's life and came close to following through with these threats. Pierre Perret, evidently a neighbor, reported that he once rescued Judith after hearing her scream for help. When he rushed into their home, Perret found Grenier clutching Judith by the throat with one hand and wielding a knife with the other. Such violent behavior was considered dangerous enough to merit a divorce.[19] If Jean Louis Girard's tantrums were less dramatic than Grenier's, they too sufficed for a divorce. Girard's wife, Jeanne Marie, filed for divorce in 1777, asserting that her husband often went into rages and smashed furniture, throwing the broken pieces out the window. Their servant further reported that, when furious, Girard would swear at his wife and threaten to break her arms. Although he had repeatedly promised to behave better, Girard persistently regressed to his violent ways. At first denying these accusations, Girard eventually acceded to Jeanne Marie's request and the two of them presented a convention by which they jointly asked for a divorce or at least a separation.[20] In striking contrast to earlier centuries, when the courts would not even hear divorce requests based solely on cruelty, women now enjoyed considerable protection from violent husbands. Had the Perret Gentils, the volatile couple of the mid-seventeenth century, lived a century later, they would not have been required to stay together until death or adultery did them part. By the eighteenth century, cruelty and misconduct could suffice for a divorce.

19. Ibid., 152–159.
20. AEN, JMN6:372–373, 375–384, 387.

In dealing with cases of cruelty, the courts at times granted separations of body and property rather than divorces. In 1802, Barbara Muller filed for divorce against her husband, Henry, claiming that he had brutally beaten her even when she was pregnant, causing the death of their unborn child. Not denying that he had beaten his pregnant wife, Muller maintained that she had provoked this violence by hiding money from him. Nonetheless, he did not oppose her petition for a divorce. Arriving at a decision in only one court session, the judges ordered a separation of body and property which was to last until Muller was capable of behaving properly and also waived the usual court costs because of Barbara's poverty.[21] As their personnel changed during the course of the century, the courts were understandably not always consistent in dealing with divorce cases founded on cruelty—at times granting divorces, at others only separations, depending on the views of individual judges. The net effect, however, was to allow women to escape miserable marriages, at least for a period of time.

It should be noted that men did not have a monopoly on cruelty in eighteenth-century Neuchâtel. In 1755, Josué Ribaux asked to be divorced from his wife, Anne Barbe, claiming that she had a passion for wine and that she had sold various household belongings—her bed, some linen and clothes—to gain the financial means to quench her thirst. Worse still, she had made several attempts on Ribaux's life and had made inquiries to hire assassins to kill him. A few months before his appearance in court, she had left the country with two Frenchmen to lead the life of a vagabond. Responding to this action, Anne Barbe retorted that it was her husband's misbehavior that had forced her to leave the household. One witness testified, however, that Ribaux had called for help against his wife several times and that on one occasion Anne Barbe attacked him in the street. The court granted them a separation for one year, after which time they were to reappear if they could not reunite. Ribaux was to pay the court costs and to provide Anne Barbe with an écu a month as support during this separation.[22] Thus, even though the burden of guilt seems to have lain with Anne Barbe, she was to receive support from her husband.

Though the recognition of cruelty and misconduct as viable grounds for separations or divorces was a major departure from the rulings of earlier consistories, an even greater innovation was the awarding of divorces for incompatibility, today's ground for divorce par excellence.

21. AEN, JMN7:833.
22. AEN, JMN5:322–336.

The cases discussed above all dealt with individuals whose lives might have been in jeopardy if they were forced to remain with their spouses. Common sense dictates that such a couple should at least be separated to preserve public order. A much greater step was taken when the judges acknowledged that, even if neither spouse was guilty of adultery, or cruelly beat the other, or deserted the household, or committed some heinous crime, some couples simply could not live together peacefully. Cited for the first time as a ground for divorce in 1769, incompatibility was listed as a motive in 18 divorce proceedings, thus constituting only 4.2 percent of the grounds cited for the century. By the end of the century, however, incompatibility had become an important reason for divorce, cited 14 times (10 percent of all motives for divorce) in the decade 1797–1806. During these last ten years before Napoleonic rule, *incompatibilité d'humeur* was invoked more frequently than all other grounds except desertion, cruelty, and adultery.

By the 1790s divorces were at times granted to both husband and wife who mutually sought a dissolution; such cases most often involved a couple who had been legally separated for several years and showed no hope of reconciliation. When Pierre and Marguerite Clottu together asked for a divorce from the Justice matrimoniale of Neuchâtel, they had been judicially separated for three years and had no hope of a reunion. Though they viewed their motives as insufficient, the justices nevertheless granted them a divorce and permission to remarry. Pierre was ordered to pay his wife 9 louis d'or per year for his child's support and to help provide the child with clothes.[23]

If the circumstances were somewhat different for Jean and Rose Marie Dessaules, the final result was the same. In 1793 the two of them asked for and received a separation based on *incompatibilité d'humeur.* Four years later this legal separation had expired, but Rose Marie did not want to reunite, inciting Jean to file for divorce for malicious desertion. Denying that this was desertion, Rose Marie asserted that Jean had not made the least effort to convince her to return to him during their four-year separation. But, considering the incompatibility of temperaments and their considerable difference in age, she found it most unlikely that they would ever be able to live together peacefully. Having considered asking for an extension of the separation, Rose Marie, like Jean, now felt a divorce might indeed be a better decision, though she respectfully deferred to the judgment of the court. Since all efforts at reunion had been in vain and Rose Marie had in effect agreed to the

23. AEN, JMN6:1262–1264.

request, the tribunal awarded Jean his divorce, ordering that all expenses be shared by the parties and forbidding them to remarry before the expiration of seven months.[24] Although officially the divorce was granted to Jean and not to both of them, there was no guilty party in this suit. Even though there was one plaintiff, both parties were treated the same and both wanted the divorce on the same grounds: incompatibility.

By the early nineteenth century, exceptional cases can even be found in which couples received divorces for incompatibility even though they had not had a trial separation. When in 1803 François Louis Courvoisier Piot filed for divorce against his wife, Marianne, he founded his action on incompatibility, expressing an "invincible repugnance" toward living with her and requesting the custody of their child. Likewise, Marianne asked to be divorced from François, requesting that the court accept the agreement the two of them had signed 30 November 1802 toward the dissolution of their marriage. In only one court session, the judges granted a divorce because of the antipathy between them and allowed both to remarry six months after this judgment. Marianne was given custody of their child until he reached the age of two years, after which time he was to be turned over to his father. François was to pay 16 louis to Marianne for the period during which she had custody of the child; once he had custody, François was to pay her 18 louis in two installments.[25]

This decision is in blatant contradiction of legal practices that had prevailed for over two centuries. Ever since the introduction of divorce in the sixteenth century, voluntary divorces had been forbidden in Neuchâtel. Plaintiffs to divorce suits based on desertion traditionally had been obliged to swear an oath that there was no collusion. Now a couple appeared in court armed with a convention aimed at dissolving the marriage—obviously a form of collusion. The recognition of incompatibility as a sufficient ground for divorce was a vitally important step in the history of marriage. For better or worse, marriage was no longer a union that antipathetic couples could never escape.

In allowing divorces for incompatibility, Neuchâtel's court authorities were far ahead of their times. The reformer Martin Bucer had earlier called for the possibility of divorce for incompatibility. Influenced by Bucer, John Milton wrote in the 1640s that affection was the principal goal of marriage, eclipsing those of procreation and the control of

24. AEN, JMV5:432–436.
25. AEN, JMN7:929–931.

sexual impulses. Whereas Milton was preaching three centuries before such divorces would be granted in England, Neuchâtel's tribunals implemented this form of no-fault divorce less than a century and a half after his time, as magistrates subtly discarded the notion that divorce had to be founded on matrimonial offenses.

To put eighteenth-century Neuchâtel's innovations on divorce in historical perspective, we should observe that England introduced its first divorce law, which allowed men to divorce their wives for adultery, in 1857. Women, however, could divorce their husbands only for aggravated adultery; that is, they had to prove that their husbands were guilty not only of adultery but also of bigamy, incest, sodomy, desertion, cruelty, rape, or bestiality. These very limited grounds would remain unchanged until 1923, when women as well as men could receive divorces for simple adultery, which was still the only acceptable reason for divorce. Thereafter, for the first time women made up the majority of plaintiffs to divorce cases in England.[26] And in the state of New York, adultery was the only possible ground for divorce until the 1960s.[27] Like Neuchâtel, reformed Holland witnessed an explosion of cases of marital breakdown in the eighteenth century. There, however, this dramatic increase in litigation consisted of large numbers of judicial separations awarded on the ground of adultery. Ever since the Reformation, Neuchâtelois had been able to divorce unfaithful spouses and to remarry, a right the Dutch "separation of bed and table" did not convey. True, in revolutionary France no-fault divorces could be received either unilaterally or by mutual consent without any proof of marital breakdown. Divorces were possible in France, however, only for the years 1792–1816.[28] Quite simply, I know of no other modern European state that awarded divorces for incompatibility earlier than Neuchâtel.

Although divorces for reasons of cruelty and incompatibility marked important developments that would have profound ramifications in the history of the family, adultery, a more traditional motive, outnumbered these grounds for the century as a whole. Cited 107 times, adultery made up 25 percent of the motives mentioned, second only to desertion. As in the previous period, adultery was cited more often by male plaintiffs than by females: 63 men as opposed to 44 women filed for

---

26. In England before 1857, even separations could be had only on very limited grounds: adultery, life-threatening cruelty, or a combination of the two; Stone, *Road to Divorce*, p. 192.
27. Phillips, *Putting Asunder*, pp. 421, 525–526, 568.
28. Schama, *Embarrassment of Riches*, p. 406; Phillips, *Putting Asunder*, pp. 175–189.

divorce against allegedly unfaithful spouses. In most ways, eighteenth-century divorce cases founded on adultery were no different from those of the previous century and a half. Many proceedings, for example, were directed against women who had given birth to illegitimate children during their husbands' long absences. And judicial authorities continued to grant custody of children to the innocent party, be it the father or the mother. When the wife was guilty of adultery, the husband received the guardianship even of young children and was generally awarded a large proportion—usually half—of his wife's property to go toward child support.[29]

Since eighteenth-century judges commonly awarded separations, some divorce cases arose from the adultery of spouses who were legally separated. The courts usually awarded separations for a period of a few years, and so many of those persons separated were unable to remain celibate. Yielding to temptation during the time of the separation could provide the other spouse with the grounds needed to procure a divorce. Legal complications arose when both parties committed adultery while separated, as seen in a case involving Abram Henry Petitpierre and his wife, Judith Anne, in 1787/88. First Abram accused his wife of adultery and was supported by a witness who had heard Judith confess to having sexual relations with several men. If this were not enough, another witness testified that at Petitpierre's request he and another man accompanied Abram one evening to observe his wife. Hiding outside Judith's home, they waited until eleven o'clock or midnight, when a man came and knocked on a window. The door then opened and the man entered the dark house. The three men hiding outside then burst into the house and surprised the couple; the would-be lover was beside the bed, as was Judith in her nightgown. Seeing the three intruders, the unidentified man quickly fled and Judith fell to her knees before Petitpierre, begging him for forgiveness. As for Abram's extramarital activities, a young woman claimed that he had twice tried unsuccessfully to seduce her. More important, evidence suggested that he may have fathered the child that a widow had given birth to. Because of the extreme animosity they had for each other and the apparent adultery each had committed, the court awarded a divorce, essentially declaring both parties guilty. Neither party was to remarry before two years expired from the day of the sentence, and even then each needed the permission of the court to do

29. See, e.g., AEN, JMV2:36–62; JMV3:397–407.

so. Custody of the children was granted to Abram for the simple reason that he had more money to support them than did Judith, and both parties were to share the expenses of the trial.[30]

In two other cases in which the fidelity of both parties was impugned, the courts awarded separations rather than divorces. One such case involved Moise Jacot, who sued his wife, Jeanne Marie, for divorce in 1746. Jacot claimed that he had not had carnal knowledge of his wife during the past four years because he suspected her of being unfaithful. Jeanne-Marie, however, had recently given birth to a son whose father, Jacot maintained, was a certain Daniel Favre dit Bulle. The midwives present at the birth of the child testified that Jeanne-Marie had declared on the *petit lit* that Favre was indeed the baby's father. Far from denying these allegations, Jeanne-Marie readily confessed to having committed adultery but argued that her sin was the result of Jacot's poor treatment and neglect. Jeanne-Marie charged that Jacot only rarely fulfilled the conjugal debt, frequently abused her physically, neglected his family, and maintained a scandalous liaison with a widow. In fact, evidence substantiated that Jacot and this widow had been excommunicated since 1743 because of their illicit *fréquentation*. Rumors suggested that Jacot did mistreat his wife verbally and possibly physically, and a neighbor reported that Jacot left the sowing of crops to his wife but did household chores for the widow. Notwithstanding the evidence of Jeanne-Marie's adultery, the court maintained that there was no proof that could justify Jacot's action for a divorce. Because of their incompatibility, however, the judges deemed it prudent to authorize a separation of body and property for three years. Jeanne-Marie received custody of the children, and the parties were to divide the legal fees in proportion to the amount of property each possessed.[31] Considering that oaths made on the *petit lit* had sufficed to convict men in paternity suits, it is surprising that such an oath was here viewed as insufficient proof of adultery.

On similar accusations of adultery, Jonas Charles Grizel filed suit in 1762 against his wife, also named Jeanne-Marie. Jeanne-Marie said that

30. AEN, JMN6:944–946, 949–957, 959, 976–979, 981–982, 1016–1019, 1022–1026, 1028–1109, 1112–1141, 1145–1146. This case shows that judicial authorities condoned spying as a means of getting proof of adultery or fornication. Both John Gillis and Martin Ingram have observed that window peeping was an acceptable means of detecting moral infractions in sixteenth- and seventeenth-century England, though Ingram maintains that such procedures were exceptional and that the right of privacy existed; Gillis, *For Better, for Worse*, p. 39; Ingram, *Church Courts, Sex, and Marriage*, p. 245.
31. AEN, JMN5:48–78, 83.

at first she considered not responding to this action since she longed for the day that she would be rid of Grizel. But since he based his suit on accusations that dishonored her, she decided not to concede victory to him so easily. In agreeing to marry Grizel, Jeanne-Marie confessed that she was guided more by romantic love than by reason and became disillusioned soon after their marriage.[32] She believed that their marriage could have succeeded if her husband had not been so obsessed with the fact that, thanks to this marriage, he for the first time had a considerable fortune at his disposal. Ruled by his own vanity, he badgered Jeanne-Marie until she finally agreed to purchase for him the title of Major (*Brevet de Major*). Because of this newly acquired dignity, he felt compelled to live far beyond his means, wasting 22,000 livres of her assets during twelve years of marriage. Finally, Jeanne-Marie asserted that Grizel himself was guilty of adultery with various mistresses. After all these counter-accusations, however, Jeanne-Marie concluded her response by confessing to having committed adultery in order to be divorced from Grizel: "If only my confession is needed to convince you, Sirs, to grant the divorce, I prefer to declare and avow that I am guilty . . . of the facts and aims of the plaintiff's cause. And I do this to avoid the tragic consequences which my life would be exposed to if I had to return to the most despicable and deceitful of all husbands."[33]

Sundry witnesses testified to seeing both parties in compromising situations with members of the opposite sex. One man claimed to have seen Grizel in the woods with a woman whose skirt was pushed up to her shoulders. Grizel had offered to pay this witness not to tell anyone about this incident and threatened him if he did so. The Grizels' servant reported that Jeanne-Marie and Jean-Jaques Montandon slept one night in the same room, though in separate beds, and she saw Montandon helping Jeanne-Marie get dressed the next morning. Despite the defendant's confession and the evidence, albeit imperfect, against both, the judges did not at this time grant a divorce but simply a separation for two years. Not until five years later did the couple reappear in court. As before, Grizel sued for divorce for reason of adultery and Jeanne-Marie, though denying any transgressions, consented to the dissolution. This time the judges awarded the divorce and divided the legal costs equally

---

32. Ibid., 984: "J'avoue à ma confusion que l'amour a eu plus de part à mon union avec Grizel, que la raison, mais il est bien difficile de penser long tems dans de pareilles circonstances."
33. Ibid., 987.

between the two. Grizel was allowed to remarry, but Jeanne-Marie would have to petition the court before remarrying.[34]

It is hard to explain why the judges awarded separations in the cases, since adultery ordinarily merited a divorce. One might think that the court was reflecting the same reservation that had led the consistory of Valangin not to award a divorce to the Perret Gentils in the mid-seventeenth century; that is, the judges may still have felt that individuals' confessions of adultery did not suffice to form grounds for divorce. Perhaps mid-eighteenth-century judges still feared that a person might try to escape an unhappy marriage by confessing to adultery, as Jeanne-Marie Grizel openly admitted. As for Jeanne-Marie Jacot's case, the judges may have viewed her oath on the *petit lit* as simply another form of untrustworthy confession. If so, however, this marked a dramatic departure from earlier traditions in which it was believed that with God as her witness a women could not tell a lie at the height of the pain of childbirth. Furthermore, this same Justice matrimoniale of Neuchâtel had granted a divorce to Felix Meuron in 1715 even though the adultery was "proved" only by his wife's affirmation and oath.[35] If in 1715 the tribunal was willing to award divorces founded on confessions of adultery, why should judges in the 1740s and 1760s regress to seventeenth-century standards, deeming such evidence insufficient? The judges' reluctance to grant divorces was probably in part due to the suspicions concerning the men's extramarital affairs. But the justices also clearly sympathized with the plight of the female defendants. Seeing two women who suffered from unhappy marriages, the judges probably believed that, if these women were guilty of adultery, their husbands' misbehavior was in part responsible for these transgressions. At any rate, both cases concerned women who confessed to adultery and complained about miserable marriages. In granting them separations, the judges allowed them to live apart from these unkind husbands, while at the same time sparing them the possible financial and social strains that being the guilty party in a divorce case might entail. It is not insignificant that, when the Grizels did finally receive a divorce, Jeanne-Marie, though technically the guilty party, was not dealt with more severely than her husband, with the exception that she needed to ask permission to remarry.

34. Ibid., 980–1018. A year later, Jeanne-Marie produced certificates attesting to her good behavior and received permission to remarry.
35. AEN, JMN3:137–140.

One minor change in eighteenth-century divorce litigation was that judges were willing in exceptional cases to allow remarriages between persons who had previously committed adultery together. The 1750s witnessed two such cases, both of which involved women who had committed adultery and filed for divorce from sexually dysfunctional husbands. Separated since 1756, Susanne Marie Borrel sued for divorce from Jean Borrel on the ground of impotence, a demand Jean agreed to provided that she pay him damages for having committed adultery. Susanne countered that in light of his condition their marriage was null and therefore her transgression not adultery but simply fornication. Though it is unclear whether the court completely accepted her argument, the judges declared the marriage null and the parties free, rejected Borrel's request for damages, and ordered him to reimburse Susanne half the legal costs she had encountered.[36] Susanne was thereafter free to marry the man with whom she had committed adultery, if she so desired.

Much more sensational was a case heard a few years earlier which was, bar none, the most bizarre divorce suit in early modern Neuchâtel. Appearing before the court for the first time in November 1752, Marie Esabeau Perrin of Noiraigue filed for divorce from her husband, Jean-Jaques Perrin, asserting that nine years previously Jean-Jaques "had mutilated himself in the most unusual and grotesque fashion, leaving himself completely incapable of having marital relations. It didn't take long for news of this operation to become commonly known. The news spread quickly from the village of Noiraigue to the entire valley of Travers. Perrin was so filled with shame and confusion that to avoid the jeers and mockery of the general public he decided to flee." Marie had received no news of him since his departure and was filing for divorce on the twin grounds of desertion and self-castration.[37]

To support her story, Marie produced witnesses who could attest either directly or indirectly to this act of self-mutilation. One of these witnesses was Perrin's nephew by marriage, who reported that when he heard about this affair he went to Perrin and asked him:

> "What have you done to yourself?" He responded that he had performed this operation on himself since he had a young wife. And since they had hidden all the knives and swords from him, he had taken the base of a little saw with which he crushed the sack or the

36. AEN, JMN5:641–645.
37. Ibid., 279.

scrotum. After having made this hole, he took the filaments of the testicle and tore them with his fingernails and removed it so. [The witness] saw one of the testicles in a little bucket . . . that [Perrin's] wife showed him but did not know whether he had torn out both testicles.[38]

Another witness reported that Perrin's late uncle had said that Perrin had castrated himself so that he would not have any more children. Yet another man, Jonas Joly, testified that shortly after the self-surgery he had asked Perrin's late brother-in-law, David Jeanneret, if it was true. Jeanneret replied that it was indeed true, and that he had seen the two blood-splattered testicles in a small bucket.[39]

Members of the Justice matrimoniale, however, remarked that there was a rumor that Marie was pregnant. Pressed to tell the truth, Marie confessed that she was indeed expecting a baby. Since she had sufficiently proved Perrin's self-castration and since Perrin had not responded to the suit, the judges granted her the divorce but, because of her pregnancy, forbade her to remarry without first receiving the tribunal's permission. This in itself was a progressive sentence, since canon law tradition and contemporary French legal practices generally did not recognize postmarital castration as a ground for dissolution.[40]

One week later, on the first of March 1753, Marie asked permission to marry François Louis Dubois. She admitted having sexual relations with Dubois after he had promised to marry her, but argued this way:

From the very moment of Jean-Jaques Perrin's self-mutilation, the deed on which she based her divorce suit, there was no longer, properly speaking, a marriage between Perrin and her. From this moment, the conjugal tie was ruptured and dissolved, considering that Perrin deliberately and maliciously rendered himself incapable of fulfilling

38. AEN, JMN: *Annexes* 412.
39. Ibid.
40. AEN, JMN5:284. Several thirteenth- and fourteenth-century legal commentators dealt with the problem of castration. Theologians and canon lawyers generally agreed that eunuchs and others whose capacity to copulate was permanently impaired could not contract a valid marriage. But William of Pagula held that if a man was castrated after marriage the union remained valid; Brundage, *Law, Sex, and Christian Society*, p. 456. In the same fashion, in Old Regime France cases of accidental impotence resulting from a wound, illness, or surgery could serve as an impediment to marriage but did not suffice to dissolve the union if it occurred after the wedding; Darmon, *Tribunal de l'impuissance*, p. 36. In referring to surgical intervention, however, French jurists surely did not have cases of self-castration in mind. In light of Perrin's willful self-mutilation, French tribunals might have considered this action to merit dissolving the marriage.

the principal duty of the conjugal union of which the ultimate goal is
the procreation of children. Or, to refer to the law, in being unable to
fulfill the matrimonial obligation, the ultimate purpose of marriage,
Perrin ceased to be [Marie's] husband in that he ceased to be a man.[41]

She further noted that laws had always regarded eunuchs as incapable of
marrying even if women accepted their proposals. Even though marriages are essentially formed by the consent of the parties, this consent
must include the desire and capacity to procreate, which eunuchs do
not have. Arguing that her marriage ended at the moment of Perrin's
mutilation, Marie asserted that she had not committed adultery with
Dubois but rather had merely anticipated the rights of marriage. After
Perrin's despicable act, it was only a question of coming before the Justice matrimoniale to receive the public confirmation of her liberty. Considering these particular circumstances, the judges permitted Marie and
Dubois to marry.[42] Though this case certainly was not typical, it serves
to show that eighteenth-century judges were flexible in regard to the
rights of adulterous spouses to remarry. In dealing with women who
had been married to sexually dysfunctional men, members of the Justice
matrimoniale showed common sense in finding appropriate solutions
for exceptional cases.

In treating more common cases of sexual dysfunction, the courts retained traditional criteria. They seem, however, to have become more
lenient on such questions during the course of the eighteenth century.
In any event, there were eleven divorce suits founded at least in part on
sexual dysfunction during the period 1707–1806. Of these, the first
four plaintiffs to such suits, all of whom filed before 1756, failed in
their quests, whereas the following seven all succeeded.[43]

In general, if one spouse accused the other of being incapable of fulfilling the conjugal debt, physicians were called on to conduct a physical
examination to determine whether there were natural impediments to
copulation. Judges required this testimony of medical experts to make
sure that an accusation of impotence was not a pretext to get out of
an unhappy marriage. In 1750, Susanne Henriette Jeanrenaud sought
a divorce from her husband, Abram Henry Jeanrenaud, founding her
action on, among other accusations, a natural impediment that prevented them from consummating the marriage. Two surgeons exam-

41. AEN, JMN5:286–287.
42. Ibid., 287–289. The judges added, however, that she would be subject to the appropriate "ecclesiastical discipline"; evidently referring to the punishment for having fornicated.
43. Two suits (1713 and 1750) were rejected outright, another (1755) was abandoned, and
the fourth (1740) received a separation.

ined both Susanne and Abram, and two midwives further inspected Susanne. Providing very detailed anatomical descriptions, these medical experts reported that Susanne, who was still a virgin despite having been married for two years, appeared capable of having sexual relations with most but perhaps not all men. Historically, this might have sufficed for an annulment, since as far back as the thirteenth century canon law had accepted the dissolution of marriages because of "relative impotence," a form of sexual dysfunction that prevented a couple from having sexual relations even though they might be able to have relations with others.[44] The physicians also maintained, however, that there was no apparent reason why Abram could not have normal sexual relations with his wife. The judges therefore rejected Susanne's request and ordered her to return to her husband.[45]

Physicians could be quite demanding in determining whether men were impotent. For example, in 1786 two surgeons examined Abram Louis Matthey Dupraz, whose wife was suing him for divorce on the ground of impotence. These physicians found that his sex organs were well formed but also asked that he give proof of his virility. Dupraz was unable to have an erection on the spot and claimed that he had suffered a fever the night before and that their presence inhibited him. To this, the surgeons responded that he should calm down; if he could not perform at that moment, he could make an appointment for another day. Dupraz returned to the physicians a few days later but told them that his state of mind had not changed and that he preferred giving *passement* to his wife to submitting himself to further examinations. Susanne thereupon received her divorce.[46]

44. Darmon, *Tribunal de l'impuissance*, pp. 38, 156.
45. The report on Susanne, signed by the two midwives and the two surgeons, read as follows: "(1) La vulve generalement un peu petitte (2) Les grandes levres petittes de meme (3) Les nymphes aussi plus petittes que dans la plus grande partie des femmes (4) La membrane de l'hymen dans sa partie superieure du meat urinaire ouverte et pouvoir y passer le doit annulaire ensorte qu'elle laisse une espace de dix lignes de diametre laditte membrane ayant environ une ligne et demi d'épaisseur et n'étant pas ouverte dans sa totalité (5) La fourchette de trois lignes plus haut que dans plusieures autres femmes (6) L'interieur du vagin assé large (7) Le méat urinaire, la partie superieur de l'hymen, et l'uretre enflamés et plus gros que dans l'état naturel, ne sachant pas si cela provient de quelqu'irritation à la suite de ces regles, que la quittèrent mercredy, ou de quelqu'autre cause, qui nous est inconnue, paroissant lui faire de la douleur, lors qu'on touchoit ces parties." The surgeons reported that Abram "nous a fair voir ses parties naturelles dans toute leur vigueur, et nous avons trouvé (1) Son membre viril de la longueur de cinq pouces quatre lignes/mesme prise du pied de ce pays (2) La circonference de cette partie à sa racine pres des os pubis, de quatre pouces huits lignes. Et par conséquent le diamètre de cette circonference est d'un pouce six lignes (3) La circonference de la même partie à la racine du gland, de quatre pouces et quatre lignes." AEN, JMN5:170–182, 191–196, 204–209, 247–278.
46. AEN, JMN6:849–851, 856–859, 883–887. Darmon found that medical experts did

On occasion, infirmities other than sexual dysfunctions were claimed as grounds for dissolution. Mental illness was cited in six of the eight cases in which infirmities were listed among the motives for divorce. Of these six plaintiffs—three men and three women—five received divorces and the sixth abandoned the cause. The other two suits involved epilepsy, and the courts awarded separations in both cases.[47] Illness, in short, cannot be said to have been one of the more important grounds for divorce during the eighteenth century.

More numerous were divorce suits based on crime. Crime or the banishment of a spouse was listed as a motive for divorce 31 times, thus constituting 7.3 percent of all grounds cited in divorce cases. Almost all plaintiffs (26 of 31) who cited the ground of crime were women, most of whose husbands had been banished from the county for some criminal act. That such cases can be found is not surprising, since the criminal courts of Neuchâtel ordered the banishment of 547 persons during the period 1707–1806, a figure that accounts for 54.2 percent of all punishments for criminal cases for this century.[48] In filing suit against banished spouses, plaintiffs had to make the usual three announcements to see if the defendant or anyone in the defendant's name opposed the action. Since banished criminals were forbidden to enter the principality, the defendants were never able to contest such suits. Consequently, virtually all plaintiffs were successful: the tribunals awarded 25 divorces and one separation on the basis of crime.[49]

Among other grounds for divorce were bigamy and deceit. During the course of the century, eight people received divorces from spouses who had remarried illegally elsewhere, and three divorces were granted as a result of deceit. One case based on deceit involved Rose nee Meuron, a member of a wealthy family who claimed in 1771 that her hus-

---

not always require allegedly impotent men to show that they were capable of having an erection. As the Dupraz case shows, when physicians did demand such proof, the accused had several privileges: he had the right to choose the date and time of the test and to get further chances in case he failed to show his virility; *Tribunal de l'impuissance*, pp. 159–183, 192.

47. AEN, JMN4:217–219; JMN5:378–397, 399–559, 561–563, 648–654, *Annexes* 413.

48. As Philippe Henry points out, Neuchâtel's penal system was based on the principle of the exclusion of the delinquent, either temporary or permanent, by death or exile. The county did not want to be burdened with the high costs of maintaining prisoners. Banishment therefore was the most common punishment; *Crime, justice et société*, p. 484.

49. It is unclear why a separation instead of a divorce was given to a woman in 1797. The fact that her husband was *décreté de prise de corps* in the canton of Bern rather than in Neuchâtel may have been the reason; AEN, JMN7:294, 302, 305–307. Of the remaining cases, there was only one rejection: a case involving a woman who was pregnant by another man when she tried to divorce her banished husband; ibid., 69.

band, David Bourgeois, had falsely claimed prior to the marriage that he possessed 52,000 French livres when he was really 2,000 livres in debt. In the marriage contract, signed in November 1765, Bourgeois promised to give his fiancée 10,000 livres, a sum he never paid. By the time of this suit, Bourgeois had completely dissipated the dowry of 12,000 livres Rose had brought into the marriage. Rose's counsel pointed out that marriage contracts are formed by the consent of the parties. When fraud or deceit is involved, however, one has not really given one's consent and the marriage should thus be null. Out of the country at the moment, Bourgeois did not respond to the suit, and the court predictably awarded Rose a divorce along with custody of their three children.[50]

Other motives plaintiffs successfully used in divorce cases were their spouses' failure to pay the conjugal debt, their conversion to Catholicism, and their obtaining divorces in foreign countries. It is rather surprising that only two instances can be found of people suing for divorce in Neuchâtel on the ground that their spouses had already received divorces in France. These both occurred during the revolutionary period (one in 1801, the other in 1802), when divorce laws in France were liberal even by twentieth-century standards.[51] Following a law passed by the French legislative assembly in September 1792, divorces could be had in France for any reason at all; and judicial proceedings were so inexpensive that divorces could be pursued by all but the utterly destitute. Replaced by more moderate Napoleonic legislation in 1803, the divorce law of the French Revolution, though short-lived, produced a veritable watershed of matrimonial litigation.[52] Considering the proximity of France, one might have expected a considerable number of cases in Neuchâtel to be responses to divorces awarded to Neuchâtelois across the border.

Divorce litigation indicates that the eighteenth century was a turning point in Neuchâtel for the institution of marriage and for the matrimonial courts. To be sure, couples who divorced remained a small

50. AEN, JMN6:122–125, 128, 131–138. The list of individuals who assisted Rose Meuron in this process gives a good indication of her lofty social status: Pierre Meuron, her father; Pierre Meuron, her brother and member of the Grand Conseil; another Meuron, *conseiller d'etat* and *procureur général;* Jean-Jaques Deluze, member of the Petit Conseil; Monsieur Sandoz of Travers, *châtelain de Thielle;* Abram Pury, *colonel;* Monsieur, son of the late *châtelain de Boudry;* and Samuel Pury, attorney at law.
51. AEN, JMV6:198–199, 300–302.
52. Phillips, *Family Breakdown,* p. 1.

minority. Probably no more than 2 percent of Neuchâtel's marriages ended in divorce in the late eighteenth century.[53] Nevertheless, the introduction of cruelty and incompatibility as grounds for divorce show that more than ever marriage entailed mutual obligations of husbands and wives which went beyond simply not committing adultery or deserting the household. Failure to respect these obligations and to live together harmoniously could merit a divorce. In allowing couples the right to divorce on the ground of antipathy, the courts finally became more dedicated to the marriage of sentiment. And women in particular benefited from this change. If the courts showed a greater concern for the affective ties between spouses than had the earlier courts, they also for the first time dealt more with disputes that followed rather than led up to marriage.

JUDICIAL SEPARATIONS

As evidence from divorce litigation has shown, judicial authorities often awarded separations of body and property as a type of consolation prize if they found insufficient grounds for divorce. In addition to these cases, many plaintiffs petitioned directly for separations. Ordinarily these actions were brought by one or both spouses, who sought to live separately for a while because of incompatibility or cruelty. Although the courts had awarded two isolated judicial separations before 1707, only in the eighteenth century did separations become an important remedy to marital breakdown.

There were 162 requests for separations during this period, outnumbered only by divorce cases and contract disputes among litigation heard before the Justices matrimoniales.[54] Although the consistory of Valangin granted a legal separation as early as 1705, this form of liti-

---

53. Pierre Caspard found that from 1801 to 1807 there were 44 divorces in Neuchâtel, while in the same period 2,619 marriages were consecrated in the principality; that is equivalent to a divorce rate of 1.6 percent; "Conceptions prénuptiales," p. 1000, n. 41, citing AEN, *Liste des sommaires de tous les enfants qui ont été baptisés, des mariages bénis, et des personnes enterrées dans toutes les paroisses de la Principauté de Neuchâtel et de Valangin,* 1761–1815. Phillips also notes the huge difference between the frequency of marital breakdown today and that of earlier times and rejects the view that rising divorce rates in recent times reflect an essentially constant incidence of marriage breakdowns; *Putting Asunder,* p. 639.

54. Police actions against fornication and adultery were more numerous, but they were made by the consistories and the Quatre-Ministraux, not the matrimonial courts. Furthermore, petitions to marry numbered 281 for the century, but the vast majority of them were heard before the Conseil d'Etat.

TABLE 13
Suits for judicial separations, 1707–1806

	Plaintiff			Outcome		
	Women	Men	Joint	Granted	Rejected	Abandoned
1707–1716	0	1	0	1	0	0
1717–1726	0	0	0	0	0	0
1727–1736	2	0	0	1	0	1
1737–1746	2	0	0	1	0	1
1747–1756	1	0	1	1	1	0
1757–1766	4	1	1	5	0	1
1767–1776	9	3	0	7	4	3
1777–1786	16	0	7	21	1	1
1787–1796	26	5	8	39	0	3
1797–1806	20	7	39	66	0	4
	80	17	56	142	6	14

gation became common only toward the end of the century. During the entire half-century 1707–1756, only 7 people appeared in court in Neuchâtel and Valangin to request a separation of body and property. In contrast, the courts heard 155 such cases during the fifty years before Napoleon's arrival (see Table 13). Consequently, during the second half of the century, requests for separations of body and property actually outnumbered contract disputes 155 to 141, a further indication that the courts now dealt more with the breakdown than the formation of marriage. Undoubtedly the same factors that caused the increase in divorces were determinants in the dramatic growth in separations—namely, the greater emphasis placed on compatibility in marriage, the growing secularization and concomitant decline in religious norms, and the economic and demographic changes that saw more people working for wages, marrying younger, and living longer.

Among plaintiffs who petitioned for separations, women far outnumbered men, 80 to 17, though a significant number of requests (56) were filed mutually.[55] In the last decade of this period, 1797–1806, petitions made by both husband and wife actually outnumbered those initiated by individual spouses. It is no coincidence that this decade, with its large number of mutual requests for separations, also had a notable

55. For five cases it is not clear who the plaintiff was. In three cases the hearing was initiated when the husband asked the court to force his wife to return to him but she in turn asked for a separation of body and property. The remaining case involved a couple convoked by the court.

increase in divorce suits based on incompatibility: most joint petitions for separations were based on incompatibility. Mutually sought judicial separations and divorces for reasons of incompatibility together served as a safety valve to ensure domestic tranquility.

The success rate of those seeking separations approached 100 percent. Excluding cases that were abandoned, the courts awarded 142 separations and refused only 6 requests. As a rule, separations were conferred for fixed periods of time, ranging from less than one year to ten years. In exceptional cases, separations of unlimited duration were given, though most were set for two to four years. For the most part, individuals petitioning for separations based their demands on incompatibility or on their spouses' misconduct: violence, drunkenness, laziness, prodigality, and so forth.[56] If evidence supported the plaintiff's contentions, the courts ordinarily accorded the separation. Among the few requests rejected was one made in 1769 by newlyweds; despite their obvious conflicts, the court did not want to give this couple a separation until they had made a greater effort to make their marriage work.[57] Such rejections, however, are simply the exceptions that prove the rule.

An interesting aspect about separation cases was the process of settling financial disputes. An issue often discussed in both separation and divorce cases was the material support for a spouse during the course of the trial. Often the tribunals required one spouse to pay the other a certain sum to provide for the daily sustenance or the legal expenses incurred during the trial. Such financial support was prescribed in the suit Julianne nee Matthey filed against her husband, Jean-Pierre Ducommun, because of his misbehavior. Claiming that her husband had possession of all their assets, Julianne asked that Jean-Pierre be required to pay her legal expenses and to provide support for her and their five children for the duration of the proceedings. The judges agreed and ordered Jean-Pierre to pay her in advance the money needed to pursue the trial and to supply her and the children with a *pension alimentaire* of 1 louis d'or per month from the beginning of the trial.[58] As one might expect, more often than not the wife, not the husband, made such de-

56. On occasion, the grounds cited for a separation were rather unusual. In 1781, Marianne Horne asked to be separated from her husband, Jonas, because of his drunkenness, impotence, laziness—all of which were probably related—and because of his bad breath. Two physicians examined Jonas's mouth and reported that, though he had cavities and exhaled the natural odor of rotten teeth, his breath was not bad enough to render living with him unbearable; AEN, JMN6:496, 512–513.
57. AEN, JMV4:1–3.
58. Ibid., 362–369.

mands. On occasion, however, a woman was ordered to pay her husband a *pension alimentaire* during the trial if she were wealthier than he or had possession of most of their mutually owned assets. Juvet Favre had to furnish such a *pension* when she asked for either a divorce or a separation from her husband, Elie Favre, because of his violent behavior and drunkenness. The justices required her to pay Elie 6 gros écus per month until the end of the proceedings.[59] The Justices matrimoniales thus tried to ensure a certain equity so that one spouse could not have a monopoly over jointly owned property during the trial. Individuals should not have been prevented from pursuing separations or divorces simply because their spouses kept tight reins on their assets.

Once a separation was granted, the courts often required one party, usually the husband, to pay the other spouse periodic sums for the term of the separation. This remuneration usually was intended more as support for children than for the other spouse. When Juvet Favre received a five-year separation, however, she had to pay her husband a sum periodically.[60] Court-ordered financial settlements for judicial separations were thus not exclusively a form of child support paid by men. In determining who was to pay what to whom during a separation, the tribunals were more concerned with a party's financial need than with his or her innocence or culpability.

When a husband and wife together asked for a separation of body and property, they generally presented a signed convention that proposed a financial settlement. Thus, when Marianne and David Louis Robert asked to be separated in 1793 because of insurmountable anitpathy, they presented an accord that called for a six-year separation, during which time the children would stay with Marianne as long as they wanted. If they wished to live with their father, they were free to move in with him. As long as the children stayed with their mother, Marianne would raise them at her own expense (she had recently received a large inheritance). David had the right to visit the children while they stayed with Marianne, and if they chose to live with him he alone would be financially responsible for them. Awarding them a separation, the judges sanctioned this agreement.[61] In 1797, Marie Madelaine and Jean David

59. AEN, JMV7:90–92.
60. The amount to be paid is somewhat ambiguous. Juvet was to provide Elie with 10 louis *par quartier.* It is unclear whether this means that she had to pay him this sum four times a year or rather that she was to make four different payments of 10 louis during the five-year period. At any rate, the fact remains that the court enjoined the female plaintiff to pay a sum to the male defendant, even though no children were involved; ibid., 266–267.
61. AEN, JMV5:227, 249–250.

Gaberel produced a signed convention that mentioned that Jean David had not brought any assets with him into the marriage. But out of the goodness of her heart, Marie Madelaine took it on herself to give Jean David 19 louis d'or per year for the term of the separation. Since he had virtually no personal possessions, she also agreed to let him use some of her household items—a bed, some other furniture, and sundry linens for the bed and table. Each party was responsible for his or her own debts contracted before the marriage, and Marie Madelaine agreed to pay those debts acquired during the marriage to which she had consented. The judges accepted this accord and awarded a separation of four years.[62]

In forming their pacts for separations, couples occasionally provided detailed accounts of how the property and personal belongings were to be divided. In 1785, Charles Petitpierre, a bourgeois of Neuchâtel, and his wife, Salomé, drew up an inventory of all their assets and debts and then noted how this property was to be divided during the separation. Obviously enjoying a fair amount of wealth, they listed most prominently among their belongings a house valued at 6500 livres according to estimates made by a carpenter and an architect. They proceeded to describe each room in the house and all the items therein and their respective values. Among the assets itemized were a small table rug on which one could play cards, worth an estimated 1.8 livres, and a clock that sounded the hours valued at 4.4 livres. In the kitchen, there were, among other things, 46 table knives, 44 teaspoons, 3 tablespoons, and 64 forks, together worth 26.6 livres. Mention was also made of the wine cellar and the quantities and respective values of the red and white wines contained therein. In all, a total of 115 assets were listed, valued at 8,101.11 livres, including the amounts three debtors owed them. The Petitpierres' own debts amounted to 3,540.11 livres, leaving the net assets at 4,561 livres, excluding their clothes, of which they both would keep their own. Having proffered this list of assets, the Petitpierres requested a separation of body and property during which time their financial interests would be completely separated; if one party acquired debts during the separation, the other would in no way be held responsible for them. Petitpierre agreed to leave his wife possession of the house and all its furniture with the exception of a bed of his choice, four bed sheets, and his carpentry tools and wood. The prices of these, as listed in the inventory, were to be deducted from the amount due him. Salomé was to be left in charge of all the debts listed in the inventory;

62. Ibid., 424–428.

for Charles's portion of the property, she was to pay him 80 livres, 10 soll tournois on the day of the separation and 2,200 livres tournois in six months along with interest at "400 per year." Household provisions not listed in the inventory were to be left to Salomé; if any furniture had been inadvertently omitted, however, they were to be shared equally between the two parties. The justices agreed to grant the Petitpierres a separation of two years and to authorize the arrangements concerning the division of property.[63] More detailed than any other convention found in the court registers, the Petitpierres' written agreement shows the practical problems many couples must have faced when they were about to separate.

At times, of course, couples could not agree on the division of property, and the court had to play a more active role in its distribution. Neuchâtel's matrimonial tribunal had to intervene in the division of assets when Suzanne Marie and Charles Favre appeared in court in 1803. Suzanne Marie, the plaintiff, alleged incompatibility and misconduct on the part of Charles. Charles replied that a month earlier the two of them along with their children had formulated an agreement for a separation of body and property. In direct violation of this convention, however, Suzanne and their children had taken from the home in his absence all the livestock, furniture, linen, even most of his own clothes, leaving him with nothing more than the clothes he was wearing, a uniform, and a black suit. He therefore demanded that his wife and children pay him a *pension alimentaire*. Describing their union as scandalous, the judges ordered that the two be separated for three years and that the accord they had written take effect. Charles was to receive a monthly payment of 1 louis d'or, and all his clothes were to be returned to him promptly. The justices further enjoined Suzanne and the children to pay Charles 3 louis so that he might purchase any necessary clothes or linen. Charles in turn was obliged to reimburse Suzanne half the court costs and to give up his home as well as all articles stipulated by their agreement.[64] Although earlier courts had considered themselves incapable of imposing such financial settlements, they now willingly intervened to ensure equitable separations of property.

As noted above, when separations of body and property expired, couples at times successfully filed for divorce; in other cases, however, couples simply asked for an extension of their separation. The courts awarded nine prolongations of separations, one of which was a couple's

63. AEN, JMN6:702–711.
64. AEN, JMN7:909–914.

second extension, all of which were made between 1795 and 1806. No such requests were denied, though a tenth case made in 1792 was abandoned. Of these various extensions, two were for an unlimited period, while the rest, including the second extension, were for fixed periods. One of the couples that received an extension had already been separated for eight years. In some ways, such renewals of separations seem rather odd. If a couple could not salvage their marriage during such a long period, a divorce would seem a more appropriate solution. It is ironic that almost all these extensions of separations were awarded at the same time the very liberal divorce law was in effect across the border in France. The French divorce law of 1792 abolished the *séparation de corps et d'habitation* that had existed under the Old Regime, leaving divorce as the only remedy for marital breakdown in France until the repeal of the law in 1803.[65] In abolishing the judicial separation, the French legislative assembly was probably motivated by the same idea that had inspired reformers to condemn the Catholics' *divortium quoad torum et mensam* two hundred fifty years before: they viewed the celibate state as unnatural for most people and therefore considered it cruel to call for a more or less permanent separation that did not convey the right to remarry.[66] One may, then, be tempted to think that Neuchâtel's courts were somewhat reactionary in ordering separations instead of divorces. In defense of the judicial authorities, however, it must be noted that all the plaintiffs, for one reason or another, asked for extensions of their separations, not for divorces.[67] The man and woman who received a prolongation though already separated for eight years, for instance,

65. Phillips, *Family Breakdown*, pp. 4–5, 11. Under the Old Regime, only women could petition for the *séparation de corps et d'habitation*. The remedies at a man's disposal were the use of a degree of physical force and the threat to lock his wife in a convent if she did not change her ways; see *Encyclopédie, ou dictionnaire raisonné des sciences, des arts et des métiers* (Neuchâtel, 1765), 15:60.

66. If the objective was to allow subsequent remarriage, however, divorcés clearly did not always take advantage of this right. In his study on divorce in revolutionary Rouen, Phillips found that only a small percentage of divorcés—roughly one-fourth of the women and only a slightly higher proportion of men—remarried during the eighteenth century. Phillips suggests that this low rate may indicate a religious influence that discouraged divorcés from remarrying; *Family Breakdown*, pp. 199–200.

67. Of all parties involved in these cases, only one expressed the desire to be divorced rather than separated, and he was a defendant, not a plaintiff. This case involved Charlotte Favre's request for a renewal of her separation from her husband, Abram, who had not foresworn his disorderly life and drunkenness. Abram preferred that Charlotte return to him. If she refused, he would rather have a divorce than a prolongation of the separation. In rendering their sentence, the justices observed that, considering the notorious misbehavior of Favre, they could not force Charlotte to return to him and extended the separation for one year; AEN, JMN7:418.

were quite advanced in age. Augustin Sagne, the plaintiff in this case, asked for the extension, saying that he still did not want to live with his wife. At this time, in 1804, he was already past eighty and his infirmities prevented him from appearing in court personally. On account of his age and poor health, Sagne clearly did not desire to remarry but merely wanted to remain separated from his wife. Seeing his plight, the court rewarded him a renewal of his separation for an unlimited length of time.[68] Evidence thus indicates that prolongations of separations conformed to the desires of the plaintiffs.

It is worthwhile to reflect once again as to whether judicial separations themselves were reactionary. As noted above, as early as the sixteenth century reformers were criticizing the Catholic *divortium,* or permanent separation, since it did not allow even the innocent party to remarry. Were the eighteenth-century tribunals taking a step backward when they began ordering separations of body and property? True, as we have seen, many couples asked for nothing more than separations and were apparently not interested in finding new spouses. Occasionally, however, couples who asked for either a divorce or a separation received the latter. Under such circumstances, one may wonder why the courts did not give divorces. In the eyes of the justices, judicial separation was a deterrent to taking divorce too lightly. Though its duration may seem exceedingly long to a modern observer, the separation of body and property must be viewed as a logical step in the evolution of marriage and divorce. Before divorces on the grounds of misbehavior or antipathy could be granted, it is understandable that couples first be allowed to live separately for such reasons. No doubt pragmatism was the motivating factor in awarding separations. Obliging incompatible couples to live together could be tormenting and even dangerous. And if after a lengthy separation a reunion was still not feasible, a divorce, if desired, might be the next step.

One may still wonder why the tribunals sometimes granted permanent separations, phenomena that strikingly resemble the Catholic *divortia.* In addition to the examples already cited, the Justice matrimoniale of Neuchâtel awarded seven other separations of indefinite duration, all granted in the decade 1797–1806. Among these seven cases, however, all but one plaintiff asked for a separation, not a divorce. Moreover, as suggested above, the age of the parties was relevant, often influencing the length of the separation awarded; indeed, four of the separations of undetermined length were awarded at least in part be-

68. AEN, JMN8:27–29.

cause of the advanced age of the parties.[69] The logic behind awarding separations of indefinite length to the elderly was that they were less capable of changing their ways and less inclined to remarry. All in all, these separations of indefinite duration do not appear to be a throwback to the *divortia* of the Middle Ages. Apart from the elderly, only couples who presented written agreements specifically asking for them received separations for an undetermined period.

In allowing couples to live apart, Neuchâtel's justices did not refer to this arrangement as either a "separation of bed and table" or a "separation of body and dwelling," two common phrases used elsewhere. As its name reveals, the separation of body and property emphasized the equitable division of wealth between spouses. In overseeing the distribution of property, judges generally tried to assure that each person received his or her fair share of the assets and debts, awarding pensions on the basis of need. Inhabitants of late eighteenth-century Neuchâtel thus should not have been forced to remain in a household simply because their spouses controlled the wealth. Some people may have been dissuaded from asking for a separation because they would have had trouble making ends meet with only half the conjugal property; most likely, some unhappy couples stayed together since they were financially more secure if their property remained undivided. Nevertheless, since Neuchâtel enjoyed relative prosperity in the late eighteenth and early nineteenth centuries and since the courts allowed poorer people to litigate free of charge, ever more people had the financial means to separate. Though the vast majority of married couples remained together, judicial separation along with divorce enabled people to overcome legal and financial barriers to escaping unhappy domestic life.

POLICE ACTIONS AGAINST MARRIED PERSONS

Neuchâtel's magistrates continued to use police actions to promote domestic tranquility and to punish moral delinquents. Such actions against married persons provide an interesting contrast to cases involving judicial separations: though married couples could now receive separations of body and property, the consistories did not brook unauthorized separations. During this century, a total of 134 police actions were made against couples or individual spouses because of the poor

69. AEN, JMN7:813–814; JMN8:112–113, 156–182.

TABLE 14

Police actions against married persons, by gender,
1707–1806

| | Convoked | | | |
	Wife	Husband	Both	Total
1707–1716	1	2	9	12
1717–1726	0	2	4	6
1727–1736	0	0	6	6
1737–1746	2	2	2	6
1747–1756	0	3	2	5
1757–1766	3	7	4	14
1767–1776	4	2	12	18
1777–1786	1	6	9	16
1787–1796	3	14	5	22
1797–1806	3	16	10	29
	17	54	63	134

domestic life they led (see Tables 14 and 15). As in the previous period, these actions were more the work of the consistories than of the Justices matrimoniales, since the latter generally heard only suits initiated by individuals or couples. Seigneurial consistories undertook the bulk of police actions for which records are extant: 81 actions were made by the consistory of Valangin, 7 by the consistory of Travers, 4 by Neuchâtel's matrimonial court, and one by the Justice matrimoniale of Valangin—an indication that even in the eighteenth century there was a certain blurring of the different tribunals' jurisdictions. Moreover, records survive for 41 police actions that the Quatre-Ministraux made against individuals or couples in the city of Neuchâtel.

Statistics for the police actions of Valangin's consistory differ considerably from those for the Quatre-Ministraux. Though the latter made three-fourths of their police actions during the final two decades reviewed here, in Valangin the numbers of such actions did not reflect contemporary demographic changes. Whereas Valangin's consistory made 11 police actions during the years 1707–1716 it heard only 8 such cases in the last ten years before Napoleonic rule.[70] There was a

70. In comparing the increase in consistorial police actions to the demographic curve, I am looking only at Valangin's police actions, since its consistory is the only one whose records are extant for the entire period. Including the incomplete records of Travers or the sporadic police actions of Neuchâtel's matrimonial court could skew the curve. The unavoidable impression from the registers of the Quatre-Ministraux is that there was a dramatic increase in police actions toward the end of the eighteenth century, and this is not simply because there are no

TABLE 15
Police actions against married persons, by cause, 1707–1806

	Désunion/ illegal separation	Domestic misconduct	Marriage initiated in scandal
1707–1716	10	2	0
1717–1726	3	3	0
1727–1736	6	0	0
1737–1746	3	3	0
1747–1756	1	3	1
1757–1766	9	2	0
1767–1776	14	1	1
1777–1786	9	3	0
1787–1796	7	3	0
1797–1806	10	1	0
	72	21	2

perceptible increase from the first half-century to the second: the consistory made 34 such actions between 1707 and 1756 and 48 for the period 1757–1806, an increase of 41 percent. But this augmentation did not parallel the population growth, much less the huge increases in other forms of marital disputes, particularly divorces.

Whereas the consistories used police actions more against couples than against individual spouses, the Quatre-Ministraux used such actions mainly against abusive or negligent husbands. The consistories convoked 56 couples, 25 men, and 12 women; the city of Neuchâtel's magistrates summoned 7 couples, 29 men, and 5 women. Even though the numbers of prenuptial conceptions were growing by leaps and bounds, the various legal bodies convoked only two couples for having started their marriage in scandal—an indication that magistrates were tacitly permitting sexual relations between fiancés. In promoting domestic peace, the consistory mentioned illicit separation or disunion 72 times and misbehavior 21 times, and the Quatre-Ministraux cited misbehavior 33 times and illegal separation only once.[71] Whereas the

extant records prior to 1715. No examples of police actions can be found during the first half-century of Prussian rule, and only ten were made before 1787; AVN, QMN1–11.

71. Two men were summoned by the consistory in 1785 and in 1802, both for their misconduct and for having left their wives; AEN, CST:89–90, *liasses*. A variety of reasons were mentioned in the eight other police actions made in the city of Neuchâtel. On one occasion in 1791, the Quatre-Ministraux admonished an innkeeper for providing lodging to a man who

Quatre-Ministraux basically ignored illicit separations, the consistories attacked them much more frequently during the second half of the century than during the first (49 to 23), a phenomenon that seems at odds with the contemporary judicial separations. If toward the end of the century the Justices matrimoniales were much more willing to grant legal separations, why was the consistory at the same time vigorously pursuing those who had separated without permission?

A closer analysis shows that the consistories' police actions against separate spouses did not contradict the contemporary practice of granting legal separations. Together, both forms of judicial activity support the theory that there was an increase in marital breakdown toward the end of the eighteenth century. More important, the sentences reveal an evolution in the treatment of separated couples during the course of the century. In the first half of the century, when a couple was convoked the husband and wife were generally just exhorted to reunite and guilty parties were subject to fines or imprisonment if admonitions were to no avail. When the consistory first convoked Abram Huguenin and his wife in 1708, the judges simply told them to return together. In 1714 the court again summoned the couple along with their female servant, with whom Abram was suspected of having an illicit affair. Ordered to send the servant away, the Huguenins appeared in court three more times in 1715/16 to account for their disunion. Testimony indicated that Huguenin continued to see the servant even after having sent her packing: two witnesses saw them talking together, one of whom also observed them playing the violin and viola together. Though this may not seem to be unequivocal proof of misbehavior, the court sentenced Abram to three days in jail for continuing this scandalous *fréquentation*.[72] When a separation was due to a man's poor behavior, the tribunals took measures to remedy this misconduct, often forbidding men to frequent the taverns if alcohol was a factor in their domestic discord.[73]

Regardless of what measures were taken against one or both spouses, during the first half-century the consistory consistently required separated couples to return together. Before 1770 only once did the consis-

---

had abandoned his wife and children, accusing the *cabaretier* of contributing to the couple's disunion; AVN, QMN8:190.

72. AEN, CSV7:33v, 56, 58r–v, 59v–60.

73. When Rose and Samuel Ducommun were held to account for their unauthorized separation in 1731, Rose complained about her husband's drunkenness and repugnance for work. Censured to live better, Samuel was forbidden to go to the taverns and threatened with a three-day jail sentence if he failed to change his ways; ibid., 130v–131v, 133v–134, 135.

tory allow a couple a certain waiting period to see if they could sort out their differences, providing them with the option of applying for a separation before the Justice matrimoniale if they were unable to reunite. This indulgence was probably the result of the couple's rather advanced age since, as we have seen, the consistory was more willing to grant separations to elderly couples.[74]

It would be erroneous to say that beginning in 1770 the courts did an about-face, freely allowing couples to live separately. Justices continued to exhort couples to live together and resorted to legal separations only when all else failed. The case of Abram Louis and Judith Perrelet shows that the consistory of the 1770s could be every bit as persistent as earlier consistories in requiring couples to return together. No less than seven times did Valangin's consistory convoke the Perrelets to account for their disunion. Even as late as 1802, the matrimonial court of Neuchâtel in a rare police action enjoined a couple to live together, declaring that their current separation was not founded on any legitimate ground.[75]

In several cases after 1770, however, the consistories allowed husbands and wives to live separately for a period of months or even longer before uniting. Such sentences were tantamount to awarding de facto judicial separations. In 1800, for example, the consistory of Valangin convoked Phillipine and David Friedrich Veuve because of their unauthorized separation. While David expressed a willingness to live with his wife, Philippine had serious reservations because of David's poor treatment of her and the dire financial straits in which he had left her. The consistory awarded a separation of body and property "for a moment," after which time they would have to reunite.[76] Although this was the only police action in which the consistory itself awarded what it termed a "separation of body and property," a few other times it did as much without applying this phrase. More important, on ten different occasions from 1770 until 1806 the consistory of Valangin explicitly or implicitly referred couples or individuals to the matrimonial court to ask for either a separation or a divorce. One of the last police actions made during this period provides insight into changing attitudes toward separations. In December 1806 the consistory asked Abram Henry Morel and his wife why they were separated. Abram maintained that he had never consented to this separation and would never do so. The consis-

74. AEN, CSV8:37r–v, 42v–43v.
75. Ibid., 121v–122, 128r–v, 131v, 132v; JMN7:821–822. Later, in 1804, Neuchâtel's matrimonial court awarded a separation for eighteen months to this same couple, Marianne and Jean-Pierre Perrin Jaquet; JMN8:26.
76. AEN, CSV8:184–185.

tory gave the wife six weeks to take the necessary steps to obtain a legal separation. If she had not taken this initiative within this time limit, she would be forced to return to her husband.[77] In this and other cases the consistory was in effect referring the persons to the Justice matrimoniale of Valangin to pursue litigation for legal separations. This is a far cry from the police actions in which the consistory ordered couples to reunite and threatened them with prison sentences if they did not. To be sure, consistorial judges of the late eighteenth century, like their predecessors, viewed separations as a last resort in dealing with marital difficulties and insisted that couples get proper authorization before separating. On the whole, nonetheless, they showed more compassion than had earlier judges toward couples whose differences were clearly irreconcilable, a change in attitude that can be found in contemporary courts elsewhere.[78]

In controlling marital breakdown, magistrates did not always wait for couples to separate illegally before dealing with domestic unrest. As before, they took action against domestic misbehavior, pursuits directed primarily against delinquent husbands: the various tribunals summoned 43 men, 7 couples, and only 4 women for domestic misconduct. Ordinarily such actions involved husbands who were violent toward their wives or whose penchant for alcohol wreaked havoc in the household or dissipated the family fortune. To remedy this misbehavior, the courts usually ordered the guilty party to treat his spouse better and often forbade him to frequent the taverns. The Quatre-Ministraux took more stringent action on several occasions, condemning 4 men to brief prison sentences and banishing from the city 2 men and 3 couples for their domestic misbehavior. Another man, Samuel Durussel, a watchmaker living in La Chaux-de-Fonds who had abandoned his wife and children and dissipated the family fortune, was stripped of his membership in the city of Neuchâtel's bourgeoisie. If ever found within the city limits, he would be considered a persona non grata and treated as a vagabond.[79] In other words, the Quatre-Ministraux were willing to resort to strongarm tactics to ensure domestic stability. Unlike their harsh sentences against illicit sexuality, however, their police actions against married persons clearly promoted the interests of women.

77. AEN, CSV9:5–6.
78. In Scotland, where divorce for cruelty and incompatibility was not possible and where judicial separation no longer existed, Presbyterian tribunals rarely intervened when married couples were not cohabiting, thereby tacitly permitting separations; Mitchison and Leneman, *Sexuality and Social Control*, p. 100.
79. AVN, QMN10:335.

The consistories, in contrast, imposed sentences that went beyond ad-monitions on only four people, all men. All these punishments—three fines and one imprisonment—were handed down during the first fif-teen years of Prussian rule. True, the sole prison sentence was an ex-treme case in which a man was condemned to eight days in prison for having almost strangled his wife.[80] Apparently none of the other wife-beaters—or the sole husband-beater—was guilty of such dangerous misrule. Nevertheless, one may still wonder why in the later decades the consistories did not inflict the more severe sentences they were entitled to give. The most plausible answer is that later in the century, as sepa-rations and divorces became increasingly possible, the courts were more interested in protecting the innocent than in punishing the guilty.

Like contract disputes, police actions and other cases of marital break-down show that there was an alliance between women and the courts in eighteenth-century Neuchâtel. Women remained relegated to a sub-ordinate position, but contemporary accounts, like the court records, support the view that a man's authority over his wife was not arbitrary. In the late eighteenth century, Samuel de Chambrier, a Neuchâtel au-thor, observed:

> The father is the head of the household and recognized as such. But if he has authority over the household, it must not be arbitrary. The wife is called on for consultation in all affairs; she can give her opin-ion, assured of being listened to. Children too are not to be left in the dark on domestic matters. They are allowed to listen and, when they have acquired some experience, they can give their opinions. The servants are consulted about many things, even those concerning culture.[81]

The Neuchâtelois Samuel Ostervald, an eighteenth-century legal scholar, also described the husband as the head of the household who was responsible for administering the family's property and revenues. Unless otherwise stated in the contract, the husband enjoyed the free administration of even his wife's property, and she had to obey him in these matters as long as he acted reasonably. He did not have the right, however, to dispose of her property without her consent. Subject to her husband's authority, a woman could not make a contract without his approval and was generally expected to follow him if he chose to move

80. AEN, CSV7:96v–97.
81. Chambrier, *Description topographique*, pp. 108–109.

his residence. If a woman refused to submit to her husband, he could attempt to set her straight, first by gentle means; then, if these proved ineffective, he could call on the magistrate for help. The husband also had to provide for the wife's material needs according to his status and means. The wife received all the rights and privileges of her husband's status and condition: his *commune d'origine,* his coat of arms. Ostervald also spoke of the mutual duties of marriage. Husbands and wives were expected to live together and to love each other. Their property was to be held in common, unless stated otherwise in their marriage contract, and both husband and wife were to practice fidelity, though it was especially important that the woman be faithful lest one question the legitimacy of her children.[82]

It is interesting that in describing the rights and duties of husbands and wives Ostervald mentioned only that men could have recourse to the magistrates if their wives were not attentive to their duties. He did not indicate whether women could seek legal aid if their husbands were remiss in fulfilling their domestic obligations. Taken out of context, this treatise could suggest that women were helpless vis-à-vis negligent husbands—an indication of the danger of relying solely on literary or theoretical works. Court records have shown that, even though they had not attained social equality, women enjoyed unprecedented rights against inattentive husbands as well as recalcitrant fiancés in eighteenth-century Neuchâtel.

The evidence from Neuchâtel's litigation following marriage thus indicates that eighteenth-century judicial authorities stressed reciprocity in marriage more than ever before, a shift that can be found in contemporary popular culture elsewhere in Europe. John Gillis, for example, has discerned greater equality in marriage in early nineteenth-century England. Rural Englishmen had traditionally used charivaris or rough music to humiliate publicly people who in some way violated the accepted social norms. Men who were beaten by their wives were subjected to charivaris, since women were supposed to be subordinate to their husbands. By the early nineteenth century, however, the charivari no longer reinforced a strict subordination of wives but now moderated domestic violence and defended reciprocity in marriage. Now it was the wife-beaters who were likely to be the victims of rough music.[83]

---

82. Ostervald, *Loix, us et coutumes,* pp. 23–25.
83. Gillis, "Peasant, Plebeian, and Proletarian Marriage," in *Proletarianization and Family History,* ed. Levine, pp. 145, 150. Gillis further states that "love ceased to be viewed as a dan-

The findings in Neuchâtel and elsewhere suggest that both popular classes and ruling authorities deemed greater equality between the sexes desirable. Viewed as a whole, litigation following marriage shows that the rights of women in the home undeniably grew during the course of the eighteenth century. The introduction of cruelty as a ground for divorce and of the separation of body and property were judicial weapons made especially for women. Through these judicial tools and the police actions of consistories, women were no longer forced, as they had been heretofore, to suffer the mistreatment of brutal husbands. That women outnumbered men as plaintiffs for almost all forms of marital litigation underscores the fact that only in the eighteenth century did the Justices matrimoniales of the principality of Neuchâtel and Valangin become essentially women's courts.

---

gerous, disruptive force and was now seen as a desirable element not just of courtship but of marriage itself."

6

The Causes of Change

In the preceding chapters I have focused on the marital disputes of a particular state for a period lasting two hundred fifty years, the beginning and end of which were clearly transitional epochs for the principality of Neuchâtel and the institution of marriage. Sixteenth-century Neuchâtel suffered intense religious conflict as recently converted Protestants clashed with defenders of Roman Catholicism. Under the influence of the political pressure of Bern, the animated preaching of Farel, and the spirited, sometimes violent zeal of his converts, the county eventually espoused the Reformed faith. With this conversion, the laity could now receive communion in both kinds, services were conducted in the vernacular, and the clergy lost its identity as an estate. Significant changes also took place in the institution of marriage: the requirement that witnesses be present at *fiançailles* effectively abolished clandestine marriages; impediments to marriage for reasons of consanguinity and affinity were reduced; divorce and subsequent remarriage became possible under certain circumstances. Though these changes did not immediately alter drastically the institution of marriage, they were the seeds of change that would later reach full fruition.

The eighteenth century was also a watershed in the history of Neuchâtel. Beginning in 1750, the principality's population grew by unprecedented leaps and bounds, and immigration and emigration increased demonstrably; nascent industrialization took root and thrived, permanently altering the county's hitherto largely agrarian economy. In the preceding discussions we have seen clearly that by the late eighteenth century significant changes had also taken place in the institution of marriage, adding support to the view that the family underwent important alterations in the early modern period. True, the similarities between sixteenth- and eighteenth-century marriages undoubtedly outweigh the differences. Be that as it may, even if in both centuries most couples consulted their parents before marrying, celebrated their *fiançailles* in the presence of witnesses, consecrated their marriage in church, and proceeded to live in their own conjugal units,[1] this does not mean that marriage and the control of marriage remained static during two and a half centuries.

To begin with, in matrimonial litigation, the sentences rendered changed dramatically since the sixteenth century. Judges of the Reformation era deemed it their duty to oblige young people to honor *fiançailles* that had been properly made, even if one of both parties had experienced a change of heart. During the Prussian era, in contrast, the courts consistently released fiancés from their engagements, provided that they had not produced children. Though sixteenth-century authorities were reluctant to allow marriages between third cousins, eighteenth-century *conseillers d'état* awarded dispensations quite liberally to first cousins. Whereas earlier members of the courts granted divorces almost exclusively for reasons of adultery or desertion, a significant number of eighteenth-century Neuchâtelois received divorces on the grounds of cruelty and incompatibility. In the sixteenth and seventeenth centuries, delinquents could be subjected to the humiliating punishments of public penance and even the pillory and, in questions of paternity, could be condemned or acquitted according to how well they tolerated torture. By the mid-eighteenth century, these practices had been abolished or had fallen into disuse. In the city of Neuchâtel a small number of women guilty of illicit sexuality in the late eighteenth century were still subjected to shame and even corporal punishments; though harsh, these rare sentences were generally imposed only on recidivists suspected of prostitution. In many ways then, the decisions of Neuchâtel's eighteenth-century courts differed considerably from earlier precedents, anticipating marriage laws that would later prevail in most of the Western world.

Change, however, was not limited to the sentences passed by judicial authorities. Earlier courts heard above all questions pertaining to marriage contracts, that is, disputes involving the formation of marriage. The courts of the late eighteenth century, in contrast, were more con-

---

1. The court evidence does not verify or disprove whether most households were composed of nuclear families.

cerned with divorces and judicial separations, conflicts concerning the breakdown of marriage. This alteration in the types of case heard reflects a change on the part of the litigants. No longer was it so common to try to coerce unwilling partners into honoring marriage engagements. In the eighteenth century, unlike in earlier periods, the large part of those plaintiffs who did try to enforce marriage contracts were women who needed fathers for their children conceived out of wedlock. More young men and women could now choose their own mates, asking their parents only for approval. Marriages of convenience certainly did not disappear in the eighteenth century, just as they have not ceased to exist today. But the marriage of choice was clearly becoming a viable alternative to the marriage of convenience. Once married, people no longer felt obligated to endure stoically insufferable marriages. Though divorces were still rare, they nevertheless ensured that there were limits to the misbehavior a spouse had to tolerate. The fact that divorce and separation suits easily outnumbered contract disputes in the late eighteenth century indicates, among other things, that people were now placing more emphasis on personal compatibility in marriage than ever before. In short, if the eighteenth century did not witness a revolution in sentiment, it at least experienced an evolution in sentiment; parallel to the changes in the courts' sentences was a growing emphasis on the importance of affection in marriage.

We should now inquire about the causes behind these changes in marriage and the control of marriage. Even those who agree that important changes took place in marriage during the early modern period do not always agree on why these modifications occurred. Some historians hold that the marriage of sentiment first became common among the working classes and resulted from economic changes, namely, the appearance of wage labor, which reduced the importance of property concerns in the formation of marriages. But others, such as Lawrence Stone, hold that upper-class couples were the first to implement the love match and to enjoy more privacy vis-à-vis kin and community and that the women of these classes were the first freed from the tyranny of their husbands. These changes in family life, Stone argues, resulted from ideological, not economic, changes.[2]

2. Roderick Phillips, for example, asserts that in traditional society marriages were held together especially by economic concerns. To avoid being monocausal, he adds that mass divorce exists today because of greater expectations of marriage; economic, social, and cultural developments that permit more marriages to break down; and increasing access to divorce; *Putting Asunder*, pp. 632, 639–640; Stone, *Family, Sex, and Marriage*.

The fact that eighteenth-century court decisions differed considerably from earlier judgments shows unequivocally that Neuchâtel's judicial authorities had a different mentality from their predecessors. Where did these new attitudes come from? New ideas on marriage and divorce could be found among seventeenth- and eighteenth-century scholars who wrote on natural law, including the Dutch jurist Hugo Grotius (d. 1645), one of the founders of modern theory on natural law. Most of these commentators favored rather liberal laws on divorce. Christian Thomasius (d. 1728), a German theorist, recognized several grounds for divorce, including cruelty and incompatibility. Likewise, Christian Wolff (d. 1754), a prominent German jurist and student of Leibnitz, favored divorce by mutual consent, provided that no children were involved. He based such a view on the theory of consensual contract: marriage in effect was a contract; just as parties to a contract could mutually cancel their agreement, so husbands and wives ought to be able to end their matrimonial contract. In cases of "irreconcilable hostility," Wolff approved of divorce even when children were involved; forcing hostile spouses to remain together would in the end be worse for the children's development than allowing them to divorce.[3]

These various German and Dutch jurists influenced a group of eighteenth-century scholars in Geneva, Neuchâtel, and the Pays de Vaud. Unlike the *encyclopédistes* of France, the Swiss-French school of natural law was neither deist nor anti-Christian but, rather, remained closely tied to the Reformed faith. The metaphysical rationalism of Leibnitz and Wolff strongly influenced the Swiss-French school through the work of Louis Bourguet, a Huguenot who served as professor of mathematics and philosophy in Neuchâtel from 1730 to 1742, and of Emer de Vattel (d. 1767), a jurist in Neuchâtel who was a great admirer of Wolff. Like Wolff, Vattel approved of divorce by mutual consent, though he felt that couples with children should stay together as long as their upbringing required. The jurist Jean de Barbeyrac (d. 1744), a professor at Lausanne who translated the works of Grotius and Samuel Pufendorf (d. 1694), rejected the church fathers' belief that celibacy was the superior state and marriage a necessary evil and contended that marriage was morally neutral. Like earlier *jusnaturalistes,* he denied that nature dictates the indissolubility of marriage, arguing that as a contract marriage was to last as long as the parties desired. Barbeyrac further held the very modern view that the purpose of marriage was as much to assure the happiness of the couple as the procreation of

3. Phillips, *Putting Asunder,* pp. 210–211, 217–218.

the race. Like Barbeyrac, Jean-Jacques Burlamaqui (d. 1748), a professor and member of the Conseil d'Etat in Geneva, favored rather progressive divorce laws, approving of divorce for reason of irreconcilable enmity between spouses. Fearful lest couples, especially those with children, take divorce too lightly, Burlamaqui became one of the first scholars of natural law to support the *séparation de corps et de bien,* a common solution to marital breakdown in eighteenth-century Neuchâtel.[4] In short, a host of legal thinkers in Neuchâtel and neighboring states espoused the view that marriage was a contract, a theory that could have important implications in cases of marital breakdown.

As far as the position of women is concerned, members of the French-Swiss school vacillated between two points of view. Some held that natural law determined that man was to rule over woman, while the general tendency among *jusnaturalistes* was to argue in favor of the equality of the sexes. Barbeyrac at times favored the former view but at others argued that, as parties to a contract, a couple could determine their own relationship. Even those who favored the subordination of women to their husbands believed that women had certain rights that their husbands could not abrogate; though regarding the man as the natural head of the household, Vattel maintained that if a man became a tyrant in his home his wife could take legal measures to ensure her rights.[5]

Neuchâtel's judicial authorities also could have been influenced by various French philosophes, who generally favored more liberal divorce laws, the marriage of sentiment, and greater equality between the sexes. Indeed, several important writers spent time in the principality in the late eighteenth century. Jean-Jacques Rousseau spent the years 1762–1765 in Neuchâtel as a refugee; Honoré-Gabriel de Riqueti, comte de Mirabeau, stayed in the county about 1777 and again in 1782; Louis-Sébastien Mercier resided there from roughly 1781 to 1785, and Jacques-Pierre Brissot visited Neuchâtel in 1782.[6] Beginning about 1770, the principality also became an important center of the printing industry and published a variety of Enlightenment works. Several printers set up shop in the principality, including the city of Neuchâtel itself: Samuel Fauche, a bookseller in Neuchâtel since 1753, ran a printshop from 1773 until about 1800, Jonas Fauche and Jérémie Witel printed

---

4. Alfred Dufour, *Le mariage dans l'école romande du droit naturel au XVIIIe siècle* (Geneva, 1976).

5. Ibid., pp. 57–58, 94–95.

6. Michel Schlup, "Sociétés de lecture et cabinets littéraires dans la principauté de Neuchâtel (1750–1800)," *Musée neuchâtelois,* 1987, 84.

works in the city during the period 1782–1785, and Abram-Louis Fauche-Borel was a printer from 1786 to 1814. During the years 1786–1790, Jérémie Witel ran a printing enterprise in the town of Les Verrières. Most important, La Société typographique de Neuchâtel, which published the quarto edition of the *Encyclopédie,* was active in the city's printing industry for two decades, 1769–1789. Though most of what they produced was intended for European, especially French, markets, the Enlightenment works produced locally clearly had an impact on the literary tastes of Neuchâtel's reading public.[7]

What did the philosophes have to say about marriage and the family? Though they were not the great liberators of women, philosophes nevertheless called for greater equality in marriage and sought to reduce the arbitrary power men had over their wives and children. In the *Encyclopédie,* the Chevalier de Jaucourt wrote an entry on women and natural law in which he argued that male domination of women was the result of civil law, not of natural law. Supporting the natural equality of all people, Jaucourt denied that men are by nature necessarily wiser, physically stronger, or more intelligent than women. Like theorists on natural law before him, Jaucourt held that marriage was a contract between a man and a woman. True, he believed that men were usually more capable in governing affairs than women and that men should thus have authority over their wives in most cases. Nonetheless, Jaucourt felt that there could be cases in which a woman had authority over her husband. Be that as it may, Abby Kleinbaum argues that Enlightenment thinkers were anything but progressive with regard to women, relegating them to an exclusively domestic role. Referring to M. Desmahis's article on women in the *Encyclopédie,* "Femme (morale)," Kleinbaum holds that philosophes actually used natural law to deny the equality of the sexes. Desmahis maintained, for example, that women were physically and intellectually inferior to men, that certain traits—such as "force, majesty, courage, and reason"—were good in men but bad in women, and that the only good roles for females were those of wives and mothers.[8]

7. As Schlup has observed, eighteenth-century Neuchâtel experienced a literary evolution similar to that in neighboring countries. This new literature began taking hold in Neuchâtel in the 1770s, stimulated in large part by the work of local printers who were producing for European markets; *Sociétés de lecture et cabinets littéraires dans la principauté de Neuchâtel (1760–1830)* [a catalogue for an exhibition in the Bibliothèque Universitaire et Publique de Neuchâtel] (Neuchâtel, 1986), p. 9.

8. Kleinbaum, "Women in the Age of Light," in *Becoming Visible,* ed. Bridenthal and Koonz, pp. 220–230.

It no doubt is true that Enlightenment thinkers excluded women from the political arena, but Kleinbaum exaggerates the negative attitudes of philosophes toward women. Even if they did expect women to be good wives and mothers, Enlightenment thinkers were progressive with regard to women by defending their rights vis-à-vis their husbands. The most important evidence to support Kleinbaum's point of view is to be found in Jean-Jacques Rousseau's *Julie, ou La Nouvelle Héloise,* in which the protagonist, obedient to her father, agrees to enter a marriage of convenience with a much older man rather than remain with the man show loves, her teacher (who was of lower status). On the basis of *Julie,* one may be tempted to conclude that philosophes not only paid little attention to the interests of women but also preferred the marriage of convenience to the love match. Most philosophes, however, clearly did not share these views. In the second half of the eighteenth century, a host of Enlightenment thinkers wrote treatises and creative works that advocated marriage for love. James Traer maintains that a

> major theme in eighteenth-century thought proposed sentiment as the key to marriage and family relationships. Dramatists and novelists contrasted the marriage of inclination, initiated by the free choice of two individuals and founded on their mutual affection, with the marriage of convenience, contracted by two families for their children and intended to further the families' social and economic goals. The idea that marriage might properly be based on sentiment or love was new. Literary tradition, from the courtly poetry of the troubadours and the myth of Tristan and Iseult through the drama of Corneille and Racine and the essays of Montaigne, had declared passionate love and marriage to be incompatible.[9]

Voltaire's *Nanine* and Diderot's *Le père de famille* both championed love matches, as upper-class male characters overcame obstacles and family opposition to marry the lower-class women they loved. In *La morale universelle,* the Baron d'Holbach argued that a successful marriage had to be based on love; any match that was founded simply on birth or wealth was bound to fail. The same theme appeared in Abbé Pinchon's *Mémoire sur les abus dans les mariages,* in which the author criticized marriages of convenience and even recommended abolishing the dowry since it hindered marriages based on choice. Notwithstanding his novel

9. Traer, *Marriage and the Family,* p. 71.

Julie, even Jean-Jacques Rousseau disapproved of parental control over the formation of marriage. In the 1782 edition of his *Discours sur l'origine de l'inégalité,* published posthumously, Rousseau condemned fathers who forced children into marriages against their will or prevented them from marrying the spouses of their choice. In his poem *Les mois,* Jean Antoine Roucher likewise spoke of unhappy spouses who were forced into marriages by ambitious and avaricious relatives and urged that they be allowed to dissolve their union and marry for love. Roucher's poem shows that the desire to replace the marriage of convenience with the love match went hand in hand with arguments for divorce; both stemmed from the belief that love was an essential component of marriage.[10]

In France, where divorce was not possible until 1792, the philosophes were virtually unanimous in favoring the introduction of divorce. The most famous writers—Condorcet, Voltaire, Diderot, Helvétius, Holbach, Morellet—dealt with the question of divorce only in a rather vague fashion. For more detailed arguments for divorce, we have to turn to some less renowned philosophes. Boucher d'Argis wrote an article on divorce for the *Encyclopédie* which he began by discussing the Catholic doctrine of the indissolubility of marriage. Then, however, he gave a historical description of divorce and noted that divorce had been possible among the ancient Israelites, Romans, and early French monarchs, thus showing that indissolubility was a recent innovation. Most of the philosophes' arguments in favor of divorce centered on the social benefits: divorce would increase the population, regenerate morality, and enhance domestic happiness and harmony. In his *Lettres persanes,* Montesquieu observed that divorce could nurture happiness and affection; "nothing contributed more to mutual affection than the ability to divorce; a husband and wife were led patiently to tolerate domestic difficulties, knowing that they were able to put an end to them, and they often held this power in their hands all their lives without using it, for the single reason that they were free to do so."[11] Montesquieu was implicitly calling for divorce for reason of incompatibility, a ground accepted in late eighteenth-century Neuchâtel and advocated in the most

10. Ibid., pp. 73–76, citing Holbach, *La morale universelle, ou les devoirs de l'homme fondés sur la nature* (Amsterdam, 1776), 3:2–32; Thomas-Jean Pichon, *Mémoire sur les abus dans les mariages* (Amsterdam, 1776), pp. 40–54; and Roucher, *Les mois* (Paris, 1771), 1:186.
11. Phillips, *Putting Asunder,* pp. 159–171, citing *Lettres persanes* (Paris, 1960), Letter 116; Traer, *Marriage and the Family,* pp. 53–54.

influential Enlightenment work on divorce, Albert Joseph Ulpien Hennet's *Du divorce* of 1789.[12]

Just as divorce was a weapon used especially by women in eighteenth-century Neuchâtel, so many philosophes regarded divorce as a means by which women could counterbalance their husbands' authority. Montesquieu favored allowing only women to file for unilateral divorce, since permitting men to do so would give them yet another means of abusing their power. In the same manner, Holbach felt that with divorce a woman could "rebel against tyranny, ill-treatment, tiresome emotions, against the continued bad-temper of a spouse, life together with whom had become intolerable."[13]

Beginning about 1770, French authors favoring divorce paid increasing attention to the plight of unhappily married women. The pamphleteer Cerfvol, for example, decried the current system in which women simply passed from the authority of their fathers to that of their husbands, arguing that divorce would provide equality between spouses and serve as a remedy to matches arranged by parents. In another work published in Geneva in 1770, Cerfvol presented arguments for divorce in the form of a dialogue between a countess and a marquise who were both unhappily married.[14] Choderlos de Laclos, author of *Les liaisons dangereuses,* responded to the Academy of Châlons-sur-Marne's essay question concerning the "best means of perfecting the upbringing of women": in *De l'éducation des femmes* he asserted that all efforts to improve the education of women were bound to fail as long as society relegated them to an inferior position to men. Laclos insisted that laws must restore women's natural equality so that they were neither slaves nor objects of property and believed that divorce was a means of promoting equality.[15]

12. Other grounds for divorce Hennet accepted included condemnation to death or to a "degrading punishment," lengthy imprisonment, captivity with no foreseeable release, exile or disappearance of one's spouse, "sterility for a specified period," incurable illness, insanity, "any crime," adultery, and "extreme dissoluteness." According to Phillips, Hennet's proposals were so similar to the law on divorce passed in 1792 that *Du divorce* was clearly influential; *Putting Asunder,* pp. 169, 173, 174, citing *Du divorce* (Paris, 1789), pp. 122–123.

13. Phillips, *Putting Asunder,* p. 171, citing Montesquieu, *De l'esprit des lois,* bk. 16, chap. 15, and Holbach, *Ethocratie, ou le gouvernement fondé sur la morale* (Amsterdam, 1776), p. 208.

14. Traer, *Marriage and the Family,* p. 76, nn. 81–82, citing Cerfvol, *Intérêt des femmes au rétablissement du divorce* (Amsterdam, 1770), pp. 5–52, and *Le parloir de l'Abbaye de * * * ou entretiens sur le divorce par M. de V * * * suivi de son utilité politique* (Geneva, 1770), pp. 1–43.

15. Traer, *Marriage and the Family,* p. 77, n. 85, citing Pierre Ambroise François Choderlos de Laclos, *De l'éducation des femmes* (Paris, 1903), pp. 13, 62.

Eighteenth-century literary evidence shows that arguments in favor of the love match, liberal divorce laws, and greater equality between husbands and wives coincided. They were all based on the notion of the companionate marriage, a union of equals based on the affective bond between them. Love was the most important element in forming and sustaining a marriage. Traer concludes:

> Increasingly during the century, imaginative literature proclaimed the importance of sentiment in human relationships. Dramatists and novelists portrayed happy marriages based on inclination or love and created by the free choice of the two spouses. They praised marriage as a source of emotional satisfaction and stressed the equality of the wife with her husband. On this basis, they argued that divorce should be available to end loveless marriages and protect a woman's liberty. In their critique of traditional religious and legal conceptions, in their emphasis in diversity, utility, and sentiment, the *philosophes* prepared the way for the legislation of the revolution and the modern form of marriage and the family it sought to create.[16]

Although we think of this period as the Age of the Reason, the emotions were not neglected: eighteenth-century novelists, pamphleteers, and philosophes strongly favored the love match over the marriage of convenience. The Reformation had enhanced the dignity of married life by denying the superiority of celibacy; the Enlightenment exalted marriage even further by making love the most important criterion in choosing a spouse.

To show unequivocally that the French philosophes or the Swiss *jus-naturalistes* influenced the decisions of Neuchâtel's matrimonial courts, we would have to find references to these authors in the court records. Such evidence unfortunately does not exist. The decisions passed were remarkably unphilosophical: usually no more than a paragraph in length, the judgments offered but a brief explanation, saying, for example, that a man could have a divorce since he had proven his wife's adultery or that a marriage contract could be annulled since the fiancés hated each other and had not produced any children. During the course of two and a half centuries, only once did the records cite an authority by name, referring in the seventeenth century to the views of Jesus on divorce. The registers also mention that before 1700 the tribunals twice asked the advice of the Genevan Compagnie des Pasteurs. Apart from these

---

16. Traer, *Marriage and the Family,* p. 78.

isolated incidents, no evidence can be gleaned from the records on the question of outside influence. Not a word can be found in the registers to indicate whether the court members ever solicited the opinions of legal savants or were swayed by treatises on marriage and divorce. Since the *procès verbaux* tell us nothing in this regard, we must look beyond the court records to determine whether Neuchâtel's judicial authorities were influenced by new ideas on marriage and divorce.

The printing industry provides significant evidence of the publications that circulated in Neuchâtel. Indeed, much of the work of the aforementioned novelists, philosophes, and jurists was available to Neuchâtel's small but avid reading public. Since printed material was still rather expensive, book lovers in eighteenth-century Neuchâtel formed *sociétés de lecture* whereby they pooled resources to purchase books, journals, and other materials. In 1750 about thirty people joined the first such organization, the Société littéraire, which served as a model for subsequent reading societies. The books were kept at a location that was overseen by a librarian and open to members a few hours a week. For an annual fee, members of these organizations could take books home or peruse them in the reading rooms some societies provided. A committee annually selected new books to purchase and sold the books from the previous year to add more money to the fund. These reading associations understandably catered to a rather small group; only the relatively wealthy had the time and financial means to indulge in much reading. Indeed, Neuchâtel's public library, founded in 1788, was not really public in our sense of the word, since only a rather small group had access to its holdings.[17]

For those who lacked the wealth or status to join these exclusive societies, Neuchâtel's reading public also formed *cabinets littéraires,* which rented out books and papers to customers who took the material home or, in some cases, consulted them in a reading room. Anyone who could afford the rental costs and respected the rules concerning the loaning of books was welcome to borrow books from *cabinets littéraires,* which were usually associated with bookstores. Though we do not have lists of those who participated in these associations, the clientele were most likely rather well-to-do.[18]

First appearing in 1750, reading societies and literary cabinets were formed, according to Michel Schlup, as a direct result of interest in En-

17. Schlup, *Sociétés de lecture (1760–1830)*, pp. 5, 22–23.
18. Ibid., p. 33. Schlup suggests that the clientele were likely bourgeois and relatively well-to-do.

lightenment thought and literature. The inventories of two *cabinets littéraires* show that the most important literature of the Enlightenment was available to Neuchâtel readers in the 1790s. For a price, Neuchâtelois could read any of several works by Voltaire and Diderot, including *Nanine* and *Le père de famille,* as well as works by Montesquieu, Rousseau, Crébillon, Marmontel, Mercier, and l'abbé Prévost. They could peruse works on natural law such as Vattel's *Droits des gens;* the popular romances of Mme de Riccoboni and Mme de Genlis as well as a French translation of Goethe's melodramatic *Werther;* or even scandalous literature, including *Les liaisons dangereuses* and Mirabeau's *Lettres de cachet.*[19] Moreover, the *Journal helvétique,* one of French-speaking Switzerland's most important literary journals in the eighteenth century, published articles by such celebrated authors as Voltaire, Fontenelle, and Grimod de La Reynière. Quite simply, Neuchâtel's reading public had many opportunities to become acquainted with Enlightenment literature.[20]

Among Neuchâtel's elite who took advantage of these literary opportunities were some members of the matrimonial courts of Neuchâtel and Valangin. In 1802, two of Neuchâtel's most prestigious reading societies, the Société du Jardin, founded 1759, and the Société de lecture,

19. Among other works listed were Voltaire's *Candide, Mémoires,* and *Lettres philosophiques;* Montesquieu's *Esprit des loix, Lettres persanes,* and *Oeuvres,* 7 vols.; Helvetius's *De l'homme, de ses facultés intellectuelles et de son éducation,* vols. 1 and 3; Diderot's *Jaques le fataliste* and *Oeuvres et théâtre de Diderot,* 2 vols.; Rousseau's *Lettres sur le christianisme* and the 34-volume collection of his *Oeuvres;* and *Les lettres originales de Mirabeau, écrites du donjon de Vincennes en 1777 à 1780,* 4 vols. Still other titles included *Le barbier de Seville, Les amours généreux, Le philosophe marié, La surprise d'amour, Défense des droits des femmes,* l'abbé Mably's *Des droits et devoirs du citoyen,* and *Le mari sentimental ou le mariage comme il y en a quelques-uns;* Bibliothèque Universitaire et Publique de Neuchâtel, MS QDD 901 and 902, Le Catalogue du Cabinet littéraire d'Auguste Fauche and Le Catalogue du Cabinet littéraire de Louis Fauche-Borel. The former list was made in 1798, and Schlup estimates that the latter inventory dates from about 1793–1796; "Sociétés de lecture (1750–1800)," pp. 99–101, and *Sociétés de lecture (1760–1830),* pp. 4, 22.

20. The *Journal helvétique,* however, was more Christian in nature than many contemporary Parisian publications. It should also be noted that Neuchâtelois had the opportunity to read some anti-Enlightenment literature. Schlup has thus described M. Linguet's *Annales politiques, civiles, et littéraires du dix-huitième siècle: Ouvrage périodique,* published at Lausanne: "A polemical journal that was opposed to the party of philosophes and *encyclopédistes,* Linguet's *Annales politiques* seems to have been much appreciated by Neuchâtel readers"; "Diffusion et lecture du *Journal helvétique* au temps de la Société typographique de Neuchâtel, 1769–1782," in *La diffusion et la lecture des journaux de langue française sous l'ancien régime* (Amsterdam, 1988), pp. 59, 68–69, and *Sociétés de lecture (1760–1830),* pp. 12, 14. Neuchâtel's pastors clearly found some aspects of Enlightenment literature offensive. In 1765 representatives of the Classe des Pasteurs appeared before the Quatre-Ministraux to complain about certain works by Jean-Jacques Rousseau. Though they listened to this complaint, the magistrates did not take action; AVN, QMN4:161.

which replaced the Société littéraire in 1802, each included at least five men among its thirty or so members who regularly served as judges for the matrimonial tribunals of Neuchâtel or Valangin. More important, Jean-Frédéric de Montmollin (d. 1812), mayor of Valangin, and Charles-Louis de Pierre (d. 1824), mayor of Neuchâtel from 1792, were members of both societies. As mayors, they also served as presidents of their respective Justices matrimoniales.[21]

The best evidence that judicial authorities were interested in Enlightenment thought is found in a list of subscriptions from 1780 for Neuchâtel's quarto edition of the *Encyclopédie*, the supreme expression of Enlightenment thought. The archives of the Société typographique de Neuchâtel contain only one list of subscribers to its edition of the *Encyclopédie*, a list that bears only six names, including "de Montmollin Maire de Vallengin" and "De Pierre Procureur Général." A bit of research reveals that the former refers to Georges de Montmollin (d. 1780), the mayor of Valangin for several years until 1778, when his son, the aforementioned Jean-Frédéric, succeeded him, holding office until 1803. The latter was Jean-Frédéric de Pierre (d. 1800), the father of Charles-Louis, the aforementioned mayor of Neuchâtel, and of Philippe-Auguste de Pierre, a member of the Conseil d'Etat and of the Justice matrimoniale of Neuchâtel. Consequently, three presidents and another member of the matrimonial tribunals had direct access to the *Encyclopédie* and therefore may well have been swayed by the thought of the philosophes.[22]

Of course, a book bought is not necessarily a book read, and the mere fact these men owned the *Encyclopédie* does not mean they agreed with

21. Among the twenty-nine original members of the Société de lecture were eleven *conseillers d'etat* and several other officeholders: Philippe-Auguste de Pierre (1768–1846), brother of Charles-Louis and a regular member of Neuchâtel's Justice matrimoniale beginning in 1801; Charles-Godefroy de Tribolet (1752–1843), regular member of the Justice matrimoniale in the 1790s through 1802; Louis Pourtalès (1773–1848), mayor of Boudevilliers and occasional member of the Justice matrimoniale in the early nineteenth century; Georges de Rougemont, *conseiller d'etat, procureur général*, and occasional member of the Justice matrimoniale. In 1802, all but one of the members of the Société de lecture also belonged to the Société de Jardin; Schlup, *Sociétés de lecture (1760–1830)*, pp. 9, 25–29; Edouard Quartier-La-Tente, *Les familles bourgeoises de Neuchâtel: Essais généalogiques* (Neuchâtel, 1903), pp. 98, 157, 197.
22. Bibliothèque Publique et Universitaire de Neuchâtel, STN, Ms 1220, No. 339. I am grateful to Michel Schlup and Robert Darnton for bringing this document to my attention. Both agree that this is the only list of subscribers to be found among the thousands of documents in the Société archives; Quarthier-La-Tente, *Familles bourgeoises*, pp. 98, 157; *Almanach officiel* (Neuchâtel, 1783), pp. 27–28. Darnton discusses this same list of subscribers in Appendix B to *The Business of the Enlightenment: A Publishing History of the "Encyclopédie," 1775–1800* (Cambridge, Mass., 1979), pp. 586, 592.

its contents. Nevertheless, since these leaders were willing to pay a considerable sum for this work (384 livres français, plus the costs of binding), they evidently had a strong interest in reading what the philosophes had to say.[23] More important, Charles-Louis de Pierre, the aforementioned mayor of Neuchâtel, was said to have been won over to liberal ideas during his youth, though he later became a fierce opponent of the French Revolution and a strong advocate for the restoration of the Bourbons.[24] Even if he opposed the revolutionary movement across the border, he quite easily could have adopted various liberal ideas, including those pertaining to marriage. Though it is not possible to determine which judges were most influential on the matrimonial courts, since the records mention only the final decision, it is safe to assume that the president would have had more say than other members. In any event, the justices of the late eighteenth century had a different mentality from that of their predecessors, and these changes in attitudes can realistically be attributed to the spread of liberal or Enlightenment thought.[25]

The extent to which Enlightenment thought influenced the worldview of Europeans has long been a major issue for scholars studying the eighteenth century. As Robert Darnton has observed, specialists have for the most part divided into two camps: those who view the Enlightenment as a broad and influential public movement and those who consider it a relatively superficial phenomenon limited to a few intellectuals. The former group includes polemicists such as Abbé Barruel, who held the philosophes partly responsible for the French Revolution. More important, de Tocqueville and, more recently, historians such as Paul Hazard and Gustave Lanson have also held that the Enlightenment had a broad impact on European mentality in general. Supporters of this view were put on the defensive by members of the *Annales* school who studied book production quantitatively. Various *Annalistes* maintain that the philosophes did not have a broad appeal, arguing that the

23. Schlup, "Sociétés de lecture (1750–1800)," p. 85. The quarto edition nonetheless was much cheaper than earlier folio editions; Darnton, *Business of the Enlightenment*, p. 274.

24. Quartier-La-Tente, *Familles bourgeoises*, p. 98.

25. The de Montmollins and the de Pierres were of course not the only members of the matrimonial courts. It would be helpful to know more about all the judges. I would have liked to study the wills and testaments of the various justices to ascertain whether their private libraries contained Enlightenment works. That task proved infeasible. Such information, if it exists, would be found in the volumes left by notaries. Notarial records up to the year 1872 occupy about 300 linear meters of shelf space in Neuchâtel's cantonal archives, roughly one-third of which date from the eighteenth century. These volumes, unfortunately, are not indexed and are arranged alphabetically according to notary. I therefore had to forego trying to discover the contents of judges' libraries in this huge mass of notarial documentation.

printing industry published the classics and religious literature in far greater quantities than Enlightenment works. On the basis of the correspondence of the Société typographique de Neuchâtel concerning the quarto edition of the *Encyclopédie*, Darnton acknowledges that Enlightenment literature did not generate much interest among the commercial and industrial bourgeoisie. Nonetheless, he maintains that the Enlightenment did appeal to the traditional elites—"noblemen, clerics, . . . notables, rentiers, officials, and professional persons"—and concludes that the impressive sales of the *Encyclopédie* show that the Enlightenment appealed on a massive scale to the upper and middle levels of French society, if not to the "masses" who made the Revolution in 1789.[26]

What was true for France was also true for Neuchâtel: simply put, there was an Enlightenment in Neuchâtel, at least among the ruling elite. The abolition of the practices of requiring fornicators to do public penance, of administering the oath to unwed mothers in labor, and of implementing torture to determine the paternity of illegitimate children were certainly examples of enlightened legislation. Although in the city of Neuchâtel the Quatre-Ministraux were quite strict with unmarried mothers, this harsh treatment was more than offset by the judgments of the Justices matrimoniales; in these matrimonial courts, eighteenth-century judges were enlightened in a way that their predecessors had not been by allowing the poor to file suit free of charge, by defending the interests of unwed mothers, by awarding divorces to chronically incompatible couples, and by permitting women to separate from cruel husbands. French philosophes would have approved of these modifications introduced by Neuchâtel authorities.

The eighteenth century brought change to the actions of litigants as well as to the decisions of judges. Why was it only in the eighteenth century that divorce action was more common than spousal litigation? Why were women for the first time the clear majority of plaintiffs who sought to enforce marriage contracts? Could it be that the common folk were imbued with the spirit of the philosophes? Some, such as the soldier who penned passionate love letters to his fiancée during the Seven Years' War, may have been familiar with popular romanesque literature. Moreover, with their subtle but perceptible move away from

26. Darnton, *Business of the Enlightenment*, pp. 286, 527–528. Darnton believes that, contrary to views of various *Annales* scholars, the Enlightenment involved more than just a small group of intellectuals; he argues that Voltaire and Rousseau had an enormous audience, at least among the upper- and middle-class French. Cf. Lucien Febvre and Henri-Jean Martin, *L'apparition du livre* (Paris, 1958).

the marriage of convenience, people such as Abraham Louis Sandoz were—consciously or unconsciously—consistent with Enlightenment thought on marriage. But it is unlikely that much Enlightenment thought filtered down to common people. The cost of even a modest novel amounted to a week's earnings for a laborer.[27] During the revolutionary period, some Neuchâtelois, calling themselves "citizens," did form patriotic societies and advocate a society based on equality and liberty, appealing to notions of natural law.[28] It is conceivable, even likely, that participants in such movements had views on marriage similar to those that led to the liberal divorce laws in France. Such patriotic societies, however, involved only a tiny fraction of Neuchâtel's population.[29]

Economic explanations are more likely factors than Enlightenment or revolutionary ideology in the changes in the actions of litigants. With the development of protoindustry, wealth became more a matter of wages than of property. Accordingly, one would expect property to play a less prominent role in forming marriages, allowing young people freer rein to pursue sentiment and personal preference in choosing mates. Similarly, since the family was less often a productive unit, the economic ties that bound husbands and wives together were loosened, removing an obstacle to the separation of unhappy couples. To prove that the quantitative and qualitative changes in eighteenth-century matrimonial disputes were related to economic transformations would require information about the occupations of the litigants: if a large proportion of the parties appearing before the courts were involved in the production of watches, lace, or printed cloth, the connection be-

27. Schlup, *Sociétés de lectures (1760–1830)*, p. 15.
28. One such group was the Société partriotique de La Chaux-de-Fonds. Two documents addressed to this organization, both dating from 1793, reveal strong democratic convictions. According to one author, a citizen is a member of a free society and is not simply a person who happened to be born in a particular state, but rather "someone who behaves in accordance with the laws and customs of the country where he is; who views it as his country and contributes as much as he can to the public welfare." The other work reveals a strong belief in natural law, which was so central to Enlightenment thought. Noting that Newton had discovered the laws of nature, the anonymous author maintained that ideas of good and evil can be drawn from the "constitution of nature"; natural law manifests that one of the most important obligations is to work for the general good of one's native country (*patrie*); AEN, Société partriotique de La Chaux-de-Fonds, Série Evénerats 1700–1799, dossier 6, nos. 22 and 23. I am grateful to Sylvia Robert for providing me with a copy of this document.
29. In the city of Neuchâtel, only once did the magistrates take action against anything even vaguely resembling pro-revolutionary agitation. In 1794 the Quatre-Ministraux convoked a group of young people for singing a song at night which included the words "aux armes citoyens." The young people were exhorted to keep quiet and not to do anything that could disturb public order; AVN, QMN9:29.

tween changes in economics and in the institution of marriage would be irrefutable. As previously mentioned, however, the *procès verbaux* only rarely tell us the occupations of the parties.

Sundry other sources have been of little help in identifying the occupations of people who appeared before the tribunals. Documents from censuses taken in the eighteenth century, for example, failed to provide the desired information. Beginning in 1750, authorities in Neuchâtel began taking annual censuses, distributing forms to be completed in all communities. Local officials filled out the forms, indicating the number of people employed in various professions listed in alphabetical order (*apothicaires, architectes, armuriers,* . . .). These officials completed other forms listing the names of the male heads of households and the number of people under their superivision—for example, the number of men and women, big boys and girls, and little boys and girls! There is, however, nothing that ties these different data sets together. We know the total numbers of people employed in different occupations, but we cannot determine which individuals worked in these domains.[30]

One would have hoped that the archival documentation on the deaths and marriages of individual Neuchâtelois might provide information on the professions of the parties to matrimonial disputes. An extensive system of cards lists pertinent information on the birth, marriage, and death dates for people who lived in the principality. Though it was common to note titles (e.g., bourgeois of Neuchâtel, *justicier* of Le Locle), it is very rare to find information about a person's line of work. In fact, such information is no more common than in the records of the matrimonial courts. Simply put, it is not possible to study systematically whether a significant proportion of litigants were involved in wage labor—the information simply does not exist.

Even though we do not have unequivocal proof of the effects of wage labor on marriage, the balance of evidence militates against a monocausal explanation for changes in matrimonial disputes. The unavoidable impression is that economic as well as ideological developments were significant. More specifically, we can say that the evidence from

30. Among the sources from the Série de Recensements I consulted in Neuchâtel's Archives de l'Etat, only one document, dossier 30, provides significant information on the occupations of individual male household heads. No information was given for women's work, not even for widows who were household heads. Even this document provides evidence that is at best fragmentary. Dossier 30 provides information concerning professions of many, not all, household heads for only nineteen of the fifty communities that filled out the forms. Even then, the material in this dossier dates from 1750, before the most important socioeconomic changes took place. See also Miéville-Sorgesa, "Premier recensement," pp. 195–208, and Cop, "Recensement de la population," pp. 128–137.

Neuchâtel suggests that the evolution of the *control* of marriage resulted primarily from ideological changes, as seen in the new decisions of judicial authorities. At the same time, transformations in the institution of marriage itself most likely were linked more to economic developments and most pronounced among members of the working classes. Far from being mutually exclusive, ideological and economic changes complemented and reinforced each other. Indeed, Schlup holds that interest in the Enlightenment was directly tied to economic developments; as Neuchâtel extended its commercial ties to neighboring countries to export watches, printed cloth, and lace, it came into contact with new intellectual trends, especially those coming from Paris.[31]

The fact that the institution of marriage evolved during these two hundred fifty years in the principality of Neuchâtel does not mean that all of early modern Europe felt similar social change. Nevertheless, the marriage laws passed in Neuchâtel during the Reformation were quite similar to those of most other Protestant states; Neuchâtel certainly was not the only principality in which Enlightenment thought might have found a receptive audience; and the development of wage labor and the social changes that accompanied it were not confined to the borders of this small county. It is therefore safe to assume that this evolution in marriage and its control was not unique to Neuchâtel. No doubt other countries underwent similar changes, perhaps earlier or later depending on the appearance of significant socioeconomic development and new ideas.

31. Schlup, "Sociétés de lecture (1750–1800)," pp. 83–84.

Bibliography

ARCHIVAL SOURCES

La Chaux-de-Fonds, Switzerland. Bibliothèque de la Ville.
Journal d'Abram-Louis Sandoz.

Geneva, Switzerland. Archives d'Etat de Genève.
Consistoire de Genève, 1542–1564, vols. 1–21.
Registres du Conseil, vol. 36, 1542.

Neuchâtel, Switzerland. Archives de l'Etat de Neuchâtel.
Actes de la Classe, 1560–1615, 1673–1695, vols. 2, 7.
Audiences générales du Tribunal des Trois-Etats, 1549–1806, vols. 3–16.
Consistoire seigneurial de Gorgier, 1639–1693.
Consistoire seigneurial de Travers, 1719–1841; Liasses, 1729, 1763–1798, 1802–1845.
Consistoire seigneurial de Valangin, 1547–1806, vols. 1–9.
Justice matrimoniale de Neuchâtel, 1551–1621, 1704–1806, vols. 1–8; *Annexes:* JMN403–428.
Justice matrimoniale de Valangin, 1700–1806, vols. 1–7.
Manuels du Conseil d'Etat, vols. 5, 7, 24, 29, 35, 42, 66, 68, 69, 71, 75–77, 86, 94, 108, 127, 129, 137, 154.
Notaires: David fils d'Huguenin Robert, Registre 6; Jean Roulet, 1662–1697.
Registres des causes de paternité de la jurisdiction de Travers, 1785–1829.

279

Série de recensements, dossiers 5, 25, 30.
Tableau général des causes de matrimoniale du Comté de Valangin en Suisse, 1547–1830.
Tables des Manuels du Conseil d'Etat, 1547–1806.

Neuchâtel, Switzerland. Archives de la Ville de Neuchâtel.

Quatre-Ministraux de Neuchâtel, 1715–1806.

Neuchâtel, Switzerland. Bibliothèque Universitaire et Publique de Neuchâtel.

Jaques-François Boyve, *Coutumier de Neuchâtel,* 3 vols. Ms A519.
Société typographique de Neuchâtel, Ms 1220, No. 339.

PRINTED SOURCES

Almanach officiel. Neuchâtel: Sinnet & Compagnie, 1773.
Almanach officiel. Neuchâtel: Fauche, Père & Fils, Libraires du Roi, 1783.
Almanach officiel. Neuchâtel: Samuel Fauche, Père & Fils, Imprimeurs & Libraires du Roi, 1788.
"Au Val-de-Ruz: Journal d'Abram Mauley. XVIIIe siècle." Edited by Auguste Bachelin. *Musée neuchâtelois,* 1887, 91–102, 119–125.
Barrelet, Jean-Marc, ed. "La situation économique dans les Montagnes neuchâteloises vers 1836: Un document inédit d'Henri Houriet, du Locle." *Musée neuchâtelois,* 1987, 237–248.
Boyve, Jérôme-Emmanuel. *Recherches sur l'indigénat helvétique de la principauté de Neuchâtel et Valangin.* Neuchâtel, 1778.
Boyve, Jonas. *Annales historiques du comté de Neuchâtel et Valangin depuis Jules-César jusqu'en 1722.* 5 vols. Bern: Société littéraire (F.-L. Davoine), 1854–1858.
Chambrier, Samuel de. *Description topographique de la mairie de Valangin.* Neuchâtel, 1795.
"Une chanson de noce à Neuchâtel au XVIe siècle." *Musée neuchâtelois,* 1909, 243–246.
"Contrat de mariage de Louis-Henri de Bourbon avec Angélique-Cunégonde de Montmorency, 1694–1695." Edited by A. Bachelin. *Musée neuchâtelois,* 1881, 237–239.
"Deux inscriptions du registre des mariages de l'église de Champion." Edited by A. Baehler. *Musée neuchâtelois,* 1920, 109–110.
La discipline des églises de la souveraineté de Neuchâtel et Valangin (1712). Edited by François Clerc. Neuchâtel: Université de Neuchâtel, 1959.
Favarger, Dominique, and Maurice de Tribolet, eds. *Les sources du droit du canton de Neuchâtel.* Les sources du droit suisse, no. 21. Aarau, Switzerland: Verlag Sauerländer, 1982.

"Institutions générales du roi au Conseil d'Etat, 1709." Edited by Jules Jeanjaquet. *Musée neuchâtelois*, 1915, 37–44.

"Inventaire du trousseau de mon épouse H.S., et que j'ai reçu le 30 novembre 1781." *Musée neuchâtelois*, 1881, 288–289.

Ioannis Calvini Opera Quae Supersunt Omnia. Edited by Guilielmus Baum, Eduardus Cunitz, and Eduardus Reuss. Brunswick and Berlin: C. A. Schwetschke and Sons, 1834–1968.

Matile, Georges-Auguste, ed. *Travaux législatifs des plaits de mai, états et audiences.* Neuchâtel: Petitpierre, 1837.

"Mémoyres de plussieurs choses remarquées par moi Abraham Chailliet, dempuits l'an 1614." *Musée neuchâtelois*, 1881, 218–220.

Ostervald, Samuel. *Les loix, us et coutumes de la souveraineté de Neuchâtel et Valangin.* Neuchâtel: Fauche, 1785.

"Prières et 'secrets'." Edited by Arthur Piaget. *Musée neuchâtelois*, 1897, 53–58; 1898, 66–68.

"Reglements d'une société de garçons [vers 1775]." Edited by Albert Henry. *Musée neuchâtelois*, 1882, 54–56.

"Relation de voyage d'un Prussien dans le pays de Neuchâtel en 1802." Edited by Victor Humbert. *Musée neuchâtelois*, 1880, 34–42.

"Relation du ministère de... Messire Jaques de Stavay..., gouverneur de Neuchâtel [1647–MDCLXXIX]." *Musée neuchâtelois*, 1865, 306–312.

"Remise d'un 'condamné' de hérésie par le seigneur de Travers aux officiers du Vautravers [1491]." *Musée neuchâtelois*, 1880, 195–197.

"Un repas de noces à Neuchâtel en 1607." Edited by Ernest de Montmollin. *Musée neuchâtelois*, 1925, 37–46.

"Requète d'un Covasson pour autorisation de mariage: XVIIe siècle." Edited by J. Jeanjaquet. *Musée neuchâtelois*, 1914, 47–48.

Rivoire, Emile, and Victor van Berchem, eds. *Les sources du droit du Canton de Genève.* Les sources du droit suisse, no. 22. Aarau, Switzerland: Sauerländer, 1933.

SECONDARY LITERATURE

Ariès, Philippe. *Centuries of Childhood: A Social History of Family Life.* Translated by Robert Baldick. London: Jonathan Cape, 1962.

Ariès, Philippe, and André Béjin, eds. *Western Sexuality: Practice and Precept in Past and Present Times.* Translated by Anthony Forster. Oxford: Basil Blackwell, 1985.

Armengaud, André. *La famille et l'enfant en France et en Angleterre du XVIe au XVIIIe siècle: Aspects démographiques.* Paris: Société d'édition d'enseignement supérieur, 1975.

Bachelin, Auguste. "La dentelle: Notice historique." *Musée neuchâtelois*, 1868, 177–181, 213–218.

———. *L'horlogerie neuchâteloise.* Neuchâtel: Attinger, 1888.

Bartel, Pierre. "La 'Religion de Neuchâtel' au petit matin du XVIIIe siècle, un phénomène unique en Europe." *Musée neuchâtelois*, 1987, 41–80.

——, Rémy Scheurer, and Richard Stauffer, eds. *Actes du Colloque Guillaume Farel.* Geneva: Cahiers de la Revue de Théologie et de Philosophie, 1983.

Béguin, Thierry. "L'influence de la Réforme sur le mariage en pays de Neuchâtel: Travail de droit entre les règles canoniques à l'époque du Concile de Trente et les dispositions du droit protestant neuchâtelois d'après les ordonnances de 1550." Mémoire, Université de Neuchâtel, 1973.

Bels, Pierre. *Le mariage des protestants français jusqu'en 1685. Fondements doctrinaux et pratiques juridiques.* Preface by Paul Ourliac. Paris: Librairie générale de droit et de jurisprudence, 1968.

Bennett, Judith M. *Women in the Medieval English Countryside: Gender and Household in Brigstock before the Plague.* Oxford: Oxford University Press, 1987.

Bergier, Jean-François. *Histoire économique de la Suisse.* Lausanne: Payot, 1983.

——. *Naissance et croissance de la Suisse industrielle.* Monographies d'Histoire Suisse, vol. 8. Bern: Francke Editions, 1974.

——. *Problèmes de l'histoire économique de la Suisse.* Monographies d'Histoire Suisse, vol. 2. Bern: Francke Editions, 1968.

Berthoud, Dorette. *Les indiennes neuchâteloises.* Boudry, Switzerland: Editions de la Baconnière, 1951.

Berthoud, Gabrielle. *Antoine Marcourt: Réformateur et pamphlétaire du "Livre des marchans" aux placards de 1534.* Geneva: Droz, 1973.

——. "La classe de Neuchâtel et les refugiés pour cause de religion à la fin du XVIIe siècle." *Musée neuchâtelois,* 1985, 195–212.

——. "Le consistoire seigneurial de Valangin à la fin du XVIe siècle." Paper presented at the Société pour l'histoire du droit et des institutions des anciens pays bourguignons, comtois et romands, Geneva, 1977.

——. "Iconoclasme à Neuchâtel." In *Nos monuments d'art et d'histoire,* Bulletin destiné aux membres de la *Société de l'histoire de l'art en Suisse,* Année 35 (1984): 331–338.

——. "Jean Crespin et les papetiers de Serrières." *Musée neuchâtelois,* 1974, 92–94.

——. "Les lettres d'Anne-Esabeau Tribolet à ses fils, 1715–1733." *Musée neuchâtelois,* 1976, 109–127.

——. "Neuchâteloises du siècle de Voltaire et de Rousseau." *Musée neuchâtelois,* 1959, 97–114.

——. "Notes sur l'école de Neuchâtel à l'époque de la Réforme." *Musée neuchâtelois,* 1964, 162–167.

——. "Valanginois au service étranger au XVIe siècle." *Musée neuchâtelois,* 1978, 121–130.

Biéler, André. *L'homme et la femme dans la morale calviniste: La doctrine réformée sur l'amour, le mariage, le célibat, le divorce, l'adultère et la prostitution, considerée dans son cadre historique.* Preface by Madeleine Barot. Geneva: Labor et Fides, 1963.

Bolle, Pierre-Henri. "Histoire des pénitenciers neuchâtelois." *Musée neuchâtelois,* 1973, 3–20.

Boswell, John. *Christianity, Social Tolerance, and Homosexuality: Gay People in Western Europe from the Beginning of the Christian Era to the Fourteenth Century.* Chicago: University of Chicago Press, 1980.

Boucé, Paul-Gabriel, ed. *Sexuality in Eighteenth-Century Britain*. Manchester: Manchester University Press, 1982.

Bouchard, Gérard. *Le village immobile: Sennelly-en-Sologne au XVIIIe siècle*. Paris: Plon, 1972.

Bourdieu, Pierre. "Les stratégies matrimoniales dans le système de réproduction." *Annales: E.S.C.* 27 (1972): 1105–1127.

Braun, Rudolf. *Industrialisation and Everyday Life*. Translated by Sarah Hanbury Tenison. Cambridge and Paris: Cambridge University Press and Editions de la Maison des Sciences de L'Homme, 1990.

Bridenthal, Renate, and Claudia Koonz, eds. *Becoming Visible: Women in European History*. Boston: Houghton Mifflin, 1977.

Britton, Edward. *The Community of the Vill: A Study in the History of the Family and Village Life in Fourteenth-Century England*. Toronto: Macmillan, 1977.

Brooke, Christopher N. L. *The Medieval Idea of Marriage*. Oxford: Oxford University Press, 1989.

Brundage, James A. *Law, Sex, and Christian Society in Medieval Europe*. Chicago: University of Chicago Press, 1987.

Bullough, Vern L., and James Brundage, eds. *Sexual Practices and the Medieval Church*. Buffalo: Prometheus Books, 1982.

Burger, Jean-Daniel. "La discipline dans l'Eglise réformée neuchâteloise." *Musée neuchâtelois*, 1967, 34–43.

Burgière, André. "Le ritual du mariage en France: Pratiques ecclésiastiques et pratiques populaires (XVIe–XVIIIe siècle)." *Annales: E.S.C.* 33 (1978): 637–649.

Calame, Henri-Florian. *Droit privé d'après la coutume neuchâteloise*. Neuchâtel: Attinger, 1858.

Cannata, Carlo Augusto. *La jurisprudence romaine*. Histoire de la jurisprudence européenne, no. 1. Turin: G. Giappichelli, 1989.

Carlen, Louis. *Rechtsgeschichte der Schweiz*. Monographen zur schweizer Geschichte, vol. 4. Bern: Francke Editions, 1968.

Caspard, Pierre. "L'accumulation du capital dans l'indiennage au XVIIIème siècle." *Revue du Nord* 61 (1979): 115–124.

——. "L'amour et la guerre: Lettres d'un soldat neuchâtelois à sa fiancée pendant la guerre de Sept Ans." *Musée neuchâtelois*, 1979, 72–91.

——. "Une communauté rurale à l'épreuve de l'industrialisation: Cortaillod de 1750 à 1850." *Bulletin du Centre d'histoire économique et sociale de la Région lyonnaise* 4 (1976): 1–35.

——. "Conceptions prénuptiales et développement du capitalisme dans la principauté de Neuchâtel (1678–1820)." *Annales: E.S.C.* 4 (1974): 989–1008.

——. *La Fabrique-Neuve de Cortaillod: Entreprise et profit pendant la Révolution industrielle, 1752–1854*. Paris: Publications de la Sorbonne, 1979.

——. "Les ouvriers en indiennes au XVIIIe siècle." *Musée neuchâtelois*, 1974, 157–168.

Chambrier, Frédéric de. *Histoire de Neuchâtel et Valangin jusqu'à l'avènement de la Maison de Prusse*. Preface by Guy de Chambrier. Neuchâtel, 1840; rpt. ed., Geneva: Editions Slatkine, 1984.

Chapuis, Alfred. *Histoire de la pendulerie neuchâteloise*. Preface by Paul Robert. Paris and Neuchâtel, 1917; rpt. ed., Geneva: Editions Slatkine, 1983.

Châtelain, Charles. "Les anabaptistes au Val-de-Ruz au XVIIIe siècle." *Musée neuchâtelois*, 1883, 147–155, 180–189.

——. "Les anciennes sociétés de garçons." *Musée neuchâtelois*, 1890, 208–215.

——. "Fiançailles rompues." *Musée neuchâtelois*, 1890, 120–121.

Chaunu, Pierre. *La civilisation de l'Europe classique*. Paris: Arthaud, 1966.

Chrisman, Miriam. "Family and Religion in Two Noble Families: French Catholic and English Puritan." *Journal of Family History* 8 (1983): 190–210.

——. "Women and the Reformation in Strasbourg, 1490–1530." *Archiv für Reformationsgeschichte* 63 (1972): 143–167.

Claverie, Elisabeth, and Pierre Lamaison. *L'impossible mariage: Violence et parenté en Gévaudan 17e, 18e et 19e siècles*. Paris: Hachette, 1982.

Clerc, François. "Survivance et transformation des instititutions canoniques après la Réforme dans le pays de Neuchâtel." *Mémoires de la Société pour l'histoire du droit et des institutions des anciens pays bourguignons, comtois et romands* 24 (1963): 307–317.

Clottu, Olivier. "La fabrique d'indiennes du port de Cressier." *Musée neuchâtelois*, 1975, 127–141.

Collomp, Allain. "Alliances et filiation en haute Provence au XVIIIe siècle." *Annales: E.S.C.* 32 (1977): 445–477.

Comité Farel. *Guillaume Farel, 1489–1565*. Neuchâtel: Editions Delachaux & Niestlé, 1930.

"Un contrat de mariage du XVIe siècle." *Musée neuchâtelois*, 1880, 292–293.

Conze, Werner, ed. *Sozialgeschichte der Familie in der Neuzeit Europas*. Stuttgart: Ernst Klett Verlag, 1976.

Cop, Raoul. "Un recensement de la population et des familles des Montagnes en 1712." *Musée neuchâtelois*, 1986, 128–137.

Cornu, James. "Chézard et Saint Martin: Essai historique." *Musée neuchâtelois*, 1879, 22–27, 43–50, 72–74, 84–88, 114–121, 137–143.

Courvoisier, Jean. "La Clusette: Contribution à l'histoire d'un tronçon de route." *Musée neuchâtelois*, 1970, 97–124, 156–171.

——. "Une fonction disparue, celle de garde-vices." *Musée neuchâtelois*, 1965, 44–47.

——. *Le maréchal Berthier et sa principauté de Neuchâtel (1806–1814)*. Neuchâtel: Attinger, 1959.

——. "Mariages et menaces de charivaris en 1807 et en 1838." *Musée neuchâtelois*, 1986, 138–142.

——. "Moeurs et problèmes ecclésiastiques dans le pays de Neuchâtel, en 1564–1565." *Musée neuchâtelois*, 1980, 80–89.

——. *Les monuments d'art et d'histoire du canton de Neuchâtel*. 3 vols. Basel: Editions Birkhäuser, 1955, 1963, 1968.

——. "Notes sur l'histoire de l'etat civil dans le pays de Neuchâtel." *Musée neuchâtelois*, 1983, 49–67.

——. *Panorama de l'histoire neuchâteloise*, new ed. Neuchâtel: Editions de la Baconnière, 1972.

———. "Premières apparitions des toiles peintes en pays neuchâtelois." *Musée neuchâtelois*, 1976, 143–144.

———. "Violences juvéniles en 1768–1769." *Musée neuchâtelois*, 1978, 131–134.

Darmon, Pierre. *Le tribunal de l'impuissance: Virilité et défaillances conjugales dans l'ancienne France*. Paris: Editions du Seuil, 1979.

Darnton, Robert. *The Business of the Enlightenment: A Publishing History of the "Encyclopédie," 1775–1800*. Cambridge, Mass.: Harvard University Press, 1979.

———. *The Great Cat Massacre and Other Episodes in French Cultural History*. New York: Basic Books, 1984.

———. *The Literary Underground of the Old Regime*. Cambridge, Mass.: Harvard University Press, 1982.

Darrow, Margaret. "Popular Concepts of Marital Choice in Eighteenth Century France." *Journal of Social History* 19 (1985): 261–272.

Davis, Natalie Zemon. *The Return of Martin Guerre*. Cambridge, Mass.: Harvard University Press, 1983.

———. *Society and Culture in Early Modern France*. Stanford, Calif.: Stanford University Press, 1975.

Demos, John. *A Little Commonwealth: Family Life in Plymouth Colony*. New York: Oxford University Press, 1970.

Diefendorf, Barbara. *Paris City Councillors in the Sixteenth Century: The Politics of Patrimony*. Princeton, N.J.: Princeton University Press, 1983.

Duby, Georges. *The Knight, the Lady, and the Priest: The Making of Modern Marriage in Medieval France*. Translated by Barbara Bray. Introduction by Natalie Zemon Davis. New York: Pantheon, 1983.

———. *Medieval Marriage: Two Models from Twelfth-Century France*. Translated by Elborg Forster. Baltimore: Johns Hopkins University Press, 1978.

———. *Que sait-on de l'amour en France au XIIe siècle?* Oxford: Clarendon Press, 1983.

———, and Jacques Le Goff, eds. *Famille et parenté dans l'occident médiéval*. Rome: Ecole française de Rome, 1977.

Dufour, Alfred. *Le mariage dans l'école romande du droit naturel au XVIIIe siècle*. Preface by L. Chevailler. Geneva: Librairie de l'Université, 1976.

DuPâquier, Jacques. *La population française aux XVIIe et XVIIIe siècles*. Paris: Presses universitaires de France, 1979.

DuPasquier, A. "Du rôle de la partie civile dans le droit pénal neuchâtelois." Neuchâtel, 1866.

DuPasquier, Armand. "Les prétensions de la maison de Mailly-Nesle sur Neuchâtel au XVIIIe siècle." *Musée neuchâtelois*, 1921, 10–20, 62–70, 89–99, 124–136, 190–206.

Duss-von Werdt, Josef, and Armin Fuchs. *Scheidung in der Schweiz: Eine wissenschaftliche Dokumentation*. Stuttgart: Verlag Paul Haupt, 1980.

Egloff, Michel, Dominique Quadroni, Rémy Scheurer, Maurice de Tribolet, and Alain Zosso. *Histoire du Pays de Neuchâtel: De la préhistoire au Moyen Age*. Hauterive, Switzerland: Gilles Attinger, 1989.

Esmein, A. *Le mariage en droit canonique*, 2d ed. 2 vols. Paris: Librairie du Recueil Sirey, 1929, 1935.

Faessler, François. "Quelques aspects de la vie artisanale au Locle aux XVIIe et XVIIIe siècles." *Musée neuchâtelois*, 1964, 179–188.

Fairchilds, Cissie. *Domestic Enemies: Servants and Their Masters in Old Regime France*. Baltimore: Johns Hopkins University Press, 1984.

——. "Female Sexual Attitudes and the Rise of Illegitimacy: A Case Study." *Journal of Interdisciplinary History* 8 (1978): 163–203.

Fallet, Marius. *Folkore [du pays de Neuchâtel]*. Neuchâtel: Centenaire de la République, 1948.

Favarger, Dominique. "A propos du coutumier Hory de 1618." *Musée neuchâtelois*, 1970, 69–72.

——. "Coutumes et coutumiers neuchâtelois à la fin de l'Ancien Régime." *Musée neuchâtelois*, 1967, 60–78.

——. "L'élaboration des lois à Neuchâtel aux XVIIe et XVIIIe siècles." *Musée neuchâtelois*, 1972, 186–212.

——. *Le régime matrimoniale dans le comté de Neuchâtel du XVe au XIXe siècle*. Neuchâtel: Editions Ides et Calendes, 1970.

Favarger, Pierre. "Une émigration de piétistes zurichois dans le pays de Neuchâtel au XVIIIe siècle." *Musée neuchâtelois*, 1909, 193–217; 1910, 25–47.

Favre, Louis. "Notre patois." *Musée neuchâtelois*, 1893, 7–13, 29–35.

——. "Rochefort." *Musée neuchâtelois*, 1879, 177–196.

Favre, Maurice. "Dix-sept journées avec Josué Delachaux de 1750 à 1753." *Musée neuchâtelois*, 1976, 128–134.

——. "Les droits individuels sous le règne de Frédéric II, vus par un bourgeois de Valangin." *Musée neuchâtelois*, 1981, 26–35.

Febvre, Lucien and Henri-Jean Martin. *L'apparition du livre*. Paris: Editions Albin Michel, 1958.

Fichtner, Paula Sutter. *Protestantism and Primogeniture in Early Modern Germany*. New Haven, Conn.: Yale University Press, 1989.

Flandrin, Jean-Louis. *Les amours paysannes: Amour et sexualité dans les campagnes de l'ancienne France (XVIe–XIXe)*. Paris: Gallimard, 1975.

——. *Families in Former Times: Kinship, Household, and Sexuality*. Translated by Richard Southern. Cambridge: Cambridge University Press, 1979.

——. *Le sexe et l'Occident: Evolution des attitudes et des comportements*. Paris: Editions du Seuil, 1981.

——. *Un temps pour embrasser: Aux origines de la morale sexuelle occidentale (VIe–XIe siècle)*. Paris: Editions du Seuil, 1983.

Forster, Robert, and Orest Ranum, eds. *Family and Society: Selections from the "Annales: Economies, Sociétés, Civilisations."* Translated by Elborg Forster and Patricia M. Ranum. Baltimore: Johns Hopkins University Press, 1976.

Foucault, Michel. *The History of Sexuality*, vol. 1: *An Introduction*. Translated by Robert Hurley. New York: Pantheon Books, 1978.

Fox, Vivian C., and Martin H. Quitt. *Loving, Parenting, and Dying: The Family Cycle in England and America, Past and Present*. New York: Psychohistory Press, 1980.

Gallone, Paolo. *Organisation judiciaire et procédure devant les cours laïques du Pays de Vaud à l'époque savoyarde (XIIIe–XVIe siècle)*. Lausanne: Bibliothèque historique vaudoise, 1972.

Ganghoffer, Roland. "Les régimes matrimoniaux du centre de l'Alsace aux XVIIe et XVIIIe siècle." In *Droit privé et institutions régionales: Etudes historiques offertes à Jean Yver,* pp. 267–283. Paris: Presses universitaires de France, 1976.

Garden, Maurice. *Lyon et les Lyonnais au XVIIIe siècle.* Paris: Les Belles-Lettres, 1970.

Gélis, Jacques. *L'arbre et le fruit: La naissance dans l'Occident moderne XVIe–XIXe siècle.* Paris: Fayard, 1984.

Gennep, Arnold Van. *The Rites of Passage.* Translated by Monika B. Vizedom and Gabrielle L. Caffee. Introduction by Solon T. Kimball. Chicago: University of Chicago Press, 1960.

Gern, Philippe. "L'approvisionnement de Neuchâtel pendant la Révolution française." *Musée neuchâtelois,* 1976, 57–86.

——. "Essai sur l'indigénat helvétique de la principauté de Neuchâtel, XVIIIe siècle." *Musée neuchâtelois,* 1966, 153–165.

Giacomini, Mariuccia. *Sposi a Belmonte nel settecento: Famiglia e matrimonio in un borgo rurale calabrese.* Milan: A. Giuffré, 1981.

Gies, Frances, and Joseph Gies. *Marriage and the Family in the Middle Ages.* New York: Harper and Row, 1987.

——, and Joseph Gies. *Women in the Middle Ages: The Lives of Real Women in a Vibrant Age of Transition.* New York: Harper and Row, 1978.

Gilliéron, Charles. "L'évolution de la preuve pénale." *Revue pénale suisse* 60 (1946): 197–208.

Gillis, John R. *For Better, for Worse: British Marriages, 1600 to the Present.* Oxford: Oxford University Press, 1985.

Godet, Philippe. "Foires, marchés et fêtes au Val-de-Travers." *Musée neuchâtelois,* 1888, 42–48.

——. "Les mariages." *Musée neuchâtelois,* 1881, 258–259.

Goldthwaite, Richard A. *Private Wealth in Renaissance Florence: A Study of Four Families.* Princeton, N.J.: Princeton University Press, 1968.

Goode, William J. *World Revolution and Family Patterns.* New York: Free Press of Glencoe, 1963.

Goody, Jack. *The Development of the Family and Marriage in Europe.* Cambridge: Cambridge University Press, 1983.

——. *Production and Reproduction: A Comparative Study of the Domestic Domain.* Cambridge Studies in Social and Cultural Anthropology, no. 17. Cambridge: Cambridge University Press, 1976.

——, and S. J. Tambiah. *Bridewealth and Dowry.* Cambridge Papers in Social Anthropology, no. 7. Cambridge: Cambridge University Press, 1973.

——, Joan Thirsk, and E. P. Thompson, eds. *Family and Inheritance: Rural Society in Western Europe, 1200–1800.* Cambridge: Cambridge University Press, 1976.

Goubert, Pierre. *Beauvais et le Beauvaisis de 1600 à 1730.* Paris: Service d'Edition et de Vente des Publications de l'Education, 1960.

Gouesse, Jean-Marie. "Parents, famille et mariage en Normandie au XVIIe et XVIIIe siècles." *Annales: E.S.C.* 27 (1972): 1139–1154.

Guillaume, Pierre, and Jean-Pierre Poussou. *Démographie historique.* Foreword by Georges Dupeux. Paris: Armand Colin, 1970.

Gullickson, Gay L. *Spinners and Weavers of Auffay: Rural Industry and the Sexual Division of Labor in a French Village, 1750–1850.* Cambridge: Cambridge University Press, 1986.

Gutton, Jean-Pierre. *La société et les pauvres en Europe (XVIe–XVIIIe siècle).* Vendôme, France: Presses universitaires de France, 1974.

Guyot, Charly. *La vie intellectuelle et religieuse en Suisse française à la fin du XVIIIe siècle: Henri-David de Chaillet, 1751–1823.* Neuchâtel: Baconnière, 1946.

Hajnal, John. "European Marriage Patterns in Perspective." In *Population in History: Essays in Historical Demography,* edited by D. V. Glass and D. E. C. Eversley, pp. 101–143. London: Edward Arnold, 1965.

Hanawalt, Barbara A. *The Ties That Bound: Peasant Families in Medieval England.* Oxford: Oxford University Press, 1986.

——, ed. *Women and Work in Preindustrial Europe.* Bloomington: Indiana University Press, 1986.

Hartcup, Adeline. *Love and Marriage in the Great Country Houses.* London: Sidgwick & Jackson, 1984.

Heers, Jacques. *Le clan familial au Moyen Age: Etude sur les structures politiques et sociales des milieux urbains.* Paris: Presses universitaires de France, 1974.

Helmholz, R. H. *Marriage Litigation in Medieval England.* Cambridge: Cambridge University Press, 1974.

Henry, Philippe. *Crime, justice et société dans la principauté de Neuchâtel au XVIIIe siècle (1707–1806).* Neuchâtel: Baconnière, 1984.

Herlihy, David. "Land, Family, and Women in Continental Europe, 701–1200." *Traditio* 18 (1962): 89–120.

——. "The Making of the Medieval Family: Symmetry, Structure, and Sentiment." *Journal of Family History* 8 (1983): 116–130.

——. *Medieval Households.* Cambridge, Mass.: Harvard University Press, 1985.

——, and Christiane Klapisch-Zuber. *The Tuscans and Their Families: A Study of the Florentine Catasto of 1427.* New Haven, Conn.: Yale University Press, 1985.

Houlbrooke, Ralph. *Church Courts and the People during the English Reformation, 1520–1570.* Oxford: Oxford University Press, 1979.

——. *The English Family, 1450–1700.* New York: Longman, 1984.

——. "The Making of Marriage in Mid-Tudor England: Evidence from the Records of Matrimonial Contract Litigation." *Journal of Family History* 10 (1985): 339–352.

Howell, Martha C. *Women, Production, and Patriarchy in Late Medieval Cities.* Chicago: University of Chicago Press, 1986.

Huguenin, Jeanne. "Une vie mouvementée, Abraham Amiet (1661–1734)." *Musée neuchâtelois,* 1923, 5–20.

Huizinga, Johan. *The Waning of the Middle Ages: A Study of the Forms of Life, Thought, and Art in France and the Netherlands in the XIVth and XVth Centuries.* New York: Doubleday, 1954.

Ingram, Martin. *Church Courts, Sex, and Marriage in England, 1570–1640.* Cambridge: Cambridge University Press, 1987.

"Inscription de mariage." *Musée neuchâtelois,* 1869, 314.

Jeanneret, Frédéric-Alexandre-Marie. *Les sorciers dans le pays de Neuchâtel au XVe, XVIe et XVIIe siècle.* Le Locle, Switzerland: Courvoisier, 1862.

Jelmini, Jean-Pierre. "La vie publique dans les communautés rurales de Neuchâtel au XVIIIe siècle, établie d'après les documents de Dombresson et de Travers." *Musée neuchâtelois,* 1972, 135–174.

Jequier, François. "Bilan des recherches de Pierre Caspard sur la Fabrique-Neuve de Cortaillod et les conséquences sociales de l'industrialisation neuchâteloise." *Revue suisse d'histoire* 30 (1980): 84–95.

Junod, Daniel. "Boudevilliers." *Musée neuchâtelois,* 1896, 269–278; 1897, 29–34, 69–76, 133–137, 157–162, 183–186.

Kent, Francis William. *Household and Lineage in Renaissance Florence: The Family Life of the Capponi, Ginori, and Rucellai.* Princeton, N.J.: Princeton University Press, 1977.

Kingdon, Robert M. "The Control of Morals in Calvin's Geneva." In *The Social History of the Reformation,* edited by Lawrence P. Buck and Jonathon W. Zophy, pp. 3–16. Columbus: Ohio State University Press, 1972.

Klapisch-Zuber, Christiane. *Women, Family, and Ritual in Renaissance Italy.* Translated by Lydia G. Cochrane. Foreword by David Herlihy. Chicago: University of Chicago Press, 1985.

Köhler, Walther. *Zürcher Ehegericht und Genfer Konsistorium.* 2 vols. Leipzig: M. Heinsius Nachfolger, 1932–1942.

Kriedte, Peter. *Peasants, Landlords, and Merchant Capitalists: Europe and the World Economy, 1500–1800.* Translated by V. R. Berghahn. Cambridge: Cambridge University Press, 1983.

——, Hans Medick, and Jürgen Schlumbohm. *Industrialization before Industrialization: Rural Industry in the Genesis of Capitalism.* Translated by Beate Schempp. Contributions from Herbert Kisch and Franklin F. Mendels. Cambridge: Cambridge University Press, 1981.

Krieg, Ernst. "Emigrés neuchâtelois en Prusse orientale." *Musée neuchâtelois,* 1934, 173–175.

Labarge, Margaret Wade. *A Small Sound of the Trumpet: Women in Medieval Life.* Boston: Beacon Press, 1986.

Lardy, Charles. *Les procédures de sorcellerie à Neuchâtel.* Neuchâtel: Sandoz, 1866.

Laslett, Peter. *Family Life and Illicit Love in Earlier Generations.* Cambridge: Cambridge University Press, 1977.

——. *The World We Have Lost: England before the Industrial Age,* 2d ed. New York: Charles Scribner's Sons, 1971.

——, and Karla Oosterveen. "Long-Term Trends in Bastardy in England, 1561–1960." *Population Studies* 27 (1973): 255–286.

——, Karla Oosterveen, and Richard M. Smith, eds. *Bastardy and Its Comparative History.* Cambridge, Mass.: Harvard University Press, 1980.

——, and Richard Wall, eds. *Household and Family in Past Time.* Cambridge: Cambridge University Press, 1972.

Lebrun, François. *Les hommes et la mort en Anjou aux XVIIe et XVIIIe siècles: Essai de démographie et de psychologie historiques.* The Hague: Mouton, 1971.

Le Play, Frédéric. *L'organisation de la famille.* Tours: Mame, 1871.

Le Roy Ladurie, Emmanuel. *Love, Death, and Money in the Pays d'Oc.* Translated by Alan Sheridan. New York: George Braziller, 1982.

———. *Montaillou: The Promised Land of Error.* Translated by Barbara Bray. New York: George Braziller, 1978.

Levine, David. *Family Formation in an Age of Nascent Capitalism.* New York: Academic Press, 1977.

———. *Proletarianization and Family History.* Orlando, Fla.: Academic Press, 1984.

———. *Reproducing Families: The Political Economy of English Population History.* Cambridge: Cambridge University Press, 1987.

Loew, Fernand. "Les mariages au XVe siècle." *Musée neuchâtelois,* 1961, 36–59.

———. "La vie quotidienne à la Sagne d'après un livre de raison des XVIIe et XVIIIe siècles." *Musée neuchâtelois,* 1976, 97–108, 145–156.

———, and Marie-José Houlmann. "Le plaisant voyage de Johann Rudolf Schinz dans le pays de Neuchâtel." *Musée neuchâtelois,* 1978, 17–35.

Lottin, Alain, et al. *La désunion du couple sous l'ancien régime: L'exemple du Nord.* Paris: Editions universitaires, 1975.

Lynch, Katherine A. *Family, Class, and Ideology in Early Industrial France: Social Policy and the Working-Class Family, 1825–1848.* Madison: University of Wisconsin Press, 1988.

M. R. G. [not identified]. "Le pilori et la bannière des Brenets." *Musée neuchâtelois,* 1901, 140–142.

MacDonald, Michael. *Mystical Bedlam: Madness, Anxiety, and Healing in Seventeenth-Century England.* Cambridge: Cambridge University Press, 1981.

Macfarlane, Alan. *The Family Life of Ralph Josselin, a Seventeenth-Century Clergyman: An Essay in Historical Anthropology.* Cambridge: Cambridge University Press, 1970.

———. *Marriage and Love in England: Modes of Reproduction, 1300–1840.* Oxford: Basil Blackwell, 1986.

———. *The Origins of English Individualism: The Family, Property, and Social Transition.* Cambridge: Cambridge University Press, 1978.

———. Review of Lawrence Stone, *Family, Sex and Marriage in England, 1500–1800. History and Theory* 18 (1979): 103–126.

Maclean, Ian. *The Renaissance Notion of Woman.* Cambridge: Cambridge University Press, 1980.

Marshall, Sherrin, ed. *Women in Reformation and Counter-Reformation Europe: Private and Public Worlds.* Bloomington, Indiana University Press, 1989.

Matile, Georges-Auguste. *Histoire de la seigneurie de Valangin jusqu'à sa réunion à la directe en 1592.* Neuchâtel: Attinger, 1852.

———. *Histoire des institutions judiciaires et législatives de la principauté de Neuchâtel et Valangin.* Neuchâtel: Petitpierre, 1838.

Mauss, Marcel. *The Gift: Forms and Functions of Exchange in Archaic Societies.* Introduction by E. E. Evans. Translated by Ian Cunnison. Pritchard, N.Y.: W. W. Norton, 1967.

Maza, Sarah C. *Servants and Masters in Eighteenth-Century France: The Uses of Loyalty.* Princeton, N.J.: Princeton University Press, 1983.

Medick, Hans, and David Warren Sabean, eds. *Interest and Emotion: Essays on the Study of Family and Kinship.* Cambridge: Cambridge University Press, 1984.

Mendels, Franklin F. "Proto-Industrialization: The First Phase of Industrialization." *Journal of Economic History* 32 (1972): 241–261.

Menefee, Samuel Pyeatt. *Wives for Sale: An Ethnographic Study of British Popular Divorce.* New York: St. Martin's Press, 1981.

Mentzer, Raymond A., Jr. "Church Discipline and Communal Pressure and the French Protestants." Paper delivered at the Sixteenth Century Studies Conference, St. Louis, Mo., 29 October 1988.

——. "*Disciplina nervus ecclesiae:* The Calvinist Reform of Morals at Nîmes." *Sixteenth Century Journal* 18 (1987): 89–115.

Merryman, John Henry. *The Civil Law Tradition: An Introduction to the Legal Systems of Western Europe and Latin America.* Stanford, Calif.: Stanford University Press, 1969.

Merzario, Raul. *Il Paese Stretto: Strategie matrimoniali nella diocesi di Como secoli XVI–XVIII.* Turin: Einaudi, 1981.

Meylan, Henri. "Un agent secret de MM. de Berne: Le curé du Vautravers, Pierre Barrellet." *Musée neuchâtelois,* 1964, 168–178.

Miéville-Sorgesa, Beatrice. "Premier recensement de la population neuchâteloise (1750) ou 'Denombrement des peuples, des pauvres et autres'." *Musée neuchâtelois,* 1988, 195–208.

Mitchison, Rosalind, and Leah Leneman. *Sexuality and Social Control: Scotland, 1660–1780.* Oxford: Basil Blackwell, 1989.

Mitterauer, Michael, and Reinhard Sieder. *The European Family: Patriarchy to Partnership from the Middle Ages to the Present.* Translated by Karla Oosterveen and Manfred Hörzinger. Foreword by Peter Laslett. Chicago: University of Chicago Press, 1982.

Moch, Leslie Page, and Gary D. Stark, eds. *Essays on the Family and Historical Change.* College Station: Texas A & M University Press, 1983.

Montagu, M. F., ed. *Marriage: Past and Present. A Debate between Robert Briffault and Bronislaw Malinowski.* Boston: Porter Sargent Publisher, 1956.

Montandon, Léon. "Neuchâtelois en Prusse orientale." *Musée neuchâtelois,* 1931, 47–48.

——. "Les registres d'état civil aux archives de l'Etat de Neuchâtel." *Musée neuchâtelois,* 1938, 31–42.

——, Louis-Edouard Roulet, Alfred Schnegg, and François Faessler. *Neuchâtel et la Suisse.* Neuchâtel: Chancellerie d'Etat, 1969.

Monter, E. William. "The Consistory of Geneva, 1559–1569." *Bibliothèque d'humanisme et renaissance* 38 (1976): 467–484.

——. "La sodomie à l'époque moderne en Suisse romande." *Annales: E.S.C.* 29 (1974): 1023–1033.

——. "Women in Calvinist Geneva (1550–1800)." *Signs* 6 (1980): 189–209.

Montmollin, Cyrille de. "L'exercice du droit de grâce à Neuchâtel sous l'Ancien Régime, 1707–1848." *Musée neuchâtelois*, 1973, 140–153.

Morel, Lydie. "Le contre-coup de la Révolution française dans le canton de Neuchâtel." *Musée neuchâtelois*, 1921, 81–88, 137–145; 1922, 23–31, 68–79.

——. "Les sociétés patriotiques de 1793." *Musée neuchâtelois*, 1920, 11–28.

Morgan, Edmund S. *The Puritan Family: Religion and Domestic Relations in Seventeenth-Century New England*. New York: Harper & Row, 1966.

Mount, Ferdinand. *The Subversive Family: An Alternative History of Love and Marriage*. London: Jonathan Cape, 1982.

Nicholas, David. *The Domestic Life of a Medieval City: Women, Children, and the Family in Fourteenth-Century Ghent*. Lincoln: University of Nebraska Press, 1985.

Noonan, John T., Jr. *Contraception: A History of Its Treatment by the Catholic Theologians and Canonists*. Cambridge, Mass.: Harvard University Press, 1965.

——. *Power to Dissolve: Lawyers and Marriages in the Courts of the Roman Curia*. Cambridge, Mass.: Harvard University Press, 1972.

Otis, Leah L. *Prostitution in Medieval Society: The History of an Urban Institution in Languedoc*. Foreword by Catharine R. Stimpson. Chicago: University of Chicago Press, 1985.

Ourliac, Paul, and J. de Malafosse. *Histoire du droit privé*, vol. 3: *Le droit familial*. Paris: Presses universitaires de France, 1968.

Outhwaite, R. B., ed. *Marriage and Society: Studies in the Social History of Marriage*. New York: St. Martin's Press, 1981.

Ozment, Steven. *Magdalena and Balthasar: An Intimate Portrait of Life in 16th-Century Europe Revealed in the Letters of a Nuremberg Husband and Wife*. New York: Simon and Schuster, 1986.

——. *When Fathers Ruled: Family Life in Reformation Europe*. Cambridge, Mass.: Harvard University Press, 1983.

Perrenoud, Alfred. *La population de Genève, XVIe–XIXe siècles*. Geneva: Société d'histoire et d'archéologie de Genève, 1979.

Peterson, M. Jeanne. *Family, Love, and Work in the Lives of Victorian Gentlewomen*. Bloomington: Indiana University Press, 1989.

Petitjean, Michel, and Françoise Fortunet de Loisy. *Les contrats de mariage à Dijon et dans la campagne bourguignonne de la fin du XVIIIe siècle au milieu du XIXe siècle*. Dijon: Université de Dijon, 1980.

Petitpierre, Alphonse. *Un demi-siècle de l'histoire économique de Neuchâtel, 1791–1848*. Neuchâtel: Librairie générale Jules Sandoz, 1871.

Phillips, Roderick. *Family Breakdown in Late Eighteenth-Century France: Divorces in Rouen, 1792–1803*. Oxford: Clarendon Press, 1980.

——. *Putting Asunder: A History of Divorce in Western Society*. Cambridge: Cambridge University Press, 1988.

Piaget, Arthur, and Jaqueline Lozeron. "Le consistoire seigneurial de Valangin au XVIe siècle." *Musée neuchâtelois*, 1939, 158–169; 1940, 20–28, 53–60.

——, and Jaqueline Lozeron. "Les ordonnances ecclésiastiques au Val-de-Travers au XVIe siècle et leur application." *Musée neuchâtelois*, 1936, 156–162, 197–204.

Pierrehumbert, William. *Dictionnaire historique du parler Neuchâtelois et Suisse-Romande*. Neuchâtel: Société d'Histoire du Canton de Neuchâtel, 1926.

———. "Les noms neuchâtelois de magistrats, fonctionnaires et employés." *Musée neuchâtelois*, 1918, 152–158, 203–211; 1919, 53–68, 99–107, 205–224; 1920, 29–45, 72–79.

Pittard, Thérèse. *Femmes de Genève aux jours d'autrefois*. Geneva: Labor et Fides, 1946.

Pollock, Linda A. *Forgotten Children: Parent-Child Relations from 1500 to 1900*. Cambridge: Cambridge University Press, 1983.

Prior, Mary, ed. *Women in English Society, 1500–1800*. London: Methuen, 1985.

Pury, Abram de. "Quelques réflexions sur l'état de notre pays vers 1769." *Musée neuchâtelois*, 1878, 258–263, 277–283.

Quadroni, Dominique. "La situation des églises dans le comté de Neuchâtel et la seigneurie de Valangin, d'après les visites diocésanes de 1416–1417 et de 1453." *Musée neuchâtelois*, 1981, 159–171.

Quaife, G. R. *Wanton Wenches and Wayward Wives: Peasants and Illicit Sex in Early Seventeenth-Century England*. New Brunswick, N.J.: Rutgers University Press, 1979.

Quartier-La-Tente, Edouard. *Les familles bourgeoises de Neuchâtel: Essais généalogiques*. Neuchâtel: Attinger Frères, 1903.

Rabb, Theodore K., and Robert I. Rotberg, eds. *The Family in History: Interdisciplinary Essays*. New York: Harper & Row, 1971.

———, and Robert I. Rotberg, eds. *Industrialization and Urbanization: Studies in Interdisciplinary History*. Princeton, N.J.: Princeton University Press, 1981.

Raftis, J. Ambrose. *Tenure and Mobility: Studies in the Social History of the Mediaeval English Village*. Toronto: Pontifical Institute of Mediaeval Studies, 1964.

Razi, Zvi. *Life, Marriage, and Death in a Medieval Parish: Economy, Society, and Demography in Halesowen, 1270–1400*. Cambridge: Cambridge University Press, 1980.

Rebel, Hermann. *Peasant Classes: The Bureaucratization of Property and Family Relations under Early Habsburg Absolutism, 1511–1636*. Princeton, N.J.: Princeton University Press, 1983.

Le refuge Huguenot en Suisse. Lausanne: Musée historique de l'Ancien Evêché, 1985.

Robert, Michèle. "Le consistoire: Inquisition des réformés?" *Musée neuchâtelois*, 1986, 9–22.

Robert, Sylvia. "L'industrie dentellière dans les Montagnes neuchâteloises aux XVIIIe et XIXe siècles: La comptabilité d'un négociant en dentelles de Couvet: Le major Daniel-Henri Dubied." *Musée neuchâtelois*, 1988, 69–95.

Robisheaux, Thomas. *Rural Society and the Search for Order in Early Modern Germany*. Cambridge: Cambridge University Press, 1989.

Roper, Lyndal. *The Holy Household: Women and Morals in Reformation Augsburg*. Oxford: Clarendon Press, 1989.

Rotberg, Robert I., and Theodore K. Rabb, eds. *Marriage and Fertility: Studies in Interdisciplinary History*. Princeton, N.J.: Princeton University Press, 1980.

Rougemont, Léopold de. "La mairie de Travers à la fin du XVIIIe siècle d'après les papiers de Georges de Rougemont." *Musée neuchâtelois*, 1914, 249–274.

Roulet, Louis-Edouard. "Le jour le plus long de la Réforme neuchâteloise." *Musée neuchâtelois*, 1973, 186–199.

Rousseau, G. R., and Roy Porter, eds. *Sexual Underworlds of the Englightenment*. Chapel Hill: University of North Carolina Press, 1988.

Ruggiero, Guido. *The Boundaries of Eros: Sex Crime and Sexuality in Renaissance Venice*. Oxford: Oxford University Press, 1985.

Rule, John. *The Labouring Classes in Early Industrial England, 1750–1850*. London: Longman, 1986.

Sabean, David Warren. *Power in the Blood: Popular Culture and Village Discourse in Early Modern Germany*. Cambridge: Cambridge University Press, 1984.

———. *Property, Production, and Family in Neckarhausen, 1700–1870*. Cambridge Studies in Social and Cultural Anthropology, no. 73. Cambridge: Cambridge University Press, 1990.

Safley, Thomas Max. "Families Unformed and Reformed: Protestant Divorce and Its Domestic Consequences." In *Regnum, Religio et Ratio: Essays Presented to Robert M. Kingdon,* edited by Jerome Friedman, pp. 153–160. Kirksville, Mo.: Sixteenth Century Journal, 1987.

———. *Let No Man Put Asunder. The Control of Marriage in the German Southwest: A Comparative Study, 1550–1600*. Kirksville, Mo.: Sixteenth Century Journal, 1984.

———. "Marital Litigation in the Diocese of Constance, 1551–1590. *Sixteenth Century Journal* 12 (1981): 61–78.

———. "To Preserve the Marital State: The *Basler Ehegericht*, 1550–1592." *Journal of Family History* 7 (1982): 162–179.

Schama, Simon. *The Embarrassment of Riches: An Interpretation of Dutch Culture in the Golden Age*. Berkeley: University of California Press, 1988.

Scheurer, Rémy. "L'économie neuchâteloise au Moyen Age." In *Histoire du Pays de Neuchâtel: De la préhistoire au Moyen Age*, pp. 263–284. Hauterive, Switz.: Editions Gilles Attinger, 1989.

———. *Pierre Chambrier 1542(?)–1609: Aspects de la vie d'un homme d'Etat neuchâtelois*. Preface by Guy de Chambrier. Neuchâtel: Société d'histoire et d'archéologie du canton de Neuchâtel, 1988.

———. "La Réforme dans les montagnes de Valangin." *Musée neuchâtelois*, 1982, 263–282.

———, and Dominique Quadroni. *Les finances du comté de Neuchâtel à la fin du XVIe siècle*. Neuchâtel: Université de Neuchâtel and Institut d'histoire, 1985.

———, Louis-Edouard Roulet, and Jean Courvoisier. *Histoire du Conseil d'Etat: Des origines à 1945*. Neuchâtel: Chancelier d'Etat, 1987.

Schlup, Michel. "Diffusion et lecture du *Journal helvétique* au temps de la Société typographique de Neuchâtel, 1769–1782." In *La diffusion et la lecture des journaux de langue française sous l'ancien régime*, pp. 59–71. Amsterdam: Holland University Press, 1988.

———. "Sociétés de lecture et cabinets littéraires dans la principauté de Neuchâtel (1750–1800)." *Musée neuchâtelois*, 1987, 81–104.

———. *Sociétés de lecture et cabinets littéraires dans la principauté de Neuchâtel (1760–1830)* [a catalogue for an exhibition in the Bibliothèque Universitaire et Publique de Neuchâtel]. Neuchâtel, 1986.

Schnegg, Alfred. "L'alerte de 1793 et les origines de l'arsenal neuchâtelois." *Musée neuchâtelois*, 1978, 145–176.

——. "Justice et suicide sous l'Ancien Régime." *Musée neuchâtelois*, 1982, 73–94.

——. "Quelques propos sur un document neuchâtelois." *Musée neuchâtelois*, 1972, 16–23.

Seeger, Cornelia. *Nullité de mariage, divorce et séparation de corps à Genève au temps de Calvin.* Lausanne: Société d'Histoire de la Suisse Romande, 1989.

Segalen, Martine. *Amours et mariages de l'ancienne France.* With the collaboration of Josselyne Chamarat. Paris: Berger-Levrault, 1981.

——. *Historical Anthropology of the Family.* Translated by J. C. Whitehouse and Sarah Matthews. Cambridge: Cambridge University Press, 1986.

——. *Love and Power in the Peasant Family: Rural France in the Nineteenth Century.* Translated by Sarah Matthews. Oxford: Basil Blackwell, 1983.

——. *Nuptialité et alliance: Le choix du conjoint dans une commune de l'Eure.* Paris: G.-P. Maisonneuve et Larose, 1972.

Sessions, Kyle C., and Phillip N. Bebb, eds. *"Pietas et Societas": New Trends in Reformation Social History.* Sixteenth Century Essays and Studies, vol 4. Kirksville, Mo.: Sixteenth Century Journal, 1985.

Shaffer, John W. *Family and Farm: Agrarian Change and Household Organization in the Loire Valley, 1500–1900.* Albany: State University of New York Press, 1982.

Sheehan, Michael M. "The Formation and Stability of Marriage in Fourteenth-Century England: Evidence of an Ely Register." *Mediaeval Studies* 33 (1971): 228–263.

Shorter, Edward. "Female Emancipation, Birth Control, and Fertility in European History." *American Historical Review* 78 (1973): 605–640.

——. "Illegitimacy, Sexual Revolution, and Social Change in Modern Europe." *Journal of Interdisciplinary History* 2 (1971): 237–272.

——. *The Making of the Modern Family.* New York: Basic Books, 1975.

Slater, Miriam. *Family Life in the Seventeenth Century: The Verneys of Claydon House.* Boston: Routledge & Kegan Paul, 1984.

Smith, Bonnie G. *Changing Lives: Women in European History Since 1700.* Lexington, Mass.: D. C. Heath, 1989.

Staehelin, Adrian. *Die Einführung der Ehescheidung in Basel zur Zeit der Reformation.* Basel: Helbing & Lichtenhahn, 1957.

Stevenson, Kenneth. *Nuptial Blessing: A Study of Christian Marriage Rites.* New York: Oxford University Press, 1983.

Stone, Lawrence. "Broken Lives: Marital Separation and Divorce in England, 1660–1860." Merle Curti Lecture Series, Madison, Wis., 28–30 October 1986.

——. *The Family, Sex, and Marriage in England, 1500–1800.* London: Weidenfeld & Nicolson, 1977.

——. *Road to Divorce: England, 1530–1987.* Oxford: Oxford University Press, 1990.

Thévenaz, Louis. "Genèse et liquidation du régime prussien à Neuchâtel." *Musée neuchâtelois*, 1957, 201–211.

——. "L'origine du franc-alleu de Lignières." *Musée neuchâtelois*, 1936, 179–196.

——. "Pour une rose: Une promesse de mariage en 1564." *Musée neuchâtelois*, 1931, 11–22.

Thomas, Keith. "The Double Standard." *Journal of the History of Ideas* 20 (1959): 195–216.

——. "Women and the Civil War Sects." *Past and Present* 13 (1958): 42–62.

Tilly, Charles. *The Vendée.* Cambridge, Mass.: Harvard University Press, 1964.

Tilly, Louise A., and Joan W. Scott. *Women, Work, and Family.* New York: Holt, Rinehart & Winston, 1978.

——, Joan W. Scott, and Miriam Cohen. "Women's Work and European Fertility Patterns." *Journal of Interdisciplinary History* 6 (1976): 447–476.

Tissot, Charles-Eugène. "La cage du château de Valangin." *Musée neuchâtelois,* 1893, 171–172.

——, and Charles Robert. "Promenades autour de Valangin par feu Georges Quinche." *Musée neuchâtelois,* 1894, 83–89, 118–124, 144–148, 191–196.

Traer, James F. *Marriage and the Family in Eighteenth-Century France.* Ithaca, N.Y.: Cornell University Press, 1980.

Tribolet, Charles-Godefroy de. *Description topographique de la juridiction de Neuchâtel.* Neuchâtel: Wolfrath, 1827.

——. *Histoire de Neuchâtel et Valangin depuis l'avènement de la maison de Prusse jusqu'en 1806.* Neuchâtel: Wolfrath, 1846.

Tribolet, Maurice de. "A propos de l'administration des possessions comtoises de Neuchâtel au XIVe siècle: Glanures diplomatiques." *Musée neuchâtelois,* 1973, 154–159.

——. "Audiences générales, Etats et Trois Etats durant la seconde moitié du XVe siècle." *Musée neuchâtelois,* 1981, 3–17.

——. "La condition des personnes dans le Comté de Neuchâtel du XIIIe au début du XVIIe siècle." 2 vols. Doctoral dissertation, Université de Dijon, 1980.

——. "Un exemple de collaboration entre mari et femme au milieu du XVIe siècle." *Musée neuchâtelois,* 1982, 283–290.

——. "La genèse des franchises de Neuchâtel de 1455." *Mémoires de la Société pour l'Histoire du Droit et des Institutions des anciens pays bourguignons, comtois et romands,* 45e Fascicule (1988): 449–464.

Trumbach, Randolph. *The Rise of the Egalitarian Family: Aristocratic Kinship and Domestic Relations in Eighteenth-Century England.* New York: Academic Press, 1978.

Ulrich, Laurel Thatcher. *Good Wives: Image and Reality in the Lives of Women in Northern New England, 1650–1750.* New York: Alfred A. Knopf, 1982.

Urech, Edouard. "La première 'crise de croissance' de la commune de La Chaux-de-Fonds, en 1706." *Musée neuchâtelois,* 1951, 162–173.

Vatin, Claude. *Recherches sur le mariage et la condition de la femme mariée à l'époque héllenistique.* Paris: Editions E. de Boccard, 1970.

Viollet, Paul. *Histoire du droit civil français.* Paris: Librairie de la société du recueil général des lois et des arrêts, 1905.

Vouga, Albert. "Une émigration neuchâteloise au XVIIIe siècle (1710–1712)." *Musée neuchâtelois,* 1889, 132–133.

Watson, Alan. *The Making of the Civil Law.* Cambridge, Mass.: Harvard University Press, 1981.

Watt, Jeffrey R. "The Control of Marriage in Reformed Switzerland, 1600–1800." In *Calviniana II,* edited by W. Fred Graham. Kirksville, Mo.: Sixteenth Century Journal Publishers, forthcoming.

——. "Divorce in Early Modern Neuchâtel, 1547–1806." *Journal of Family History* 14 (1989): 137–155.

——. "Marriage Contract Disputes in Early Modern Neuchâtel, 1547–1806." *Journal of Social History* 22 (1988): 129–147.

——. "The Marriage Laws Calvin Drafted for Geneva." In *Calvinus Sacrae Scripturae Professor,* edited by W. H. Neuser. Grand Rapids, Mich.: Eerdman's, forthcoming.

——. "The Reception of the Reformation in Valangin, Switzerland, 1547–1588." *Sixteenth Century Journal* 20 (1989): 89–104.

Wendel, François. *Le mariage à Strasbourg à l'époque de la Réforme, 1520–1692.* Strasbourg: Imprimière alsacienne, 1928.

Wheaton, Robert. "Family and Kinship in Western Europe: The Problem of the Joint Family Household." *Journal of Interdisciplinary History* 5 (1975): 601–628.

——, and Tamara K. Hareven, eds. *Family and Sexuality in French History.* Philadelphia: University of Pennsylvania Press, 1980.

Wiesner, Merry E. *Working Women in Renaissance Germany.* New Brunswick, N.J.: Rutgers University Press, 1986.

Wrightson, Keith. *English Society, 1580–1680.* New Brunswick, N.J.: Rutgers University Press, 1982.

——, and David Levine. *Poverty and Piety in an English Village: Terling, 1525–1700.* New York: Academic Press, 1979.

Wrigley, E. A. "The Growth of Population in Eighteenth-Century England: A Conundrum Resolved." *Past and Present* 98 (1983): 121–150.

——, and R. S. Schofield. *The Population History of England, 1541–1871.* London: Edward Arnold, 1981.

Yver, Jean. *Egalité entre héritiers et exclusion des enfants dotés: Essai de géograhie coutumière.* Paris: Editions Sirey, 1966.

Index

Library of Congress Cataloging-in-Publication Data

Watt, Jeffrey R. (Jeffrey Rodgers), 1958–
    The making of modern marriage : matrimonial control and the rise
of sentiment in Neuchâtel, 1550–1800 / Jeffrey R. Watt.
        p.   cm.
    Includes bibliographical references and index.
    ISBN 0-8014-2493-3 (alk. paper)
    1. Marriage—Switzerland—Neuchâtel (Canton)—History.
    2. Domestic relations—Switzerland—Neuchâtel (Canton)—History.
    3. Divorce—Switzerland—Neuchâtel (Canton)—History.   4. Adultery—
Switzerland—Neuchâtel (Canton)—History.   I. Title.
HQ653.W38   1992
306.81'09494'38—dc20   92-52775